Very magical as it unfolds. I love how all the characters are introduced and then weaved to the central core of "our intimacy with God", how each plays a part in unraveling the story. It is very powerful and written with immense control, yet freedom of a style that is engaging and thought-provoking. I felt the passion and energy as I read, and I just love the flawless storytelling, weaving and weaving that intricate carpet of life on Earth.
~ Harjit Kaur, Senior Lecturer

Prophecy will be fulfilled & pass away. As for knowledge, it will pass away and lose its value and be superseded by Truth. But love never fails, never fades out, or becomes obsolete, or comes to an end. This book is written by a woman who loves you enough to lay her life open before you.
~ Kristen Daria Zuriel, Missionary

The wealth of knowledge and experience Tahira shares in this book as she explores the choices we have for our future inspires one to start thinking about his or her own. An important book to read in the journey of self-discovery.
~ Sanmuga Thavamoorthy, Online Magazine Editor

This book is very powerful and thought-provoking. Tahira is right when she says "There are somethings that can only be received from God in silence". Through the experiences, I see this. Thank you. Thank you for sharing and keeping things simple enough for us to see and feel.
~ Shikha Tuli, Educationist

Forewords by Ameerali R. Jumabhoy
and Dr Eric Wilding

THROUGH THE *Golden* DOOR

*The Doorway to
Our Advancement*

TAHIRA AMIR KHAN

Copyright © 2015, Tahira Amir Khan

Door photo: Shikha Tuli
Photographs of the Author: Nicola Gastadalli
Artist for the illustrations: Tahira Amir Khan

All rights reserved. This book may not be reproduced in whole or in part, or transmitted in any form, without written permission from the publisher, except by a reviewer who may quote brief passages in a review; nor may any part of this book be reproduced, stored in a retrieval system, or transmitted in any form or by any means electronic, mechanical, photocopying, recording, or other, without written permission from the publisher.

Disclaimers

The author has tried to recreate events, locales and conversations from her memories of them. In order to maintain their anonymity in some instances the author has changed the names of individuals and places, she may have changed some identifying characteristics and details such as physical properties, occupations and places of residence.

Although the author and publisher have made every effort to ensure that the information in this book was correct at press time, the author and publisher do not assume and hereby disclaim any liability to any party for any loss, damage, or disruption caused by errors or omissions, whether such errors or omissions result from negligence, accident, or any other cause. In addition, the material and quotations specified in this book is mainly for analysis or criticism only. The quoted material is only a small portion of the overall work and is not the "heart of the material."

This book is not intended as a substitute for the medical advice of physicians. The reader should regularly consult a physician in matters relating to his/her health and particularly with respect to any symptoms that may require diagnosis or medical attention.

ISBN: 978-9-8109-7077-2 (sc)
ISBN: 978-9-8109-7081-9 (e)

Printed by: Lulu.com

Publisher: AskSphere LLP
14 Robinson Road, #08-01A Far East Finance Building. Singapore (048545)

Email: tahira@throughthegoldendoor.com
Web: www.throughthegoldendoor.com

Lulu Publishing Services rev. date: 12/18/2015

Contents

Dedication vii
Epigraph ix
Forewords xi
Editorial Notes xv
Preface xvii
1 – The Old World 1
2 – To Simply Be 9
3 – Growing the Spirit Man 23
4 – Intertwining with Nature 40
5 – Everyone A Healer 62
6 – Reaching Zero Point 81
7 – Loving Unconditionally 91
8 – No Fear, No Anger 106
9 – No Lies, No Secrets 129
10 – Vision of the Golden Door 146
11 – Doing What We Love 153
12 – Master Creators, Master Alchemists 169
13 – Making Technology Responsible 197
14 – Making War Unthinkable 219
15 – The New Commodity 247

16 – Unity 261
17 – Free, But Responsible 277
18 – Thriving, Not Simply Surviving 299
19 – The Golden Door Opens 324
20 – The Secret Key 353
21 – Your Personal Golden Door # Action Plan # 366
Epilogue 379
Bibliography 381
Acknowledgments 383
Contributors 385
Glossary 387
Theories and Definitions 391
Alphabetical Index 393
About the Author 401

Dedication

A tribute to my beloved mother, Anisa Mirza Khan:

I learned about the undying, unquenchable unconditional and divine love from my own mother. While the years posed a mountain of challenges, she taught me how to overcome fear and to become bold and resilient, to overcome my health challenges and more. It's not easy for her either as she had gone through decades of trials and tribulations. She made bold steps to train teachers for new schools for children in the rural parts of Pakistan. She showed bravado as she organized English Plays written and directed by herself to children who could barely speak a word of English. I saw for myself how she radically transformed their lives. How many people would do what she did and take such great risks? Very few. And she is fearless. She would take any challenge, anywhere without fear and hesitation. Ironic as she always felt "fear" was one of the greatest setbacks in her life. How untrue I would say.

A tribute to my beloved father, Taher Amir Khan:

If there was anyone who was a living breathing miracle, it would be my father. When struck with illness, he faced up to it to heal himself through a regimented healthy eating and exercise routine as well as a positive mental attitude. He kept to his routine for decades relentlessly. Even business-wise, he worked with tenacity to build a business that went down and up again despite all the hurdles he was up against. My father is a man who can make anything work. As a father, he is a exemplary. A true believer of education, nourishing and quizzing us when my siblings and I were just young minds.

And he did this with the grandeur of information every single day. Moreover, his religious and spiritual dedication daily was a guiding light for us. As such, the achievements we have now, we owe so much of it to him.

A tribute to our beloved Founding father of Singapore, Mr Lee Kuan Yew:

His time came on the 23rd March 2015, but his deed was done. He left Singapore to be one of the pantheons of city states on Earth. Technologically, soon to be a Smart Nation. One of the most economically and politically stable nations in history. Decades of awards from the best airport in the world, busiest port etc etc. I could give a long list of accolades of what his leadership has achieved for Singapore. A man of fortitude who was not afraid to be who he was, and not afraid to set rules and standards to build Singapore from ground up. The world admired him greatly. Some say that he is even greater a persona than some of the top world leaders, while many have scorned him for having an iron fist. Nonetheless, his approach worked and was suitable for creating a strong foundation. But this era is now coming to a close, as we enter a new one. The transformation and creation of the Golden Planet. To pave the way for a new approach, led by new politicians and new leaders. A new approach that suits a more evolved society of people. A new generation of people formulated by Lee Kuan Yew's foundation building – free, responsible and knowing what do and what not to do.

Epigraph

*A Woman
Is the Glory of a Man.*

*Heaven on Earth
Is the Glory of Mankind.*

~ Tahira Amir Khan

Forewords

Foreword by Ameerali R. Jumabhoy:

Whilst reporting on what can be succinctly described as a profound and moving set of experiences, Tahira Amir Khan manages to maintain a close relationship with the reader, bringing them back to her true message, in the heart of every chapter. When you encounter each chapter, at first the message seems to whisper to you, so softly that you may not hear it if you do not pay close enough attention. As you delve further and you read with concentration, you pick up on Tahira's perceptiveness and delicacy of language that make this book the joy to read that it is.

There are too many paeans to the power of spirituality that do not resonate with contemporary life. This book is not one of them. Tahira relates her experiences in a way that endears you to her and at the same time challenges your perceptions on the way the world is viewed by modern society. She augments her hypothesis with scientific explanations which bridge the gap between the seen and unseen. Her vision of society is also a model that has universal application and builds on common themes of morality that are often forgotten in modern society. The chapters in this book serve as a blueprint as to how to live a more calm, peaceful life imbued with a spiritual awareness and a strong but quiet sense of resilience. The greatest legacy of this book is one of the focus on Unity. Unity through the intimacy with God as well as through the interconnectedness of the world we live in today.

That Tahira has so brilliantly portrayed her experiences and the world we live in is a testament to her clarity of thought, her tenacity of spirit and her honest objectivity. Readers will find this an accessible account of a life which is far from ordinary.

Ameerali R. Jumabhoy, Singapore

Foreword by Dr Eric Wilding:

The autobiographical journey of Tahira Amir Khan navigates the challenges and elations of her life, especially over the decade. With a head full of ideas, a heart full of dreams and eyes full of visions; she traces her own development with a vulnerable transparency. Each chapter is peppered with encounters of people—both old and young—who serve as mentors, inspiring her growth as a person. She is willing to look wherever the light is guiding her. The journey is not simply subjective; Tahira grounds her experiences in the latest scientific knowledge, while simultaneously allowing ancient wisdom to be part of the foundation. With a fluid literary style, she allows readers to observe a narrative tapestry of technology, mathematics, geometry, philosophy, psychology, sociology, literature and spirituality.

There are encounters that will challenge empirically minded readers. However, if readers open themselves, these gems will expand in their hearts and minds. Many readers, like the author, have been seeking a greater experience of the ultimate reality. They have most likely attended seminars, retreats and gatherings as well as read books, articles, and pamphlets on the next thing that will lead them further on their path toward enlightenment. The author will be a welcome companion as readers compare their travels with hers, exploring the puzzles, paradoxes and mysteries of existence.

Tahira Amir Khan is also an Futurist-Innovator. She envisions a world where we have learned to confront and overcome our anxieties, fears and animosities—replacing negative emotions with positive ones. This approach can help impact multiple sectors of societies. The technologies she sees can be used to aid humanity in its development of knowledge and compassion. The focus on healing the whole person (body, soul and spirit) could have implications for healing diverse cultures: families, businesses, religions, countries and ecosystems. What we view as miraculous or supernatural could be a regular occurrence as we come to understand personal and collective identities and their mutual interdependence.

The journey comes towards a climax as Tahira soars in mystical encounters. The flow of the journey is guided by a deeply relational love. There is a joy and peace as she becomes increasingly aware of the selfless Unity that she has with nature, animals, humans and God. Moreover, she regards this as a praxiological possibility for others. The transformation of the author may be transferred to the readers as they join hands with the author to experience walking through the Golden Door.

Dr Eric Wilding,
Professor of Language and Religion,
Centennial College,
Toronto, Canada

Editorial Notes

First a short, and admittedly simplistic, allegory to get us on our way; on a sunshiny day a man waters the plants in his backyard. He twists the nozzle on the hose, changing the water flow from jet to spray, adjusting it to where the water becomes a curtain of the tiniest possible droplets, no longer a facsimile of rain but of mist and fog. And upon this curtain, this hydro-screen, he now observes the appearance of a rainbow. In the construct of light and atmosphere, the rainbow was ALWAYS there, but for the limit of human sensory perception, which hides more than it reveals, denies more than it allows. Alter the conditions, tweak the settings, energize certain variables and comprehension of reality is released from the prisons of our physical senses into the realms of the cosmic and the spiritual.

Every so often, the "powers that be" send particularly unique, courageous and gifted individuals to help us in our journey towards universal awareness and self-discovery, hopefully managing to convince us along the way that these are one and the same thing. Or to put it another way, the not so different aspects of the One. For a greater part of her life Tahira has gravitated towards cerebral pursuits. Mathematics, technology, spirituality, art and entrepreneurial imperatives define not only the paradigm of her passions but the focal point of an instinctive drive. Several years ago certain encounters of a very unusual kind had her question the status quo and at a crossroads in life she chose a path rife with risk and sacrifice, to answer the call of a higher purpose. Within these chapters Tahira shares discoveries, interactions, illuminations and revelations and delivers the message she was meant to deliver. So dear Reader, proceed with an open heart. Let Tahira show you the rainbow within the mist. At this crossroad let Tahira gently and lovingly, nudge you towards a path that promises gilded horizons.

By Adil Naeem
Co-Editor

At some juncture in our lives, we all reach a point where we start to question if there is more to our daily rigors. This book details Tahira's journey to find the answers so many of us search for.

Having known Tahira for more than thirty years, I was very touched when she asked me to help edit her book. Many in school remember Tahira as the athlete. In university, she was the polished computer nerd. In the business world, she is the bold entrepreneur. To me, she is one of my closest, dearest friends who has always been there for me. Tahira is a very giving person who puts her heart and soul into everything she sets her mind on. And, she often chooses the path less traveled. Most great minds often do.

For the past three years, Tahira has conscientiously devoted the most part of her energies to finding the answers to a more meaningful life. During her search, she encountered a series of spiritual revelations which she wanted to share with as many people as possible. And what better way than through a digital book, which is limitless in its reach?

This book beautifully recounts Tahira's experiences, which explore symbolism, philosophical, scientific and spiritual teachings. I have learnt so much from her and welcome all of you to embark with her, on this journey of discovery.

By Flaviana Chelliah
Co-Editor

Preface

The colors were a little brighter.
A warmer, more loving world,
Where life made sense.

I resisted change. Resisted it for years. But there I was. A technology entrepreneur trapped within the confines of a one dimensional state of being where Practicality ruled above all else.

A naturally curious person with big ideas and big plans, I was researching on planetary civilizations and their advancement from a purely logistical and scientific angle. The primal driver was my discomfort with an old world of the current and a craving for the new. The Hand of God came in to shift my thinking around. He had to intervene. I was on the right track with a passion and an agenda but I was a little off the mark. He had to come in and set it straight. The stigmata, the divine encounters, the supernatural abilities, the audible and visual messages and revelations. The foreboding question on my mind was where were we heading as a planet was forced to take a slight twist. A New World redefined from what I thought it would be. What was this New World? Just as what is the "old you" and the "new you"; the "old me" and the "new me"?

It was early 2011 when I began coming out of the woodwork. Still deeply entrenched in the world of business where image consciousness was paramount and earthly values were the measure of all things. Yet somehow life appeared to have come to a grinding halt. I had lost all sense of who I was. Then one day in April 2012. The strangest of encounters. The most curious of visions. A divine wake up. And a subsequent farewell to an existence both mechanical and subservient. Followed on by the year 2013. A pivotal year. A booming voice of authority broke through the silence in my bedroom.

Commanding Voice, 'God is sending a lot of messages to a lot of people right now!'

I was completely alone at the time. Whose voice was this? Shocked and startled, little did I realize that there was so much more to come. A river of mind-altering communiques cascading through words, visions and surreal encounters. Month after month, year upon year. At first I could not understand why, but over time I began to see its underlying purpose. I was simply receiving what I had asked for. I had asked an umpteen number of questions over the years. Somehow I was ready for the downpour of answers now. My turbulent life prior to this point had been good training ground; hardships having prepared me well as it turned out. So when the time came it was not so difficult for me to open myself up to receive that which would be, indeed needed to be, revealed. The blinders came off, comprehension came naturally and the truth that there existed an entirely new mode of thinking became palpable in March 2014. A fortuitous vision that set the precedence for everything that unfolded from there onward - the vision of a Golden Door.

Around the Golden Door was a circumference of many other doors, which though, were as mere shadows in comparison to the magnificence and grandeur of the Golden Door. The Golden Door was closed. I questioned why this door was shown to me. If there were Keys to opening this door, what were they? I imagined God sculpting the Keys. Without these Keys, we could continue to go around in circles, repeating the same mistakes endlessly until we got it right. I was trying to make sense of it all at least in my own life moving up (or down) an imaginary scale. If this new world was through the Golden Door, would I be part of it? Or would I stay on the barren road of stagnation and struggle?

The deluge of revelations was unceasing and relentless. The people. The startling information. The unforgettable visitations. The life changing experiences. All leading to the discovery of the aspects needed for the Uplifting. I realized that these were guides for not only my own transformation but for all of humanity collectively. This led to a journey of invaluable interactions with people as I lived and traveled from my homeland in Singapore to Malaysia, Bali, and Pakistan. Both ordinary and extraordinary people who were living breathing catalysts to the world, giving life and meaning to the discoveries that unfolded before me.

Then came March 2015. The vision of the Golden Door once again, but this time I saw the door opening gradually, luring me in to show a glimpse of a hitherto unknown world. A New World. Accompanied by a sense that it was different this time; the glowing sights, the colors vivid and bright. The whispering sounds. We looked brighter.

The vision of the New World motivated me all the more to discover the Keys to this world - the next level of our civilized existence. I imagined my transcendence collectively with all of humanity, synonymous of a machine-like environment going through a massive upgrade with Keys at each level. Each of us as individuals conjointly with the Planet Earth attempting to make an upgrade as a sum total, almost as if it is happening all at the same time. The Old World moving onto the New World. The Old World fraught with calamities and upheavals that have been hurled upon us with greater intensity the past few decades. The Old World with our old selves reaching an expiry date. The inflated human egos and deepening thirst for power that has led to world wars, terrorism and unending strife in so many forms on a global scale. Including the financial crises of the last several decades motivated by greed leaving hundreds of millions of people debt ridden and struggling to survive. The use and misuse of technology from weaponry to nuclear energy. The barreling of corporate and political scandals as well as senseless territorial disputes between nations. An eternal agenda to control by creating irrational fear.

With the spiritual movement that has been going on for some time now, I thought about how more and more people have been aspiring for their own spiritual uplifting, how the internet and mobile and social networks have been bringing people together; how there is a greater concern for the downtrodden, the poverty-stricken and the environment. Were we moving fast enough in the right direction? Or was this just an endless crusade for our betterment? Although so much good has already happened in the world, as the ripple effect of elevated human consciousness travels across countries and continents awakening the minds of many, so much more work still needs to be done. The awakening had to accelerate.

God preparing me alongside everyone else, for the next stage of human and planetary uplifting. An amalgamation of change in our inner and outer worlds, collectively as each of us sheds the veil and sees with clarity. A chain reaction that resonates and bounces off one person to the next, and on to the next – becoming a huge crescendo that is the revealing of the New World. Where would the New World launch itself first, if it happens? Will we miss the boat? As events unfolded, I could see the pieces coming together - Heaven on Earth, or shall we call it the Golden Planet? But firstly and most importantly, before we even deem to arrive there what are the Keys to opening the Golden Door?

My Role, Your Role

It was only when I was given a preview of the flip side of myself, my alter-ego, my second Self, indeed my True Self that I started questioning all that is or appears to be. My role is to be a conduit through these experiences. My role is to make you question all that you and I are meant to be. My role is to open your eyes on what needs to be done. Many of these facts you probably already know, and perhaps some you may even disagree with. The Truth is that there really is no right or wrong. Sometimes things need to be shown and sometimes things need to be experienced. It's like saying that you can swim, but when you are thrown into the waters you start to struggle and you may even drown. I was pushed into the waters and I was drowning till I was forced to open my spiritual eyes and embrace a vision of a True Reality (which may sound fantastical to some). It was God who gave me that hard push. It was God who helped me to open up and receive this other side of my Self with the innumerable signs have made their justification.

Did people believe my story before I wrote this book? Yes and no. Some shirked while some embraced in awe. Some responded with skepticism, some with joy and elation. I do not know why God orchestrated all the events and experiences, in such perfect harmony. He has His ways. Will you as the reader believe these experiences and allow them to transform your life? I leave it up to you.

The narrative has been crafted in the form of a story, with some situations, locations, descriptions and dialogues adjusted / created to fit the flow. However, they are founded on real experiences, backed by what people say harnessed by their own experiences and supported by our ever evolving scientific theories. And then there are times when there is no empirical evidence per se, simply a Knowing in the Spirit. Science says to question. Spirituality says to experience. It is hoped that a potent marriage of a questioning experience shall lead to greater understanding, greater altitude and greater freedom. It is through this questioning that we develop new insight. It is through these experiences that we derive a fuller understanding. It is this journey of questioning that leads us to a holistic discernment of things and events that lie beyond practical application and abstract theory.

In order to make sense of these visions and personal encounters, I have tried to remain an impartial observer, evaluating through verified theories or, at times, extemporaneous theories of my own. There are a few occasions where I attempt to quantify with a gnosis with as much simplicity as possible; the thoughts and revelations with God's building blocks of the universe: mathematics, quantum mechanics and astrophysics. On other occasions, some of the thoughts and ideas may be speculative as I may not have scientific proof for everything. So many of these visions, encounters, events and experiences would be termed as supernatural or even preternatural (defined as beyond what is normal or natural, perhaps within the paradigms of some cultures), which means that they fall outside of the paradigm's ability to test by scientific experimentation.

As you read through this book, you may observe that I may have, on few occasions, arrived at some of my own conclusions. However, in full embrace, I open it up to you as a reader to evaluate and explore the theories that I have shared, and to even look at other theories which I may not have explored so as to draw your own conclusions.

Allow the story to flow with ease as discoveries unfold seamlessly. As with the fictional characters, they are based on a combination of a few real people. This world is magical as I perceive it - for our learning and testing, to come out of it unscathed, coming out of an Old World to a nascent New World. And as you embark on this magical and mystical journey uncovering the cypher within my words, do bear in mind that it is important to read this book from beginning to end.

The Old World

A world that reflected
A denseness that we had resigned to.

The uncanny likeness
Of an upside-down world,
With its boundaries and limitations.

In contrast to the anguish of facing deprivation and the daily struggle to secure bare necessities as faced by my parents and their ancestors in their early years, my siblings and I enjoyed our childhood in a life of prestige and comfort. As third generation Singaporeans, with origins from Pakistan and Afghanistan, we knew only about living in large bungalows, live-in chauffeurs, and a cadre of top notch household help. Since the 1980s we resided in a highly coveted neighborhood in Singapore close to the bustling frenzied Orchard Road. Image consciousness was everything to me and to those around me, infinite energies were expended in maintaining the facade of "we've made it" to friends, neighbors, acquaintances and business associates. We resided in a realm which was above the rest.

So that was the center of my universe in my youth. In my early 20s, worldly ambitions took precedence. I was in awe of the corporate world where I could see opportunities for myself to create in manifold, add my signature and make my proverbial mark. However, as in all things seductive this glittery world was a double-edged sword, rife with office politicking, each person left to fend for themselves. From childhood it was the realm of the upper-class, and moving onto adulthood it was the realm of dissatisfaction and deception, always wanting for more.

There was the materialism of my childhood. And there was the materialism of adulthood. There was nothing else. When I look back upon it now, it seems as totally fictitious and illusory. The worldly desires of the mishpocha. Yet the true desires of my heart and the hearts of my family remained secret and hidden. To make things worse, I was always unwell, plagued with numerous allergies. If the dissatisfaction of the world reflected on my health, it did so very well. It was as if I was allergic to life itself! I was living too much in a world that was empty. The world of void. My single-minded purpose to stand out and impress got me nowhere in terms of inner peace.

The turmoil was universal as I saw the world at large in a state of stress and upheaval as well. I was bewildered at the rise and fall of people and nations and the highly destructive and negative broadcasting of world events by the media. There was too much to read about, to understand. Unswayed by the ethos of culture and what was commonly believed in and practised, I sought to find the answers everywhere. I became the curious analyzer. From scientific explanations about consciousness, to quantum mechanics as well as the study of the universe trying to reason how my small inner world would relate to the expansive outer world. In the process, I tried to make myself an unofficial expert in Fengshui, Astrology, Astronomy, Palmistry and more.

My curiosity was unquenchable, sometimes up for 16 hours at a stretch trying to figure out the intricacies of every topic; laying my hands on everything I could find to feed my curiosity. I had a great need to develop a deep knowledge in all the facets of spiritual teachings and their intertwining with scientific thought and discovery. So great was my curious inquisitive nature that even as a young child my mother would marvel at how I had to touch and feel everything to figure out the what, how and why about it. As the years passed, spiritual teachings touched the very core of my being.

At an early age, I was naturally inclined towards religion feeling a common interest and commitment I shared with my family and ancestors. I wanted to know God deeply and I was a true believer of His existence. At the age of 19, I took a year off prior to starting university to study the interpretations of the Holy Q'uran. Consequently, through the years the Buddhist Sutras and the Holy Bible became areas of interest. However the cosmic perspective was my greatest draw, as I saw God as the ultimate Physicist and Mathematician, crafting the universe to perfection, with messages and meaning laying layer upon layer.

Despite the consuming interest in religion, spirituality and science, there was still this emptiness within me. Wasn't all that supposed to fill the void of the world? This was the eternal question on my mind. The current, or shall we say, Old World did not make sense. As the years passed, those questions became more and more prevalent in my mind.

When I would voice my feelings out, I would get the usual, 'Focus on the real world!'

I wanted to answer back and say, 'But this real world as you call it is not real! It's an illusion.'

Too many people did not understand that statement then, though many are beginning to understand that now. The limitations, especially in terms of mindset and belief systems: 'You can't do that.', 'That's impossible!' or 'I refuse to believe that.'

There I was - so much of a misfit. I imagined a different world and I wanted to be part of that. The conflicting polarity of life. As the imagery of strife, starvation and then affluence, abundance, comfort shuffled like a deck of cards through the crevices of my waking mind, I likened it to the movement and changes of the world.

And then the question arose, were we moving forward or backward? If we were going through a spiritual evolution, there had to be a simultaneous planetary evolution. As I mulled over all this, there was still no sign of the withering of my topsy turvy world. A world where false appearances spoke volumes. A world ruled by dollars and cents. I went back to searching, trying to claw my way through.

Consciousness is the ground of being. Consciousness is not material, but an aspect of God's nature. It converts possibility into actuality because it does not obey quantum physics.

Quantum is the minimum amount of any physical entity involved in an interaction. The word "quantum" comes from the Latin "quantus", meaning "how much."

Quantum mechanics is the science of the very small: the body of scientific principles that explains the behavior of matter and its interactions with energy on the scale of atoms and s*ubatomic particles*.

The first Sign, the first Prophesy

Singapore
June 2008

The year 2008 was all I remembered it to be – a life that was dense and heavy, as if I was part of a world that was resigned to carrying an enormous weight. When things went wrong, the sensation emotionally and physically was intense. Despite years of occasional meditation and prayers, chaos was a regular visitor to my life, triggering a cataclysmic array of negative emotions. At times I found myself craving the release of resultant endorphins. A momentary satisfaction, but the after effects made me feel "out of sync" with my true Self. I was still driven towards an edacity to bring sense to this upside down world. If visualized as a painting, I was like a tiny speck obliterated by the feet of millions of wayfarers.

At home, I created a small corner adorned with a vibrantly colored yet intricate Persian silk rug where I would immerse myself in spiritual, self-help and autobiographical texts. I took little steps to carve out some joy in my life - reading and decorating were some of the ways. Even bringing up a smile became an effort, an act to please the world when within there was a deep and pervasive sadness.

Yet somehow, I sensed there was an inner knowing, a depth embedded within those emotions that I had to release and pour out. And so I did just that through artistic expression. After all, other than the colors of the adornments of my home, the only colors in my life were the colors on my paint palette. Not a trained painter, or artist per se, but relatively adept with charcoal pencil and water color, I poured out what was bottled within those pent up feelings. Initially clumsy and awkward, I would create dark shadows around the drawn images as Darkness was what I understood best. Very soon, I found myself swimming in the rhythm of a visual expression, flowing with colors from within me, like a rainbow caught in the wind, all in a combative effort to counter the prevailing melancholic mood.

Singapore
March 2011

Three years on in 2011 and I was still in discomfort, still agonizing over an earthly living. I would refer to my painting from time to time wondering why I sketched and painted those ancient-looking white statues - ethereal beings standing with authority and stature. And why those arcane door openings surrounded by a neon-green glow leading toward a blood red center? Finally, whirling around the apparent symbolism were rotating strips of patterns, shrinking in size counterclockwise - specifically curval shapes of sacred geometry filled with aquamarine. Everything engulfed pictorially within a xanthous background of yellow, orange and gold.

I was baffled to say the least and certainly lost for words on the meaning behind the colors and the imagery. What was leading me?

Moreover, little did I know that by the month of March I would get my first real revelation of my impending journey of awakening and discovery through such an ordinary yet idiosyncratic encounter with nature.

It was one of those "very long day at the office" days. The monotonous daily activity of inserting the keys into the door knob to enter my home. That nondescript activity was changed forever by the presence of an uninvited bug. A praying mantis to be exact. It was the size of a long pencil and had placed itself conspicuously on the inner-handle of the door knob. It turned its oversized green head up towards me, rotated its compound eyes slowly and curiously to focus its gaze upon me. The body of the mantis was elongated to the point that it occupied the entire door handle. Yet, I had no fear of the large creepy crawly.

The eyes were distinct, exuding a wisdom beyond the levels of a mere insect. Conveying a profound intelligence, I felt that it telepathically guided me to keep calm and be at peace. As soon as I turned around, in a flash it disappeared. Where did it go? In the first place, how did the mantis get into my home? Did it get through one of the windows? I remembered that I had shut them all. It was probably just my imagination acting up. No, it felt very real, almost too real to be dismissed. Perhaps an illusion of an insect to cover up what really was. Maybe it was perfect timing to get into the being, the core of me, so a seed of knowledge could be planted. I was vulnerable and open at that point of time.

An explanation that I found from teachings of animal spirit guides - 'The action of the praying mantis is not guided by others, but rather by an inner force that is guided by Self'.

Like a warrior, teaching the art of self-control, the science of stillness. The mysterious praying mantis was a sign for me to simply "Be" - to stay calm, centered and focused in times of chaos and confusion. And as for the painting, when I look back to 7 years ago, from the year 2015, the peculiar artwork was truly my first "accidental" prophesy. A prognostication of an imminent spiritual journey.

The Painting of an Accidental Prophesy

The overt borders
With recurring curval patterns,
Spinning, and expanding in size.
Sacred geometry
Of a blue aquamarine.

Four arcane wooden doors
Opening on all sides,
With a neon-green glow,
Surrounding the center
A blood red crimson shade.

Above the xanthous background
Of yellow, orange and gold,
Stood three Beings in White,
Regal & imposing;
Of the Ancient,
The Current & the Future.

Tahira Amir Khan

The Painting of an Accidental Prophesy

To Simply Be

To simply "Be" in the moment,
In the midst of noise,
Trouble or hard work.

To be calm in the heart
Meditating in God's name.

Invisible revelations
Start to come in,
Like trickling downloads.
With one complete download,
And then another.

Opening up a new belief system,
Firing up a new intention,
As we prepare ourselves
For the New World.

Singapore
March 2012

'You have been chosen!' the stranger exclaimed, 'Pray! Start praying and meditating. Don't waste any more time!'

He looked like any average South Indian man dressed in standard office attire, but with a slight twist - he was frenetic, or worse appeared possessed. At that time, I was with a friend and we were ready to board the MRT train at the Redhill district of Singapore, towards the city center. Amused and judgmental, we tossed our heads and laughed at the ridiculous behavior of this man. My friend looked at me and shook her head concurring with me that he was out of his mind.

My incredulous and somewhat sarcastic response as I crossed my arms over my chest, 'Alright, so which religious organization do you represent?'

Embarrassed and dismayed the stranger retorted, 'None of all that! I am a technical manager at a tech and infrastructure company based here in Singapore.'

He scrambled through his pockets to get his business card and then shoved it into my hand. The words in large – Halliburton, a global transnational, with his name and designation written in smaller print at the bottom.

He then said, 'I honestly don't know why I need to share this information with you, or where this is coming from. All I know is that you need to take my words very seriously!'

His Chinese wife called him from the distance and pointed at her watch impatiently. The stranger exclaimed, 'So do it now. Meditate and pray. Time is short! They have given you extra time.'

I asked curiously, 'Extra time for what?'

Before we knew it, he scurried off never to be seen again.

The next morning while I was getting dressed to go off to work. I took at long hard look at myself in the mirror. Why would I be chosen? And if so, for what purpose? I was puzzled. I was just an ordinary woman, who was so immersed in my work, that there was no room for anything else. Like many Singaporean women, I had no children and work and career consumed my life. As an entrepreneur, I was faced with business expenses which were so high that I allowed myself to become a slave to my company. Occasionally, I would suffer from bouts of negativity and confusion. A powerless inability to remain centered. Though I felt bound by the shackles of daily survival, God was always on the back of my mind and I was craving for the intimacy. I wanted to speak to Him and have a response. I wanted to see his face. But nothing.

I recall in my 20s during bouts of depression when youthful relationship issues haunted me, I would send Him an email expressing my grievances asking Him for help. When the email would not bounce back, it gave me a sense of solace as I knew that He did receive it. Even when I became deeply entrenched in the fast-paced business world, I would continue with the prayers in my heart. But still the emptiness remained.

Crazy as it sounded, I knew the stranger (I had named him the MRT Stranger) I had stumbled upon was making some sense.

His frantic message had weight, 'Meditate and pray daily …'.

I had thoughts of God with occasional prayer in my heart and meditations about once a week, but it was never daily. And so I decided to proceed onto the task assigned by a random stranger, recording the date of March 2012 as a milestone for the beginning of this important task. The commencement of daily prayers and meditation.

Discovering Stillness

There are some things
That can only be received
From God in silence.

I was in my solitary safe zone, in front of my bedroom dressing table mirror, mulling over the events of the day. So what was a Chosen One supposed to do? I wanted to laugh as it sounded like it was straight out of a movie.

If it were real, I had to get back on track. I was so involved in surviving financially day-to-day, that I was losing sight of my purpose – whatever it might be. There was this sadness that hung over me. I had to shift out of it and simply "Be", to be in the present, to be aware of and to be connected to the omnipresent God. So determined to pursue this spiritual quest, I aimed to follow through on the instructions of the MRT Stranger. He could have been an Angel unbeknown to himself. I searched for his business card but it had disappeared. The strange association with the mysterious praying mantis, who was there one moment and then the next moment gone.

The signs were there. To stay vigilant always and to move away from giving excuses for not following instructions. Recording the beginning of a spiritual journey, I placed a bangle on my left wrist as a form of a visual milestone. The choice was a raw marble stone bangle, iconic of my own rawness at that time. I began my prayers with those that were most familiar to me. Instead of being sporadic and inconsistent about my prayers in the past, I would practise them daily this time. I recited the *Ayatul Kursi* and at times the *Surah Yasin*. Recitation of the 99 names of Allah was conducted as a ritual every night. From *Al-Wasi, Ya Malik* to *Al Khaliq* requesting for forgiveness, abundance and assistance from God and His Angels and more. I would recite many more amongst the 99 names of Allah, the Vast, the All-Embracing, the Omnipresent. Sometimes taking on a spiritual randomness devoid of any methodology, simply going with what made sense to me. When I was done with the recitations, I would dive into silent meditation, pushing myself into a state of "no thought", "blankness", entering a world of stillness.

The stillness was enjoyable. It made me feel complete and fulfilled. I meditated and I imagined myself as one of those infinite number objects, part of a Whole which was blanketed in a process of unification of everything - part of something as infinite and eternal as God. Black the color of mystery. Bringing "Black" and "Whole" together - a Black Whole - this gives greater meaning to what we know of as the Black Hole, the gravitational well in the fabric of space, the eternal mystery. Imagining that all objects across the universe to be centered by stillness, through prayers and meditation I was hoping to embark onto a journey to rediscover the innate stillness within myself. To develop a harmonious connection with God as the Almighty creator of all the Black Wholes.

Still looking for an overriding completeness and fulfillment, the euphoric sense of the Black Whole, I began to consult a Thai Buddhist Forest-Monk. I had heard of one through word of mouth who would make monthly visits from Thailand to Singapore. He would come to give private and group guidance on Buddhist meditation and chanting while explaining their purpose and significance. He was a small, frail man in his late fifties, adorned in a dark orange robe.

The Buddhist Monk was sitting quietly in his room, which he used for meditation and to provide one to one consultations. A light shone in from the window of the room creating an oasis of calm and peace around him as he sat barefoot on the floor. I sat down in front of him and I shared my life experiences asking him for his guidance.

He spoke in Thai as a female interpreter explained the best she could in English, 'Meditation is about silencing the mind. It's about Discovering Mindfulness.'

Reaching out for a book by the Venerable Acara Suvanno Mahathera (1920 – 2007), titled "Striving to be Nobody," he said, 'Read this, and learn about The Four Foundations of Mindfulness.'

I turned to the page he gave and read the abstract:

'... For the purification of beings, for the overcoming of sorrow and lamentation, for the disappearance of pain and grief, for reaching the Noble Path ....'

Pasted neatly on the wall of the small room was a large paper poster of Tibetan art. A psychedelic mix of primary colors, a golden yellow meandering pathway amongst the objects and figurines stood out. The end of the path was a beautiful destination.

I observed pointing at the poster to give it attention, 'The Noble Path, the Golden Road. I would like to be on that golden road.'

The Buddhist Monk smiled silently for a brief moment and then said, 'Remember the 3 divisions of achieving the Noble Path: wisdom, ethical conduct and concentration.'

Way back in 2003 when I learned Kundalini meditation, I was taught that when we close our eyes and silence our mind, we allow a Universal energy to come in. That was more than 8 years before consulting the monk. The meditation technique at that time involved what was called the Kundalini Awakening. It involved a primal energy physically moving up the central channel to reach the crown of the head. I recall practicing it regularly for a year. I had visions but most times they were of darkness filled with obscurity. I remembered why I stopped. I was not fulfilled. There remained a lingering visceral emptiness within me. No answers. No real connection. And so with time, I fell out. Perhaps the timing was not right.

The MRT Stranger and the Thai Buddhist Monk were the two mystical catalysts in my new spiritual journey. With a firm agenda, I began to meditate and pray daily. The Buddhist Monk said 'meditate and pray daily' not just meditate or pray. So not just one or the other, it had to be both and it had to be daily. I would do it cross legged in the lotus position or sometimes just sitting or standing. When I went into meditation, there were times when I found myself racing through an elusive wormhole, a fiercely twisting tunnel. If I did not stay focused on its track, I would lose it trailing behind only to start over so that I could catch it again. I had to train myself and build upon it as a skill. With time, it started to come more naturally, though at most times it was a struggle with rampant displays of random images. I began to seek meditation like an addicted recluse, sometimes twice or three times a day.

Black hole is normally thought of as a massive object (i.e. a star) which has collapsed under its own gravitational force, creating a "hole" in the space-time continuum; a gravitational well in the fabric of space with infinite curvature. Such a curvature is theorized to produce zero volume with infinite density at its core. **Galaxy** is a gravitationally bound system consisting of stars, stellar remnants, interstellar gas and dust, and dark matter.

Black Whole uncovers scientific proof that we are One. The work of physicist, Nassim Haramein, provides insight into the structure of space-time and a new coherent model of the universe. Nassim Haramein redefines a black hole as a "black whole" as it both absorbs and radiates coherent information. His physics describe everything to be centered by stillness, that in effect, everything from protons to the universe itself is a black whole.

Space-time is any mathematical model that combines space and time in the following way. Events are defined in terms of four dimensions: three of space, and one of time. With one coordinate for each dimension, there is a continuous shift along the time dimension.

Discovering the limitless Vortex

Many weeks would pass till one day when I was shown an uncomfortable vision. It was uncomfortable because it reflected my own world. Clouds, trees, plants in reverse, creatures with the appearance of armadillos. The creatures were weirdly hanging upside on the trees, with their eyes peering down. Every thing and every being was upside down in the vision. It was the first time I was shown something so real and clear. A prophetic message tied to the given vision. Armadillos are symbolic of the existence of boundaries and limitations. My old world of limitations. This current world with its perceived limitations. Structures, rules and limits. The name I gave for the vision was apt. I called it the Upside Down Kingdom.

The next time I met with the Buddhist Monk, I described the turning and twisting tunnel.

His immediate reaction was to say, 'Go deeper!'

Go deeper? His answers were always brief. He spoke not to impress. I wondered what he was trying to imply here.

'When you see the tunnel again, just go deeper and deeper, and see what you discover,' he added.

I went on to describe to him about the Upside-down Kingdom vision.

I explained to him, 'I feel the world I was shown is descriptive of the world we are living in right now. An upside down world with boundaries and limitations.'

I was so sure of myself as I continued to say, 'I feel that it is also my own world that is upside down and limited.'

He acknowledged my words through a gentle nod. The Old World I was part of – imbalanced, heavy and disconnected, a mirror of Planet Earth as I viewed it. A heaviness all too palpable, with its divisions, racism, disagreements, deceit and struggles and more.

'The world is in chaos. I am in chaos. How will this end?' I spoke pleadingly.

The Buddhist Monk smiled reassuringly, 'I believe that the positivity in the world is still greater than the negativity in the world. So we will be okay. Just do your part of being more and more positive, and you will be part of that New World which will be better.'

Wondering why he would travel to Singapore every month from Thailand just to mentor a small group of disciples in Singapore, I was just itching to ask.

'Why do you come to Singapore every month? Why don't you just focus on mentoring students in Thailand?' I asked.

The Buddhist Monk replied, 'Because people in Singapore are more ready.'

More ready for what? What was he talking about? As brief as always, he left me hanging.

The translator spoke this time, and said, 'Someone else is waiting to speak to his Holiness. Hope it is okay that we end the session now?'

'Yes, of course. Just one last thing, if you don't mind. When I meditate I feel this shooting pain in the middle of my left palm. Only my left palm. And I feel an energy vortex coming out of there,' I replied.

The Buddhist Monk turned to the translator, and then looked at me and said with a broad smile, 'Be prepared. Maybe something is coming?'

The pieces of some kind of puzzle were slowly beginning to come together. First I was told I was chosen for something. Then the obscure vision of our current world. Next the striking pain in my palm. But what was most intriguing was when he said that Singapore was more ready. What was it ready for? All that got me excited. Me, society, my country, the world – it was all interlinked. I took on a new challenge to start researching on planetary civilizations feeling a natural inclination toward the topic.

There was one area which I was most drawn to due to its astrophysical perspective. It is called the Kardashev Scale. It is a scale that measures planetary civilizations primarily on their energy disposal levels. The Type Zero civilization is a fossil fuel based (oil, coal, gas) economy, with its ethnic, religious and national divisions. Type I (One) civilization uses all available resources on the home planet, that is, Planet Earth. Though it is a hypothetical scale, I was drawn to the idea that the Type I civilization was the start of access to an unlimited energy supply. Naturally, I felt the association with the energy emanating out of my left palm. In fact, in terms of that astrophysical scale, researchers say that we are now at the tail end of the transit between Type Zero and Type I.

The threats of war and economic collapse contribute to the bleak and heavy hopelessness of the planetary society in the present era. If our planetary society was going to remain overwhelmingly dense, I could not imagine it completing the transit to Type I. For the planet to be less dense, we had to be lightened in all aspects of ourselves. We had to do the inner work so that we could contribute to tolerance, peace and harmony in a society.

That research challenge shifted gear to become a new project. Perhaps I would write a book on my real world insights about the shift from Type Zero to Type I. But then again, what was I thinking? I knew some but I did not know everything that was needed for the shift. If based on textbook knowledge and some of my own knowing, yes. Nonetheless, I placed the challenge on myself and stuck by it.

I said to the Buddhist Monk, 'I was thinking of writing about this Old World shift to New World.'

'Hmm. I see. Perhaps you will receive more information when you meditate,' he said.

'Yes. Maybe I will,' I replied.

I thought silently for a moment and said to him, 'Sometimes when I meditate, I get a flood of thoughts that confuse me sometimes. How do I differentiate?'

As my faithful mentor, the Buddhist Monk would always attempt to give me an answer.

'Go with your inner voice. Differentiate between your inner voice and voice of Ego, which often gets mistaken with the inner voice. The inner voice has stillness – neutrality, no right or wrong. The voice of Ego has compulsions,' his faithful reply.

'Well, I find it very hard to differentiate,' I complained.

'It takes practice. Go into stillness daily. Maybe then you will be able to differentiate,' replied the Buddhist Monk.

He then asked out of curiosity, 'What will be the title of your book?'

Thinking through for a few moments, I replied, 'Perhaps ... Transit to Type I?'.

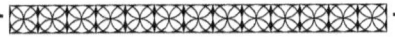

Kardashev Scale A hypothetical scale which puts energy consumption in a cosmic perspective. With 3 base classes, each with an energy disposal level: Type I (One), Type II, and Type III. The Type Zero civilization is a fossil fuel based (oil, coal, gas) economy. It has ethnic, religious and national divisions. Type I civilization uses all available resources on the home planet, that is, Planet Earth. Type II harnesses all the energy of its star with a planetary communication system, planetary culture and economy, planetary flow of knowledge, energy and other resources. Furthermore, it uses the world energy grid using planetary resources such as wind, wave, geothermal as well as energy from outer space. It also has the ability to modify weather. Type III goes another step further by harnessing the energy of its galaxy. This scale was originally conceived in 1964 by the Russian astrophysicist, Nikolai Kardashev (who was looking for signs of extraterrestrial life within *cosmic signals*).

Removing What's Unnecessary

Thanking the Buddhist Monk graciously. I was ready to move forward. Not only was I all set for a great journey of penmanship through writing a book entitled "Transit to Type I", I took on a new mantra to close off the past and to simply "Be" in the moment.

To break the old habits of living a reactive life. Rushing for as many tender proposals as possible, drowning myself in operational matters and simply letting time slip by without considering my true intentions. Forging full steam ahead looking for results in things which I felt had to be accomplished, when all the while it was not matching my highest purpose. I was running through the pathways of life blindfolded, and many times going through the wrong ones.

The endless chores, the accumulation of things, the robotic need to expand the business.

If my physicality could speak, it would have said, 'This is hurting me. Leave it!'.

And if my soul spoke, 'You are many dimensions. Discover them!'.

But that was not all. Being in the moment was one thing, I had to let go of the old of the past that was dragging me down. The people, things and even past memories that were toxic and harmful to me needed to be trimmed away - from people in my life who were easily offended, who leeched my energy, as well as staying away from company that would corrupt the new good habits that I picked up. I thought that once I adopted these new beliefs, I would no longer struggle the way people struggle now.

The words of the Buddhist Monk, 'Our ultimate goal on the physical plane is to expand the goodness of ourselves and expend the negatives of our being.'

All boiling down to learning to let go.

He added, 'Let go of situations and possessions that do not support your new way of being.'

We have been so conditioned to hold and have a desperate need for the future, which ties into the need to accumulate things. It is interesting how human life on Planet Earth has always been about possessions. So many of us are being pushed to realize that it really is much more than that. Human happiness more than domination and pride. Buckminister's vector equilibrium showed its essence in this perspective mathematically. It's 64 perfectly stacked tetrahedrons represented rebuilding ourselves as an immaculate New Human by spirit. The dark energy between the points of the vector equilibrium being the stress points, the points of my inner change. My inner change, your inner change as well as everyone else's on Planet Earth.

Our minds must be renewed to the understanding that the materialism of the world is not real but an illusion. While we often dream of purchasing grandiose homes and expensive cars, but if we decide to shift to the New World, we have to be prepared to downsize, and become more sustainable and harmonious with

Planet Earth. The emergence of the Minimalist Human who can do without. The trimming of the dead wick. To refill the lamps of ourselves with the oil of a renewed consciousness, equipped with a focus on transforming of our minds. As I started the process of letting go, looking at the big picture I imagined families, societies and nations being pushed to Let Go.

> *'No problem can be solved from the same level of consciousness that created it'* ~ Albert Einstein

Nevertheless, I began to cut the rope – venturing beyond my comfort zone. The commencement of the shedding and shredding everything that was unnecessary from all aspects of my life. The extravagant office scaled down to a smaller one. Out went old clothes and numerous knick-knacks from the home and office all given away. But more importantly than all of those material things was the separation from and abandonment of old ideas, old values and old beliefs. I was willing and ready to start Empty.

'I know that I don't know' as I recited aloud to myself, 'God is the All Knowing'.

Delving into stillness, I sensed that something spectacular was going to happen. I did not know how to put a finger on it. Whatever it was, something was coming.

Vector equilibrium is the most primary geometric energy array in the Cosmos. According to Buckminister Fuller (1895-1983), the vector equilibrium is more appropriately referred to as a "system" than as a structure, due to it having square faces that are inherently unstable and therefore non-structural. This is part of synergetics, a metaphoric language for communicating experiences using geometric concepts. In its broadest sense synergetics is Fuller's hypothesized coordinate system of universe - both in its physical and metaphysical aspects. Fuller's system of epistemography and mathematical-physics attempts to disclose how nature actually operates - "operational mathematics". Fuller claimed that synergetics could be understood by child*ren*.

3

Growing the Spirit Man

As Golden Souls,
Reaching out to
The very heights of our Spirit,
Body, mind and soul.

Like glowing beacons
Standing on tiptoes
Arms open wide.
Holding onto the Light.

Singapore
May 2012

Very quickly, meditation became a daily disciplined habit. It became part of my life, just like I had to have breakfast in the morning or brush my teeth before going to bed. It gave me solace through the creation of stillness, despite the occasional dark, gloomy foreboding visions. Those left me uncomfortable.

First, the previous vision of the Upside Down Kingdom which left a queasy feeling in my stomach. A week later, this was followed by a vision of a burial ground with people dying with their skeletal remains. They were grieving and in pain. The depiction of Hell came to mind. Further along the timeline, an unsavory vision of a scaly reptilian being - large, stout and strong, staring at me in the face.

With all those unpleasant visions, I was just craving for my visions to be light, bright and beautiful. Some of the meditation experiences were so depressing that I just wanted it to be finished and over with.

The Buddhist Monk encouraged me in a soft voice, 'Just continue. They are there to stop you. Don't give up.'

Finally in May 2012 my perseverance paid off. After a good two months of repetitive effort.

I was sitting on a wooden park bench at the Gardens by the Bay overlooking the glittering Marina Bay sea waters. It was an early evening in Singapore and the skies were already dark. I was entering into meditation as I felt light water droplets on my skin as a serein started to drizzle. The cool winds blew against my face as I stayed calm and centered.

In the midst of it all, and totally unexpectedly, a circular portal emerged out of the darkness. It was colossal, almost cloud-like with transparent shades of white and gray. Floating close to this prodigious portal looked like souls, human souls. They were large and they were golden! As I locked in my focus on the vision, I could see that these large Golden Souls were going through that portal. In fact, they were at the front of a queue while lagging behind them were gray-colored, dim and misty souls. I did not notice them at first, but I could see that they were much smaller in size, hunched and appeared sadly defeated. It was as if, with the quintessential qualities of the Golden Souls, they were perhaps given a higher priority over the gray souls.

Moving images on a reel like a scene out of a 3D paranormal movie, projecting out in space. By instinct somehow, I sensed that they were human souls of our planet. If I was right, just the visual manifestation, which was clear and tangible left both my senses and comprehension reeling. A soul has never been seen under an electron microscope, nor spun in the laboratory in a test tube or in an ultra-centrifuge. The soul certainly did not look like life is just the activity of atoms and particles, which spin around for a while and then dissipate into nothingness like a dust funnel. Initially stunned by the vision that appeared for an instant, I was puzzled and saddened about the marked difference in the colors and the dimensions of the different soul energies. My own sadness leading to my detriment! Were one of those gray misty souls a reflection of myself at that moment?

> *The self-organized queue*
> *Of Golden Souls*
> *Luminous & standing tall,*
> *With shrunken Gray souls*
> *Trailing behind.*
> *Hunched and miserable,*
> *Of an achromatic gloom.*

I felt that there was something very real going on there. It was much more than a vision - more like a very real event taking place. Maybe there was something much deeper happening to the soul or the spirit? Maybe a prophesy of things yet to come? If so, why was this shown to me now? So many questions that left me in a state of paranoia. With reverence, I opened up to the Buddhist Monk about the visions. As usual, his response would keep me hungry to see more.

The Buddhist Monk said, 'It could be a portal to another realm, another world, or it could be a reincarnation portal.'

Placing his finger on his chin, he thought through for a few seconds and said, 'Where was this portal located? Was it in front of you?'

Thoughtfully, I replied to make sure I was accurate, 'No, it was on the left. This huge portal was on my left.'

He guided, 'Something was going on and you were there to bear witness to it. The true meaning behind the vision is for you to determine. It is shown to you at this time for a reason.'

If that was true, it was certainly timely as I had prodded through years with agonizing questions of the purpose of my infinitesimal life on Planet Earth within the grand scale of things.

For one thing, I was still unclear about the differences between the soul and the Spirit. Some experts say that the gate to the Soul as "imagination", "conscience", "memory", "reason" and "affections". They say that the Spirit receives impressions of outward and material things through the soul, where the Spirit is the projection of the soul.

If it was the spirit and soul that confused me, the anomaly that beleaguered my mind with a flurry of questions was the portal. Was the portal a reincarnation tunnel for those departed souls, according to Buddhist beliefs? Alternatively, was it a gateway into a different dimension? Perhaps, a symbolic message that either we transformed ourselves to a higher energy vibration and moved onto a lighter brighter world; or simply remained where we are in this denser civilization. A compelling answer that recoiled back at me. A clear visual representation that we have two important choices to make: we could either become souls shining with radiant golden energy field, or be distressed and depressed souls with a dull gray misty energy field. Two contrasting versions of the Spirit Man (Spirit Woman).

I reflected candidly on my life. An intrinsically deep yet reluctant acceptance that if my soul were stripped away from my body, a weak gray energy field would be revealed. Ideally, I wanted to have a shining golden Spirit Woman. A rude wake-up call to face the reality of my present state. In fact, I imagined that in this world billions of us would be living in this denser civilization where we were our denser "gray" selves.

In the recent years, through the recurring financial crisis' and the growth of militants and terrorism, the concept of a structured life has been destroyed for millions. People were either losing or have lost their homes, their regular incomes disintegrated and their stability gone. Many are left with nothing to cling to. For those who are not used to stepping out of their comfort zone, they were enveloped in fear. This was an Old World that was amassed by gray misty souls. On the other hand, there were the handful of Golden Souls. Could they have developed their inner strength, inner wisdom and were prepared for the massive changes? Maybe their absence of fear have made them pillars on which others could lean on when nothing made sense anymore. From another perspective, were these Golden Souls emanating with cohesive and integrating energies, moving away from the negative energies which were causing separation and segregation?

This compelled me to research even more. A lonely journey of research and analysis as I bounced ideas in my head, compiling, assessing and speculating. The gray misty souls, the Golden Souls and the undefined and unknown Portal. Was that it, or was there much more to this? How would the knowledge of this impact us and the Planet Earth as a whole?

One of those fundamental rules is that everything is made up from little bits, and that we were the little bits, like particles. Material objects are made up of particles, but also the forces that keep those objects together (and apart at the same time to prevent collision). Light, other than making things visible, was the electromagnetic force keeping electrons tied to the nuclei of atoms, and atoms tied together to make molecules and finally objects. Similarly, as humans we are like the electrons tied to our families (the atoms), which is further tied to a country (molecules) and then to the object, in this case, planet Earth.

"Light" being the ultimate consolidator of this molecular structure made up of all those particles. So assuming that we were all Golden Souls, then everything would come together to create a hypothetical Golden Planet. I was getting into hypothesis again, but it was fun exploring, and the destination exciting. I continued my research and analysis. In both Islamic and Biblical Scriptures, God is often referred to as Light. Most exegetes focus on the metaphorical value of these statements. But as we realize that all forms of matter are in fact solidified light (energy, as in $E=mc^2$) and the electromagnetic force. This brings us back to the notion that we need to be Light personified, which also means in the image of the One True God Head.

Other than Buddhist meditation techniques, I had spent some time studying the Sufi traditions. Sparks of the Spirit of God, according to Sufi tradition, synonymous with the highest level of our human soul. Logically speaking, only then could we become the facilitators for an integrating force bringing everything within the planet Earth together to the highest level. If a majority of us were to remain as those hunched gray misty souls replete with darker energies, there would be no hope of unifying and stabilizing our planet. The intensifying breakages and collapses of anything and everything from the economy to the ecology would persist.

The elusive question was, what was the highest level of the soul? There must have been Golden Souls that existed before in history. Were they appropriate examples for this era? If not, were we going to become like Golden Souls like never before in recorded history?

If the answer was 'Yes' to the former question, then some of the legendary figures who graced the masses over the centuries across the continents may be the treasured Golden Souls. Socrates, the most recognized philosopher of all time, who taught that people should focus their lives on self- development and gaining knowledge. Moreover, Plato, the philosopher and mathematician, was Socrates' prized student who wrote enduring philosophical literature that has influenced almost every culture that has read them. Mother Theresa, who was the greatest inspiration of the concept of giving wholehearted free service to the poorest of the poor. Gandhi, the father of the Indian independence movement who spent a lifetime preaching *satyagarha*, a non-violent way of protesting against injustices.

My instincts were beckoning that we were moving towards a far greater advancement both spiritually and physically than ever before. I wanted to call it the New World. It could be an aspect of a Type I civilization or beyond. Holistically, it could be a reflection of Heaven on Earth. And if we did reflect on our achievements, for example those of Albert Einstein whose creative intelligence and intuitive insights opened up our minds to the way the universe operates, I sensed that our past accomplishments would appear elementary from where we were heading to.

From Carbon to Crystalline

I stood at the last row of a Christian conference. I was in an investigative mode. I wanted to understand what and to where this Portal was leading to and I was trying to explore all avenues to get my answers. If it was a Reincarnation Portal, then well and good. But if it was not, I had to keep exploring. I managed to grab a seat on the last day. There was such an information overload that it just swept over my head with little understanding of all the symbolism, terminology and quotations recited in memory by the speakers.

One of the assisting speakers was introduced as Marianne Smith. A vivacious short-haired brunette in her late 50s, she wore a tailored dark blue pant suit which slimmed down her well rounded figure. She added a little feminine touch to her image with an orange persimmon flowered blouse. Marianne was visiting Singapore all the way from South Carolina of the United States. I could see that she was exhausted from a full day conference she had completed. But she was glowing, glowing like a beacon. I went straight up to her for that sole purpose and to find out why.

Flustered but happy that she was done for the day, she remarked in a Southern accent, 'Oh, its the Glory!'

'What is that?' I asked.

'Come for my next conference and I will tell you more about that. By the way, what's your name?' she said.

'Tahira,' I replied.

She said with a smile, 'A lovely name. What does it mean?'

I was asked that question many times before, and answered, 'It means "pure" and "holy" in Arabic.'

Marianne replied, 'Very interesting. That is exactly what everyone of us is supposed to become. Holy like the Saints. Our hearts pure and undefiled.'

One of the male participants of the conference approached her and she turned to attend to him.

I spoke quickly to catch her attention, 'Oh, could I ask a question? Just a quick one.'

She said, 'Of course!'

I asked, 'Your presence is glowing as I said, but why is your skin sparkling with gold? Is that some kind of mineral makeup?'

She shook her head and said, 'Nope!'

I added, 'Then? I have not seen that on any person. I am not sure about the others though.'

I paused realizing my intrusion and said, 'I apologize. I have a naturally curious mind. Being a bit of science freak myself, these things need to make some sense to me logically.'

She replied, 'That's perfectly fine.'

I said pleased with Marianne's response, 'I just like to know and see that there is a symmetry and meaning to everything. Correction, not everything as some things can't be explained. But still, there must be some underlying justification to everything.'

She grabbed my hand excitedly and said, 'Tell you what. Let me wash up a little and I want to share something with you over dinner.'

Combed and washed up, she returned in half and hour from the Ladies.

Marianne said, 'Let's have some Thai food. Over dinner I will share something which happened to me. And here in my iPad I am carrying some of the evidence. And I want you to help me out to find out more.'

The conference was at the Orchard Hotel. It was 7pm and we walked the streets of Orchard looking for a good Thai restaurant. With many in the vicinity, we found one round the corner. As soon as we were seated, she ordered some of her and my preferences which were mostly light but spicy dishes. In moments, Marianne started opening up about a turning point in her life.

Marianne explained, 'My life entered a whole new paradigm several years ago. I was standing on a platform while ministering with passion and intensity about the Glory of God and taking the path of Jesus. An unexpected moment struck when I was getting a lot of gold dust on my skin and it was growing more and more on my palms.' she continued, 'The gold dust was in between the palm of my skin. Not on it. Not below it.'

She was trying to tell me that the gold dust was interwoven as if it was the very fabric of her skin.

Marianne explained enthusiastically, 'What amazed me even more was how through the skin the gold dust fragments were actually growing; heat was in my hands, so intense that my skin started peeling off,' she added, 'I kept the skin sample sealed in a bag. Then several years passed, I noticed that skin barely decomposed, almost remaining intact. Of course I was even more determined to investigate what was really going on. I went to a laboratory to get the skin clinically examined and analyzed by a scientist.'

With heightened excitement, she shared, 'The microscope was too small so the lab scientist took me to a bigger one located in another room. He checked the top and then the bottom of my skin. Structure of the gold dust was a symmetrical triad of 10-10-10. Not sure which measurement whether it was troy ounces or grams or pennyweight,' she continued, 'Well, the laboratory scientist who studied my skin said that it could not be classified as human skin since all skin loses its shape over time, but the finger printing of my skin remained through the years. Believe me, I always did have normal skin throughout my adult life. However, it was after that incident that my skin quality has transformed to something that was beyond ...' Marianne paused acknowledging her own disbelief that she was a living testimony, 'beyond explanation ... beyond what the scientists had ever witnessed in any living human being!'

Fueled with a fire to unravel the mystery, while having dinner with Marianne, I opened up my iPhone with her permission to research while on the go. I was such an avid searcher that I could do it fast while eating.

She said, 'Yes, this is exciting stuff and almost emancipating that such levels of transformation perhaps in human is happening. I am really eager to find out what you discover. So please ... go ahead and do what you need to understand more about this.'

Crisscrossing with analysis as I went through online articles and studies on our DNAs and the Truth behind them. What she shared could be a sign of the impending crystallization of her skin. There are some theories that claim that we are being changed physically from carbon-based being with 2 strands of DNA into crystalline beings with 1,024 strands of DNA (eventually) because only crystalline substances can exist on higher dimensional levels. Furthermore, Carbon is necessary to form all DNA, which is part of the chemical code of life as it currently exists. And the Carbon atom has 6 electrons, 6 neutrons and 6 protons. Periodic Table of the Elements, the atomic number for the Carbon element is also 6. Interesting, from 6-6-6 the mark of the beast (as in Scriptures) to 10-10-10 the sign of perfection.

Are we moving from beast to beings of Light? Were we heading towards the perfection of our physical bodies? Or was it more accurately a metamorphosis of our physicality to perfectly align with a renewed mind, spirit and soul?

I went further to read what Dr. Max G. Lagally did with regards to clinical research on silicon membranes. A certified BS, MS, Ph.D, he was a Professor of Surface Science at the University of Wisconsin–Madison. In 2006, he began developing silicon membranes in the Department of Materials Science and Engineering at the University of Wisconsin, Madison. In his research, he has discovered that the surface of a silicon membrane can be functioned to become biologically sensitive. He theorizes that it could bind DNA.

In other words, silicon can support life.

As she saw me thinking deeply over the information, Marianne looked at me and said, 'Explain to me simply. I don't really understand all that scientific jargon.'

Putting down my iPhone on the dinner table, I said, 'Here is a simple analogy to explain the idea. When a log of wood is placed in a fire, it burns down until all that remains is the Carbon element. But if a diamond is placed in a fire, its structure is retained. So all of our cells must be transformed from carbon to silicon crystal so that we can withstand the tremendous amount of Light that will be streaming into the planet.'

I picked up my indispensable smartphone and did another quick search on mystics and crystalline. I uncovered some evidence showing recent discoveries of mystics who have passed on, yet their dead bodies were well preserved, with whole muscles and inner tissue, soft joints and skin – remarkably without any signs of decay. So these mystics may have crystalline bodies that do not rot. I showed the information I dug up through the Google search and showed the well preserved bodies of the mystics to Marianne.

She said, 'Yes, I believe that this is just the beginning. We may all become like that. I am not the expert, but you need to find out more.'

Were these mystics so enveloped in the Light of God that facilitated the crystallization process? If the DNA "Carbon to Crystalline" is the theory behind the "embedded in the skin" gold dust, there could be a possibility that the Marianne's DNA position could be within the crystallization process itself. Nonetheless, she did not physically look any different in terms of the general physical structure of an average human being. However, as a human being becomes more and more crystalline genetically, he or she may be more radiant in subtle ways, but internally they will develop greater depths of emotion, perception, intuition, and sensitivity.

Radiance was an understatement. And she showed great depth in the emotion of love. As soon as the bill was paid, we both walked across the restaurant towards the door. Marianne was shining like a beacon as always, and several people from various tables turned to look at her. They looked like they were a mix group of Singaporean Chinese, or from Mainland China, or maybe even Burma and Thailand. They were grinning with joy looking at her and some of them gregariously opened their arms wide for a hug.

I turned to her puzzled and asked, 'Do you know these people?'

She responded with a positive intensity, 'No! I have never seen them before in my life! But this happens to me all the time. People look at me and they just want a hug!'

It was not just those people, who apparently were perfect strangers to her, but the waiters and the manager at the restaurant who joined in too. It was a hug one-to-one and sometimes a group hug. She ran to each of them as if she had not seen them for years, shining with love and joy on her face. One hug after another.

She said, 'Just look at this. These people tell me that they are Buddhists, Taoists, Free Thinkers. But they could all recognize the Love of God shining through me. They do not know me - I am not famous nor have I ever visited Singapore before! But they recognized God. The Love of God that breaks all barriers!'

I was convinced that Marianne was a living example of a golden soul. She was shining like a beacon with arms opened wide radiating a presence larger than life. She was like an evolving crystalline being shining with the Light. I felt jubilant just by knowing her and what I learned which was invaluable. Wishing that we could interact more often so that I would learn from her, I promised that I would try to check out a local laboratory here in Singapore to do further tests on those skin samples.

As I reflected on her physical transformation, I recalled the weeks of my own bodily pain which commenced soon after those disciplined prayers and meditations. Every night, my arms and legs felt like they were tied to a moving tow truck pulling with great force. I would be groaning with pain at times begging for it to stop. Unexplained by my doctors, instinctively I knew the initial DNA changes may have had a role to play. Through the regular prayers and meditations, I had opened myself up to receive downloads upon downloads of new information, words of knowledge, revelations, insights. Something had sparked the release of higher vibrational energies, which I felt was the catalyst for the DNA changes.

The human DNA contained the secret code, and I went deeper to learn more. Human DNA has been found to have two codes: big code and basic code. Though the word "junk" riles a lot of people in the scientific field. If Junk DNA is like a computer basic system upgrade, is God flipping the switch now? Like a sleeping giant, our DNA was just waiting to be fully activated. Once it is activated, experts say that it brings about the heightened awareness and the new human abilities. Heightened awareness by developing a deeper connection with God, this bringing about financial breakthroughs, a touch on personal relationships, release from addiction and more. Supernatural abilities such as the healing touch and miraculous creations and breakthrough ideas.

Crystal crystalline solid is a solid material whose constituents, such as atoms, molecules or ions, are arranged in a highly ordered microscopic structure, forming a crystal lattice that extends in all directions.

DNA (Deoxyribonucleic acid) as a molecule that encodes the genetic instructions used in the development and functioning of all known living organisms and many viruses. DNA is made up of four chemicals, abbreviated as letters A, T, G, and C. Much like the '1's and '0's, these letters are arranged in the human cell like this: CGTGTGACTCGCTCCTGAT and so on. The order in which they are arranged instructs the cell's actions.

Junk DNA Human DNA has been found to have two codes: big code and basic code. Junk DNA is hidden and dormant upgrade of our basic code. Junk DNA was like a computer basic system upgrade from which the user can then download and adapt it to suit their needs (most ordinary people only use a very small fraction of their computers potential, but will be familiar with upgrades). Some microbiology experts tell us that over 97% of our DNA is apparent*ly unused (junk).*

From Soul to Spirit-driven

Some experts claim that it is not just we as humans who are changing, but all life forms on Earth are becoming crystalline. All the fish in the sea, the flowers and trees in our garden, and the birds in the sky. Everything is changing, while some will move ahead with the change faster than others. Nothing will die or be destroyed, for we are all moving together into a new state of being. Could this be Darwin's theories being disproved?

The theory of the Evolution of Species debunked as the DNA molecule is just too complicated to have arisen by natural mutations. Dr Francis Harry Compton Crick (1916 - 2004), one of the original discoverers of the DNA molecule, later proved mathematically that it is absolutely impossible for evolution to have ever even begun to produce DNA in the short amount of history that we have as a planet.

Impossible? What was the missing link that caused the massive jump start forward? As I wracked my brain for an answer, I continued to consult Marianne.

She raised a point, 'We have been very much soul driven. We have reached a point of time that it is now about developing the Spirit Man or Spirit Woman.'

Something within me began to resonate as she spoke about the Spirit Man (Spirit Woman). The human mind and soul is plagued with anxious thoughts, troublesome feelings, and impure intentions, however it is our spirit that is our innermost part with which we contact God and substantiate all things of the spiritual realm. The faculties of the spirit are attained through "faith", "hope", "reverence", "prayer" and "worship".

Marianne said, 'Our Spirit Man (Spirit Woman) is growing from the inside out, and one day it will grow so big that it will break all the yokes surrounding us'.

A laudable statement. The Golden Souls I saw were almost double or triple the size of the gray misty souls trailing behind them. Then it occurred to me that the elongated Golden Souls could be a radiating expression of the renewed Spirit Man (Spirit Woman). As a result, a critical need to raise our frequencies so that we can enter the New World.

History tugging me back again for a cross-reference. Even if we are going to become like Golden Souls like never before, there must be something in the past that was done to aid the process. Besides it was all over the History Channel on the TV. Ancient history recording the building of structures to raise the vibrations of the human soul to bright golden energies. These structures may have been designed to expand the Spirit Man (Spirit Woman). *Angkor*

Wat of Cambodia, the pyramids of Egypt, Macchu Picchu of Peru, Borobudur of Indonesia, to name a few acting as generators to raise the energy frequencies. They were designed based on the Golden Mean so that these structures may become like resonant chambers that amplify the vibrational energies.

If that was the case, why did we move backwards? Were there fewer Golden Souls on this planet relative to the Darkness? Although the Buddhist Monk was positive when I asked him this question before. Common sense guided me that those pyramid shaped mechanical structures played but a small part in the enhancement of vibrational energies. There was much more. Besides, external manipulation to raise vibrational energies has a temporal effect. Since the Spirit, is the innermost part that we contact God with, we have to cleanse ourselves internally so that we no longer become physical containers for darker energies. Like Marianne, we had to become lighter, and go closer and closer to becoming like Light, in the image of God. I was a child of God, but I was not reflective of the image of God. I did not need anyone to tell me that. My plagued mind, body and soul were a testament to that. So I began to explore all the ways to expand my Spirit Woman.

Empowering the Spirit Man (Spirit Woman)

To remain centered always as I had already learned through stillness. To be free from stress, from abuse, free from addiction, anger, fear and many other negative influences. To reduce stress by letting go of work situations that no longer serve. To make healthy choices in the associations with people as a conducive fellowship raises my vibrational energies. To come back to the priorities of regular prayer and soaking in the words and guidance of Scriptures of God.

The to-do list was getting long and there was still so much more. Physically, I had to lighten and strengthen my body through oxygenation, hydration, occasional fasting and any activities that induced the removal of toxins. Eating raw or live foods, moving away from heavier foods. I read about the resurgent popularity of macrobiotics, a term originally coined by Hippocrates to refer to individuals and communities of people who were healthy and long-lived. Essentially, growing the Spirit Man (Spirit Woman) was all about frequency – linking everything together, mind, body and soul.

Marianne's words, 'The purpose of the mind is to empower the Spirit Man (Spirit Woman) to function.'

'If you want to find the secrets of the universe, think in terms of energy, frequency and vibration,' ~ Nikola Tesla

Are we moving on up energetically? Moving into a new position? The divine signs were there and they were shown to me personally. Considering the tumultuous state of our world today, the timing seemed right. There was a sense of urgency. There was a Russian quantum biologist by the name of Dr Poponin who had conducted a DNA Phantom Effect experiment which gives an interesting perspective on how the New World was a very ready reality and that direct human influence is not involved. We simply needed to switch into that physicality. Just a switch? A too simple an answer to a complicated issue. If these DNA activations have been going in the recent years, then it could mean that Planet Earth is now at its proper frequency position.

Was this another proof of God's divine plan? These words permeated through my mind.

'An eternal echo that still keeps going. Let there be Light!'

We need to be prepared to bring in the New World. It's time to pave the way for the illuminating Spirit Man (Spirit Woman) within ourselves. It's about ensuring that human beings with illuminating Golden Spirit Man (Spirit Woman) make up an overwhelming presence on Planet Earth. Along the way, if we advance in unison in the right direction, the existence of gray misty souls with respect to the majority on this planet would become smaller and smaller in proportion. Armed with new learning on the Spirit and DNA, I had to endeavor to take all the actions necessary. The list was long and I was lost as to where to begin. Finally, something led me to nature.

DNA phantom effect is an example of subtle energy manifestation in which direct human influence is not involved. Dr. Poponin put DNA in a tube and shone a laser through it, and to his surprise he realized that it actually captured the light and caused it to spiral through the helix, as if it were a crystal. Even more amazingly, when Dr. Poponin removed the DNA, the light continued spiraling on its own. For light to form a DNA helix on its own should of course be impossible, unless the light itself had become harmonically tuned to some naturally existing frequency in the energy of space around it. This could mean that the spiraling light energy of DNA was there first, and the physical molecules simply formed around the spiraling energy once the planet was at the proper frequency position.

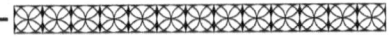

4

Intertwining with Nature

As the mysteries of nature open up
More of God
More of the New World
Is revealed.

Bringing forth the creation
Of a renewed home.
No longer
A sense of hiraeth.

A home truly connected
With the animal kingdom,
With plants and trees,
With all forms of nature,
On land and sea.

Ubud, Bali, Indonesia,
July 2012.

The time-stamp was July 2012. It was a mere two months after the vision of the Golden Souls at the Gardens by the Bay. I allowed circumstances to push me with a big hard shove to experience a radical change in environment. The change was long overdue. Earthly transitory needs and wants had taken precedence for far too long. After four weeks of thinking about Bali, a moment of truth and a decision to move and live there was made. An enviable dream destination for many. Who could imagine? I had visited Bali before on short 3 or 4 day trips, but this move was going to be a completely different experience with a completely different purpose.

Soon it was all bags packed for Bali. Just a two hour flight away, the island shared the same time zone as Singapore, yet it manifested a totally different existence. Singapore had business running through its veins, Bali had nature and leisure woven in its ancient fabric. Incidentally, it was also a decision made by close friends with their families, spouses and children, all making the same dramatic and sudden shift. An asynchronous move in tandem. The beginnings of a new adventure.

We spent the first few months in central Bali, up in Ubud, a quiet yet iconic tourist village. I stayed in a villa managed by a friend by the name of Olga who is a Reiki healer. Her home is a villa tucked away deep in the Bali forests, decorated with all the little healing spa comforts. She had given up city life in Singapore (and her homeland in Armenia) to nourish her soul in the natural tranquility of Bali. Although she would commute to Singapore monthly to meet her clients, she was quite satisfied making her home in a rustic open-air villa surrounded on all sides by the tall trees of a deep enchanting forest.

As we walked up the partially cobbled earthen path towards her villa, we could see her sitting at the porch with a coterie of animals surrounding her protectively. The villa had an open concept design except for the bedrooms and bathrooms which were walled for privacy.

She received us with a beautiful effervescent smile, 'Welcome! This is my humble abode. All in the open with the birds and the trees. Come sit in the outdoor living room lounge and just soak in the ambiance!'

Excited I made myself comfortable at the open living room where the only modern amenity was a large plasma TV. The rest of the furniture was simple weatherproof bamboo sofas and tables. Long curtains were draped to create a separation between the rooms – adjacent to the living room was the healing room.. With a few paintings from the local Balinese artists, the fuss-free set up of the home emphasized the natural surroundings in every way.

Olga brushed aside the long fringe of her shoulder-length hair and pointed happily at her son who was playing with the animals in the garden.

She said, 'Ah, there he is. Remember my son? He has grown into a big boy. These animals are like his brothers and sisters. See how he plays with them!'

Her son was basking in the Sun as he rolled in the garden with the dogs and the cats, talking to them and giving them his full attention, totally oblivious to the people watching him. As a single mom, Olga adored her son and showered him with the immense love and care of a mother. She was an animal and nature lover and had a perpetual love affair with both. A rare woman who was so deeply connected with the Earth, that it was the very oxygen she breathed.

I enjoyed the feel of the place, with the occasional distraction from the roosters that would crow at random times of the day.

Olga shared her personal story as we listened, 'I was living in Singapore for a few years, and felt the lack of nature at that time. Each year it became increasingly difficult for me. It reached a point that I literally felt I could not breathe. I had the overwhelming need to be close to trees and to touch the earth with my feet. The Botanic Gardens was among of the few places in Singapore where I could recharge myself ecologically.'

Then her voice broke as she opened up, 'I remember the painful day in Singapore, when I lost a few members of my family. I prayed to God to ask Him to show me the way. This song started playing in my head … "I'm coming home. I'm coming home. Tell the world, I'm coming home." I knew that it was a message from God - giving me a final push to Bali, my new home.'

Her personal trauma appeared over and her aura was radiant, as red and vibrant as her fiery red hair. It was clear that she had no regrets. Living in an environment that was so infused with nature, she felt happy, healthy and grounded.

She said, 'Here the natural energies needed for my healing sessions are magnified. And for my own healing too.'

The sound of crickets and bullfrogs all night was deafening. A large slippery gecko that refused to budge from the roofless bathroom, would perch itself on the top of the wall projecting a commanding presence. There were other non-human visitors as well. The occasional visit by the village dog, who would come in for a romp around the garden, take a dive in the garden pond and then leave. The stray kitten that decided to make the villa her home and would join Olga in healing sessions. While Olga laid hands on her patients for healing, the kitten would sit on her lap and lay her paw in a similar fashion with Olga's, eyes closed and purring. In the meantime, the cow and the pig that lived next door made their presence known audibly. The multitudinous creatures that lived in the forest trees; they were invisible to the eye but their presence and aliveness was neither to be denied nor ignored.

Olga said, 'I rarely feel alone here. Every minute that passes is awe-filled with an abundance of life brimming within this place.'

A dual maternal and paternal presence from nature itself. Refreshing yet warm and comfortable, open and expansive yet tender and protective.

A city dweller all my life, this made me look at homes from a totally different perspective. It was such a pity that there are some cities where the amount of greenery is limited by intent, with priority given to concrete structures, be they residential or commercial. Furthermore, interaction with animals is limited to pet ownership for those who decide to have them at home. Here, there were animals everywhere, some domesticated and some free. Some like the gecko had just invited themselves over and decided to become part of the household.

Olga said, 'Did you know that human beings are one of an estimated 2 to 30 million species of animals living on Planet Earth today? Yet, we create disconnect through our urban living by designing it to disconnect with nature,' she continued, 'Of course, a lot of homes are being designed around nature. But there is so much more that can be done.'

Olga reached out for a magazine she was reading, which was sitting on the tabletop at the living room.

She flipped the pages to one article, 'Just look at this article here. Some research indicated that those who grow up in a city have a two- to three-fold higher likelihood of developing schizophrenia. Earlier studies show that even after reaching adulthood, city living raised the probability of contracting anxiety disorders and mood illnesses, such as depression.'

I scanned through the article and gave my views, 'I suppose being around nature helps us advance or progress in a way.'

Olga replied, 'Precisely. I received many revelations through my prayers and meditations while surrounded by nature. It gave me clarity of mind.' she continued, 'My mind opened up. I could connect with God so much better than before. I learned about forgiveness, which I greatly needed to learn. I was in a mental block before. Or shall I say my heart was blocked!'

Shifting over to talk about forgiveness, Olga said, 'Well that was the one thing that saved me. I discovered the answer while living in Bali,' she continued, 'FORGIVE ! We are able to forgive only if we take responsibilities for our choice. Without the approval of our soul, nothing can happen. Gratitude is just as important. To practice GRATITUDE daily. That is the essence of my daily prayers. Forgiving others and offering gratitude to God.'

Pointing to a small tree at the far end of her garden, she said, 'I conduct all my prayers while sitting on the grass under that tree. The green grass is my natural prayer rug. I love it!'

Closing her words with a broad smile. Suddenly, an all important thought stuck her that she needed to share with me.

She said, 'I need to warn you. Because of the thick presence of nature, with all those regular Balinese rituals of prayers happening around this village, the energies around this area are very intense.'

I asked, 'What do you mean – intense?'

Olga shared, 'If your heart is mostly filled with purity and goodness, these positive energies will be multiplied here. However, if you heart is mostly filled with the impure energies of hate and anger, these negative energies would be multiplied too,' she added, 'I have seen apparently nice people get into a fit of rage, while some others become even nicer than ever. It depends on what is in their heart rather than their external behavior. If your heart is filled with unforgiveness and bitterness, then I would not want to be around when the magnification of those negative energies happen!'

She laughed, 'You see, we can't pretend while you are here,' she continued 'I believe that we were all sent to Bali to start the cleansing process.'

'Really?' I questioned.

Olga said, 'Yes, like the kidney of the Earth.'

If that was the case, I was excited and prepared for the detox. I was filled to the brim with toxicity. Since this was the start of my journey, Bali would perhaps play a role in the purification process.

Fortunately, for her and me, I felt calmer and more at peace with myself than ever before. I could almost feel the cleansing within. From a physical aspect I felt as if the natural streams of fresh waters in Ubud were a hydrating sustenance for my body, with the life and it's functions so intimately intertwined with nature. I felt elevated. Much more so then ever before. A fresh, crisp, lasting feeling.

Olga said, 'Our vibrational energy is kept at an optimal level when we have a regular interaction with nature. Everything that has consciousness is connected and gives life to each other,' she continued, 'Ever since I could raise my vibrational energies by practicing forgiveness and gratitude, I started to feel an overwhelming feeling of love within me. And it has been a year now since I moved to Bali. I feel much more alive than I ever did before!'

Multidimensional beings of consciousness

It was one of those uncomfortable mornings. A recurrence of my allergies. Olga looked concerned and placed her hand on my shoulder comfortingly, 'Your soul is crying.'

Initially, I felt that was a very peculiar statement. I had never looked at my soul that way.

She said, 'I know what you are thinking. Our soul speaks to us in strange ways,' Olga paused and said, 'And so do our bodies. I have had this strange sensation the past few weeks. It is hard to describe. Today this mysterious sensation finally peaked.'

I asked curiously, 'Tell me more.'

Olga answered, 'When I would look at anything, I found that I could see people's energies, just like nocturnal animals seeing in the dark. At times, I would see their faces in one way, and then sometimes I would see their faces in another way. And it would shift from one face to another.'

I asked with a barrage of questions, 'Did you see different colors? Or just one color? And when you saw the faces, did you think you were shown their "true face" beyond a face they project to the world – like a mask?'

Assembling my questions to be answered, she replied consistently, 'Different colors like auras. I saw people as energy beings. Regarding the faces, yes, they would flip from one to another. Maybe showing their "true" face. I don't know. This is new to me.'

A strange phenomenon indeed. Possibly a clue to something bigger – the ability to unveil. Digesting what she just said, I felt the looming in of the majestic trees that covered the village, as though they were listening to our conversation.

Some of the trees were so close to the villa surrounding it completely that they appeared a mile high. Looming, protecting, shielding - almost human-like - multidimensional beings with consciousness. Trees with their own unveiling abilities, pushing me deeper into an unceasing and unrelenting research. I was aware from prior research that a tree's antennae stretch off the Earth to pull down energy from the electromagnetic field to be used in certain ways for the purpose of growth and expansion, for the purpose of communication and forming a network, or grid in a sense, over the entire planet, at a certain frequency that supports life of all kinds. They are considered in that way a kind matrix of energy, antennae that moderate a particular pulse of energy that supports the ability of life to express itself on Planet Earth in all forms.

I was no expert but I knew instinctively that different trees had different frequencies – as would multidimensional beings with consciousness. Especially larger older trees like the Redwood Tree or the Banyan Tree. I read that one of the most notable, is the General Sherman, a Giant Sequoia located in the Giant Forest of Sequoia National Park in California, at 11.1 meter (36.5 ft) along the base. These giant trees were the ambassadors of the tree world. Each tree as if an atom within a larger communion of trees, in a constant state of information exchange, by breathing on what they give off and breathing on what we give off, assuring the energetic bond between us that allows for the support of life - the communion of all the cells in our body and the cells of the tree. This is achieved not only electromagnetically, but at the molecular level as well. As I wrote down my findings, Olga looked on inquisitively.

She said, 'Each tree has a unique frequency. So do we. We all have a unique frequency.'

Synthesizing all that I had discovered, it was clear that the closer nature and humans are, the greater the Life-Giving manifestation. It helps alleviate loneliness, it is uplifting and gives us a greater feeling of connectedness. Not a coincidence that ancient cultures from all over the world just happened to encode the same geometric structure of the fabric of universe into their architecture, and monuments. The universe, a 3D holographic fractal moving infinitely both ways, of perfectly spaced spheres. Based on fractals which prove self-similarity, the universe with its overlapping spheres can be seen as this connectedness and life-giving force.

In fact, I discovered another research report that proved that large old trees are critical in many natural and human-dominated environments. It was disheartening to read in the report that populations of these trees are declining rapidly. The alarming decline in old trees in so many types of forest was stated to be driven by a combination of factors, including land clearing, agricultural practices, man-made changes in fire regimes, logging and timber gathering, insect attack, and rapid climatic changes. The authors of the report made a call for an urgent world-wide investigation to assess the extent of large tree depletion, and to identify areas where big trees have a better chance of survival. What a waste that I had taken trees for granted all this time.

I awoke the next morning with a vivid dream. Whether it was by sheer coincidence, or because my thoughts were so much on trees, my dream was about the Giant Tree. More specifically, it featured the close-up of the tree trunk of a Giant Tree. It appeared as a looming dark brown conscious being exuding strength and stability. After which, the dream switched scenes to show me the skyline of the Singapore city, across the Marina Bay coastline. It was the Gardens by the Bay at the Marina Bay, where I was shown the glowing Golden Souls.

Just a quarter to seven and the morning in Ubud was as bright as ever. I did not even have the chance to really think through the dream before Olga's 12 year old son entered the bedroom I slept in.

Her son asked coyly, 'Would you like to go on a tour of this village? We can go all around to see the paddy fields.'

I replied, 'Of course my dear. I will be more than happy to.'

Accepting the invitation with enthusiasm, I got myself ready quickly to join his little tour. Nimble with his white bike he set off in a scurry while his eager dog followed to keep an eye on his master. Comfortable among the relatively docile wildlife of Bali, Olga's son weaved across the muddy tracks. A large white crystal gemstone necklace given to him by his mother would bounce on his chest with each movement over the uneven tracks. He knew exactly where to go and how to take care of himself. I trailed behind on foot lumbering in my bulky track shoes.

I was shown a view of sporadic villas, some with contrasting designs nestled across the fields. An eclectic mix of people lived in the neighborhood. Some were local Balinese who spent almost all of their time outdoors - from eating to bathing the traditional way, equipped with buckets and all. The local Balinese were usually also the owners of the more opulent villas occupied by their mostly expatriate tenants. The expats were from all over. An American couple who had made Bali their home, while the husband would travel to New York to handle work-related matters every two weeks. A German family who were writers, an Australian couple and the list went on. Every family compound would have its own family temple, where they would go to worship several times a day. Within the neighborhood, there was harmony despite the diversity of the people living together.

Intertwined with nature, a peaceful serenity filled the air. The gecko stalked on the villa rooftops act as surveillance, making sure that nothing alien enters the villa grounds. No Balinese family would be complete without a dog to guard the front door, and a handful of roosters, which are sacred animals in Bali and used for fighting and for ceremonies. The tall trees act as custodians with their watchful presence as they stay in fixed permanence. The Balinese village elder ensures the rules are followed amongst the village members. Each person, animal and plant (tree) had their allotted task, which they fulfilled both dutifully and peacefully.

As soon as I returned to the villa, I rested on the bamboo couch in the living room porch. Olga joined me as she had just finished a Reiki healing session.

I told her, 'I am writing this book. I guess it's about how we are shifting towards a new planetary civilization. I simply refer to it as the New World.'

She nodded and listened as I continued, 'I am trying to work out the blueprint of this New World in my head. Here is what I envision from my learning in Bali. People will be using more and more of the spaces outside their homes. People in neighborhoods will be brought together, they and of course animals, creating a natural form of surveillance. The environment shall be beautified to provide an inviting habitat for God's creatures.'

Olga agreed and gave some points of her own, 'Countries around the world should take Bali as an example for its interconnectedness with nature. Oneness with not only ourselves, but with nature and all of God's creations. In fact, some research proves that the more vegetation there is in a neighborhood, the less crime. I know it sounds radical, but it's true.'

Since the Giant Tree oneiric, I was captivated to learn more about such trees. Perhaps to discover some divine purpose. Moreover, I imagined that in the New World the symbiotic relationship between humanity and nature would reach its optimum manifestation once many of us start dwelling in such accommodations and environs. An ascended and highly evolved residential norm, with our vibrational frequencies elevated through nature as one contributing factor.

Electromagnetic is a type of physical interaction that occurs between electrically charged particles. The electromagnetic force usually manifests as electromagnetic fields, such as electric fields, magnetic fields and light. **Electromagnetic force** holds all atoms together.

Fractals prove self-similarity at various scales. Magnifying a fractal reveals small-scale details similar to the large-scale characteristics. Imagine consciousness as a fractal, starting from source and then multiplying infinitely out through self-*similarity*.

Deriving the Wisdom From Animals

South Bali, Indonesia,
September 2012

Moving down to South Bali, I met with a gentleman who worked around the area. He was an American who, like Olga, had chosen to make Bali his home after the demise of a flourishing business in the United States. A youthful looking 60 year old, he fashioned a healthy tan and washboard abs thanks to daily surfing on the beach. He introduced himself as David. A pioneering and visionary businessman who bought a plot of beach property, two decades ago when its only asset was a couple of coconut trees. Now the plot of land he owned was teaming with resorts promoting open and natural living.

One of his new hats was as a philanthropist, which he wore with pride. He worked with vigor to financially support various animal activist projects in Bali and around the world. His plans were to urge Indonesia and other countries around the world to free the dolphins. Campaigns were launched to open the eyes of society about the importance of banning traveling circuses from using dolphins in their shows as these noble and sentient earthlings suffered greatly in captivity.

David shared, 'All my life, I would act on my freewill and my choices made my destiny. This, of course, has always pushed me to work a lot harder. Though I must say that I have had my share of supernatural experiences showing me that there could be something more.'

Driven to understand what motivated him, I probed further, 'We have some things in common. I have had my fair share of visions and some amazing ones which have made me question. But do tell me more of yours.'

David replied, 'Well, where do I start? Let's say, I felt some kind of Universal Source leading me. The Universal Source as many of you would call God. It really got me thinking'.

Reminiscing, he shared, 'I decided to remain in Bali and never to return to the United States to live. This was over 20 years ago as I was out on the beach with my two Golden Retrievers enjoying the evening waters. I was thinking about starting anew in a Bali after a previously traumatic time of being framed and cheated in business,' he continued, 'I recall at a far distance, I saw two dolphins jumping through the sea waters. They caught my eye and I felt myself filled with strength. Now dolphins are found only in the purest waters. Of incredible swiftness in its motion, the dolphin is an emblem of absolute strength. It was said that it could not be controlled except by its own love for man. The dolphin's affection for man was said to be so great, that it proved not only most docile to any one kindly approaching it, but would follow the fishermen, recognize them individually, and frequently warn them against storms by changing its usually frolicsome gambols into straight motion towards port.'

David lost himself in the moment as he shared his heartwarming tale.

He said, 'In Hindu mythology, the Ganges River Dolphin is associated with *Ganga*, the deity of the Ganges river. The dolphin is said to be among the creatures which heralded the goddess' descent from the heavens and her mount, the *Makara*, is sometimes depicted as a dolphin.' Bali was famous for its unique *Balinese Hindu* culture.

David added, 'On another note, the idea of the dolphin as light-bearer, representing Jesus Christ, the Light of the world, has been preserved in Christian art to a late date. Constantine gave to the Basilica of John Lateran a candelabrum of purest gold, with eighty dolphins.'

I commented, 'You are also well versed in religious history.'

Flattered, he smiled and said, 'Well, yes. Almost like seeing Light while being in the dark, I saw the dolphins as a sign from Jesus giving me hope and strength. Jesus' rising and resurrection was my rising and resurrection from the death of my old Self.'

David paused a moment and then opened up, 'This is when I became fearless. I mustered up some courage and took a huge gamble to invest the only two thousand US dollars I had on that plot of beach land. It was all or nothing. I practiced complete faith and my life turned around completely', he added to prove a point, 'Wildlife needs to be protected as they are God's way of using nature to direct us to the right path.'

I could relate to him recalling the incident of the mysterious praying mantis that guided me towards stay centered. His were the dolphins; they saved him, and led him to carry out a new purpose to invest in protecting wildlife to the best of his abilities. The Dolphin project became just one of the many projects that he had decided to give his time and money to.

God's signs to him, to me and to so many of us. I researched that throughout Mankind's existence, divine signs have been coming through animals. All the more that wildlife needs to be made more accessible to humans. Distancing nature and wildlife from our lives only distances our connection with God. Hence in a practical sense, wildlife (for example, through zoos or natural habitats) should be made much more accessible and decentralized, as in every neighborhood, village, town or city, big or small. The emphasis must be that the methodology of our relationship with nature (and animals) must be in a much more egalitarian way, and not through subjugation and domestication (control).

Desired is an in-sync blossoming of the "Flower of Life", taking it to the next level of the union between all living beings. Plants and trees may become as one with household appliances as we have never seen before. Animals may flourish as friends and be part of the family, where they are not owned. Maybe no one will have pets, but only animals as friends. Perhaps a New World founded on a symbiotic relationship between all earthly creatures.

Flower of Life which is an infinite array with spheres around forming an infinite flower of life holofractographic lattice structure, according to the Holographic Universe Theory. The Flower of Life can be found in all major religions of the world. It contains the patterns of creation as they emerged from the "Great Void". Everything is made from the Creator's thought.

The Flower of Life is part of **sacred geometry** can be described as a belief system attributing a religious or cultural value to many of the fundamental forms of space and time. According to this belief system, the basic patterns of existence are perceived as sacred, since contemplating one is contemplating the origin of all things.

The **Holographic Universe Theory** is based on the fact that the universe is a consciousness hologram. Reality is projected illusion within the hologram. The hologram is created and linked through a grid matrices based on patterns of sa*cred geometry.*

Demise of the toxic

As David and I strolled along the beach, I noticed a large area of the beach further up that appeared dark and murky. That cross-section of the beach was littered with gross garbage from plastic bags to syringes. It was upsetting to see the natural beauty of the beaches blemished by man's negligence.

Noticing the look of disgust on my face, David kept my hopes up by saying, 'There are a lot of projects on-going (or about to start) to handle pollution issues. In fact, I am evaluating whether to be actively involved in a project that researches the impact of dispersant sprayed onto oil spills in relation to the impact on sea animals like the dolphins, turtles and others. Another one which I am already involved in is to protect the Rainforests of Bali,' he continued, 'Countries that have abused nature in one form or the other, will find nature abusing them. This has been going on for too long. The sad fact is once a tipping point is reached, I can't imagine what the consequences will be. It will be detrimental no doubt.'

Acknowledging, I said, 'I suppose so. But it is no longer just about protecting Planet Earth, it is also to protect ourselves. From what I can see from your experience and mine, nature plays a part in our uplifting, and it is doing so right now. Intimacy with God through the presence of nature.'

He replied, 'I agree. Let's pray the world steers in the right direction.'

Pretty much sold by what he shared, I was even more supportive of David's activities.

'He who understands nature walks close with God,' ~ Edgar Cayce

To feed my growing hunger to learn about trees in the vicinity, I asked, 'Tell me more about your Rainforest protection project.'

David replied, 'Of course. I am a volunteer for the Indonesian Rainforest Foundation. We have started various re-forestation programs which involve and support local indigenous families and groups so they may develop methods of achieving economic independence while maintaining their forest lifestyles. We give them the choice to protect and maintain the future of their rainforest homes while reaping rich resources such as natural plant medicines and extracts, artisan goods and other forest products which can be marketed and shared with the world on equitable terms,' he added, 'The Eastern Java-Bali Rain Forests are found on one of the most active volcanic islands in the world. Once the home of the extinct Javan and Balinese tigers, these forests still contain one of the most endangered and high-profile songbirds in the world, the Bali starling. Almost all of this eco-region's natural habitat was cleared long ago by logging interests and for agriculture and settlements to provide for a rapidly expanding, dense human population. Only tiny fragments of natural forests remain, and these are also disturbed.'

While David displayed the profundity of his nature and wildlife knowledge, I was reminded about the soul stirring story of my maternal grand-uncle from Pakistan. His radical transformation as he was lost for several months in the forests of Bangladesh left a legacy. Probably the only known arboriculturist in the family, the natives of the forests found him huddled under a tall tree in a fetal position struggling to survive. As he acclimatized to more normal living conditions after being saved, he emerged transformed. He became what Pakistanis called a *peer*, a holy man. Because of his survival and his new enlightened demeanor, he was revered by the natives. When my mother would relate the story about him, she would describe him as superbly generous at heart knowing nothing else but to give. Since his transformation, he was protected with great reverence by the natives around him.

The little information I knew about the story of my grand-uncle, regardless of how much was true, it was evident that his being lost in nature played a part in his transformation. This could explain the great draw to immerse in nature as the forest monks did. My mentor the Buddhist Monk shared his 'meditating in the forest' experiences with relish whenever he could. So it was not nature simply battling for its rights to co-exist with us, but more poignantly our need for a relationship with nature if we are to progress and ascend. Nature raising us up to connect with God.

While I was walking and absentmindedly thinking about my eccentric grand-uncle, David stopped for a moment and turned to his left.

He spotted his beach-side home from short distance and said, 'Let me show you my home. If my wife and children are around, you can meet them too.'

We walked over to the entrance to his Spanish hacienda style house with strong Balinese influence in its design. His wife was busy working out the business accounts at her desk and the children were still in school. She gave me a warm smile to receive me. The home was unusually beautiful. Similar to Olga's it had an open concept, with a twist that he created a bubble design with the rooms. Curved walls joining like a circle of about 180 degrees, and the front of the room which would be the entrance being completely open. No door, just no front wall. Each room was like a separate annex with a patch of garden in between. Ferns were growing on all sides of the circular walls of the rooms and sprawling over the roof.

David pointed to a tree that was embedded in one side of the wall, 'You see this tree here. It's over 50 years old. When I designed this house, I made sure that this tree was not cut down but becomes part of the design.'

A masterfully designed home with its intermixing of vibrant plant life.

David was a notable example of a human being who understood his duty to reclaim and restore the natural environment. Add to that, he was a walking-talking encyclopedia, as he continued to surprise me with new information.

'Remember those tall trees and the giant Banyan Tree you were so fascinated by while in Ubud? Don't be surprised if they are nature's sentient cellular network.'

I responded, 'The life-giving Giant Trees?'

He said, 'They are for communication and healing, and maybe more.'

How true, and so are we. I imagined us becoming more and more connected than ever before - expanding our Spirit Man (Spirit Woman) with each other and with the Planet Earth more than ever before.

He added, 'Nature may be only 5% of what we know. There are still a lot of unknowns,' he continued explaining with greater insights, 'Nature is not off-the-shelf, ready-made or an instant solution. By bringing nature into the equation, we are no longer at the mercy of mental degradation promoted by mainstream media. Nature is not stagnant. It's very dynamism breaks the barriers for creative thinkers to think critically and to limitless capacities.'

I shared my two cents worth, 'There are no limits to nature. Just as there are no limits to ourselves.'

He acknowledged my words, 'You got that right.'

'Look deep into nature, and then you will understand everything better'
~ Albert Einstein

As I admired the fern carpeted walls of David's home, I noticed there was a perfect alignment of the leaves on those ferns. They were spiraling in a counterclockwise direction based on the Fibonacci sequence, the numbers in the following integer sequence 0, 1, 1, 2, 3, 5, 8. This formula governs the placement of leaves along a stem. The Fibonacci also reflects the Golden Mean, which coincides with the perfectly designed pyramid structures, as well as the human body and the Cosmos.

I reflected back on the painting I did in 2008.

'The overt borders
With recurring curval patterns,
Spinning, expanding in size...'
~ *from the descriptive prose of the painting*

How the divine message on repeated patterns and numbers was so evident back then. The abundant and ubiquitous nature of God's perfect numbering sequence, showing how everything is perfectly designed, and that nothing is by coincidence. Of course! Nothing is by coincidence. I was in Bali for a reason, just as David and Olga were led to Bali for a reason before their lives transformed. If the dream of the Giant Tree was a divine sign, then the magnificence of the trees I was shown and educated on in Bali reinforced it.

The mysterious Giant Tree. David's words on nature - '... only 5% of what we know ...'

Like a black box to be unraveled, I was just beginning to understand the significance of the Giant Tree. The answer flowed naturally as if I was guided to it. It was not a voice, but a message downloading as words: "roots", "sap", "soul", "tree", "God".

Assembling as the rest of the word gaps were filled - ' ... to grow your roots deep into the soil of your origin. To draw the sap - the core of your soul, undergoing change the same way that the sap of a tree is chemically transformed in the trunk of the tree.'

I felt that the sap was from God, and I had to continue to draw the sap so that I would be chemically transformed. It was an encouragement to keep going with my meditation and prayers. But this time, I felt led to add the visualization of a Giant Tree as part of my meditation. I would imagine myself sitting under it as my secret place to converse with God.

> *My meditative Secret Place*
> *Communing with God,*
> *Resting in Him.*
> *As He shields me,*
> *Heals me*
> *And transforms me.*

Immensely satisfied with my new-found learning, I took the drive back up to idyllic Ubud bidding farewell to the beaches and bustling seaside fun activities of South Bali. Within two short hours, I was in the village of where Olga resided in chilling out in the Zen atmosphere. I felt almost bucolic as I lay back on a make-shift hammock tied between two tall trees in her garden. I began to truly see the impact of nature in our lives and how protection and integration is one of the fundamentals of our planetary advancement. According to Scriptures, God's original job for the first man Adam was to take care of the Garden of Eden. Henceforward, it has been our responsibility to manage the plants, trees, and animals created by God, and not to allow them to deteriorate. Because if they do, we will deteriorate alongside with them.

So there I was, cradled in the hammock reflecting upon my visions, revelations and new learning from all the amazing people I had met so far. The spectacular vision of the Golden Souls. The crystallization of Marianne's skin. The thought-provoking dream and the revelation of the Giant Tree. What was shown so far was exciting, yet I knew instinctively that this was just a preview.

Fibonacci sequence the numbers in the following integer sequence 0, 1, 1, 2, 3, 5, 8, 13, 21, 34, 55, 89, 144. The first two numbers in the Fibonacci sequence are either 1 and 1, or 0 and 1, depending on the chosen starting point of the sequence, and each subsequent number is the sum of the previous two.

Golden Mean represented by the Greek letter phi, is one of those mysterious natural numbers, like e or pi, that seem to arise out of the basic structure of our Cosmos. Unlike those abstract numbers, however, phi appears clearly and regularly in the realm of things that grow and unfold in steps, and that includes living things. The decimal representation of phi is 1.6180339887499.

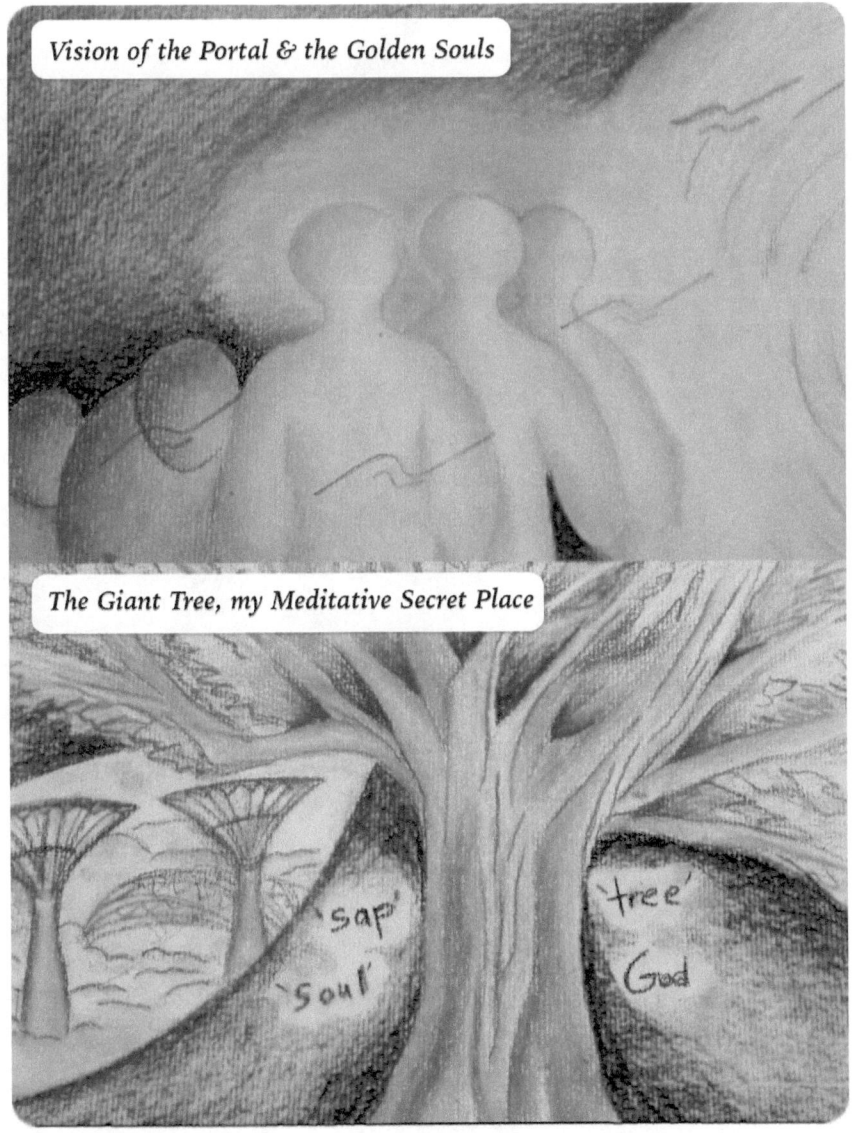

5

Everyone A Healer

The new paradigm of healing,
A self-empowered renewal,
Of spontaneous rejuvenation
And divine realignment.

Singapore,
Jan 2013

Regardless of the travel back and forth to Singapore for work every fortnight, Bali was a rejuvenating getaway. An alternative working and living arrangement that helped develop another side of myself, slowly and surely waking up the dormant multidimensional being I was supposed to become.

The highlight of my long stay in Bali was the discovery of the Giant Trees, their purpose and their place on Earth and their place in our personal lives. But what was even more intriguing was how in that same year Singapore had launched itself as the land of the Super Trees, just south of the Marina Bay East Garden at the same spot where I used to meditate and saw the "Portal and Golden Souls" vision. It was being constructed at that time. By mid 2012, the Marina Gardens by the Bay was fully complete and the South Garden opened up to a stepping stone into Pandora, a 101 hectare verdant wonderland as depicted in James Cameron's epic Avatar, highlighted by the imposing canopy of 18 steel Super Trees, mechanically constructed ranging from 25 meters to 50 meters high.

Awed by the botanic transformation, it was good to be back in Singapore. It was December 2012 when most waking hours of the day were about settling back in and completing household and business chores. More operational work in the business world of technology. In my heart, I was not happy to be going back to old ways. Had I really thought of a new way of living? No. Though I kept to my daily meditations and prayers, I slipped back into that mechanical subservient life which played a part in bringing me down in the first place.

It was on my birthday when I was given further divine guidance. The date journaled in my diary - January 17th 2013. It was a hot sweltering midday in Singapore, hotter than the heat I already felt burning beneath my skin. As the internal body heat persisted, it gave prevenient signs of a fever. A short while after, I was hit with profuse sweating which lasted an uncomfortable two or three hours. To my relief there was a brief period of normality; though this did not last long as there was a second rapid rise in temperature followed by the appearance of a red rash that spread over my arms and legs.

Whatever was going on with my body, I had to get it diagnosed quickly. I walked down from my apartment to search for the nearest polyclinic, and found one just around the corner. With just three patients waiting in line, time moved slowly as I convulsed with the spasmodic pain that began to surface behind my eyes, my legs feeling as if they were being ripped apart and a terrible itch all my skin. Shortly, the nurse called my name for the general practitioner on duty to see me. I walked into the doctor's clinic looking malnourished as I had barely eaten the entire day. The bitter taste in my mouth made cooked food, in particular, atrocious to the taste buds.

After evaluating my condition, the lady doctor said, 'You have the symptoms of dengue. If your blood platelets continue to breakdown, you may have to be hospitalized.'

I was afflicted with dengue fever for the first time. It was the most uncomfortable sickness I had ever experienced in my life.

The doctor said, 'I will need to put you on some medication ...'

Before she could finish what she had to say, I impatiently interrupted her but in polite manner.

'It's okay. I don't need any medication. I can heal myself.'

She asked, 'Are you sure?'

I spoke with certainty as if led by a greater force, 'Yes, I will be healed.'

She looked at me for a second and saw how confident I was in spite of my disheveled appearance.

She said, 'If that is what you want, I need you to promise me that you will come and see me everyday so that I can check on your progress. The nurse will call you specially to remind you.'

I answered obediently, 'Yes, definitely.'

I struggled to walk back home. There was such a great certainty within me that I could heal that I could not understand it myself. There was an inner voice telling me that I could self-heal. Since the visionary spectacle of the Golden Souls, I believed that anything was possible. After nourishing myself with a bowl of fresh fruits, which was the only thing that tasted good, I went back to work at my desk. A habitual self-confessed workaholic, I pushed myself to get back to work as that week was one of the busiest weeks of the month with a lucrative Bahraini government tender that had to be submitted. My birthday downsized to a short lunch out with family as I was too depleted of strength for a prolonged celebration.

An instant message came from our Bahraini business partners, 'The deadline is by midnight today but we need your proposal by 5pm so that we can consolidate our portions.'

I stayed quiet and I did not reply to that message as I was struggling to hold myself up on the chair. Noticing my silence as I was not too pleased to hear about the stringent timeline, he said, 'Hope that you can make it? Unfortunately, the extension for submission was turned down. So sorry for informing you about this government tender so late.'

Appreciative of his apology, I answered amicably, 'No problem, I will try my best.'

I said that as I felt that there was just too much that needed to be done, I could not even give myself an hour or two to rest. I had to keep at it. In the end, I pushed myself to the point that I completed the tender proposal to the best of my ability, keeping it to a 3 page simple document and emailed it across to the business partner as I pressed the SEND button with my crimson rash covered hand.

With that strenuous task completed minutes before the 5pm requirement, I collapsed to my bed relieved that I could finally work on some meditative self-healing. I had still more work the next day with another deadline. It made me wonder if I was listening to what the Buddhist Monk had advised me which was to let go and simply "Be". I could have let go of the tender, but it was an obsession that I had to overcome. To chase after every deal that came to the table, when really I had to learn to think of myself and my capacity and simply pick and choose.

I sat on my bed in a meditative cross-legged position with a plan to start a self-healing process. I did not know of any method other than pursuing an approach of stillness with commonsense mental affirmations. At times the pains would get so bad that I would unlock myself from that cross-legged position and lay down flat on the bed. The afternoon went by as I remained in bed unable to move an inch. Then evening set in till finally it was 11pm at night when an unexpected phenomenon took precedence. My body, like a separate conscious being, decided to take over and make a decision to heal itself.

It was as if my body was saying, 'Enough is enough, I will take over now. You lie down and relax and just watch the show.'

Almost instantaneously, the itch in my palms surged in intensity, convulsing all through the night. I was literally pushed and shoved to sit up and my arms pulled out with the palms outstretched, irking and pulsating with the pain. Not only was it a torturous experience as the pains surged with intensity, my mind was also marred with confusion of what was really going on. I had no choice but to surrender to the process as the prickling discomfort engulfed my swollen red hands. The poison from the dengue infection that felt infused into my blood stream started vaporizing into the air like invisible toxic fumes. The vortex in the middle of my left palm, extended itself to form a second vortex within my right palm, transforming them to become like two incredible biological healing devices.

Fast forwarding 4 hours. The rashes on my legs were mostly gone. The pains subsided. It finally came to my realization that I was witness to a spontaneous self-healing based on a decision made by my own body, if that was a correct observation. It never occurred to me that I had any form of healing ability. Somehow, it felt as if it was willed by some other living entity – my own body like a conscious being or maybe an activation of my DNA or maybe even a release of healing instruction encoding from within my DNA, perhaps the "junk" DNA for that matter.

And this conscious being had pressed some kind of empyrean button that launched a four hour excruciating self-healing process that was completed successfully. An unconventional comparison but I felt very much like the Balinese gecko that broke its tail and could grow it back! My muscle aching legs felt brand new. It was unbelievable to think that in just one day I could be healed of dengue fever which usually lasts two weeks to a month. In my case, it was resolved in little over one night. In several unforeseen sequences, I was cured. The intervention by something or of something which I could not quite understand.

New Human "Healing Factor"

A preternatural self-healing experience that had a silver lining. I was just coming out of the Old World thinking that the physical world controlled us, when in actuality the reverse was true. I was beginning to see that we through our own consciousness control the physical, and that includes our bodies. I was embarrassed to recall that I was at one time doubtful of the idea of divine healers assuming that it was either a hypnotic trick or simply targeted patients who amicably agree that they were cured as part of a staged showmanship.

Overall, I was happy to discover a new found ability - a mutant power of accelerated "healing". Was it a DNA activation of some kind, maybe a release of instructions in the code of the Junk DNA, or possibly angelic intervention or perhaps something else? I had made positive intentions to heal myself in the past but the results were never as dramatic like this – not even for the common cold. The aspirations of extra-human healing and longevity was exciting. As the months passed since that self-healing phenomenon, the long list of allergies that plagued most of my life also lessened significantly.

I saw it as a sign that we could be entering a new era of self-healing, moving away from simply laying healing hands on people. As soon as I got home, I checked on Olga to hear her thoughts about this. She was still in Bali pursuing her Reiki healing work.

Olga shared, 'We are supposed to learn to start healing ourselves. They told me that the power is within us and we need to work on being positive, happy and joyful. The joy in our hearts will release that healing.'

She referred to "they" as divine beings who spoke to her telepathically while she was in meditation or prayer.

Olga said, 'They told me that God is teaching us to live in good health, through our own efforts. People may get healed through the laying on of hands by a healer like myself, or rush to a doctor who prescribe medicines and treatment, but how long will the healing really last?'

Trying to imply the message of self-empowerment, she emphasized, 'We need to unleash our own power of healing from within. It has been untapped.'

Several months later, an associate company to our firm had a series of business meetings with a group of clients who had flown into Singapore. The clients were represented by middle aged men, accompanied by an entourage of spouses. I had a little part to play in those meetings as I was simply invited to meet with the wives. The meeting place, the posh business lounge of the Intercontinental Hotel with the usual pleasantries and orderings of coffee and tea. I joined in only at the tail end of the day-long meetings at the time when their wives would come in. They were high society women from India decked in Louis Vuitton and Cartier, well manicured with perfect hairdos. At times they would speak with crisp and perfect English with all the correct grammar in place, and at other times it would go out in a toss with a gauche. Still, I enjoyed their company as they were open to listening and curious as I boldly shared about the twofold dengue self-healing and Golden Souls phenomenon, no holds barred.

There was one lady who was particularly inspired.

Rather matronly dressed and clearly older than the rest, she doddered over to the table closer to me and complained sorrowfully, 'My knees are in so much pain, I feel them crumbling.'

I may have aroused her curiosity so much that she had to ask, 'Can you heal me?'

I was a little reluctant at first. I was ready to give a thousand and one excuses that I was totally new to divine healing and may not be able to provide any results at all. Besides I had never laid my healing hands on anyone.

Then I remembered Marianne's words, 'The laying on of hands is the foundation of the church.'

Although I had no association with any religious organization, Marianne's statement sounded plausible.

The lady said, 'My husband has health issues too. Maybe you could work on him first before me?'

I replied, 'Sure, by all means.'

I took it that she was inquisitive to watch what would happen. It was certainly not a novelty as laying on of hands has been around for centuries with there being an accelerated escalation of divine healers all across the globe in recent times. Furthermore, she was coming from India where it was part and parcel of her culture.

Anyway, I laid my puzzlement aside as I started off with her husband. He appeared to be a successful businessman from Hyderabad, India. Heavy set with a Chevron-style mustache, his words were almost overly friendly with an eagerness to please. He began giving me a background history how of his business had started and how it was going through a decline resulting in his health being affected. The tremendous strain in his work environment brought about chest pains and other medical issues. His wife tried to cut short his potentially long story as she hand signaled that he was ready to start.

The lady said, 'I place my husband in your good hands. I trust you.'

I broke my mental agreement not to give excuses by replying sheepishly, 'I am doing this for the first time. I am certainly not a healer. Like you both, I am a businessperson and I never expected to be laying healing hands on my business associates.'

Her husband laughed, 'Haha, we understand. We totally understand.'

He reassured me speaking in a nasal voice enriched with a distinct Indian accent, 'Don't worry. It's alright. We have faith in you.'

And so my first patient was all ready to begin. I was doddering trying to figure out which procedure to follow and if there was any fixed method. Unsure of the method and the words to say, I did what came naturally to me. I called on God and His Angels for assistance. I named Archangel Raphael as I read that he was the angel of healing. I also called on Jesus' name due to the association of Jesus Christ to miraculous healing throughout history. Then something peculiar began to happen. There was a gradually increasing energy emerging from within my heart to flowing towards my hands, creating some form of invisible field surrounding my body. It was my Spirit Woman coming alive and stretching bit by bit over the space. As I made mental and verbal intentions that he should heal, I felt the further growth of my Spirit Woman. I sensed that this energy field was engulfing him as I lay my hands on him.

By the end of the session, he felt a peaceful solace wrap around him. Though he was not cured completely, he felt a small amount of physical and emotional pain leave him. The session took about half an hour during which time I was pleased to receive several visual and symbolic messages for him. He was delighted to hear them as he said it would be helpful to him in resolving the current issues in his life. With those messages passed on, I was beginning to see how through my Spirit Woman, I unleashed a divine healing tool that was untapped. I may have acted as a conduit for a higher frequency vibration and by laying hands on this lady and her husband, their vibration frequency was also being raised. Similar to those ancient pyramids, which some researchers and scientists have discovered acted like free energy wireless power generators.

I imagined those healing abilities being available to everyone - whether a teacher, or a waitress at a restaurant, the neighborhood bakery owner, or our business accountant or lawyer. Laying on of hands may be available as a skill to all. Of course, for some people it would be a greater gift, possibly measurable on a scale. But what was most exciting was the spontaneous self-healing. Spontaneous self-healing incidents like mine may escalate across the world and predominate eventually. If we stayed on the right path of our uplifting, and did not fall back to the denseness of old ways and beliefs, we may be privileged to be part of such a health-wise empowered New World.

Satisfied, the lady's husband spoke graciously, 'Thank you! I feel a little lighter and much more at peace. Thank you again. Let's see if we can do some business together. We have some information technology projects coming up.'

Naturally, he went straight to talk about business.

He said, 'Maybe this business would interest you? Here's my card.'

A courteous offering from him with two hands outstretched, I fumbled to read the small text on his card as it was filled with details on various certifications and awards plus a lengthy name.

As his wife eyed my confusion, he said 'Just call me Siva. We will be happy to hear from you.'

Although Siva's words were kind, I felt some kind of dread about him. In the past, I would always be angry with myself for those sudden cringes and unexplainable bad feelings about people or situations.

I decided to ignore my sensitivities and went on briskly to ask his wife if she was ready for her turn. That momentary cringing switched over to a tinge of joy as I saw another side of myself emerging; a multidimensional being falsely entrenched in a one dimensional life all this while.

The Self Healing Paradigm

It was an early evening at the popular East Coast Park of Singapore. The beach on the east side of Singapore was not as exotic as what South Bali had to offer. However it had its own charm with spotless park grounds and sands. With amenities all around and designated walking and cycling lanes, it was a fuss free quasi nature abode, while still being very close to the city.

Taking a leisurely walk along the jogging pavement beside the bicycle track, I thought I would keep going further east, thus shifting gears to a brisk walk towards Changi Village, a modern village which was once a ghost town. Since its revival, it was still peaceful with its relative openness and greenery all around. I spotted several hornbills perched on two rain trees growing side by side. A rare sight with their stunning yellow beaks as they made the ambiance more alive with their loud bird calls. The majestic rain tree is one of the most commonly known trees native to Singapore. Drawn to the family of hornbills, I sat down on a well cut grass patch under one of the umbrella-shaped rain trees for some shade.

With my iPhone in my hand, I logged onto Facebook to find an old friend Yasmine who was online at the same time. Coincidentally, she was the very person who had joined me for a walk at East Coast back in 2009 when she came to Singapore on her first trip from her homeland, Jaipur, Rajasthan in India. She was part of a corporate delegation attending a major conference organized in Singapore. At that time, we made a strong connection as we both had deep interest in spiritual matters. I was in the midst of a phase of intensive book reading, regurgitating facts and figures from bestseller authors such as Robin Sharma, Gregg Braden, Dr Bruce Lipton and many other influential figures. We were also passionate about healthy eating, yoga, and more - the full works. The all-encompassing pathway which we were both seeking towards enlightenment during those years.

I said 'Hi!' instantly when I saw her name online.

We were in touch on and off over the four years, and we continued to share spiritual insights from time to time. I was most impressed with Yasmine from the beginning. She was a go-getter who overcame many sicknesses and ailments (my conditions were mild in comparison) which had led to multiple surgeries – none of which seemed to defuse her brio.

It was not long before I opened up to Yasmine about the supernatural and preternatural experiences that I had recently shared with the entourage of Indian businessmen wives. That triggered a conversation about the latest illness that hit her, the Big C - cancer. In the past year I did see her posts opening up about being inflicted with the Big C. Though I added comments of encouragement to her Facebook posts, I did not approach the topic privately with her until she made the first initiative.

As we chatted while I sat under the cool shade of the rain tree, she surprised me by saying that she had recovered quite significantly. That was a big relief. So it seemed that we both had good news after all.

Yasmine said, 'I started by practicing visualization techniques to heal my body with affirmations and forgiving and loving myself. I did everything from the Louise Hay "Heal your life techniques". Healing and meditations for forgiveness and emotional freedom using the ancient *hawaien* anger and forgiveness techniques.' she elaborated, 'I never thought of myself as sick or ill. This was even when I was feeling physically weak. I refused to acknowledge the weakness in my body. I imagined as many times as possible that each cell in my body was glowing with health and cancer free.'

She endeavored to explore surrounding herself in nature as a healing method too.

Yasmine said, 'I visited Mount Kailash and Mansarovar lakes in India which was an eye-opening experience. The feeling of sheer power and energy combined with the beauty of the place, seeped and became at one with my body simply blowing me away'.

She shared how she had begun to perform deeds of derring-do to keep her spirit going, 'Helping others and spreading the awareness of surviving cancer helped me. During my sickness, I wanted to be able to be productive, anywhere and anytime I could. I gave talks in public forums on cancer and how to be strong and positive, eat and stay healthy. Most of all, I endeavored to cut cords and ties with negative episodes and negative people.'

By removing negativity from her life and filling it with love compassion and forgiveness.

Yasmine expressed, 'I am learning my lessons and accepting each day as it unfolds. I try not to think about yesterday or tomorrow, just today, just this moment right now!' she continued, 'I did everything that made sense to me – from practicing *yoga nidra*, a sleep like state which yogis practice during this meditations - very much like lucid sleeping which is among the deepest possible states of relaxation while maintaining full consciousness. In addition, I enhanced my meals with a more alkaline diet. And I did not stop there. I attended a very powerful divine retreat for inner healing in India, and learned about letting go, forgiving myself and others.'

She confessed, 'I had a great deal of emotional baggage, which is why I started doing inner child mediation for healing my past by being in contact with my spirit guides and healing Angels to guide me and take me to my life purpose.'

I listened intently as she opened up about the many-faceted and 360 degree approach she took to self-healing.

Yasmine went on to share a life altering supernatural experience.

She shared, 'I had visions of white healing Light entering and healing my body. I was in a garden full of fragrant flowers and beautiful trees which energize and heal. There was a brilliant purple Light in my natural eye area, removing heaviness and negativity and filling it with hope and lightness,' she paused for a moment absorbing the feeling of that tender moment and then continued, 'I have such immense gratitude about an unforgettable night. As I recall it was around 3am. I was at the divine ashram during this inner healing. I literally felt His presence and I felt protected and in His care. Suddenly, I felt all the fear that enveloped my heart had vanished. An unraveling sensation of feeling all cleaned up from inside, all emotional baggage dropped and I was free of the imprisoning hold of cancer cells.'

She felt touched and healed by Jesus, and she continued, 'I handed over my problems and I felt light. I felt guided on the right path as I explored all avenues of cancer treatment.'

Everyone a healer. While I healed myself, so did she. She healed herself significantly. Though she chose to proceed with chemotherapy, I was still most impressed with her. But more than anything, I was glad to see that she was alive.

I recall the words of Marianne, 'We need to heal ourselves through the divine and through the natural.'

And that was exactly what Yasmine did. A holistic approach of healing that worked. In all the media and social network updates I have read, there was an undisputed corroboration of a rapidly growing number of cases of critically ill people worldwide who completely left out any involvement of intrusive medical treatment. And those numbers have been going up at an incremental rate which was promising.

As I thought through my discussion with her, I could not help but realize how one day if I had the privilege of being part of the New World, perhaps we would look back and shake our heads at how barbaric some of our medical treatments seem by comparison to these energy-based techniques. The chemotherapy Yasmine went through was very painful. Each treatment would take her several days if not a week or more to recover. She was very wise to couple her treatment with energy-based methods, affirmations as well as divine healing. I also believe that as we become higher vibrational energy beings, as we transform ourselves to emulate those Golden Souls, we will have an enhanced ability to communicate with the cells of our physical body. DNA manipulation would be a simply a matter of self-healing or with the assistance of divine healers.

As we finished our online chat, I turned my head to look up towards the outstretched branches of rain tree that covered me with its loving embrace. A protective Giant Tree; I envisioned the rain trees in Singapore forming the top tier (among others) of the natural sentient network. Its similarity with our DNA. Some researchers say that the human DNA displays itself like a biological internet superior in many aspects to the artificial one. I came across articles talking about experiments done by the military, where leukocytes (white blood cells) were collected for DNA from donors and placed into chambers so they could be measured for their electrical changes. The study talked about how the donor was placed in one room and subjected to "emotional stimulation'" consisting of video clips, which generated different emotions in the donor. The DNA was placed in a different room within the same building. Both the donor and his DNA were monitored. As the donor exhibited emotional peaks, so did the DNA. There was no lag time and no transmission time.

The fluttering of a flock of small birds swooped in and out as a unified group under the trees at the park as sunset began to set in. My thoughts still on the human DNA. The bond that tied the DNA with its donor, like an invisible umbilical cord. How truly connected we are, bringing the word "Unity" to the forefront. Living cells probably communicating through a currently unrecognized form of energy - an energy, not affected by time or distance. This energy of this field that may have healed me as well as Yasmine – this non-local form of energy, an energy that already exists everywhere, and all of the time. It began to make sense. The ubiquitous and all-encompassing energy, the One True God Head.

There may have been an indoctrination in society and incomplete teachings that make us feel that we have to depend mainly on the external to resolve the internal. Here is where I discovered something interesting. Going down to the very basics, according to quantum physics by definition an atom is made of energy. There is no physical construct to it - the atoms are assembled into the molecules and the molecules are assembled into the cells, and these cells are assembled into our bodies. Having read the cellular biologist Bruce Lipton's (PhD) books, he claimed that if we do not include the invisible energy spectrum as relevant to our health and human body, then we are leaving out one of the most important factors that control life on

Earth. The energy which physicists refer to as the field, which we live in and immerse ourselves in.

> *"The field is the sole governing agency of the particle'* ~ Albert Einstein

The field, the invisible energy around us, is the sole governing particle of the physical that we see in front of us. So if we want to understand the nature of the physical, then we need to understand the nature of the sole governing agency. God the Sole Governing Agency! Our God heals. A fact so evident. A fact so clear. Maybe that is why we are destined to become self-healers. With God within our DNA, how can it be disputed? The fact that everyone of us has the capacity to heal ourselves is as true as our ability to see, taste, speak, touch and hear - like a 7th or 8th or 9th sense waiting to be tapped into. But what was this consciousness that took over and resulted in the spontaneous self-healing? Was the Junk DNA responsible, or something else?

Marianne's words, 'RNA brings the material of Heaven to Earth to materialize Heaven on Earth.'

I read that RNA was the decoder, the regulator of our DNA. Prior or at the moment of the "spontaneous self-healing" phenomenon, was my gene expression modified or the DNA decoded to allow for that to happen? Did the hours and weeks and months of prayer and meditation spark that change? Did I activate a new kind of DNA technology by spending more time with God, in my meditative secret place under the Giant Tree?

Alternatively, there may have been a decision in the heavenly realm to show me spontaneous self-healing so that I would have it as a testimony; a testimony of what we are meant to be. Probably released through the RNA, the biological messenger.

Above all, we had to have faith, and the substance of that faith is hope, the very essence of the substance of Heaven, and to desire it and to visualize it to bring it into our lives. I did all that! I had developed a stronger faith in God than ever before. I had hope as I pulled my way through the most difficult times maintaining my faith. The aspirations of being part of the New World was at its uttermost. But last but not least, I had also willed myself to heal as I had so much work to do that week that it triggered the spontaneous self-healing. In a way, a placebo effect creating the positive thought vibration. Thought, a vibrational energy, where some say that vibration is more important in influencing the physical body than the chemistry!

More profound words from Marianne, 'God does not bring sickness. There is no sickness in the heavenly realm,' she added, 'The frequency of our lives is in resonance with the Presence of God. Everything is in harmony as in Heaven.'

I was still new to the concept of Heaven. I had never seen it nor experienced it. Heretofore it was fascinating and it gave me a sense of hope.

RNA or ribonucleic acid, helps carry out the DNA's guidelines. DNA is like a blueprint of biological guidelines that a living organism must follow to exist and remain functional. Of the two, RNA is more versatile than DNA, capable of performing numerous, diverse tasks in an organism, but DNA is more stable and holds more complex information for longer periods of time. Basically, everything is made up of DNA and RNA. DNA holds the body together and RNA is what causes the DNA to be bonded together to form physicality. The RNA World theory of evolution says that life originated from RNA or a very similar polymer. Based on that, RNA came before proteins and DNA, because RNA consists of molecules that can be a gene and an enzyme as well.

Entry of the Spiritual Doctors

Human consciousness has been proven through experiment to have an effect on the molecular structure of water. Dr Masaru Emoto (1943-2014), Japanese author, researcher and entrepreneur, believed that water was a "blueprint" for our reality and that emotional "energies" and "vibrations" could change the physical structure of water. Dr. Horowitz, among Dr. Emoto's leading scientific supporters, explains this metaphysically by relating the power of "love" in human hearts to the power of God to respond to prayer and heart-felt loving intentions to heal the world and be helpful to one another.

The same is true for humans who are ready to receive the healing energy. As a result, I imagined that the new spiritual doctors or medical healers would be incorporating "sound" as an integral part of healing process. I read that high frequency sound helps realign the cells in our body to an optimal pattern and frequency so that the body triggers self-healing. Music tuned into A = 432 Hertz is not only more harmonious and luxurious to the ears, but also induces a more inward experience that is felt inside the body at the spine and at the heart to facilitate healing. It has been found that the healing energy sent through stringed instruments really does change the physical oscillations of the instruments.

Our hearts emit electromagnetic fields that change according to our emotions. The human heart's magnetic field can be measured up to several feet away from the body. Positive emotions create physiological benefits in our bodies. We can boost our immune system by conjuring positive emotions. Negative emotions can create a nervous system chaos, but positive emotions do the opposite. Nikola Tesla (1856 - 1943), Serbian American inventor and futurist best known for his contributions to the design of the systems for modern alternating current, claimed that if we could eliminate certain outside frequencies that interfered in our bodies, we would have greater resistance toward disease. Possibly, the new medicine where we look at the harmony of resonance, frequency and vibration.

I imagined that as long as we take on this path, we may see a role-reversal in terms of drugs and divine healing where divine healing may play a primary role, and the drugs and/or surgery approach a secondary role. This is in line with Dr Bruce Lipton's claim that our bodies are not designed for regular use of drugs, which is the main reason why drugs are given in small quantities. Thus, as our bodies become more and more crystalline, the dependence on drugs or surgery may fall away.

As Yasmine endeavored through her multifaceted healing and as I discovered through my own spontaneous self healing experience, we are moving towards healing through the divine and through the natural. The natural would be through nutrition, energetic healing activities since we are vehicles of Light, as well as emotional healing, exercise and non-intrusive medical intervention. The emergence of self-healers within all of us. The emergence of spiritual doctors or medical healers, characteristic of the New World medical professionals.

Based on that notion, I imagined that a day might come in the future (the New World) when self-healing would be so spontaneous and instantaneous with our vibrational frequencies so high, that sickness would be practically unheard of. And during the transition, we may be healing each other with simply our shadow. There are a rapidly growing number of people who can do that now. After all, we are vehicles of Light. I imagined sickness as Darkness and where there is Light, there is no Darkness. Golden Souls as vehicles of Light.

With new knowledge gained on the new paradigm of healing, what was next? My thoughts went back to the words of the Buddhist Monk which was said many months before, ' … Something is coming!'

Something even greater and bigger was impending.

Dr Emoto's water crystal experiments Emoto believed that water was a "blueprint" for our reality and that emotional "energies" and "vibrations" could change the physical structure of water. Emoto's water crystal experiments consisted of exposing water in glasses to different words, pictures or music, and then freezing and examining the aesthetic properties of the resulting crystals with microscopic photography. Emoto made the claim that water exposed to positive speech and thoughts would result in visually pleasing crystals being formed when that water was frozen, and that negative intention would yield "ugly" frozen crystal formations.

6

Reaching Zero Point

*Pushing us to collapse
Till we are reduced to the 'seed'.*

*The seed geometry
Of what becomes,
With more and more octave growth.*

I learned how my body could miraculously and spontaneously self-heal. I discovered the underlying workings of DNAs and how RNA acts like a biological messenger from Heaven. But at the soul level, I was still not done yet.

Singapore
7th September 2013

A fateful day in September. A day of a full release of a mountain of sadness, disappointments, fear and anxiety. Crisis after crisis hurtled me down an abyss. That was the sensation. I was crashing on a hard rocky bottom, where the mask of my Ego was shattered to bits. My breakdown from the external world, creating a breakdown within.

An inexplicable sadness reached my very core. An overwhelming sense of grief that was so intense, prolonged and yet somehow liberating at the same time that as the emotions subsided, a startling appearance of a spot of blood emerged from the center of my left palm. A bright crimson puncture wound that mysteriously appeared and then disappeared a few seconds later. A euphoric purge or a release of something I could not understand. With family members around me, they were just as astounded as I was. One of them shouted a word that resonates till today, 'Divinity!'

The experience left me in a daze. There was no physical pain. In fact, I felt light and in some strange way renewed. That itself motivated me to understand the depths of the unusual phenomenon. Historical documentation called it stigmata, most notably recorded by St Francis of Assisi in Christian history. Some articles state that in the eight centuries since then, there have been about 400 additional reported cases. Stigmata was recorded to be experienced by many women in history, primarily those who suffered dreadfully.

My stigmata experience was analogous to the self-healing experience during the dengue episode, as they were both spontaneous. It has also been long debated by many who believe stigmata is a psychosomatic effect brought on by intense prayer. Scoffers often try to impute it as a product of religious fanaticism, a product of the mind of the believer, however unconsciously done. Other say it is self-induced perhaps brought about by a psychokinesis. All this reasoning made no sense to me as I had no interest in Jesus' crucifixion at that time. My focus was on planetary civilizations more than anything else. Although I questioned the experience thoroughly, there was a veritable and tangible Truth tied to it.

Almost hard for me to explain in words, there was however one saying that described it aptly - 'There is an end to everything'.

The stigmatic experience marked the end (or the demise) of my old Self and it signified the resurrection of my new Self. Even from the Islamic spirituality point of view, based on what I knew, we can experience death before we die. With death we awaken with necessity. A true giant of a Person within me making its first attempt to emerge.

I endeavored on with my research. I discovered that stigmatics (as they are called) were considered to be co-suffering with Jesus Christ and that they were the chosen few to save the world from great sins. Some articles also state that alongside stigmata were the other unusual phenomena - the gift of prophesy, bilocation or the ability to be in two places at the same time as well as healing, levitation and inedia (breatharianism) or the power to forgo nourishment. Prior to the stigmatic experience, I was experiencing divine healing and prophetic abilities. The transcendent vision of the Portal and the Golden Souls was the most profound so far. My intuitive perspective that human abilities were resurfacing. The limits of what we set on human abilities could be surmountable. In my case, I had to allow this giant of a Person within me to come out through a continued surrender – a surrender and release of intensely painful emotions.

Rebirth

Singapore
Late September 2013

It was the middle of a hot Saturday afternoon. As light from the blistering hot sun that day seared through the windows, a loud audible voice broke the silence in my bedroom.

Commanding Voice, 'God is sending a lot of messages to lot of people right now!'

The resounding voice pierced through from the back of my head like a bolt of lightning. Commanding and authoritative, catching me unawares. Was it an Angel passing a message from God? I turned around and I saw no one behind me.

I was not surprised by those words as during the past week I was toiling over some hard questions. Too many people I knew were going through upheaval in their lives. And I worried for them. Whether it was due to my overreaching concern, I don't know, but I knew that my thoughts were being heard and I was getting a serious response.

As I was being reduced to zero point, so were many others I knew personally. Possibly a brief window for a rapid acceleration of a multitude of souls from rebirth to beyond. So much talk circulating around the globe about the rebirth of humanity. Some call it the shift towards the New Earth. Some say Heaven is invading Earth and we are forced to change if we want to be part of it. Some speak about how fast we can potentially transform and what kind of people we could become. Some say it is all part of a carefully planned operation by conscious beings that are "not of this world". Needless to say, our old belief systems are being tested and challenged, broken down and dissipated to where we have nothing but the equivalent of a blank slate.

As I sat on the floor of my bedroom still shaken by the Commanding Voice, my mind played on the words "a lot of messages" and "a lot of people". I closed my eyes to meditate on those evidential words. Within moments, I was shown the vision of the universe with its galaxies stretching and expanding infinitely. The universe expanding and its energy density growing less and less. Particles that had a large mass became tougher to sustain, and so they were becoming extinct. I saw how the killing went on until only the smallest particles remained. Then suddenly the dying ceased. Vast planes of space stretched out ahead in distances no one could have known were there. At that moment, I opened my eyes.

Depicting an era of a quark slaughter which some scientists say has been part of our universe's history. For some reason which is still unknown, the balance of matter and antimatter shifted slightly in favor of regular matter. This shift resulted in a minute excess of regular matter and while all other matter and antimatter canceled each other out, the excess of regular matter survived. All of the matter that makes up our universe today, including planet earth and her dwellers was present at the birth of time and survived the fiercest era of destruction our realm has ever known.

Prevailing in the atmosphere of silence, I tried to make sense of this vision. The quarks or elementary particles were comparable to beings of consciousness. Us. Humans. I assumed that those smallest particles were those people amongst us (including myself) who were crushed to zero point. The sudden ceasing of the dying leaving behind vast planes of emptiness stretched out ahead in distances no one could have known were there. Suddenly there was room to travel as the survivors were a truly minute part of all the particles that ever existed. Like solely surviving a great disease that wiped out an entire city, being left with nothing but space. Alive in a realm of unprecedented grandness; alive without the prospect of ever having to die. But that wasn't all. There was something else.

The haunting words came to mind, 'Do or die. Change or simply fall away.'

The Old World; the old, heavy and dense moving towards demise. The demise of those who refused to adjust, who refused to change. Then there were the survivors. They were the truly minutest parts of all the particles that ever existed. There was room to travel, with minimal bombardment with other particles. There was freedom to move fast and with ease. It was as if they were solely surviving a great disease that wiped out an entire city, and there was nothing left but space.

The "Quark Slaughter" vision was the name I gave this phenomenon. Was it a galactic interpretation of the transition towards the New World? If so, the underlying message was a reassurance. I was being reduced to one of the many minutest quarks amongst the billions (or trillions) of quarks, and that it was a good thing. Something to be grateful for. Perhaps also the vision answered the objective behind the divine message spoken by the Commanding Voice. A universal message to Mankind to surrender and allow for the demise of their old Selves so as to lead to mass rebirth or renewal. Any attempts to resist, hold onto our Egos, or to hold onto old ways for self-preservation may just result in delays or worse have detrimental effects.

Attempting to quantify the experiences, I felt that the Buckminister's vector equilibrium mapped the surrender, demise and resurrection rather well. The dark energy between the points of the vector equilibrium being the stress points, the points of inner change. The inner change sparked by the fall of our Egos. Some Spiritualists would describe it as "The Dark Knight of the Soul". The death of my old Self bringing forth a rebirth from zero point. Zero, the center, the null point, the true unknown. I was pushed to this seed level. I had become this "seed". It was the zero point for happenings or non-happenings in my life, my state of being. An empty theater, an empty circus, an empty universe ready to accommodate any act, any experience and any audience.

But what I found peculiar was the sudden ceasing of the dying of the quarks. If associated with our world, it may reflect the final ceasing of war, great disease, grand corruption and large scale poverty. Certainly a greatly awaited moment. Perchance the result of Planet Earth's reaching its very own zero point, pushed to become an empty theater to receive a fresh audience of renewed citizens, of Golden Souls.

I named my stigmatic experience the Stigmatic Zero Point. Corresponding it with the Quark Slaughter vision, I could see God's purpose more vividly. Although the latter did give me a bit of a scare when I saw how the quarks were being reduced to mere nothingness, however the eventual destination was vast and free. So it was positive.

Antimatter is the stuff of science fiction. *Star Trek*'s starship Enterprise uses matter-antimatter annihilation propulsion for faster-than-light travel. Antimatter is also the stuff of reality. In particle physics, antimatter is material composed of antiparticles. Antimatter particles are almost identical to their matter counterparts except that they carry the opposite charge and spin. When antimatter meets matter, they immediately annihilate into energy.

Quark is an elementary particle and a fundamental constituent of matter. Quarks combine to form composite particles called hadrons, the most stable of which are protons and neutrons, the composite of atomic nuclei. Quarks appear to be truly fundamental. They have no apparent structure; that is, they cannot be resolved into something smaller.

Quasars are among the most luminous, powerful, and energetic objects known in the universe, emitting up to a thousand times the energy output of the Milky Way, which may contain 200–400 billion stars. Quasars are clearly on the opposite side of the spectrum of *quarks*.

The Journey

Singapore
October 2013

A month whizzed past. Time was moving quickly. It was the middle of the work week, and our new office address was registered at Raffles Place. Considered the heart of the Central Business District and also known as the Wall Street of Singapore, Raffles Place's trademark was its polished glass skyscrapers externally and its hallowed halls of professionalism internally. As part of a cost-cutting measure, our new office was tiny as compared to the old one. However, its proximity to the business hub and its small size was good enough for business meetings and the like. The rest of the time we would work at home.

Once I was done with collecting some contractual paperwork for a new consulting project, I left the office to sit on the side benches located on the centralized grass patch surrounded by the skyscrapers. Looking for a little breather, I dug my hand into my bag to pull out my sketchbook. I had a large black sketchbook which I carried everywhere with me in case something useful transpired. If and when that great thought or idea would sink in, I could doodle it out with an artful pizzazz. Inspired by the great Leonardo Da Vinci (1452 - 1519) whose personal sketchbook was filled with visual designs of the inventive and artistic genius. Fidgeting with my charcoal pencil, the first thing I did was start sketching the galaxies with a random stream of dots to resemble stars. Then I drew the outline of my left palm, and scribbled a circle in the middle as the mark for the Stigmatic Zero Point. I linked the two drawings with a line – from the view of galaxy to the tiny red circle on my palm.

The little red dot of my rebirth,
The Christ Consciousness,
The vast Galaxy within
Aching to be explored.

As I sat there in the growing dusk in the city, like a little child whose mind had been awed by the meaning behind the visions, the office crowd of Raffles Place was busy flooding the pavements to grab a bus, taxi or an MRT to head home. Disturbing me from my thoughts, a lady who was walking by briskly slightly brushed her high heels against my feet by accident. Undeterred, she continued staring at her mobile phone texting furiously. If I guessed correctly, she was in the midst of a virtual argument. Little did she realize that there was a paraplegic gentleman on a wheelchair right smack in the middle of her path. This obviously led to an unpleasant collision which could have been easily prevented. The poor man was in shock and in pain. The impact of her knee hurt his right shoulder quite badly. Cold and callous to what had happened, and oblivious to the looks of anger by the passersby around her, she had her eyes transfixed on her mobile phone. She simply turned two steps to the left and kept on walking. No apology. No concern.

The arrogance and coldness of her demeanor gave further depth to the meaning of the supernatural visions and experiences. We are mere quarks in the vast universe of God's power. Some of us care, while some of us don't. This lady was an example of members of Mankind still lost in resolving the smallness of their worlds and failing to understand the deeper essence of ourselves as Spirit Man (Spirit Woman). Failing to observe the works of God who could gloriously splash the dusky sky with such grandeur, and then to wipe it clean in a moment. With the continued neglect and focus primarily on earthly matters, we could allow for Planet Earth to be wiped clean in a fleeting moment too.

Mindful of the vast galaxy within, I wanted to say to her, 'If you only knew that there are far greater things than this, there are far greater plans.'

Turned off by what I just witnessed, I placed my things in my bag and headed off to catch the MRT. Squeezing my way to enter the crowded train, I was lucky to get some standing room. Amidst the activity around me, people were quietly minding their own business. Many had their headsets on as they watched TV serials, while others were browsing the internet.

As the crowd lessened, I was eventually able to get myself a seat. I took out my sketch again, separating myself from the people huddled in the train with me. Allowing my thoughts to flow naturally, I found myself drawing an animation strip, marking a timeline of the advancement of humans and events with the galaxies in the background. Perhaps a timeline that was in parallel with the Quark Slaughter vision. Then I drew an arrow circling back to the beginning to signify a repeat. Instigated by the behavior of the cold brisk walking lady, I was reminded of Mankind experiencing "repeat" procedures. The whole host of problems – the wars, natural disasters and economic crisis recurring again and again. The problems in our personal relationships repeating again and again. Each time unique, each time we are struggling to correct our mistakes.

Earth, alive with its own innate consciousness, going through its journey from zero point, while we as its planetary citizens synchronize with its journey. All going through repeat procedure until we learn the lessons and with each graduation, progress further in our evolution. Was this the final "repeat" before this New World would be allowed to come in? Or were we just too busy staring at our mobile phones and not working on ourselves fully to play a part? From the far-fetched Upside-down Kingdom to a Brobdingnagian Quark Slaughter vision, we are on a transition moving towards a threshold. There were going to be tests and tribulations to challenge, to distract and to slow us down. There were also going to be the facing off with the dominion "villains", that is, the negative energies, entities and emotions, the adversaries, or our Ego.

As a helping hand, we will have our mentors and guides to help us through. On my journey so far, there was the MRT Stranger, the Buddhist Monk, Marianne and Yasmine the Cancer Survivor, also the enigmatic praying mantis. I was determined to change and move upwards. If upwards meant shifting from a mere quark to a large luminous quasar, I sensed that it would be contradistinctive. A different pathway altogether.

7

Loving Unconditionally

Unconditional Love,
The organizing principle of the Cosmos,
The over-arching purpose
For the advancement of our planet.

Bearing fruit
To the harmony in families,
The growth of nations,
With Heaven on Earth
Within our reach.

Kuala Lumpur, Malaysia
2nd week of November 2013

A neon green ball of Light glowing as it floated in front of me. A split second later, it burst into flames. I stumbled a few steps back in shock before its final transformation into a man. A fleeting moment before I could catch my breath. Luminous white hair cascading softly on his shoulders. A pearl essence pouring from the crown of his head, creating a wonderful crescendo of cascading light through his very being. Dressed in a beige cloak, his face was luminous - projecting an aura of benevolence. The brightest blue aquamarine eyes looking deep into my eyes, pouring in a fountain of liquid love.

I was on a short visit to Malaysia and had plans to return to Singapore in a week. The neon green ball of Light. The flaming fire. The luminescent face. An apodictic encounter with divinity. Was it an Angel, or even greater an Archangel? Or was it the visitation of an ascended master or a Divine Being? Was it the extraordinary visitation of Jesus Christ? The presence was supreme, mesmerizing and beyond true description. There was a serenity in the Divine Being that transferred to me that eased my breath. I felt my heart flooding with unconditional love - an outpouring from the Divine Being's eyes and an in pouring into me like a river of love.

The fire took me by surprise. What was that? Christians associate the fire to the Holy Spirit of God. Then there was the ball of Light. The color of the ball of Light, the color associated with the heart according to Spiritualists as well as to the Holy Spirit of God. A momentary experience that was so healing and so heartfelt that it made sense. So much love that made me reflect back on the love of my parents - an unconditional love that was there despite the ups and downs. Was this arranged as I was badly in need of love and healing at that time? I was at my lowest and I had to come up. In that sense, the timing was pivotal.

It was a little over two months since the Stigmatic Zero Point experience. The healing neon-green ball of Light, the Fire, the loving blue eyes filled me with overwhelming emotions for many months onwards, and each time I looked back on the incident.

'Sacred geometry
Of a blue aquamarine.

Four arcane wooden doors
Opening on all sides,
With a neon-green glow ...'
~ from the descriptive prose of the painting created in 2008

I sensed a subtle hint of a prophesy coming true from the painting. And considering the sacred geometry, so intrinsic in the painting, I felt it was reflective of the Divine Being too.

The Divine Being felt analogous to harmonious living fields of Light – a quantum field of all possibilities. A kind of divine light vehicle. A counterclockwise rotating field of Light generated from the spinning of specific geometric forms, simultaneously affecting the body and spirit creating a powerful shape called the Merkabah, like wheels within the wheels - spirals of energy as in DNA, which transports the spirit/body from one dimension to another. I imagined that the more the unconditional love fed through us, the greater the energy field of the sacred geometry extended around our bodies. The lack of it in our lives, the smaller, and the dimmer it becomes as if a metaphor for the shrunken gray misty souls I saw floating in the "Portal and Golden Souls" vision while meditating at the Gardens by the Bay.

Whatever or whoever the Divine Being was, the presence was the personification and the magnification of unconditional love. The ball of Light, the Fire and the Diving Being – appearing in that order milliseconds apart. A paternal and maternal presence of unconditional love, the creation of a dominion of spinning shining light of sacred geometry that was at its greatest, and its brightest. My ocular description of the "aquamarine eyes flowing with liquid love" reminded me of my own earthly father. The huge reservoir of love my father gave. It was also the lovingly nurturing from my own mother. A father-mother duality of the feeling. An overwhelming completeness that I was striving for. The Divine Being touched me in that respect, and I wanted more of it.

Merkabah also spelled Merkaba, is the vehicle of divine light vehicle allegedly used by ascended masters to connect with and reach those in tune with the higher realms. "Mer" means Light. "Ka" means Spirit. "Ba" means Body. It is the holy grail in ancient times containing the knowledge of unified physics. Mer-Ka-Ba means the spirit/body surrounded by counter-rotating fields *of light.*

Blossoming Of Divine Love

Singapore
Beginning of 2014

The year 2013 came and went, and 2014 started with some necessary and inevitable beginnings. My family and I were invited to a Sikh wedding. It was my first and I was looking to forward to the new cultural experience.

I walked up the stairs at the entrance of the pristine white *Gurdwara* and was directed towards a large white main hall called a *Darbar Sahib*, where the *Guru Granth Sahib* is seen, a holy text current and perpetual Guru of the Sikhs. At the head of the hall sat a Sikh Priest with his head wrapped in a white turban, as he gazed wide-eyed at the audience.

Soon after the young couple getting married walked in slowly from different directions. Dressed in intricate finery of white, gold and red, they sat about a meter apart, on their knees with their heads down conferring respect for the priest. Behind them was a glitterati of guests dressed in the most vivacious colors, watching in anticipation. The Sikh priest set his eyes with intensity at the young couple. His motive was only to make it clear to them that they were embarking on the institution of marriage which was a spiritual one, and not to be taken lightly. As I sat there in the middle of the *Gurdwara* attending a wedding solemnization ceremony, I listened to the meaning of his words, with the mystical Punjabi music playing in the background.

The highlight of the morning wedding was the speech by the Sikh Priest on divine love.

The Sikh Priest spoke in Punjabi, 'The coming together of a man and woman, equal regardless of their gender, not one greater than the other - as two bodies and minds merge to become One. United in divine love,' he continued, 'Divine love is the highest form of love, a step above romantic love. It is the essence of the true bond of marriage.'

With the utterance of those words, I felt an instant elevation. Those words resonated with me so perfectly that I felt a firing up of my Spirit Woman, like a meteoric shooting star. The sensation of a white Light that enveloped me, from my heart and outward through my palms to the crown of my head. My very soul and spirit ignited. The words "divine love" with such a meaningful explanation behind it, combined with the remembrance of the eyes of the liquid love of the Divine Being sparked that sudden uplifting. My Spirit Woman was within a split second absolutely humongous. I felt larger than life than ever before.

That was when I discovered more and more how God was in control and I was simply the conduit. His control was giving me so much guidance. I could see more clearly that a very strong foundation is created when relationships are based on divine love. Tighter bonds within families - an integration, a Oneness - making lives focused within the family unit; where any possibilities or visible signs of division fall away. When divine love exists, fear and anger has no place. And vice versa, if fear and anger exist, there is no room for divine love to reside in our hearts. As the ceremony ended, everyone got up to leave the premises for dinner at a large hall in the basement. It took me a moment to collect my senses before I picked myself up from the floor. As soon as I did, a lady approached me. She said that a friend of hers who was sitting two rows behind me saw a white Light cover me. I wish I could have seen it on myself, though I had felt it very strongly.

Still drifting with the beingness through the rumination of "divine love", I gently nudged myself back to reality as I walked slowly down the corridor toward the main entrance following the rest of the crowd at the wedding. I passed by a framed picture decorated with yellow chrysanthemums.

The picture stood out like a placard with the words, 'God is One'.

I thought of God, the Divine Being and the Oneness of the new married couple. A sense of hope that there was such a thing as unbreakable divine love.

As I admired the beauty of the simple message on the picture, partially lost in my thoughts, relishing the momentary elevated feeling, a passerby commented, 'Not everyone can become truly One.'

A dampener to the cruel reality of division. But that did not deter me. In all my adult years, I was blind to the fact that "divine love" would have such a special meaning to me. That very special and very brief moment in time, when I was transformed into a golden soul, towering in height.

Unconditional forgiveness

Kuala Lumpur, Malaysia
Beginning of 2014

Unconditional love. Divine love. Still there was more to be uncovered. The intermingling and overlapping, the base of it being forgiveness in its totality. It was an Indonesian Mystic who gave me a greater perspective on this. I was still keen to investigate who the Divine Being was, though I felt it was Jesus. But why now? And what was the purpose?

I thought I would consult a local Pastor who could shed some light on the visitation since Marianne had returned to the United States. I asked around for a suitable guide that could explain my supernatural experiences, and fortunately I was given one very quickly. As I spoke to some members of the attendees at the Sunday Service, I noticed a slim tanned lady dancing in a deep trance just like the Sufi mystics. I was told by some people that she had been in that trance state for awhile, from the beginning of the worship and praise till the end of the service. A good two hours. On occasion she would cantillate in an incomprehensible language. Later, I discovered that she was speaking in the mysterious language of the Spirit – or speaking in tongues as it is otherwise known. A murmuring mixture of unintelligible phrases and fragments of melody, while being completely zoned out and disconnected from her immediate physical reality, until finally she collapsed on the floor in a state of limbo.

That raised my curiosity, making me more determined to meet her. While I waited for her to wake up from her state of unconsciousness, she rolled on the floor to the left and to the right trying to regain her senses. In her early 40s, she had a girlish radiance of a 20 year old. Svelte, dressed in skin tight denim and a deep red turtle neck, she finally got up rubbing her eyes with her fists. Slowly getting up, she saw me waiting for an introduction.

Shyly nodding, she said, 'Hello.'

Noticing her hesitation in speaking English, I shared with her that I was quite fluent in Bahasa. Feeling comforted, she introduced herself as Adriana.

I asked, 'How do you do it? I mean get so deep in trance. Where do you go?'

She smiled and replied in Bahasa, 'I go to Heaven!'

I asked again with a polite cynicism in my tone of voice, 'It's that easy?'

Adriana explained, 'Yes and no. Hopefully, through my personal experience you will understand. Though it is a long story, let me explain very briefly. I have come to Malaysia to earn a living to support my children. My children are still in my village in Indonesia and I only see them once a year while my parents take care of them. My husband disappeared and till today I have no idea where he is and who took him. There was a lot of evidence that he was kidnapped and possibly killed,' she sighed and said, 'I just hate the thought of that. Well, anyway, since his disappearance, I was left penniless and I had to take care of myself, my elderly parents and my three children. And well, the story continues.'

I consoled her and said, 'I am really sorry to hear what you went through.'

Solemn but still smiling, Adriana said, 'Well, to summarize, it was a life of poverty, loneliness and everyday just craving for my children,' she continued, 'My life was like a walk through the gates of Hell. To make things worse, I saw Hell in my dreams regularly. It was bad enough to experience it in real life, and then to see it while asleep.'

Adriana was reluctant to describe the details of what she really went through, but these were her words, 'Our focus should be to experience Heaven,' she paused and elaborated further, 'While in Indonesia, we were so poor that we lived in the smallest quarters you can imagine. It was not the kind of life I wanted to give my children,' she continued, 'Who could I turn to other than God? No one else could help me at that time. Certainly not my parents. In fact, I had to support them financially too. Even though I came to Malaysia to work as a domestic helper, I am not earning much. My parents and I are always under the water with loan sharks chasing us almost daily.'

Throughout our conversation, she did not speak one word of bitterness against the people who may have been responsible for taking her husband away from her.

Adriana's pious reply, 'These people who were involved, whoever they may be, I have forgiven them unconditionally. I still pray for them asking God to bless them and to show them the Light,' she added, 'You must understand that, in terms of forgiveness, it should not be just in words, but you have to forgive deeply in your heart. It should be so complete that the pain that they have caused you should not bring out feelings of anger, resentment or blame any longer.'

While Adriana struggled through a life of poverty and pain, it was through her emotional prayer to God craving to experience heavenly love for the first time, and for a lifetime onwards that changed everything. That act of emotional persistence and unconditional forgiveness granted her the sovereignty to visit Heaven.

With a beaming smile, she said, 'Children don't bear grudges. So we need to be like children. That is what I discovered that unless you become like a child, you will not be able to enter Open Heaven.'

This ordeal in her life was indeed a blessing in disguise to help her come to this realization. I never imagined loving unconditionally and praying for the same people who had hurt me the most. Initially, it sounded like a masochistic pursuit. However, with the earnestness that showed on her face, I was convinced wholeheartedly.

The topic of Heaven was an ambiguous one. Her presence and transformation proved it. As we continued to talk, little did I realize that she would sharing one of the secrets to entering and seeing Heaven – while still being alive. I always thought that one could only go to Heaven after death.

'I can enter Open Heaven at will,' she said.

She held her head up high with a humble pride, still maintaining the gentleness in her voice, 'It's like I have been given the authority to enter.'

Unconditional love was the irrefutable secret. And tied to this unconditional love is unconditional forgiveness going hand in hand. It sounded too simple in theory, though difficult to achieve in practice.

'Why "Open Heaven"?' I asked.

Adriana replied, 'Open Heaven. "Open" because it is open for entry. But ... ' she paused, 'you need to have sovereignty to have access to Open Heaven. You do not have the authority to enter if you do not have unconditional love in your heart.'

Would I ever be granted sovereignty? Would I ever be able to attain unconditional love in my heart? I had to tackle the residual bitterness in my heart. The unforgiveness of a lifetime of hurtful experiences was still simmering within me. There was a need for an atonement through apology and forgiveness to reach closure.

Intuitively Adriana said, 'So whatever unforgiveness you have in your heart, give it to the Lord.'

I listened obediently. I placed the intention in my heart with the desire to see and visit Open Heaven. I wanted to feel and experience it on my own.

Adriana reached into her bag and pulled out a plastic box. Modestly, she opened it to reveal 6 to 7 gemstones of different sizes, sparkling in vibrant reds, yellows, blues and greens.

Stirred up by the delightful show of shining splendor, I exclaimed, "Wow! Where did you get this?'

Adriana replied succinctly giving a playful wink, 'Gemstones from Heaven. They appeared out of nowhere. Sometimes when I am sweeping the floor or dusting the cabinets.'

Puzzled, I answered 'But why are these gemstones being shown to us?'

She replied, 'Proof of Heaven.'

I asked skeptically, 'Proof? Most of us already know that Heaven exists. Why do we need proof?'

Leaving me hanging, she replied, 'Maybe you will find out why.'

I answered, 'I hope so.'

She pulled out a tiny aquamarine gemstone and held it up to show me, 'This is for you. Keep this. The Lord told me to give it to you.'

At first dumbfounded and lost for words, I held the sparkling gem in my hand clutching it securely as it was so small that I was afraid that I would drop it. I thanked her graciously. I did not understand the meaning behind the gemstone but I was hoping to find out.

The Love Quantum

Adriana and I made a collaborative effort to meet again. It was an eye-opener that she had no formal education and had come to Malaysia on a domestic worker employment contract. I tempted her with a serious proposition, that with the knowledge she gained and her wisdom, she could become a very good personal coach.

Adriana's reply, 'I used to struggle before but since I started experiencing the realm of Heaven every night in prayer or when I went to sleep, I found that I brought the vibration of Heaven onto Earth for my own life. I love taking care of newborns, so I found a great employer who lives in a beautiful sprawling home in the Malaysian countryside. They cover all my travel and expenses. So right now, all I do is help the mother take care of her newborn twins until they are old enough for her to take care of them herself,' she continued, 'Sunday is my break from work. I have no desire to hang out in stores like many others do. I spend my entire Sunday at the church from morning to evening, either in prayer or clearing the place up. Who do you think keeps the church clean?'

Before I had the chance to ask her any further questions, she said abruptly, 'Hold on. Listen. Did you hear that voice?'

As I strained to listen, 'No. Nothing,' I replied with disappointment.

Adriana turned to me with her eyes transfixed on my eyes, gazing softly just as the Divine Being had.

She began to recite a quote by memory, '1 Corinthians 13 – 'If I speak in human and angelic tongues but I do not have love, I am a resounding gong or a clashing cymbal. And if I have the gift of prophesy and comprehend all the mysteries and all knowledge; if I have all faith so as to move mountains but do not have love, I am nothing.'

A chill ran down my spine as she said that. It was exactly what I needed to hear. The Beatles hit single 'All You Need Is Love' rang in my head. I was putting in so much time and energy trying to understand the mysteries of the universe, when the answer and the solution to all was in essence LOVE.

For some it would be a preposterous thought that an illiterate domestic worker could have such words of wisdom. But she broke all definitions of entitlement. She visited Heaven so frequently that she began to reflect the persona of a citizen of Heaven. It was beginning to make sense to me. Open Heaven was in the atmosphere to show us a preview of a possible manifestation of Heaven on Earth. By having a daily taste of Heaven, she was bringing that frequency into her own life. A spinning MerKaBa shining from within her heart just as the Divine Being had. She was so bright, which explained why I was drawn to speak to her. The New Humans endowed with ethereal wisdom, purity and inner beauty – with an energetic state that radiates out miles away, to others even beyond what the eyes can see.

Love was the answer. It was part of the basis of Heaven on Earth. Heaven and Earth becoming One. So "love" had to be my intention. I had to think, speak, act and even breathe love in my life. I had to start reassessing all my relationships – family first, then friends. I had to imagine that intention being transmitted by an unknown energy signal; warping space-time much like gravity, creating pathways for connection. With the intention of love, it would infuse a connection into my life. Love has the highest vibrational frequencies. When we are filled with love in our hearts for God, for ourselves, our families and fellow mankind, it affects our actions towards society, towards our planet. A stepping stone towards transforming into bright Golden Souls. Towering Golden Souls for that matter.

I began to delve into books and YouTube videos by experts on how to make the best out of relationships. Though I had done it umpteen times before, I wanted to raise the bar this time. To my surprise I discovered that even relationships have a quantum attribute. So if we view a relationship from the quantum perspective, knowing that anything could happen at any moment, we would be more likely to experience a freedom and detachment that could serve the moment currently playing out. The fascination of the quantum world where anything could completely change spontaneously at any moment. The gift of renewal. To live and love in the Now. Since the Stigmatic Zero Point, the visitation of the Divine Being, I felt like a renewed person. Now, I had to renew every aspect of my life particularly in my love and family relationships. I imagined that intimate relationships being the most intense and therefore, the easiest to measure change within. To never force others to come around to our way of thinking. As we transform for the better, we let others be infected by it.

Summed up by Adriana's simple words, 'Just be the change. Be the Love.'

In a Quantum world, there is no separation. Particles that were once together, though seemingly separated, forever are joined (and entangled) and dance as if they are One. The mysterious phenomenon of quantum entanglement where two quanta can become entangled or influence each other regardless of distance. The "love" quantum.

Quantum entanglement a special connection between pairs or groups of quantum systems, or any objects described by quantum mechanics. Briefly, 2 quanta (photons, electrons, etc.) can become "entangled" that is, influence each other even across vast distances. Physicists were blown away by this because it seemed like these particles were communicating faster than the speed of light. This led to the notion that on some level these quanta are existing without location, thus no "speed" is needed. Since this is so contrary to our experience and how we have been taught to view things, it can be a bit mind-boggling to think that somewhere particles are "speaking" to each other, where this is no *location*.

Unity in Love

Thinking aloud, 'God in me, through me and as me - One life, One Mind, One Spirit'.

I meditated on the reality of the love of God in me, so that I would become the full embodiment of it thus infecting the bonds of love in my personal and family relationships. To view the moment as the highest expression of love, and thus the outcome becomes the highest expression of love. If I perceived harmony, that too is confirmed. A common agenda to transform ourselves for the

New World in the intimate areas of our lives. Relinquishing of all judgment, surrendering of all criticism. To be open and to listen and to be relentless in expressing unconditional love to our loved ones and family. A training ground for the expansion of our own hearts.

Since the visitation of the Divine Being, I felt a greater wisdom guiding me. The words "surrender" kept coming forth. Toying with the learning - 'Surrender to God', 'Surrender our love relationships.' Experts say that with the onset of surrender, a relationship starts to bloom and become beautiful as divine love is allowed to enter into our lives.

A touching abstract I came across, 'With surrender, we allow ourselves to start falling in love with ourselves, and when that happens it magnifies into divine love entering our lives. The vibrational frequency of the relationship may reach the state of divinity, the pure God-child love.'

I imagined the souls, different but equally matched in frequency, becoming one – an elegant dance of differences coming into play. Divine love giving the grandest power, maximizing the creative powers resonating between the couple. Almost like the Midas' touch, everything the couple or family touches becomes beautiful and turns to gold. Moreover, to love thy neighbor as thyself. Any love, parent to child, between siblings, between a man and a woman, between friends like the radiating circles of sacred geometry that spread outwards in concentric rings of joy, touching everything in its path and magnifying as it spreads. The effect of a stone in a pond, love touching souls as it radiates outwards spreading the joy of connection in its purest form. A MerKaBa of golden energy frequencies.

Olga messaged me saying that she had exciting news.

'Remember I spoke to you about how I could see people like energy beings? You know like the way nocturnal animals do?' she said.

I asked imploringly, 'Yes?'

She said, 'This is different, almost like the reverse. Now people can feel my energy very strongly. It was very intense the past couple of days. I went down to an event a couple of days ago, people would come to me and hug me. They would say 'I love you!' These are strangers I have never met before! I thought I was just imagining things. The day before and then today the same thing. People I have never met before coming up to me, saying that they feel so connected to me! Both men and women!'

Just like Marianne, she became a shining beacon of Light, at least for a short period of time.

I asked, 'Why do you think this is happening? What triggered it?'

Olga said, 'I don't know. But since I healed my heart of all the pain of the past, and discovered peace in nature, with my daily prayers to God, I found that the growing love within me was also reflecting outside. Suddenly it peaked. People were responding to me with the same amount of love I had in me.'

Olga was experiencing reflections of love from her healed and loving heart. She was literally creating a reality filled with love.

I asked, 'It's still there?'

Olga replied sounding a little disappointed, 'Now? No its gone. I had anxiety issues all over again. That could have taken that power away.'

God and His universe responding kindly to those who manage their mini-universes (themselves and their family units) well, with dedication, compassion – an outpouring of love. I envisioned a New World with an abundance of love. A glimmering aquamarine blue river of liquid love flowing in abundance. In other words, striving to create rivers of love in all aspects of our lives.

Love, the fulfillment of the law of creation. Unconditional love. Unconditional forgiveness. Divine Love. Love in totality that is nurturing, healing and secure. I imagined that when individuals become secure in love, societies as a whole become secure and happy, and this pushes forth progress of Planet Earth to the next level. Creating societies and nations of leaders driven by love. With those surreal breakthroughs about love, the thought of Open Heaven was perpetually on my mind.

8

No Fear, No Anger

Fear and Anger,
A destructive duo
Of low vibrational energies.

Feeding off each other
Causing us more harm than charm,
Than ever before.

A shift is needed,
From react and destroy,
To create and resolve.

Kuala Lumpur, Malaysia
Late December 2013

'You have a beautiful smile. You need to smile more,' this lady said to me, fashioning a smile herself.

Moving back a little to the end of 2013. It was a charity gala in a Kuala Lumpur, an eleemosynary treat of colorful song, drama and dance organized by a global charitable organization. An eclectic mix of Malay, Indian and Chinese performances with a tasteful touch of an international flavor from the West. Enjoying the fusion of cultures, she was sitting and swaying softly with the music while conversing with the people at her table.

The lady leaned towards me as the newbie in the group and continued, 'When we force ourselves to smile, our hearts smile, and then we find that our whole body smiles.'

I rarely smiled. I allowed the thoughts of a difficult past dull my present moment, stealing my own smile away from me. She was a graceful lady with fair Pakistani, Indian or even South American looks with her waist length wavy jet black hair.

She apologized and said, 'Sorry for not introducing myself. I am Faryal.'

We sat next to each other at the table while she shared about her spiritual journey, the one thing we had very much in common. She had a very kind voice, soft spoken and eloquent. In fact, so soothing, so mellifluous that her voice itself would leave a smile on anyone's face.

Faryal said, 'I live in Kuala Lumpur now. I am originally from Pakistan.'

Dressed elegantly in the local dress, a green with yellow gold silk *kebaya*, she had a polished and classy demeanor. Her aquiline nose and high cheekbones were a perfect combination of allure and innocence. However, she was painfully thin with a noticeable strain on her face.

I replied, 'Oh, my mother is from Pakistan too. But I was born and brought up in Singapore.'

Faryal replied, 'I see!'

With a contented smile, she said, 'Well, I left Pakistan and found what I was looking for in Southeast Asia.' she continued, 'Before my shift to Malaysia, my life was not short of turmoil. I was ridden by fear. Born into a family of landlords in Pakistan, I grew up with a silver spoon,' she added, 'There were great benefits too. Benefits which come from loyalty to a *zamindar* or feudal land owner as you would call it. We had adoring village maids-in-waiting who did everything for us. From dressing to feeding to ironing our socks and placing them on our feet.'

I said, 'I see. Generally, anyone would say, "Lucky you".'

She continued, 'Yes, sounds wonderful I know. But it was a privileged life caged in the prison of family expectations.'

I replied, 'True.'

Faryal said, 'But please don't get me wrong. My father is a great man. His conversations are peppered with Sufi anecdotes, Buddhist sutras, Biblical Scriptures and more. He has a very diverse knowledge. It's just the culture where the decisions or the freedom of a man tends to override a woman's. It's changing, well maybe not so quickly in my family but all around me I see it. Yes, all over Pakistan.'

The greater prison was the suppression by the men in her family who disallowed her to do anything on her own, without their prior permission. Faryal was in her late 40s. She had been bound to Pakistan for over twenty years living at the mercy of the men who held tightly onto all the money she earned, leaving her practically penniless. A truly "wealthy-poor", her life was a deception. She started a new life as a social worker to reach out to women from broken families and to those in need. Naturally, it affected her health. The very prominent lines on her cheek and her thin and frail physique a clear giveaway.

She said, 'Little did people realize that though I was from the crème de la crème of society, I was not really living. I was like the living dead! I had to do something. I had to break those chains. I became a victim of fear because I was in a society where the truth was that men were afraid of women. The more men are afraid of women, the more they want to control them.'

The fear and the attempts at control are directly connected. Women have a great power, the feminine beauty, sexual attraction, the ability to earn. That is real power and men know that. But it continues in more subtle ways. It is women getting paid less for the same job. It is subtler now. One has to look much harder to find it. The discrimination of women continues in few parts of the world. The "fear" of women began to make sense. Based on what I had read and through my personal interactions, more women than men were leading the change in the world spiritually.'

I asked as I was keen to know about her views, 'You must be aware that there is so much talk about humanity being in the cusp of the Golden Age?'

She said with a knowing smile, 'Yes, as a matter of fact I do.'

Realizing that I was speaking to the right person, I went on, 'The cusp, the harbinger of the New World. What are your thoughts about a shift towards this New World?'

Faryal answered promptly as though she had thought it through for hours, 'I believe that our shift into the New World will happen when we reach a point where it is about men and women sharing power. That happens when there is no gender fear'.

Finally, she spoke about that one life-changing day when she finally took up the courage to overcome fear. Fear of change. Fear of breaking out of her prison.

Faryal said, 'I felt that I was led by the Spirit to come to Kuala Lumpur. It was the perfect place for me, an Asian setting with some of the freedom of the West,' she added, 'I live alone with my two dogs. But I don't feel alone anymore. Not like before when I was surrounded by many people from maid servants, relatives and what-not, yet I still felt alone because I did not fit into their thinking, their bias. I am fine now as I have relinquished my fears and I know that I have God always with me where ever I go.'

When she shared this, I began to understand why she felt liberated. She was finally free and, most importantly, free of fear.

She said, 'And because I felt imprisoned, I was full of anger,' she continued to explain, 'Fear (and anger) feed on each other. My health deteriorated as a result'.

Her skin was wafer thin and her cheeks were carved with deep sunken lines. A worrying frail composure battered by years of wear and tear from fighting her inner demons. Thankfully she was generally healthy as she claimed to be.

Faryal said, 'This is the philosophy I follow now. If I am angry, I channel that emotion into positive action. To get some real resolution to sift through that anger. And if I am fearful, I work on transforming that into courage. I try to convince myself to carry out an activity that is either brave or out of my comfort zone for that day.'

Listening to her ritual, I could not help comment that it took a lot of discipline.

I commented, 'Turning anger into positive action. Fear into courage. You must be very controlled and disciplined.'

She replied, 'It's not easy to be aware of our emotions. It just takes practice.'

Throughout our conversation, I could not help noticing the wrinkle scars left behind on her beautiful face from the abysmal strain of the past, she did the same as she cross-examined my forehead detecting my premature grays and sallow skin.

Faryal gave me another mantra to follow. Besides fear, I had to conquer anger issues too. Destructive emotions that lead to various unnoticed problems. Recognizing when anger first occurs is a key factor in determining what to do when it rears its ugly head. I researched that emotions such as anger impact the body in a different area compared to the emotion of fear, disgust, happiness, love, depression, and more. Each individual emotion had its own unique part of the body that correlates to it. Feelings of fear are concentrated around the chest and low abdominal area. Alternatively, feelings of anger are concentrated in the head, chest and arms. Here we are as vulnerable humans creating all of this anger, hate, fear and resentment, and as a result getting very sick as it manifests physically into our bodies – starting from viruses or worse cancers and other psychosomatic conditions.

If we decide to delve deeper into the consequences of fear and anger, it breaks down into the vestiges of chaos, lawsuits, lack of compromise and more. If we lock into the negative vibrations, which are low and dense, we will lock into that particular reality. A dichotomy as I imagined that the New World would have no place for lower vibrational energies. As long as emotions of fear and anger are present, or any emotion closely linked to them, we will not be in-sync with the vibrations of the New World. What if this mismatch remains, would the shift be delayed? A question I was hoping to get answered.

It was surprising to discover that though she was coming from a vastly different background as I did, she too had an interest and concern for Planet Earth and its advancement.

Faryal explained, 'We need to have so much joy within us, and in our hearts so that we can be part of the advancing Planet Earth.'

A devout Muslim, she remained open-minded believing in cohesiveness amongst religions and spiritual practices. In between, she spent time in Sri Lanka training up on her new passion in divine healing.

'I really wanted to learn everything I could about divine healing so that I could bring it to Pakistan during my yearly visits,' she continued, 'And speaking as a Muslim woman, I believe that there is a lot of Truth behind divine healing.'

As soon as she said that, I could not help impress upon her my spontaneous self-healing experience with dengue. I shared with her my viewpoint about how I felt that everyone would be capable of self-healing with the faith in the divine.

She responded with coherence, 'Well, then I will add to that – there is a lot of Truth in self healing too - spontaneous self-healing as you pointed out. Once we release the fear of opening up our minds, then we can start to break all limits on anything. God is great!'

Faryal spoke passionately about her personal research on the late American Prophet, Edgar Cayce. I had heard a lot about him too. Edgar was the father of holistic medicine, pioneering the concept in modern times that we are indeed spiritual beings having a human experience'.

She said, 'Edgar Cayce readings assert that we are at an important juncture associated with the transition to a new root race.'

I discovered that the term "root race" refers to the gene pool in the human family. In older, esoteric literature and in legend, terms like life streams, life waves, new people, or even advanced beings. More coincidences from various perspectives that we were heading to a jump in our advancement.

A new root race unblemished of all emotions of low vibrational frequency - emotional anguish, anger, frustration and worry. Supported by the Law of Vibration, with love having the highest and fastest vibration, it brings about joy which is the greater "Flow of Life Force" through our mind, soul and body. This "Life Force" is God, His energy, His intelligence. This explains the vacuum or sense of emptiness that we feel when fear and anger is reverberating through us. Faryal was right about wearing a smile. I was glad that she was saved from her domestic imprisonment. And I was glad that she saved me in a small way by reminding me to smile. The inner smile of positive vibrational energy, sending loving energy to someone, even oneself!

Law of Vibration a law of nature that states that 'nothing rests; everything moves; everything vibrates.' The lower the vibration, the slower the vibration; the higher the vibration the faster the vibration. An alternate perspective of the Law of Vibration states that anything that exists in our universe, whether seen or unseen, broken down into and analyzed in its purest and most basic form, consists of pure energy or light which resonates and exists as a vibratory frequency or pattern. All matter, thoughts and feelings have their own vibrational frequency. The thoughts, feelings and actions we choose also have their own particular rates of vibration. These vibrations will set up resonance with whatever possesses identical frequency.

Joy, A Perpetual Natural State

Lahore, Pakistan
January 2014

Meeting Faryal was an inspiration. Her transnational move being "led by the Spirit" was brave and bold. I wanted to learn that level of surrender to God that she practiced. The kind of surrender that requires very strong faith - a new lesson for me to live by.

Faryal was planning to visit her homeland Pakistan and it gave me an idea. In the past years, my mother had taken up a position as an expat educationist in the cities and rural parts of Pakistan. A bel esprit in the field of education, my mother completed her stint and she raved about the experiences especially in the rural areas. I wanted to experience that too, simply to visit those rural parts of Pakistan. It would be an enriching experience.

I asked Faryal, 'When do you plan to go?'

She replied, 'Around the end of the year around November, maybe December. If you are willing to wait till then?'

I was too impatient and excited. I felt it was the right time and I was ready to go earlier. Nonetheless, the stumbling blocks were there, and they were mounting. The Pakistani immigration delayed my visa as they were concerned why I was visiting the country after so many years since my last visit. More tests to prevent me from going. Tests also of my greatest weakness - fear.

Words of discouragement from all around - 'It's dangerous!', or 'Don't go or you will have problems visiting other countries.'

Yet, the urge so strong to visit my maternal ancestral homeland from which I had taken a 10 year absence from, simply because of fear. Coaxing myself to go for it, this eventually led to a home run with plans confirmed and Pakistan visa issued and ready for collection.

Upon arrival in the city of Lahore, I went straight on a road trip to a colony in rural Pakistan. I shared a vehicle, a black four wheel drive with two other women who were heading toward the same rural colony. It was a pleasant drive passing by mostly chick pea plantations. The countryside was scorched desert with flat scrub, all sand-flats and dust-devils. The driver decided to make a pit-stop half-way for lunch. Covering our heads with our scarves, we got out of the car and walked towards an outdoor eating place. There were turbaned men eating while sitting on large bamboo benches. The men watched us almost interrogatively. We sat as far off as possible, in a isolated corner, so that we could avoid those glances and eat peacefully and undisturbed. With the sound of crows in the background, we had a decent meal of *chicken tikka* and *nan* before heading back into the car to complete the rest of the journey.

I had a pleasant surprise that in the midst of this desert town, there was a vibrant and growing co-educational junior school. At the time of my visit, there was only the one school. It was primarily a school for the rural dwellers, from the destitute to children of landlords. It was a rarity as it catered to both the rich and poor. As far as I knew there was only one restaurant and one convenience store. Just outside the colony, was a sprawling village that, as far as I knew, no city dweller (let alone a local Pakistani) would consider exciting to visit. It had little to offer other than some ram-shackled stores that sold the bare necessities. The only major excitement in the village was when the locals discovered that a foreigner had come to pay a visit. Then, of course, one would get a bevy of curious onlookers.

The car that we were in stopped in front of a conventionally built concrete two storey house surrounded by unusually high brick walls. Painted in lackluster shades of brown, the gates of the house were opened slowly by two servant girls from the village. They were wearing a large dull colored *depatta* wrapped around their shoulders and faces to emulate a *burqa*. Basically cloaked from head to toe, I noticed their eyes aflutter, peering through.

They rushed to get my bags and insisted that I not enter the bedroom yet as they were still preparing it for my comfort. The older servant girl led me to the dining area. She was probably about 17 years old, while the younger one was about 14. As she removed the *depatta* to reveal her face, I was pleased to see a broad toothy grin on her face displaying her happiness.

She said trying to speak some English which turned out to be mostly monosyllabic, 'Eat, eat!'

There was a delightful spread of local cuisine on a table decorated with a bouquet of flowers, folded napkins and candles.

'Haha, very romantic. Thank you!' I teased the twosome.

Before I had the chance to eat, they persuaded me to see the bedroom.

They said almost in unison, 'Come, come!'

So I climbed up the stairs with them. The two storey house was very bare with some simple decorations to add that homely feeling. The two girls huddled together with an escalating excitement as I pushed to open the bedroom door.

'My goodness!' I exclaimed with delight, 'This looks like a honeymoon suite!'

The bed was strewn with red rose petals and with a lingering rose fragrance in the air.

They giggled with amusement. I could see that they had picked up a thing or two from all the Bollywood movies they were watching, probably the only entertainment in that isolated colony. On the right of the bed, the girls had gingerly laid out a big jar filled with raw honey and a large bowl of freshly picked pomegranates.

So happy to receive their warm assistance, I decided to affectionately call them my two little birds. A well-suited name for them as they would flutter from completing one task to another with pure joy and exhilaration.

Speaking in Urdu, the older girl said, 'The honey comes fresh from the bee hive of our village farms. The pomegranates come from the farm too.'

'Farm?' I asked.

The older girl replied, 'Yes, in the village just outside the colony. We can get fresh honey and pomegranates for you every day if you like.'

Addressing me respectfully like an the older sister, '*Baji*, would you like some milk?'

I asked curiously, 'Milk from where?'

She said, 'From our cow. We have our own cow just outside the colony where my family lives. We will milk the cow first thing in the morning and give it to you.'

My stomach was certainly not ready for raw milk. I was so used to pasteurized milk from the supermarkets. But the way they attended to me was a pleasure on its own. They were giving me an abundance of what came naturally to their village. An abundance of food and an abundance of love. I shared with Faryal about the warm welcome I received. She would occasionally come online while she was busy setting up her new home in Malaysia.

Faryal said, 'Those girls didn't have to do that for you. Most of their earnings goes to their parents anyway. You will see that the sheer love they expressed is sincere and not because they want money from you. Of course, with some few exceptions. But most are not.'

In the following days, I was invited to the homes of almost every family that lived in that colony. Each time a lavish meal was prepared and it went past eight course meals at times. And their invitations were genuine as I was not there on work nor for any business purpose. Although I was surrounded by love, there was a general disarray and it was hard accomplishing anything constructive. Thankfully, I was not there on work or I would have been very frustrated with the below average standards of productivity that abounded. Either the electrical power was down or there was no water, and things would take ages if not days to repair. Those were the rare days, even when I was in Bali, when I felt the need to rush back to Singapore.

Faryal said, 'Too much love amongst the ordinary folk, but too little infrastructure and too much corruption. Now see what happens a week before you leave.'

Faryal left me in suspense. The days passed with each day greeted with those same toothy grins and bringing fresh of food and milk. They wanted to join me for walks at the one and only park and the one and only school within the colony. They became my little bodyguards as we walked the empty roads of the rather barren area. Repeat invitations from the families in the colony would keep pouring in endlessly.

Faryal's explanation of all this, 'It's just in our hearts. There is a natural desire to give.'

Sure enough, on the last week of my stay in the rural colony, the drama of involvement and interference intensified. The sadness of the village helpers in the home I stayed in was so heartfelt and genuine. Not for a tip or extra wager as they never asked for anything. Within a short time of three weeks, I was considered part of their family. And my leaving was for them just like a family member leaving on a long trip. This included my two little birds, the families at the colony and the teachers at the school.

'*Baji*, when are you coming back? We will miss you!' speaking with sorrowful faces wishing for my quick return.

From the very efficient Singapore, a tiny red-dot a ne plus ultra in systems and infrastructure, to this rural colony in disarray. On that scale, that part of Pakistan would be on the opposite side of the spectrum compared to Singapore. However, efficiency aside, the love and joy they gave was in abundance. The villagers who served at the home I stayed in, showered me with love and care regardless of whether they were getting anything in return. Nosy as they naturally where, they would want to know everything about my life, and to be involved. I reflected back that this was a huge contrast to big city living where many times attention and care need to be bought.

The colony was in a location of rural Pakistan where many Pakistanis themselves would not even consider visiting. It was too isolated, far out from the city and it was not too safe either. However, the love and joy that filled my heart from the villagers made me forget the potential danger. Faryal shared my sentiments exactly, and so did my mother who had spent some time at the rural colony.

My mother said, 'I have been showered with flowers, cards & even tears of joy when these people see me. My heart felt so warmed with so much love,' she continued, 'In the rural areas, the love and affection the children & teachers have given me is awesome. The teachers are young enough to be my daughters and the students could be my grandchildren. I thank God for such blessings. The warmth & love here is unsurpassed!'

Faryal shared, 'Well, we see great hospitality amongst the people in the cities of Pakistan, and as you go down the income brackets or out in the villages, the warmth and love is even greater,' she continued, 'I guess people in very advanced countries have become less emotional,' she added, 'I think city people need to learn about sharing and caring from the simple village folk. Don't you think?'

I agreed wholeheartedly.

But for a moment I was puzzled and asked Faryal as I wanted clarity, 'If there is so much love here that you tend to forget your fears and anxieties, then why did you leave Pakistan?'

She replied, 'Yes, the love all around is very healing and supportive, but I left because I was looking for freedom.' she added, 'I still do come to Pakistan every year to get my healthy dose of love. But freedom is most needed to get rid of that one fear I have always had. As I shared with you, I always had things done for me, and I started developing a fear of doing things on my own. I wanted to release that fear.'

I replied, 'I see. Then you are doing the right thing.'

Faryal said, 'It has felt right so far, and I have never retracted back.'

I said, 'I can sense your firm commitment.'

She said, 'I refuse to get myself stuck in a loop and go back to being a victim of my fears.'

Faryal said, 'You are very fortunate to be born in Singapore. You have so much in place to contain the daily anxieties we Pakistanis face in dealing with some very basic needs. Furthermore, with its refined processes, it is easy to get things done as people are so much more trustworthy. A clean society where you can just soak in the freedom of it.'

I agreed, 'That's true.'

Faryal said, 'But then again. Fear and anger come from all around most times regardless of where we live. I could be brought up and living in Singapore where everything is functioning perfectly, yet I could still be fraught with fear and anger.'

Releasing Fear and Anger

It was my last three days in rural Pakistan before returning to the city of Lahore. Other than the usual house visiting, I had a little more time to get to know the my two little birds who worked at the house I stayed in. The younger one who was 14 was already engaged to be married to her first cousin, an arrangement made by her parents. Up to now, her life had been dedicated to serving and it would continue for the rest of her life. The older girl was not yet engaged and arrangements were being made desperately for her marriage. She painted a very painful life living in a traditional family setting. She shared how one of her first cousin was burnt to death by her uncle for disgracing his family, as well as numerous stories of her female relatives disappearing, most likely kidnapped and probably raped. Unfortunately, there was no sign of their reappearance, and at most times, and though reports were made, very little was done.

I was not surprised at all by what she shared as over the decades there have been books and media filled with articles about such abusive suppression of women. I understood a fragment of how the women felt through my own close encounter. I was visiting Pakistan at the age of 13, and I found myself in a situation where I was forcibly grabbed and taken away by two men in the late hours of the night. With God's grace, I got away in the nick of time before anything could happen. Yet for years on, I was so traumatized by what had happened that I kept silent about the experience till my 30s. The mocking words while in captivity by those men taunted me so much that some of that fear remained in me till adulthood. Nonetheless, what I went through was pittance compared to these Pakistani women. Despite the pain that infringe into their lives, the moment by moment joy that they focused on, was admirable.

The words of the Buddhist Monk, 'Our Ego assigns blame.'

With fear and anger comes Ego. I wanted to blame others for my experiences, but I had no one to blame, not even myself. I made the mistake of locking the fear and anger inside me for too long, when I should have released it long ago. The Upside-down Kingdom, the world of agitated gray misty souls. With such severe problems these women in Pakistan were facing, I realized that I was part of a community of city dwellers who allowed the slightest issues to break us or embroil us.

Common statements such as 'I hate that person', or 'I trust no one', or 'She's is driving too slow!', or 'Why aren't things placed the way they are supposed to be?', or 'I am scared'.

City dwellers fraught with irritation and impatience, spewing out words pitted with anger. It would be an exaggeration to say that it happens all the time. Of course, that was just my observation as a city dweller myself. However, this could apply to anyone, anywhere. In fact, I have seen uncontrollable fear and anger come from people from all sorts of backgrounds and walks of life.

Proud words of threat such as, 'Haven't you seen my temper?', or 'Don't push me!', or 'Don't get on my wrong side!'

People who think they have the right to be angry when others have broken a rule. There are others who find themselves getting angry often, usually about small things that do not bother others. Then there are those with sudden angry reactions that are explosive like thunderstorms on a summer day. They zoom in from nowhere, blast everything in sight, and then vanish.

Finally the fearful ones, like myself, where the self-defeating phrase "afraid of" was a regular part of their vocabulary. With fear comes anger, both feeding on each other. The destructible duo like emotional living beings completely devoured my mind and heart from taking positive steps forward, and this was regardless of where I went whether it was Singapore, Malaysia, Bali or Pakistan. For centuries, fear and anger has been indoctrinated in our societies. Everything that we have interacted with since childhood is loaded with elements of fear. Education systems, corporations, financial institutions, the media and the list goes on.

Olga words as I remember, 'Fear and anger are there in all of us. We can trigger it or we can disassociate with it. For many of us, it has become a part of our identity.'

Subjecting ourselves to fear and anger hinders our advancement keeping us locked as gray misty souls. A reminder to simply "Be" moving away from reactive-based living where everything bothers us and everything becomes irritating.

Adriana's words of wisdom, 'There can be no room for love in your heart if you still have fear or anger in you. Release those emotions as they are still there.'

Adriana's authoritative yet caring words that held the secret or one of the secrets to getting the authority to accessing Open Heaven. And entering Open Heaven was my focus.

I had to continue dealing with my fear and anger issues. I decided to try an exercise which Faryal shared with me. It involved spending some time alone writing down my thoughts on all the causes and damaging consequences of fear and anger as a form of a therapeutic release. Scribbled in poetic grace to soften its traumatic undertone:

Fear and anger
The destructible duo
That locks us in the past,
Causes disruptive chaos,
Prevents compromise.

It halts negotiations,
Ends business collaborations.
Results in failed completion.

Triggers lawsuits.
It stops rational thinking,
Blocks our intuition,
Disrupts creativity.

It hinders progress,
Damages our health.
And creates disunity.

I put down my pen while releasing my breath as I had kept it held throughout. I put aside the written note with a plan to dwell on it the next time I dived into my meditative secret place. Little did I realize that even though I took my prayer and meditation ritual seriously, at times it would fall back to becoming a ritual rather a connection. Especially when I was traveling, I allowed the distraction and busy-ness to slacken the act with less focus and concentration. Furthermore, when faced with worldly or earthly issues, I would allow the impact of those issues to take precedence over the state of my heart.

It was one afternoon when I received my wake up call on this matter. Once again, I was filled with anxiety. I had received a call from Singapore that an urgent matter had to be resolved. I was going to lose some of my precious valuables! Drowning in my self-created atmosphere of consternation and worry, I felt handicapped on how to resolve the matter. I was still in Pakistan and even if I were in Singapore, I could not resolve the matter instantly. Though there was care and concern from the people around me, I could not alleviate the flood of anxiety within me. I was so disappointed with myself. I knew all the theory, and I had learned the importance to simply "Be" – to "Be" in the moment, to "Be" calm in the midst of chaos. On top of that, I had the beautiful and loving encounter with a Divine Being who made me feel assured that I was not alone and I was taken care of. Regardless, I was still regressing.

I spent the whole night tossing, turning and worrying. As I awoke the next morning, I saw a tiny black dot sitting on the top mount of the palm of my right hand. It was a queer black spot, maybe a trifling. However, as a passionate hobbyist in palmistry for several years before, I knew that it meant that I had a blemish within me and it would continue to slow down my spiritual uplifting. My heart was tainted with anxiety, a very low fear-linked vibrational frequency.

I had to cry out with all my emotions to God. To speak to Him and say, 'God how do I know you so that you can show me the way?'

I had to raze out those negative emotions once and for all if I wanted to continue walking along the straight path. Wising up to my mistake, on that same night I meditated and soaked myself under my imaginary Giant Tree. As a light tingling sensation set in, God was making His presence felt, He was working on healing me. I carried on with a prayer asking for His forgiveness for deviating from my path. Through my wasteful anxieties, I was not demonstrating complete faith in Him.

Energy levels of emotions Dr. David R. Hawkins, MD, PhD developed a "map" of the levels of human consciousness (also called the Scale of Consciousness) that uses a muscle-testing technique called Applied Kinesiology to document the nonlinear, spiritual realm. The Hawkins scale is arbitrarily from 1-1000. The key level of 200 corresponds to 40 megahertz. According to his scale, fear resonates at an energy level of 100. Anger vibrates at an energy level of only 150. The vibrational frequency of sadness and grief is a very low vibrational frequency of approximately 75 Hertz compared to happiness and joy which are possibly as high *as 540+ Hertz.*

Replacing Fear with Love

I awoke the next morning and noticed an odd change on my right palm. The black spot had disappeared! The color black appearing and disappearing in less than a day, something I failed to previse. God was speaking to me through colors and the palm of my hands. First the stigmata, then the black spots. I opened up my mind to the mechanics of the universe to derive the answer.

When I thought about the black spots, the first thing that came to mind was sunspots. My once-dormant passion for university physics rose to the surface. I imagined my body (the mini-universe) resembling the peculiarity of sunspots. According to a scientific journal, sunspots are caused by all of this uneven movement of the gases at different rates resulting in the Sun's magnetic fields to be distorted and twisted, similar to how our bedsheets get all bunched up and wrinkled if we move around a lot while we sleep. The twisted magnetic fields have so much power in them that they're able to block the hot gases from rising to the Sun's surface. This results in a sunspot, a dark spot on the Sun, which is cooler and darker than the surrounding gases.

The sunspots and the black spots on my palm had something in common. They represented the blockage of Light – a hurdle towards my spiritual advancement. I was blocking the Light of God into my life through fear. The worry and anxiety (linked to fear) had manifested in my physicality as a "blemish". The divine message was to become holy, without blemish from within. And so the way forward was to pick and probe and remove them from my emotional system. To channel feelings of fear into love; and if I had any feelings of anger, to channel the anger into action.

An avouchment thought aloud, 'I will endeavor to flush out all feelings of fear and anger from within. I shall channel such feelings into love and positive action instead!'

When fear arises,
Think of Love.

When anger arises,
Think again of Love.

Then finally "Joy"
To be in a perpetual state
Of Love and Joy.

Discovering the Love Frequency

While I had to deal with my fears, so did Faryal. It may have been created by the way we were brought up, or through our experiences, our environment or perhaps it was seeded into us. For myself, it was mostly my worldly experiences and for Faryal primarily her upbringing. It's the seeding that has affected most of us. The media still acts as if its purpose is to spread fear among people all the time. Visual images representing fear and anger constantly being screened in front of us. The reports of war, rape, child molestation, murder, robbery and assault are in the mainstream media daily. Unfortunately, the media does not take the time to balance them appropriately by location or by population numbers. The daily diet of horror stories subliminally act on the psyche of the viewer and leave an impression that the world is a very dangerous place.

We need to be selective of what information we choose to expose ourselves to in order to move into the New World. Resorting to forced censorship and control is not an answer as we are in an age where everything is connected and everything is available in the media and on the Internet. As much as possible, we need to take this on as a personal responsibility, to be selective and to use discretion. We need to also ensure that the information available to us and projected to society through media and the environment we set up within our families and neighborhoods is filled with the positivity of peace, love and joy. In that sense, we create environments which foster positive emotions, the seeding for our internal and external well-being.

The Love healing frequency (528 hertz) was one of the things that helped Yasmine in her healing from Cancer. The same Love frequency I felt during the visitation of the Divine Being. 528 resolves to a 6, the icon for physical manifestation. That is, $5+2+8=15$; and $1+5=6$ (using Pythagorean math). The mark of the beast 6-6-6 elemental components of Carbon, representing physicality on Earth. So more love frequencies of 528, more creation in the physical. I read that some people view the symbol '6' as a reflecting of the 'spiraling down from Heaven into the wholeness of Earth.'

Fear and anger are both at an extremely low frequency. Hence, the indispensable formula is to let go of all fear and anger, and to let go of all relationships and associations which are based on fear and anger. The black dot appearing and disappearing signified the need to renew our minds to clear the blemishes within us. As we take on the mind of God, we have to choose not to worry, not to fear and not to anger. Furthermore, when we are sad, fearful, upset, angry, or frustrated we are not in the best place to make important decisions, because the decisions would be manifesting out of a low vibration. But when we raise our vibration first by growing our Spirit

Man (Spirit Woman), we make decisions and take actions where the results are likely to be more positive and long-lasting. It is integral to use our cognitive flexibility in order to shift our thinking or attention in response to this new goal for humanity of becoming a love-powered golden soul.

With that new information, I tried to teach myself that whenever I felt angry or fearful about something, I would have to make a conscious choice to act out of love. By doing this, I would raise my vibration from one of "anger" to one of "love". Additionally, if anyone evoked negative emotions in me, I would first try to look inward. People could only trigger fear and anger if those emotions were already in me. I realized that God puts people in our paths to test us and to trigger those flaws within us, emotions of fear and anger to test us, so as to give us opportunities to heal our old wounds, blockages and insecurities. Adriana was correct that I had to learn to forgive, and to keep forgiving as well as to ask for forgiveness on a daily basis. I had to learn that everything is worth an apology. Faryal was also right that I had to smile more and emanate "joy" in my heart. A fine example were the joyful and simple village servant girls.

After all, humanity was not meant to grovel in fear, begging for crumbs of life, and we were also not meant to rage in uncontrollable anger. I imagined the shift into the New World would involve bringing this loving bond across all societies and locations across Planet Earth - big or small, urban or rural, accessible or isolated. Embracing love and joy over worldly matters, the passage to an effervescent and perpetual joy within our hearts wherever we go. Love and joy, the "Life Force", the building block of God's work - the highest vibrational frequency.

It was 10pm in the ever so quiet colony and it was my final day and I had said my goodbyes to the rural dwellers. The next morning I would be taking an almost full day drive back to the city of Lahore. Done for the day, I placed myself on a *charpoy* in the balcony on the 2nd storey of the house to complete my night prayers.

The scribbled note in my hand with the words, 'Fear and anger, the destructible duo!'

I made the repeated prayer for the release of those negative emotions. I visualized my Giant Tree and being in communion with God.

The provincial balcony gave me an open-air view of a large empty patch of land. When I looked up, it was a tranquil scene of the beautiful starry night sky. And when I looked around to my left, I spotted my two little birds mischievously hiding behind the window overlooking the balcony watching me pray. As soon as I finished, I turned around and saw them laughing again. They must have been wondering what I was up to. I ran up to them to tackle them as I playfully caught the younger one. They continued to laugh with amusement. A tiny sparkle on the forehead of the younger girl caught my eye. I looked closer to see. It was a speck of gold dust!

I was puzzled for a moment. It could have been a divine sign that those village helpers were blessed as they taught me a good lesson on how to be content and happy always. I took it to also mean that it could be a sign that I was on the right track in dealing with my fear and anger issues. I reflected back taking a bird's eye view of my travels. In Bali, I soaked and went through some healing in the raw elements of nature. In Pakistan, I was introduced to the joyful outpouring of genuine love from the rural dwellers. Overall, I realized that it was unsustainable to be dependent on the external environment to resolve emotional issues. I had to create that "joy" within myself wherever I was. I had to be a personification of "love" just like the Divine Being.

Remembering to keep fear and anger under control, I had a deepening desire to see what God had in store for me next.

Marianne's words, 'Desire is the catalyst for everything.'

I asked aloud in prayer, 'More of your teachings and guidance God. Reveal to me your secrets. You can trust me.'

Love healing frequency is of at least 528 hertz. According to internationally known public health authority Dr Len Horowitz, it is the frequency that is central to the musical mathematical matrix of creation. A frequency of 528 Hertz means that there are 528 cycles of vibration occurring every single second. Dr. Horowitz, working with mathematician Marko Rodin, advanced the mathematical relationship to genetic structuring, as DNA segments reflect Rodin's 'infinity pattern', that some researchers predict will revolutionize everything. Horowitz also claimed that supposing we were to play the 528 hertz "Love" frequency, that energy would go out and would probably touch the hearts and open the hearts of people who may have had closed hearts before. Math scientist Victor Showell describes 528 as fundamental to the ancient Pi, Phi, and the Golden Mean evident throughout natural design. Victor Showell together with John Stuart Reid, a pioneer in acoustic research and cymatic measurements, have proven that 528 is essential to the sacred geometry of circles and spirals consistent with DNA structuring and hydrosonic restructuring. 528Hz is also the *"miracle"* note.

9

No Lies, No Secrets

An expanding and escalating
Inner desire of humans
To want to know the Truth,

And with all of us connected
Within a universal field of consciousness
The Global Mind
Nothing can be truly hidden.

So no more lies, no more secrets.
Advancing ourselves as we go through
The Golden Door of Truth.

Rural Pakistan
February 2014

A full moon night and a dead stillness filled the air. It was my last night at the rural colony and it was also the tail end of a chilly winter. The nights were still cold outdoors, but always warm and toasty indoors. I slept soundly in the bedroom of the guest house.

It was in the wee hours of the morning, approximately 4am, when something strange happened. I felt a slight buzz permeate through my body, strong enough to have awaken me. Then the buzzing sensation doubled to become a mild electrocution of my entire body. Suddenly the numbers '0's and '1's appeared before me, flooding my entire vision. A bizarre visual attack of binary code! No voice, just code. Peculiar as it may sound, I felt like I was a device receiving a transmission signal, my brain acting like a traditional radio receiver. What was going on! Was my brain intercepting a communication signal or maybe some kind of a secret code? Perhaps I was going overboard with a wild imagination or perhaps it was a manifestation of Truth. It felt as real as ever. The question was - why was this happening to me now? The strange electrocution and binary code. Binary code, one of the earliest form of communication or a method of counting, is the code which is what computers think by.

By 5 am, the *azan* was sung by the Muslim cleric of the only *mosque* in that colony. Day break had come and I was still reeling from the incident. By 7am, my two little birds came knocking on my door asking if I was ready for breakfast as in a couple of hours the car would be coming to take me back to the city. I said 'Yes', and shortly after the older one came into the bedroom with morning breakfast and tea presented on a tray. Enjoying the pampering, I finished breakfast quickly so that I could finish my packing and be ready for the car. I did not share anything about the electrocution with my helpers or with the people in the house, as I thought that it would be beyond their comprehension. Maybe in the city, I may find some opportunities to share my experience and somehow find the Truth behind it.

Lahore, Pakistan
February 2014

I was hoping to spend a couple of days in the city before returning to Singapore. From the quiet rural colony to the busy city of Lahore, it was a welcome change. In fact, the very next day when I arrived, I was invited to an aristocratic though somewhat long drawn luncheon by the city's high society. Along with several friends, we drove up and arrived at a sprawling home with a perfectly manicured lawns and gardens.

We were received at the door by a traditional butler who led us into a lavish study heavily decorated with British colonial artifacts. Two elderly gentlemen and a lady were sitting in the study. As we warmed up to each other, the conversation meandered through colorful and intellectual themes and topics, ranging from politics to philosophy. As I expected the topic of God and spirituality came up soon. First as little ripples as one person or the other was talking about practicing yoga to transcendental meditation. A foreigner could have easily falsely assumed such topics would be out of place in an Islamic country like Pakistan, when the Truth was that it was perfectly normal while sipping *kahwah*, the local herbal tea with Pakistanis.

Heavy discussions which were no farce and contradictory to what some would assume.

'I am an Atheist, and you know why? Because I have seen religion tear this country apart!' a fierce remark by one of the elderly gentlemen.

In his late 70s, happily retired, he was a daring adventurer who traveled around the globe. One could easily tell by his red cheeked complexion and his forceful presence.

The elderly gentleman shared, 'I have traveled the world from Boston to Brazil. Where religion is dominant, there is strife. I have only seen it take humanity backwards!'

As soon as he said that, there were fervent replies back and forth. In spite of the passionate responses, the discussion was civil and healthy with no abusive remarks.

I waited for the ripples to die down before I shared with him privately, 'I feel that we are questioning more now because we need to shift from simply being aware of God's existence and His Word, as religion teaches, and move towards a deep intimacy with God. It will take us forward for the advancement of Planet Earth, and not backward. God's close guidance every step of the way, always teaching and guiding.'

Impatient for answers, the elderly gentleman queried, 'Intimacy in what way?'

I paused for a moment so that I could give him a reply that made sense.

I explained, trying to justify my words, 'Well, for instance, just during my short trip in the rural part of Pakistan I had this bizarre "electrocution" experience. Perhaps it could have been arranged by God to teach me something or to activate something within me. Or perhaps it could be something else. But prior to that experience, I had asked in prayer for God to reveal His Secrets to me. For ages, I have had a deep desire in my heart for those answers. And sure enough I have been getting them step by step. It's been amazing.'

The elderly gentleman asked, 'How did you get the answers?'

I replied, 'I asked. Sometimes I was given hints to derive the answers and sometimes the answers would come direct. Either through a voice, or visually through symbols and visions, through repetition especially through numbers, also through people who I believe were arranged to meet me and pass on messages to me, and then finally a knowing in my spirit that an answer that was not there before is now there, crystal clear. All this has come when I was ready and the time was right.'

I was very careful with my answers and tried to remain as diplomatic as possible. I did not want them to feel that I was arrogant and that I had all the answers, when the reality was I had so many "spaces" and "blanks" to be filled in.

Wanting validation he queried further, 'What makes you so sure that it was arranged by God?'

I replied, 'For one thing, there is knowing. Another indicator is that He made sure that every incident was unique and in perfect sequence.'

I joked, 'God is very systematic, very structured. He is a mathematician, a quantum physicist, and much more of course. As we say, He is All That Is. In fact, one incident would happen, and then the next to add to the learning from the previous. It was like I was going up from kindergarten and then graduating to primary school class 1, 2 and upwards. New information adding to the previous, and sometimes completely replacing the old information.'

A little fascinated, he said, 'Interesting. He is teaching you and upgrading you at the same time'

I replied, 'Quite correct. Many times I had questions. Is this all my imagination? No. If it was, why did these incidents happen one after another only after I started seriously meditating and conversing with God as a person? Once I gave Him my undivided attention, He took over my life and showed me what I needed to be shown.'

He said with wishful thinking, 'I need to develop that level of focus.'

I said, 'God cannot reveal Himself to us if our minds are so full of distracting thoughts about earthly matters.'

This piqued the interest of inquisitive ears at the dining lounge area. A remote coincidence that a younger gentlemen in his late 40s had an unusual hobby of tapping into and listening to radio signals from channels around the world (and beyond). I could see a striking father and son resemblance between the elderly gentlemen and this younger man.

Without wasting the chance, he jumped in, 'What's this electrocution incident that you had?'

As I described the entire event in detail, he looked startled.

He said, 'I think it is unlikely for brain waves to interfere with radio waves. Brain waves are too slow and too weak, and they're extremely hard to measure.'

Whether the younger gentleman was wrong or right, the incident happened and I knew it had a profound reason to reveal something to me. If he was right, it could have been an activation within my DNA (with the RNA) releasing binary code. Mathematics and biological data tend to have a synergistic relationship. Hence, a very possible theory too. After all, there is so much evidence that God is within our DNA.

At the same time, I was grateful to him that he interrupted the previous heavy topic on God, shifting to something less political like science. From what I heard, he was a trained physicist although he was adroit at explaining terms in simple layman words.

The younger gentleman clarified, 'Electromagnetic radio waves are energy sent as pulses in basically binary code. Radio waves and brain waves are both forms of electromagnetic radiation — waves of energy that travel at the speed of light. Binary code translate into pictures for instance, like Digital TV. Did you see any visions or pictures appear after those '0's and '1's?'

I shook my head. Perhaps, I was not alert in those early hours. He was referring to visual pictures based on symbolism as shown in my visions and dreams.

He said, 'You were definitely receiving some kind of transmission, either local or extraterrestrial.'

I asked, 'How about if it came from a "deeply" local source, like from our own body, our own DNA?'

He replied, 'Hmm, possible.'

I researched that DNA in our cells is very similar to an intricate computer program. The sequencing and ordering of the '1's and '0's is what makes the computer program work properly. In the same way, DNA is made up of four chemicals, abbreviated as letters A, T, G, and C.

The younger gentleman asked, 'Did you hear about the mysterious radio waves from deep space?'

I shook my head.

He expanded, 'Well, there was an unknown radio signal, which may have come from a black hole, colliding neutron stars (or – for those who "believe" – alien life), has been picked up by astronomers live for the first time ever. Its origins remain mysterious. The fast radio bursts are quick, bright flashes of radio waves that last only milliseconds, but still emit as much energy as the sun in an entire day.'

The younger gentleman glanced at his phone as he received a Whatsapp message from his *peer*, a Pakistani fortuneteller, who was advising him whether he should travel or not to London that week to negotiate a project contract. For a man of science, he was still very traditional by regularly consulting his *peer*.

'Could it be a binary transmission from God?' he asked, returning his focus on our intellectually stimulating discussion.

'Could be. After all, the God spark is within our DNA,' I replied.

'And our DNA as an instructional script, a software program, sitting in the nucleus of the cell. Who knows, you could have been receiving a new instruction,' he added.

The younger gentleman caught the interest of the rest of the people at the tea, so he lectured, 'Let me explain. What is real is what you can taste, touch, feel and hear. These are just electrical impulses. The mind is like a television screen. It is receiving a signal. It is receiving input. It is decoding an energetic frequency into what we call a physical experience, or as physical reality.'

Linking back to the Matrix, this Holographic Universe. Symbols of communication being transmuted through the Matrix? I knew that symbolism had been a part of Scriptures from the beginning because it is the vehicle of revelation and the language of faith. As vehicles of revelation, symbols summarize and interpret human experience and interaction with God. Was this divine revelation in the form of binary code coming through as downloads?

A framed quotation by Persian poet Rumi, became my brief fixation.

'The wound is the place that Light enters you,' ~ Rumi.

The binary code '0's and '1's, matching the first two numbers in the Fibonacci Sequence. Probably this signified a new beginning for me. Whatever it was, since that electrocution day, I was more vibrant and energized than ever before – both mentally and physically. Information would run through my mind a lot faster as I deciphered it while I conversed with people. My ability to perceive things heightened. If it took me 5 seconds to understand something in the past, now it took half the time. I was more in tune with information, as if hidden cards on a table were suddenly turned over to be revealed. Pleased with the revelation, I secretly hoped that the elderly gentleman would get the same joy ride as I was experiencing. After all, he was an adventurer looking for a great discovery just as I was.

Tapping within the layers

I stumbled upon some research that we are entering into a world where there will be no more secrets. Our minds are going deeper into the layers as we are opening themselves up to limitless power. Researchers give indicators of how more and more of us will be tapping onto a field of information for communication. Just suppose we could know what others are thinking. Suppose we had access to information inside every other person's brain and they had access to ours. What would it mean in the New World? Just as I was receiving the binary code at that moment, we may all become like living breathing radio wave receivers, with our potentially new DNAs, thereby becoming a world without secrets.

We are all immersed in the Earth's magnetic field. According to Wikipedia, the United States Census Bureau estimates that the world population exceeded 7 billion on March 12, 2012. Hence, the human species is about 7 billion conductive brains all sharing this field, all connected yet without each of us being aware of it. This field contains enough energy to store the experiences of every human being who has ever lived. In fact the strength of the magnetic field induced in every brain matches closely the earth's magnetic field as all brains are considered almost identical with the strength that each brain generates. Between the Ionosphere and the Earth's surface a matching 7.83 Hertz pattern. The intensity and natural frequency is similar between the Ionosphere (region of the upper atmosphere of the Planet Earth) and the human brain. What's interesting is that much of modern technology (for example, the Internet) is pulsed with the human brain. Homogeneous fields that all of us are exposed to.

The human brain of approximately 7.8 Hertz (its alpha and theta states). The ionosphere of approximately 7.8 Hertz. Technology communication fields also match around the same frequency. My imaginative creation of a numerical string of 7-7-7 which I called the "Mystical 7". The Number 7 is the most potent of all symbolic numbers signifying the union of three and four, the completion of a cycle, the perfect order, the perfect number.

If we have access to information, we can get it from anywhere. Imagine the possibilities. We just need to know the mechanism as we open up the layers of our mind. New Humans with renewed and delayered minds, tapping onto channels anywhere in the world and maybe across the Star Systems and more. Opening up our present senses and developing new senses so that we can tap onto fields of information and communication. The question is will we reach a point where we will perhaps see too much? A sensory overload that we as people wouldn't care about and begin to become oblivious to the flood of information out there? The mind of the New Human may reach an advanced auto-pilot state, extracting the essence, like picking up a needle from a haystack, but done with absolute ease. I could see that happening right now through the ever expanding flood of data out there on the Internet and social media.

Still seated, I turned left and right to look for the younger gentleman. He was away at the food table, picking up a piece of chicken from his plate, munching on it thoughtfully.

As he returned, I asked, 'What are your thoughts about the progression of data and communication systems?'

Thinking for a few moments, and then returning to his seat he explained, 'The first time Alexander Graham Bell generated a signal across the room, it was audibly scratchy. He could barely hear it. Now we have one of the most sophisticated technologies in the history of the mankind – we have the telephone and mobile communication system.'

I probed, 'How about "Us" as the new communication system?'

He nodded, "Interesting, yes why not?"

The new technology of the New World to be practiced by New Humans may be enhanced telepathic abilities, as part of daily life. I imagined that all of us would be tapping onto this unified field. The Holy Grail in physics is the Unified Field Theory, a formula that states how all disciplines of physics and physical law, all forces in nature from particles to galaxies and space time, are unified in a mathematical formula. A Oneness that makes us all connected.

Schumann Resonances are a set of spectrum peaks in extremely low frequency of the Earth's electromagnetic spectrum. In fact, the brain researcher Michael Hutchison calls 7.83 Hertz the electromagnetic matrix for all life on this planet, the frequency at which all life forms have developed and, until a few decades ago, the prevailing electromagnetic frequency at which all life took place. The natural frequencies of the human brain are: Beta waves (14 to 30 Hz) Alpha waves (8 to 13 Hz) Theta waves (4 to 7 Hz). The human brain in a healthy state has also been shown to oscillate at 7.83 Hertz, in a natural state of resonance with the Planet Earth. The resonant tone of Earth it is C# (tone vibration of the Earth) - amplification wave.

Unified Field Theory sometimes called the Theory of Everything (TOE, for short) is the long-sought means of tying together all known phenomena to explain the nature and behavior of all matter and energy in existence. In physics, a field refers to an area under the influence of some force, such as gravity or electricity. A unified field theory would reconcile seemingly incompatible aspects of various field theories to create a single comprehensive set of equations. Such a theory could potentially unlock all the secrets of the universe and make a myriad of wonders possible, including such benefits as time travel and an inexhaustible source of clean energy, among many others.

The Global Mind

I was pleased of course as the conversations were well received and free flowing. Hoping to take advantage of the situation and hear what this impressive group of people had to say, I brought up another topic.

'Do you know much about remote viewing?' I asked the group.

A silver haired and well-dressed elderly lady in the group spoke this time. As she sipped her tea, she replied calmly, 'I do practice transcendental meditation. But remote viewing? I have heard of it but I am not sure what it is.'

I explained, 'Remote viewing is the ability of a person to describe a remote geographical location up to several hundred thousand kilometers from their actual physical location. In any case, I have experienced it. This was a little over a year and half ago, around November 2012. I had just flown in from Bali for a short one week trip for some work in Singapore.'

She asked, 'Oh, you were living in Bali?'

I replied, 'Yes, for a short while before I returned home to Singapore.'

That was a time when I felt that God was teaching me with snippets of information about the mechanics of the universe. I had just learned about Unified Field Theory. I could relate it better symbolically as a Global Mind which we had to tune in and tune out of. I went on to describe the whole incident.

I described, 'The vision appeared as a black and white movie on wide-screen, comparable to a TV screen with bad reception, suddenly tuning into clarity. I saw thousands of people dressed in white moving chaotically, but yet in accompaniment with each other. They were crying with expressions and moans of grief. I could see a dead body of an old man being carried by several people also dressed in white. The body was covered in white clothing. The body was long, depicting a tall man. He had a white beard and very defined features. I thought that it was very odd that he was adorned with dark squarish sun glasses!'

'Who was this?' the lady asked.

I replied, 'I had no clue at the time. So what I did was I asked my family and I was told that the funeral was for a well-known religious leader from Pune, India, which was going on that very same day!' I continued, 'It was very strange to me as I had never even heard of that person before, let alone did I turn on the TV or read the newspaper or connect to the Internet to get any information on this. I had just woken up in the morning, gone into my usual meditation and this was what was shown. Why? I still don't know.'

The man turned out to be Bal Thackeray, of whom I had never heard of until that day. He was an Indian politician who had founded the *Shiv Sena*, a right-wing Marathi ethnocentric party active mainly in the state of Maharashtra in Western India. His followers called him the Hindu *Hriday Samraat*, a fearless leader who stood tall in Maharashtra. The lady was intrigued by what I shared and so was the elderly gentleman. For me, that was real evidence of the Unified Field Theory, that all our thoughts are shared thereby creating the Global Mind.

I imagined that almost every thought, idea and event, resided in a cloud, like the Apple iCloud for iPhones and iPads to upload and download data. I may have just downloaded a Bal Thackeray Funeral event from this Global Mind repository. A method widely practiced by central intelligence agencies to extract secrets and track down wanted men in hiding or objects concealed from the public eye. The Bal Thackeray Funeral event may have been an event that was open for my access, downloaded and for my perception. As we go within the layers of our minds, we may be able to receive more and perceive more.

I vocalized my speculations, 'Perhaps we may achieve a world where there will be no more lies and no more secrets.'

The elderly gentlemen responded with comedic sarcasm, 'Haha! Well that would be the day. I hope that I am still alive to see what would happen to this country!'

The laughter infected the whole room with more spicy comments about the comical politics in Pakistan.

The New Human abilities as a threat to secrecy. With so much false information and documentation and with so many cover ups worldwide, a shift would be timely to finally break out and head towards the Truth.

I recall what Adriana the Indonesian Mystic shared during one of our interactions as a privileged regular visitor to the heavenly realms.

Adriana words, 'In the heavenly realm, you can read my mind and I can read yours.'

Thoughts like words are vibratory and have frequencies. At higher frequencies, they may become translucent. Our Hearts see, while are our Minds are mere storage devices. If Adriana's observation is true, does it mean that the blueprint for Heaven on Earth will be put in place or is already there? If so, where were they located? Is the blueprint imprinted on the structure of Planet Earth itself or placed on certain countries and cities to become launch pads or early prototypes? Or is it a blueprint within the DNA of Golden Souls, as they become infectious launch pads for the transfiguration of others who interact with them?

I left those thoughts and questions aside and placed a formal request to God to have answers. For now, the Global Mind was for my scrutiny. The Global Mind, like a Big Data storage device. The Heaven and Earth reflections, where the inner desire of humans to want to know the Truth is finally satisfied. The creation of Wikileaks, in 2005, an online document archive with the slogan "We open governments", Youtube and Facebook posts fraught with conspiracy theories and video footage that expose the Truth of the what-when-who-how, as well as successful whistle-blowing attempt by Edward Snowden, an American computer professional who leaked classified information from the National Security Agency, since June 2013. Even in Singapore, politicians toppled due to an array of sex scandals as well as religious leaders who siphoned large amounts of money for their own purposes without the knowledge of their ardent followers.

With all that happening, as we move through the transition, there is a need to make a proactive effort to mold our characters to speak the Truth, and move away from deception and lies. To do away with the sycophants within ourselves, misleading and swaying influential people for material again. To shift away from lying that serves our own selfish purposes.

Furthermore, I imagined that our true mind should be in our hearts, not our brains. Our brains act like storage devices for access and analysis. This is why our tripartite being is considered body, soul and spirit. The "mind" may already be part of the heart within the body, linked to the soul and spirit; and linked to the brain as storage device. If so, maybe it would be more accurate to say that it is a Global Mind repository of an interconnected body, soul and spirit, since it all comes together, with the interconnected storage devices with emotion and power infused.

And perhaps, this Global Mind with the Holy Spirit of God, coming together for another layer deeper into the revelation of the Truth.

Only the Truth Prevails

Singapore
Early March 2014

I was finally back in Singapore. It was a useful one month trip to Pakistan, covering the city and the rural parts. The highlight was the night of the "electrocution" phenomenon and the fruitful discussions which occupied my mind as I settled back home. To me, just the thought that we were so connected, and how one day if we keep moving in the right direction so that nothing can be kept secret anymore, was exhilarating. Almost like a dream come true as I had grown tired of the deception I faced in business and in the corporate world. A surer possibility that it could be the end of the Upside-down Kingdom, and towards a New World of Truth.

Incidentally, Siva the Indian businessman who was originally from Hyderabad got in touch by email. He wanted to meet to discuss some business. I remembered him quite well as my very first prospect for "laying on hands" divine healing. He kept his promise and he was as enthusiastic as ever.

Siva wrote, 'A good project we can bid for together has come up in Dubai. We are looking for a good consulting firm. Thought of your company.'

Words on a friendly business email. Since my personal session with him wearing the hat of a divine healer rather than a technologist, I remained uncomfortable with him. A clinging haunting feeling that I could not shake off. Since the Bal Thackeray Funeral event was shown to me with such vivid clarity, I knew that could make some headway by incorporating that new ability in my work.

I asked God to reveal to me the Truth about Siva. In minutes, I felt my senses become more acute, the surface of the skin on my face tingling along with my palms and the base of my feet. Moments later, a vision of him appeared sitting on a chair, body and shoulders slouched forward. A Darkness loomed over his head. As the vision made itself more clear, a number of snakes appeared on both sides of his head. A reptilian crown formation of an eldritch face distorted out of shape. Siva's own face was blanked out, while the face above him showed an ominous facade. Snakes signifying deception and manipulation.

I mentally tuned myself out of that state hoping to quickly cast off that ghastly image from my mind. It was clear to me what I needed to do. I decided to do run a professional check on the company. According to business filings, the company appeared clean with a decent financial record and more. If it was the old me, this would have been enough to accept his business invitation. However, led by the Holy Spirit of God, I was shown the Truth between the layers and so I sent him a polite decline. Shortly after, as if with the opening of a can of worms, it was exposed that Siva's company was engaged in questionable business practices. I was thankful that I had been saved the hassle of being cheated as since his company turned out to be deceptive, we would have suffered from their business moral obloquy.

As my prophetic abilities surmounted, this was my first test of faith in God.

I felt these words filled my mind as a guide, 'Unlock your mind from conventional thinking.'

John Samuel Hagelin, PhD (Harvard), an American particle physicist and Professor of Physics at Maharishi University of Management (MUM) made this claim that the mind is structured in layers. Just as the universe is structured in layers. From superficial to profound, and that if we use the mind in a very superficial level, we will have very limited power. Based on this, we can barely move a speck of dust across the tabletop without using our hands. To go beyond the superficial levels of our own minds, we need to tap the layers deep within.

As the Buddhist Monk said in the past, 'Go deeper!'

Just like removing the layers of skin of an onion one by one. With each layer the pungent olfactory sting is stronger, but a greater potency is revealed and unleashed. Once unleashed, nothing can be held back; neither the Truth nor the potent power within ourselves. By unlocking my mind from conventional thinking, I would be releasing an increased magnitude in my power than ever before.

The Truth, the power as well as a new way to communicate. Just scan through the ages. People used to interact more verbally and a person's word would be taken as honor. As technologies progressed, part of this verbal communication was replaced by handwritten, then by SMS texting. Now QR codes as large as chunks of words and pictures shift to symbols through their prevalent use. Now as we progress further, the use of traditional alphabets may be gone. We may reach a point where we have broken through the layers so that it is no longer about honoring a person's "word" but about honoring a person's "thought".

The New World, an era where a lot of verbal and written messages may be communicated telepathically. Either it being purely a human ability or enhanced with man-made technology. Thoughts, binary code, numbers, symbols, all zigzagging through the unified field we are immersed in. A New World where even white lies can be seen out in the open. Any system that chooses to operate based on the old human nature will be in trouble or will become non-existent. Our thoughts which were once kept in secret and our real intentions masked by a disguise, will be out there and wide open for all to see. We may be forced to realize that the Truth can never be hidden. There may be no more place for the lying politician, the deceiving businessperson, the gossipy neighbor or a cheating spouse. There may be an evolution of the thought agreement, from the conventional written agreement. A thought-based covenant that we have with each other, which is as important as the covenant we have with God.

To work towards a transparency never known before, where one human would just look at another and would know exactly who they are. A world where it is difficult to keep secrets from one another. There may be no need to be defensive as everything is out in the open. Lies and secrets may be considered a facet of the past. After all, sooner or later the Truth will come out. It will always be about coming clean. Forgiving and asking for forgiveness will become a daily practice that no one can do without.

The words of the haunting song by Police, 'Every breath you take. Every move you make. Every bond you break. Every step you take. I will be watching you ...'

To finally rinse off the blemishes of falsehood and lies, and move towards Truth, where speaking and acting on the Truth comes from within the totality of ourselves.

10

Vision of the Golden Door

From Quarks
To Quasars.

From Gray Misty Souls
To Towering Golden Souls.

The Golden Door was closed
Waiting to be opened,
For the new Me,
The new You,
For the New World.

Singapore
Mid March 2014

First it was Stigmata in September 2013. Then the Divine Being visitation in November 2013. Followed by the electrocution experience in near barren land in February 2014. And before all that, the meeting with Adriana about the concept of Open Heaven. I was just back from Pakistan, and recounting the superlative experiences, the thought of Open Heaven was so deliciously tempting that I could almost feel it in my taste buds.

The potentiality of myself being a visitor of this Open Heaven had to be possible. In my mind, it just had to be. It became a daily obsession. In all fairness, a healthy one as I placed that intention so deep in my heart. So deep that I could almost imagine it spiraling through the Holographic Universe, waiting for the right moment for God to answer my call. Pondering with some amusement, I was beginning to understand the way God works. He would give me the answer or show me something when I least expected it. Of course I was pleased with that, because it made my life so much more magical.

An eventful day just past the Ides of March. A frigorific feel in the air left me chilled to the bone. The cold wind penetrated the skin of my palms transmuting into an mild electric current. I stayed in that presence for a while. A long meandering road arose in front of me leading toward a Golden Door. The road was of a golden hue, a glorified version of the yellow brick road in the storybook fantasy "Alice in Wonderland" coming alive. Trees with a luscious golden canopy along each side of the road. The view and the feeling were magical. Golden Souls floating in and out of a realm, appearing and disappearing. And this was going on in slow motion.

Was time slowed down on purpose so that I could see in greater precision the attributes of those Golden Souls? The last time at the Gardens by the Bay, they were much further in distance and were passing through a giant Portal. This time, I was given a close-up of how it looked like. Almost 10-12 feet tall or maybe even more, these golden Spirit Man (Spirit Woman) appeared visually like a rippling sea of golden energy with a rounded silhouette of the human body. They were tall majestic beings. Towering Golden Souls. I reached out to touch them as they were just a few inches away from my fingers. The spectacle just blew me away.

A stunning spectacle
Of Towering Golden Souls,
Floating in and out of a realm,
So close, almost touchable.

Was I hallucinating? No, it was far too real. I was standing with my palm opened face up in prayer just like the time when I had the encounter with the Divine Being. Furthermore, it was not a flat 2-dimensional vision. My sense of taste and hearing became highly acute, and my mind was in the Now. The realm could have been in 4th or 5th dimension or even much higher. There was a fresh yet faint scent of something I wish I could remember, perhaps the scent of frankincense. The sights were too awe-inspiring for me to even be aware of my other senses.

Questions filled my mind. Is this how our Spirit Man (Spirit Woman) would look like if we become Towering Golden Souls? Or is this what we will be in the future when we become energy beings? There was such an aliveness. Tears rolled down my cheeks as I continued to stay in that presence. I was shown a world that existed but did not exist at the same time. Like the red pill, blue pill of the Matrix movie, a switch between different realities.

A poignant quote from the iconic movie, 'You take the red pill, you stay in Wonderland, and I show you how deep the rabbit hole goes.'

I was in red pill mode when I stepped into that golden realm of a reality. I wanted to remain in it but either I could not sustain it or I was not allowed to.

Just like in the words of the movie, 'You take the blue pill, the story ends. You wake up in your bed and believe whatever you want to believe …'

Throughout that ethereal experience, my upper body - hands, arms, chest, face - were vibrating with an even greater intensity, a very high vibrational frequency. But all of a sudden, I swooped out of that rabbit hole and I fell back into the "lower frequency" realm of the real world.

Then these words were spoken, 'There are many doors waiting for you. But there is one very special door, the Golden Door. It represents a very beautiful path, and it is waiting to be opened.'

I interpreted is as the doors representing the many options and opportunities available to me. Amongst them, there was that which was very special. The "Golden Door" was a symbolic entity that was very real and ripe for its manifestation.

> *The Many Doors*
> *Representing many opportunities,*
> *Countless physical realities,*
> *Yet there was only*
> *One Golden Door.*

The elusive door of choice toward a warm, brighter, more loving world where life made sense. Was this the door to my own personal transcendence? Or was this also the Golden Door for the Planet Earth, the New World which I could enter and be part of?

'It is entirely possible that behind the perception of our senses, worlds are being hidden behind which we are unaware.' ~ Albert Einstein.

A world hidden and all this time I was incognizant of the Truth. Mulling to myself on the aftermath, if I get there again and if I could just stay there for a little longer so that I could explore. But, no, I was shown what I needed to be shown. Was that a glimpse of Open Heaven? Or was it a reflection of what I perceived as Heaven in my heart? According to Adriana, unconditional love and unconditional forgiveness was the secret to getting access to Open Heaven. However, was that enough to create heavenly reflections on Earth towards planetary advancement?

My mind in a state of flux. I kept thinking of the many doors and the single Golden Door expressed to me in spoken words. Whatever choices I made, would result in a totally different outcome and a vastly contrasting life. Simply by one choice, picked from a lottery of different permutations leading to either a progression or a digression. I imagined that the most elusive door, the Golden Door, would be the most beautiful pathway for myself. Alternatively and concurrently, it may also be Heaven on Earth (the return to the Garden of Eden) as described in the Scriptures. Alleged by some that a "new Heaven and a new Earth" await us, it is a renewed Planet

Earth that has been purified, renovated, reconstituted – a need that resulted from contamination by sin. Some say that evidence demonstrates unequivocally that the expression a "new Heaven and the new Earth" is uniformly used in the figurative sense.

However, there are optimistic and reassuring passages in the book "Romans" in the Bible depicting that, quote '... the sufferings of this present time are not worthy to be compared with the Glory which will be revealed to us.' unquote.

Or was this the next level of the Kardashev Scale of planetary civilizations as I was researching and writing on? I imagined Planet Earth moving up (or down) a planetary advancement scale, while we moved up (or down) the scale of our human advancement. If a comparison were made between these Scriptures and the Kardashev Scale, both may have their commonalities: purity, infinity (no limit) and a renewed structure. Resources that are pure and with no limits. Cleansed and purified at zero point or rebirth. If those qualities applied to Planet Earth, then those same qualities would have to start within each of us. The purification of the Human Soul. The harnessing of the limitlessness energy within us. As part of the purification, the tests that we encounter testing us as we graduate up our evolution. A possible Human Uplifting Scale where we push our own consciousness to change and grow as our Spirit Man (Spirit Woman) extend and expand outward. A resurrection of the power of God within us as the earthly blinders unveil.

There are forces of nature against us, against intolerance, terrorism and war. These are all hindrances to reaching a Type I civilization and beyond. These natural and man-made forces are testing us and Planet Earth; collectively hindering and at the same time re-calibrating our (and the planet's) graduation up the scale towards a heavenly state of limitlessness, abundance and Unity. Coming back to confronting and cleansing ourselves of the emotional forces of anger, fear and other negative qualities from within; so that when we take it to the marketplace we can carry out our deeds with the right thoughts, words and actions.

A far cry from the 1900s when my ancestors were thwarted by suppression when simply surviving to be alive would suffice. There was great pride in being a war hero. There was acceptance in strict religious and cultural doctrines. An era when scarcity, restriction and control dominated. Maybe now, we are reaching the end of an era with the avail of the Golden Door before us. A transit out from an old era to new one.

The Stigmatic Zero Point of myself, the quark slaughter of ourselves to the lowest possible denominator.

'... And they heard a great voice from Heaven saying to them, Come up here ....' ~ Revelation 11:12

Adriana was visiting Open Heaven nightly. I imagined how she was becoming like a citizen of Heaven as she was so light and ethereal herself, so different from everyone else. Hence, through the Golden Door I imagined that we would be transfiguring interstellarly, as tripartite beings – body, soul and spirit. Quarks aside, we may become like quasars, the cosmic version of the Towering Golden Souls. So a fresh new question arose. What are the Keys to opening the Golden Door?

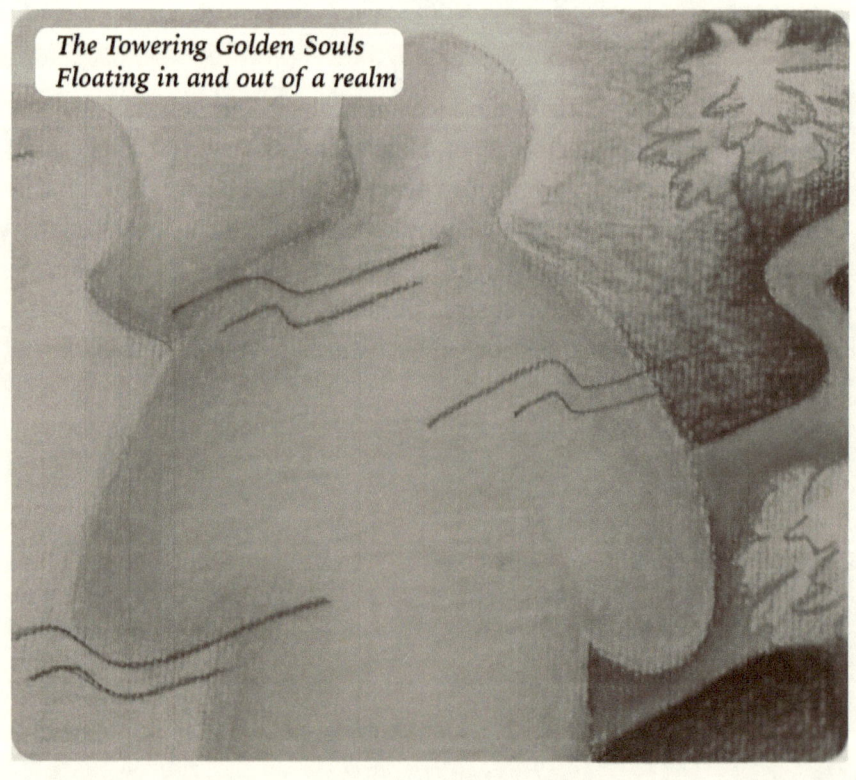

Doing What We Love

We are entering into a time
Where we need to take a break
From chasing shadows.

Expanding ourselves
With the vision of our Hearts
The source of our creativity.

Sharing our passions,
Igniting a contagion,
Carrying out our true purpose,
Losing all sense of time.

Everyday an accomplishment,
Everyday our first love,
Every moment alive in the Spirit.

Singapore
April 2014

There was projection of white Light over the foot of my bed. Three ethereal beings presented themselves as though they were emerging from a portal. The vision of beings framed within the portal space created the effect similar to an overexposed picture with subtle hues of pastels and white. Silhouettes with luminous human faces chiseled like the classical Greek sculptures – all three of them with an even leveled forehead and a dignified straight nose. They were dressed in white. A resemblance to the Prophet Elijah who was known to be amongst the boldest of God's prophets.

Perhaps a time portal that acted as a gateway to other times, dimensions and realms. As these Divine Beings looked down upon me enveloped within this whitish cloud-like ethereal space, translucent in their physicality, they shook their heads in disappointment. Their placid facial expressions showed a loving concern as they spoke to me telepathically. I did not catch the exact words but I knew what they were trying to imply.

Their telepathic words, 'Why so much sadness? You need to be happy in the heart so that you can do your task.'

I looked at them with guilt written all over my face. I nodded.

The brevity of the visitation made me think. First, there was the loving and healing presence of the Divine Being who I felt could have been Jesus. Similarly, these three ethereal beings showed their love with that same care and concern. Even though I was absolutely sure that I had never met "them" before, they seemed so familiar to me as if I knew them from before. They were silently watching me from another realm.

Two visitations and both were soulfully beautiful. Just before this second one, I had stepped up on my meditations spending more time in my secret place. I continued on the written affirmations. My emotional roller coaster rides were lessened by at least half or one third of what they were before. Although I was a lot more stable and stronger, I would still find myself from time to time waking up in the mornings with no clear direction of what was my true purpose. Occasionally, I succumbed to weakness with a lack of focus and the encumbrance of daily distractions.

Other than being aware of my flaws, I questioned who "they" were. Were they members of the Heavenly (Divine) Council monitoring my progress? The Scriptures defines the Heavenly

Council as a symbolic ruling body consisting of God as the supreme monarch with an assembly of supernatural servants gathered around his throne in a heavenly place. Alternatively, could they be the Men in White Linen as described in Biblical Scriptures? I read that they were the said saints who were now spectators of the race that we run. Was I failing the race which was why they were shaking their heads in dismay? This was an important time, a crucial time for the transition of the human race and the Planet Earth. I would love to have them cheering me on.

Or were they ethereal beings of some kind of Galactic Council? I learned that there were some galactic councils that facilitated decisions of the Galactic community. They aided in Mankind's dealing of difficult problems such as the Planet Earth's current situation, inspiring innovative strategies for resolving conflict as well as the education of youth and inspiring humanity with the possibilities of extraterrestrial contact. In addition, they were promoting the growth of crystal children, peace education, exposing elite manipulation, promoting improved global governance, and diplomacy and conflict resolution. If it was a Galactic Council, it made sense as I had interests and concerns about all those planetary issues. If it was the Heavenly Council or perhaps the Men in White Linen or even Angels that made sense too from all the heavenly experiences and encounters. "They" were concerned about our shift, our waking up and rebirth to become our new Selves.

Retrospecting intensely, I remembered I had actually sketched out three beings in white way back in 2008! So not just a painting, a Prophetic Painting.

> '... Stood three Beings in White,
> Regal & imposing,
> Of the Ancient,
> The Current & the Future ...'
> ~ *from the descriptive prose of the painting*

The mere painting which was originally an emotional outlet, turned out to be a truly an accidental prophesy. With the three Men in White displayed prominently, I was being led by the Spirit all the way back then. And I had no clue! It was so clear now that it was the unveiling of a prime agenda with God directing the way.

Moreover, referring to these Beings in White, "they" were referring to a task. What was this task and was this the same one that was "urgent" as alerted by the MRT Stranger? Whatever it was, they were compassionate beings and they were preparing me for something. I had to catch hold of my maven mind and stop it from the obsession of trying to figure out who they were and to simply absorb that personal message for me. I was surrounded by Angels who were assisting and guiding me. I had a one-to-one supremely loving encounter with a Divine Being. Wasn't that enough? Why was I failing again and again?

Now this was the second time round. An external intervention by beings who were always watching! Their official visitation was a sign that I had to take control of my emotions, my life once and for all and it was a serious matter. I was failing the basic test too many times. I was shown how some of the simple village folk in rural Pakistan could achieve this as they enjoyed with contentment the basics of life. I was shown how Adriana, the Indonesian Mystic, could do it when she forgave unconditionally those who caused her hurt. I was shown how Faryal found joy with her new found freedom and by confronting fear in her life.

Despite all that, I still had some fragments of fear and anxiety within me that would disappear for weeks but then suddenly arise and take hold of me. Just like the mysterious black spots on my palm, appearing and disappearing like sunspots in my inner universe. How many times did I have to have stigmata to realize that I had divinity within me, and with this divinity there was no such thing as fear? When would I finally breakthrough from this chain habit of negativity? I had to be a pillar of strength. "Joy" had to be a very essential part of my being.

It took me a couple of hours of reflection and retrospecting before I could see clearly why I had fallen. The prayers, worship and meditation played their part, but when I was not carrying those activities, I would spend most of my earthly time doing things that dragged me down. Just as Dr Popoin discovered through the DNA Phantom Effect, the New World was a very ready reality and I had to match that elevated energy by living my highest excitement 24 hours a day 7 days a week. By not aspiring for and harnessing the highest vibrational frequency available to me, I was allowing for a kind of life that I did not want to take precedence. A purposeless life floating around like a leaf in the wind.

I was hungry to know more about God's plans. I was told by the MRT Stranger to hurry as he had said previously, ' …. they have given you extra time!'

Extra time for what? Flummoxed on how to begin, I figured I would start off with baby steps. First by doing what I loved, that made sense. I enjoyed innovating – from formulating a new concept and bringing it to fruition. In the early years of business, I used to work furiously in conceptualizing and launching technology startups. However, I neglected that for many years when I focused mainly on operational matters. I had to go back to my first love, my forte. Other than just that, I loved crafting out the written word to communicate new ideas, new thinking - a futurist of some sort. That was the epitome of "me". In fact, it came so naturally as I researched and penned my thoughts for the book "Transit to Type I". Unfortunately, I had succumbed to the "real world" focus on survival and not thriving. I had pushed it aside as less important while I devoted most of my time on business operational matters.

In essence, commanding the power of the pen and innovating, and doing that during every waking hour of the day. A passion, perhaps an untapped gift no longer to be left aside to grow moldy. Incidentally, it was all linked to the use of my hands. It was my palms that would get divine messages. It was my palms that would get the vibrations, the feeling of a vortex and the appearance and disappearance of spots. Those hands were tools to be used with seriousness and urgency.

Taking a deep breath, I typed out my new mission on my iPhone notepad:

'To transpire the heavenly message across as my thoughts and ideas dance between science and spirituality; to mingle them with answers deep within the mysteries of the universe, and finally suffusing them into the real world so as to express what we need to do on Earth. To conceptualize and bring that idealism into the marketplace.'

It was still very broad and vague. However, it was a starting point and with time I would discover a clearer pathway. Perhaps a Writer-Futurist-Innovator.

Thinking back on the three compassionate ethereal beings.

I was hoping that they were nodding their heads in approval saying to themselves, 'She's finally got it!'.

To work towards a new endeavor. To be caught in a rapture forgetful of my qualms. Joy, passion and hunger would come together as a peaceful energetic orchestra, a geometric energy field of Light activating and spinning counterclockwise within my heart. A grand plan, almost too good to be true.

Spreading the Love of Work

Kuala Lumpur, Malaysia
Early May 2014

A bright sunny Saturday morning in Kuala Lumpur, Malaysia. I had taken a five hour coach journey up from Singapore to the Malaysian city to visit several relatives and friends. Staying at a family home in the outskirts of the city, I let the day pass lounging on the sofa toying with the idea of the new mission. It was still rather vague though it was a good starting point. I noticed a DVD glistening at the right side of a long table top below the Plasma TV screen in the living room. The DVD was titled "The Agony and the Ecstasy". An eternal classic about Michelangelo Buonarroti (1475 – 1564), the renowned Italian sculptor, painter, architect, poet and engineer of the High Renaissance. The legendary figure who exerted an unparalleled influence on the development of Western art. In the film, he personified wholehearted surrender to his great love for artistry.

I could connect with Michelangelo's soul and spirit. He would live life indifferent to food and drink, eating more out of necessity than for pleasure and that he often slept in his clothes and boots. A reckless abandonment which I could understand as I would myself forget about everything around me when I was researching, innovating or writing. Food and drink would become a mere sustenance. Convinced, I remembered that I had the book by Irving Stone. And so I got up from the sofa and searched for it in the scattered bookshelf in the reading room. Hidden beneath a pile of other old books, I found it. Keeping the book with me always, it was for my completion and a source of inspiration.

Whispering softly to myself, 'My hunger and faith – flowing like multiple rivers, no longer hidden, no longer enclaved.'

I imagined that by doing what we love and by sharing the passion, we trigger the magical quality of quantum entanglement to its greatest potential. It is based on the theory that two particles can be entangled if they come close together and their properties can become linked. Even if you separate those particles, they remain connected. When I share my experiences with others, it can spread like a contagion depending on how much heart I put into it. Myself as the particle with others as a particle. As they hear my testimony and my revelations, it plants a seed into their thoughts and their lives in one form or another. Just as Michelangelo did with his works, which had a great influence on painters, sculptors and architects for many generations to come. Einstein called it "Spooky action at a distance". Scientists are still dumb-founded by how quantum entanglement works.

The shared passion creating a contagion, where even the most ordinary person would be extraordinary. Yasmine became a shining beacon as she relished speaking in seminars on how she healed herself. Adriana who entered Open Heaven daily, which even a Government Member of Parliament may not have access to. Marianne who was a positive contagion just by her presence. One hug from her with her vibrational frequency so high, I felt healed.

They were all loving every moment as they pursued their sublime endeavor. I imagined that discovering our unique gift gives us a greater intimacy with God. It prepares us for the New World; as we would be able to push those gifts to full bloom as we blossom alongside as Golden Souls.

Beyond gifts, it is also how we handle the most mundane day-to-day tasks so that our vibrational frequencies are always at their peak. Such as sweeping the floor, fixing a car, washing dishes or beautifying a home. Venerable Acara Suvanno Mahathera was a fine example. Sweeping was his form of meditation. Venerable Acara's words, '... you must do it slowly and mindfully.'

Faryal was another inspiration in this respect. As a homemaker, she took interior decoration and even dish washing to another level.

That weekend, while I was still in Malaysia, Faryal invited a group of us to her quaint little home. The inviting gold gilded mirrored entrance. The delicate white French furnishing in the living and dining room to match. The sparkling New Orleans-inspired dining sets with slight gold trimmings. The pearly marble floors and soft white intricately papered walls that embraced all the contents of the home creating a beautiful wrapping for display. But what caught my eye the most was a lovely prayer rug in the far corner, depicting the Tree of Life. It emerged to be seen from the floor almost with a life of its own as it stood out amongst the polished spotless furnishing.

'Everything looks so impeccable. A pluperfect arrangement of such a divine collection of artifacts, furniture and all. Nothing is out of place!' I exclaimed with admiration.

She said with a beaming smile, 'I do all the decoration, arrangement and cleaning myself, yes, every item. Everything is precious.'

'That's so evident in your home. And I just love that silk Tree of Life carpet that you have there,' I said.

'I absolutely adore that piece. I use it as a platform for my prayers,' she said cooing with contentment.

Faryal's home was a quotidian example compared to all the other homes I had ever visited. This place had an unusual feeling about it.

She said, 'When I buy anything for my home, I would always meet the person who sold me the items. Maybe for coffee or lunch. I would build a long-term relationship with that person. We become great friends,' she paused to reflect and said with a profoundness, 'Like the Tree of Life – all of us connecting, supporting, nourishing each other.'

She would nurture the relationship with the source of the object she purchased the items from.

Faryal said, 'I was driven by the searching for something other than just the norm. Even with the smallest piece, I can get easily excited, because I know that the creator of the piece is driven by his or her own passion to create, be it from an artful inspiration or perhaps life experiences or perhaps spiritually. Since I left Pakistan, I have now traveled quite a lot. I love meeting people and getting to know their beliefs and culture, and to discover what inspires them. So in the culmination of all my years, I finally get to express my own definition of decoration as the passion was embedded within me. Through this passion, I am able to connect with people on different levels.'

As soon as we finished tea, she piled up the dirty cutlery perfectly in the kitchen basin.

I could not help but say to her, 'Not long ago, you told me that you were a helpless woman who was dependent on servants to even put on your socks and to comb your hair. You said that you had not even fried an egg.'

I opened up my arms like an expressive Italian to show my amazement, and said, 'And now look at this? Home décor extraordinaire!'

She smiled back humbly. I realized that I was disturbing her concentration. Her eyes were closed. Delicately plate by plate, she washed each plate tenderly with careful strokes. She was in a trance-like state while listening to Tchaikovsky playing in the background. The act of washing plates was her daily meditation. And through that meditation she magnified it to become a noble duty. The act itself sanctified the cleanliness of her home, as she took herself to a higher state transmitting the vibration of Love into her home, giving it a splendidly fresh and calming feel.

Working Agelessly

Singapore
June 2014

Faryal's new role from a confined lady of luxury from Pakistan to a marvelously talented homemaker and decorator in Malaysia, while globetrotting to Sri Lanka and other places of her fancy. Even at the most scabrous points in her life, it looked like she whisked by undeterred as she channeled herself through the love of home cleaning and decoration. A love so great that she appeared to lose track of time. It was funny that as Faryal danced her fingers down every dish that she cleaned, I imagined Michelangelo playing his paint brush with philharmonic strokes in the same way.

The saying, 'Time flies when you are having fun'.

Blissful states of people who enjoyed every moment. My own realization that when you can feel time, you age. As they lost track of time, their youthfulness was frozen with the stillness. The gift of agelessness for consistently doing what they love.

On my return to Singapore, I met with a Qi Gong Master in her senior years. An art enthusiast and culturati, she was waiting for the opening of an Asia-wide art exhibition. I met her while we were both standing at the entrance. As we talked, she shared how she enjoyed the myriad of artistic and creative events organized by the Singapore Arts festival, which was promoted by the Singapore Tourism Board. It was an annual exuberant affair with visitors pouring in from around the globe.

Without exaggeration, she looked more than a decade younger with supple skin, and youthful and nimble presence. Her couture was Balinese inspired adding diversity to her authentic Chinese name, Mei Ling.

'I am a trained and highly experienced Qi Gong Master,' said Mei Ling.

'I have delved in a quite a number of areas, but Qi Gong is very new to me,' I confessed.

Mei Ling said, 'Really? I'll give you the highlights,' she continued to explain, 'Qi, defined as natural energies. Qi Gong is about the connection to the different densities of Qi ... the indulgence in a space of stillness which I would deepen with breath, and enter into the centers of the subtle energy vortexes. And as the energy vortexes move through me, I move with it becoming one with them.'

The exhibition opened and we made our way in. It was in the main Convention Center at the Marina Bay Sands, and this mega art exhibition had been held there every year the past few years. I walked along with her so that we could continue our conversation. The exhibition hall was so huge that it was segmented based on the countries of origin of the various artists. Most of them were from Asia. We passed by Japan, South Korea, Indonesia and headed towards India and China. Artists originating from Singapore were also featured prominently at the exhibit. We were at the China exhibit segment when Mei Ling caught me admiring a sculpture of three galloping horses burnished in gold and bronze.

'Stunning piece! I have a soft spot for horses,' she said.

It was described as an Akhal-Teke, the most beautiful Golden Horse. A creature with bountiful energy that charged with speed and tirelessness.

I recited thoughtfully, 'The bountiful energy of Akhal-Teke ...'

'I feel filled with that level of energy while I do what I love. And that is Qi Gong, of course,' Mei Ling added to my words.

As soon as she said that, a faint distant sound of thunder was heard coming from outside.

'If we can hear that all the way inside this huge convention hall, that lightning strike must be a big one! Thank goodness I have my umbrella,' I remarked.

In Singapore it could rain anytime, though the rains are usually short and intermittent.

'There you go, one of the basis of Qi, which is best explained as a type of energy very much like electricity. The Schumann resonance, caused by lightning strikes,' she continued, 'Lightning pumps energy into the brain-earth-ionosphere space and causes it to vibrate or resonate creating standing electromagnetic waves that are reflected from the ionosphere, back to Earth, back to the ionosphere, and so on,' Mei Ling said.

The brain-earth-ionosphere matching resonance of 7-7-7.

'Anyway, this is my expertise, my passion. Other than horses of course,' she added, 'Whatever I do, I give it all my might and I have zero expectation of the outcome,' Mei Ling said.

'No expectation of success?' I replied.

'Nope. Expectation is a distraction, it creates anxiety and disappointment. Intention is important, yes, so is hunger and passion. If the work or task makes me happy, that is enough. Usually that itself places me in the right frequency to bring great results,' she replied.

I looked up on the Akhal Teke in Wikipedia. The horse was of an uncommon breed. It was the national emblem of the Central Asian nation of Turkmenistan. Shiny and metallic, this breed was hardy and capable of running all day without tiring.

I reflected on the threefold visitation of the neon green ball of Light, red flaming Fire and the Divine Being. Since that evening when it happened, I felt a subtle ignition of an inner fire like the Akhal-Teke. Coupled with that "electrocution" phenomenon in rural Pakistan. I wanted to spark that Fire to its full potential. From igniting the Fire, to fueling the Fire to greater strength bringing out an unbridled energy. Marianne had this unbridled energy which she called the Fire of God. It allowed her to minister non-stop for hours at a time, sometimes a full day without rest. Mei Ling was in her 50s but did not looking anything above 40. At the same time, she had no physical ailments whatsoever. I was told that the Fire of God is with those who are so filled with the Holy Spirit of God. I wanted to be like that.

Doing what we love, even the most mundane tasks, joyfully with this intent: that we connect to the higher energy realms. Creating a shadow of Heaven on Earth where nothing ages, nothing breaks down. Both Mei Ling and Marianne looked at least 10 years younger than their chronological age. Faryal was only discovering that agelessness at that time as the decades of pain and trauma had led to her previous poor health and the deep lines on her cheeks. At least now, she was reveling in much better health than she had before. For all of them, time stood still as they pursued their passions. I imagined myself emulating that and becoming unstoppable like the Akhal Teke.

I imagined that as early versions of crystalline beings start to emerge, aging may transcend to something other than what we can possibly imagine right now. The number of such ageless persons may grow so rapidly that it would be hard to differentiate between a 25 year old in this time, with a 50 year old in the future. Middle age may shift to the 100 year old and beyond. A senior citizen in the future may have the physical attributes of a 40 year old as diets and lifestyles change. Perhaps the influx of a new generation of the "100 year old Experts", the new middle age. As the purification of our body, soul and spirit continues, it may go way beyond that. Alongside "chores", the word "retirement" may soon be an outdated idea. The common concept of a senior citizen or the silver-haired population may take a dramatic turn as the definition of "time" in the New World may take on the value as in Heaven.

Radical in a Positive Way

I had a clearer picture of my heavenly task on Earth. I had to start on it immediately and let it evolve towards refinement. I had to be almost radical, infused with risk and passion, and sparked with the Fire of God within. A timely moment to commemorate this new milestone for my own remembrance. Removing the marble bangle I had on my wrist, I replaced it with a purple amethyst crystal bracelet. Purple amethyst known by the ancients as the "Gem of Fire" carrying the energy of fire and passion, creativity and spirituality yet bearing the temperance of logic and sobriety. A perfect emblem for a task to achieve greater things.

The results came quickly as I was indulging the newly discovered (yet still budding) task by reading and meditating on the concepts, attending events and seminars and surrounding myself with like-minded individuals. Soon I was on a roll going through a full blown transformation. My concentration became more and more focused. That was my own radical behavior rising to the surface, just as I imagined it was with Michelangelo.

We need to start asking ourselves this question: Has any great change happened on Earth without being radical? Positively radical, that is. In other words, has any great change happened without going against the norm? Looking back in history Giordano Bruno (1547-1600), the Italian priest who reinforced the heliocentric theory that the Earth was not the center of the universe, a theory that challenged popular belief at that time. Apparently, Giordano believed that there were more things in Heaven than on Earth. He claimed that there were unseen elements and untapped energies governing the Cosmos that, if comprehended and perhaps even harnessed, could have world-transforming results. Was Bruno way ahead of his time in predicting our shift towards the New World? I believe so, which means that we need to be radical, in a positive sense with a positive agenda.

I sensed that it was the Spirit Man (Spirit Woman) rather than the soul that fuels radical behavior. The spirit represented by the fire, just as the flaming Fire, the Holy Spirit of God makes its presence greater. The heart (not the brain) is the link between body, soul and spirit. Since the heart generates the largest electromagnetic field produced in the body, there is a kind of emotional information encoded into this electromagnetic field. So, by shifting our emotions, we are changing the information that is encoded into this electromagnetic field that is radiated by the heart. This can impact those around us. As a result, spending a majority of our time doing what we love, opens up the radical side of us pushing us to go against the norm. By doing so, we may have a bigger impact on others and the environment around us. Towards the New World, we need positive radical change and it needs to come quickly. If most of us are going through the daily drudgery of life doing what we consider just acceptable or tolerable, it would just slow down the process of favorable change.

Furthermore, the heart's electromagnetic frequency arcs out from the heart and back in the form of a torus field. The axis of this heart torus extends from the pelvic floor to the top of the skull, and the whole field is holographic, which means that information about it can be read from each and every point in the torus. This also connects on the sacred geometry level where our heart center is composed of a star tetrahedron, connecting the energy together. By doing what we love, it brings out a multiplicity in our energies and our ability to create.

Revisiting Buckminister Fuller's tetrahedron, where all the vectors lines are of equal length and equal angular relationship, an ultimate and perfect condition is created wherein the movement of energy comes to a state of absolute equilibrium, and therefore absolute stillness and nothingness. The zero point, the Unified Field, the "vacuum of space" or simply the pure potential which, according to contemporary theory in physics, contains that infinite amount of energy. We start becoming like personal portals to Open Heaven, the gateway towards the highest realms within ourselves.

Mei Ling's words, 'We have been at war with our brains and our bodies for too long, it's time for us to do what we love.'

Her words had strength as she allowed her body to slow down aging as she went with the flow. To do everything we do every single day at our highest excitement, releasing the distribution of more of God's gifts upon us, and thus fueling our body, soul and spirit with a tireless energy, being infectious to others just by living our lives. To do everything in a loving embrace, even if they are mundane tasks for the day so that the aging phenomenon may slow down so rapidly that we would hardly notice it.

It is primarily the passion, the hunger. Hunger redefines our DNA and pulls us into a greater reality. Hunger causes us to move outside of what seems safe. With the hunger, downloads start to come in, and we start being filled with good things, from gifts, ideas and more. After all, we are not just individuals going to work every day, we have been given revelatory gifts for a purpose. It is a sign of what God wants us to do. We need to wake up and be present and listen. To discover our true Selves and derive the source of our Aliveness. When we are doing something that we are truly passionate about, it places us in a higher energetic state that lifts up the soul, making us more aligned with the DNA of God. And with that, whatever we touch and feel would radiate back that corresponding vibration of God. Like musical notes played on piano keys, it echoes back a captivating melody. No more rushing through things with a strain on our faces, or lashing out with a common complaint of having too much to do. To spend most of our time acquiring new skills and knowledge, to consistently enhance our gifts as the pendulum swings back to the specialist.

Above all, to have zero expectation of what the outcome will be. The excitement itself will be the driving force, as more and more opportunities are created bringing more and more excitement. To keep pushing to the best of our ability until life becomes an ecstatic flow of synchronicity – in aid of creating a New World where there is such a wealth of new wonders to experience, explore, and invent that the notion of boredom and apathy would be absurd.

Torus in geometry, it is a surface of revolution generated by revolving a circle in a three-dimensional space about an axis coplanar with the circle. The torus opens up a continuous sea of infinite energy. Wiktionary describes the torus as a space in 3-dimensional Euclidean space: a shape consisting of a ring with a circular cross-section: the shape of an inner tube or hollow doughnut. The energy flows in through one end, circulates around the center and exits out the other side. We can see it everywhere – in atoms, cells, seeds, flowers, trees, animals, humans, hurricanes, planets, galaxies and even the Cosmos as a *whole*.

12

Master Creators, Master Alchemists

We need to start
Looking at ourselves as if
We have God in our DNA.

To be egoless, compassionate,
All forgiving, and so much more.

Creating and manifesting instantaneously,
With the purest intentions,
With Zero expectation of the outcome.

Reflecting back on Bali
August 2012

I had journeyed to Bali in 2012. Then rural Pakistan in 2014. In between I was in Singapore with the occasional crossover trips to Malaysia. The impromptu trip to Bali sparked a soul cleansing immersion in the realm of nature, while in rural Pakistan I was shown true joy of the heart, oblivious to the pervasive poverty, chaos and fear.

Besides Bali's breathtaking nature, there was another aspect of the island that left an indelible mark on the mind. The colorful and vibrant dances I had witnessed in August of 2012. It was late at about 11pm at the rice field imbued part of Ubud. It was *Galungan*, Bali's major feast held throughout the island. An annual event in the *wuku* year, which is part of the Balinese ceremonial calendar. During this ten day period, Balinese claim that all the their gods, including the supreme deity *Sanghyang Widi*, come down to Earth for the festivities. The last and most important day of this ten day festival is *Kuningan*, during which the chanting and dancing shamans cover their faces with bright, colorful masks of demonic imagery and dance akin to tarantism. The use of drums is similar to the Nepalese, Native American as well as the Mongolian shamans. At times they would use smoke for space cleansing – smoke from opium, cannabis and frankincense.

As the fragrant smoke of frankincense permeated the air, these festivities were going on throughout the island of Bali and they are taken very seriously by the local folk. It was a radical shift in mindset to what I was used to at that time. While the shamans looked primitive in their clangorous song and dance rituals, my prayers and meditations were done in a very quiet and differential manner. The more lettered folk in the village shared that the combination of the words in the chants, and the resonance of the smoke was to drive away the lower vibrational negative entities. That made sense as frankincense has a very high vibrational frequency of 147 Hertz. Their ancient methods had the support of science.

Still skeptical, I continued to watch the performances. I became all the more curious about the difference between Meditating in Stillness versus Meditating in Movement. I had other questions too. Looking back, I wondered if the Balinese shamans had glimpsed Open Heaven, or their version of it, alongside with heavenly visitations. I wondered if they believed in Heaven on Earth, and the blueprint of the New World. There were some stories amongst the Balinese village folklore that there was a shaman who turned himself into a ball of fire as spectators looked on. Some said it involved the dark arts. Some said that it was illusion, while others said that it was the human mind manipulating matter.

I remembered watching the performances, impressed with their dedication. Their worship with song and dance was an eye-opener. As I indulged in the tribal Polynesian atmosphere of Bali in 2012, the captivating *Qawwali* music in Pakistan came to mind. My all time favorite is the *Qawwali* or Sufi music performances by the legend Ustad Nusrat Fateh Ali Khan (1948 - 1997). I had the privilege of attending his performances during my childhood visits to Karachi, Pakistan. He had also come to Singapore at one time. What was special about Sufi devotional music is that the *Qawwal* will continue each verse trading off lines with the other singers. A simple verse-and-chorus format, where each verse builds to a crescendo, then passionately returns to the chorus, over and over again, sometimes up to twenty minutes.

Some people would say that the words are repeated until they lose meaning, as in, '... leaving only the music and the spirit behind'.

They say that when the spirit is left behind, the audience is brought to an elevated state. They described a change in the atmosphere. The legend's voice, heavy with the emotion poured into the singing, combined with the repetition put the listeners in a trance-like state. Nusrat's very presence was a mystical experience that created a high frequency atmosphere. During each performance, his hands appeared to float on the surface of unseen sound waves. I had experienced this myself and it was absolutely elevating. It reminded me of the whirling Turkish dervishes, also within the Sufi tradition, who would swirl continuously in a counterclockwise motion to take them to a higher elevation - the same trance-like state.

Marianne shared that there are groups in almost every part of the world carrying out meetings where the people would lose themselves in worship. Including worship conducted in churches or even in the privacy of peoples' homes. The worship would open up the Glory Realm, a very high frequency dimension with the possible access to Open Heaven. That was what she was refers to when she is ministering with passion and intensity about the Glory of God and taking the path of Jesus.

The greater the emotions they would pour into the prayer, with focus and repetition and combined with music, the greater their ability to manifest thought into reality. A sensation of drunkenness in the Spirit of God. The Glory realm was preached with fervor since the 1990s by its founder Ruth Ward Heflin (1940 - 2000), a Christian worshiper who had holy gold flakes appearing on her face while she worshiped in prayer, song and dance. An alien concept to many. She claimed that she was experiencing the fruits of the heavenly realm.

Some would say it is a Pickwickian view of the heavens. Others would say that the gold is a deception. Deep in my heart I knew that it was leading toward the Truth, no matter how frivolous the gold manifestations may sound to the skeptics. The path to the Extraordinary is never ordinary. And since my preview of Open Heaven (which I knew came as a formal invitation), the proof of the gold-embedded crystalline skin of Marianne, as well as scientific fact that gold is superconductor of light, I was not going to close the door on that concept. My early research, focus and interest was on planetary civilizations as I craved to be part of the illusive New World. I knew instinctively that my invitation to Open Heaven and the witnessing of its fruits were very tightly linked. It would have been foolish to decide to close my mind taking it back to old ways of thinking when I had an abundance of proof as arranged by God and His helpers.

Meditating in Movement

Singapore
Late June 2014

So that was Bali back in 2012. It was 2014 and so much had happened since. The "spontaneous self-healing from dengue" phenomenon, the stigmata, the floating neon green ball of Light with the red flaming Fire and the Diving Being encounter and then the visitation of the 3 ethereal beings emerging from a portal, either the Heavenly (Divine) Council or a Galactic Council. And finally, a preview of what I perceived as Open Heaven. Counting 1,2,3,4,5 – 5 out of this world experiences. I was so thankful to God for the amazing journey so far. From the daily drudgery, life was becoming more and more magical!

Lured towards another heavenly encounter, this time seeking more than just a preview; I stood in the middle of the garden. My palms stretched out and standing still. For a moment I felt ridiculous.

Thinking aloud with a smirk, 'This feels so primitive.'

I stopped and went over to sit for a while. What was I doing? I coaxed myself to continue. I walked up barefooted to the garden again and turned on some music. I closed my eyes and moved slowly and awkwardly.

Unexpectedly, I felt a sensation on both my ankles. Something pushing my ankles up so that I would be on tiptoe and move! My dancing, which was stiff and nondescript, became a modern dance that was fluid and sensual. I recall friends and family saying to me, 'You hardly dance!'

I suppose I was too self-conscious and too serious about life. The more I danced, the more naturally I moved with the music. At times, I would pick up speed and spin myself around, inspired like a swirling dervish. Worshiping for the first time – a close-eyed symphonic approach to giving undivided attention and praise to the Almighty. Moving like a river rapid, reaching a higher and higher velocity. With minutes of continuous movement, I would gradually slow down and come to a standstill, like the stillest of waters. In that stance, I would allow meditation to take over. Throughout, I was barefooted, conscious of the coolness of the grass I stood upon. A liberating sensation as I felt every atom in my body simmering in a reverberant field of energy. I felt powerful.

'Music is a moral law. It gives Soul to the universe, wings to the mind, flight to imagination, and charm and gaiety to life and to everything.' quote Plato

Whether it was an Angel encouraging me to dance, or my own sentient DNA inducing the movement, I was beginning to comprehend the primordial and infinite force behind it. I was being led well. Nature, song and dance were the epitome of my short experience of living in Bali. I could now take that new learning anywhere I went. It made me realize that, in a strange way, worship and dance played a part in our advancement. Our true mind is in our heart, and our heart is the seat of the soul. I felt that through worship we would tap into the layers of our minds, and that would elevate our soul and spirit to another level.

Giving us a greater power, as highlighted by John Hagelin's statement, '… if we use our mind in very superficial or ordinary manner, we can barely move a speck of dust across the tabletop without using our hands …'

I realized that all this time, we have been emphasizing on structure, systems and rules to take us forward, when the uplifting of our soul through the right tone, frequency and prayer activity was equally important. Some research state how music directly reflects the geometric structure of space-time. When there are variations in music, there will be the corresponding adjustments to space-time. Sound, frequency and pitch are factors that can take us to different dimensions and realms. Raising the octaves can achieve a similar result as well.

To sum it all, I imagined that the access to the Glory realm would prepare us to dwell in those higher frequencies, to habitat in them. The interstellarly transfigured New Humans who would resonate at those higher vibrational frequencies. The eventual matching between the humans on Earth with the heavenly realm, yearning for the long awaited manifestation on Earth. Heaven coming down as the blueprint of the New World. There may be a possibility that as we reach higher and higher in the realms of Heaven, we may bring in higher and higher levels of the New World.

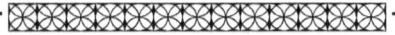

Octave a series of eight notes occupying the interval between (and including) two notes, one having twice or half the frequency of vibration of the other. Through the use of higher octave music where some notes are almost undetectable to human ears. If one note has a frequency of 440 Hertz, the note an octave above it, is at 880 Hertz, and the note an octave below is at 220 Hertz.

The Power to Create

As 2014 progressed, I noticed something unusual. A repeated appearance of the binary three digit code numbers 111 and a four digit version 1111. It was about once every 2 or 3 days. But enough for me to notice it. I could not understand the significance of it really. I looked at the meaning in the Scriptures. 1111: The balance, the new beginning, the birth of light. Each time this would happen I would pause in whatever I was doing, take a moment to let the thought vibration of it sink into me. Maybe there was a need to raise my vibration to the overall higher vibration, the higher intention, the moment of balance and alignment that is 1111. Then there was the possibility of the release of the binary code from my DNA. Perhaps a genetic wake up call? A passage from Scriptures was beginning to make so much sense here:

'In the beginning, God created the Heavens and the Earth ...' ~ *Genesis 1:1*

Creation and new beginnings. And so it was, as a landmark day presented itself to show me in reality the crystallization of the theory on instantaneous creation. That fateful day was on the American Independence Day of the 4th of July 2014.

Singapore
4th July 2014

A day signifying the release and breaking away from the shackles of an old way of thinking. I called it my "first new creation" date. That night a blue gemstone materialized out of nowhere. I had barely tucked myself in bed as it appeared in the air and laid itself distinctly on top of my white quilt. A tiny gemstone, a shining aquamarine! I was more than happy to receive it, perhaps even rhapsodic. My cynosure for the rest of the evening as I gazed upon it adoringly. It was exactly the same size and color as the gemstone Adriana gave me. How extraordinary! Wishing to examine it further, I placed it on my left palm and almost instantaneously gold dust formed under it on the palm of my skin! The formation was within the Great Triangle of the palm, as some expert palmists would call it, symbolic of creation.

I was completely taken aback. This was the first time I had experienced anything like this. Why was this happening now? However, in a few moments it became clear. Incidentally, earlier that day, I had made an emotional request to God to be shown of miracles, and it was my first prayer of such a nature. In the past, I would have written off miracles including gemstones as the works of a counterfeit. My alter-ego of the past refused to acknowledge that creative miracles can exist. This was very real. What was most enchanting was how the blue gemstone and gold dust would just emerge out of nowhere.

I had a renewed sense of hope that God was truly listening by demonstrating a miracle, but the same time, I questioned how the gemstone and gold materialized and where they came from. I loved jewels though I certainly did not have a big craving for them in the material sense. My main desire was to see the fruits of Heaven, to understand its attributes as well as what the citizens of Heaven would be like, at least from the perspective of where we were heading towards planet-wise.

Hounded by those mixed thoughts and feelings, I was determined to verify the quality of the gemstone and to understand more about the gold. I could go get the gemstone tested, but the gold dust, which appeared embedded in the skin, was only visible for a few brief moments.

And so I took the gemstone for an evaluation at a gemologist in a store in Singapore. After a brief examination, they claimed that their gemological testing equipment was simply not responding to the gem I had shown them. They were surprised that the gem was not acting like any other gem. Was this a gemstone given by an Angel, or was it a product of spontaneous creation just like my spontaneous self-healing experience? Angels were a possibility. However, the latter was very possible too as quantum mechanics proves it so. In the quantum world, there is a sense that things don't like to be tied down to just one location or one path. A quanta (with reference to the blue gemstone) can be here or there, but nothing in between - defying space and time.

The Gold,
The Crystal Gemstone,
Perhaps spontaneous creations
Defying space and time.

Perhaps, the scene of the Glory of God is in us. A jolt of realization within me, as my thoughts crossed over to my spin dancing in the Glory realm. The spinning MerKaBa of energy. Quantum physicists discovered that physical atoms are made up of vortexes of energy that are constantly spinning and vibrating. From what I knew, matter at its tiniest observable level is energy, and human consciousness is connected to it. Human consciousness can influence its behavior and even re-structure it.

'What we have called as matter is energy, whose frequency has been lowered, as to be perceptible to the senses. There is no matter,' ~ Albert Einstein.

The universe has already been constructed for us to do it. So in a way, we are all capable of becoming mystics like Adriana, in various degrees of course. That day, 4th July 2014, was the opening of a veil for me.

I held the blue gemstone in my hand to dwell on the thought of its spontaneous creation. If the gemstone was not given by an Angel, then the power of manifestation could be within me. Perhaps the new DNAs opening up dormant abilities. Regardless, I felt that the spontaneous and instantaneous creation was to prove that things which are seen were not necessarily made out of pre-existing materials, as required by theories of chemical and cosmic evolution. Was God teaching me something new?

That power of manifestation is the Glory of God and I had to be extra careful with my thoughts, words and feelings. I had so much of my negative feelings of fear and anger under control, now I had to deal with words and thoughts. The two words "I AM" the name of God as revealed in the Scriptures. The more intimate our relationship with God, the more powerful the response. A reminder to myself. The real power of "I AM" may not exist in the gray misty soul. It may be void in its ability to create through its disconnection from God.

A reminder to myself to say "I AM" and to always use it in a positive context.

Henceforth, moving forward by thinking aloud with another affirmation, 'I AM able to achieve and create anything. I AM special. I AM a success. I AM healthy and vibrant!'

So with that power of God within ourselves, we can defy the laws of nature. Our minds, like the governor of the realm of matter, converting energy into reality. These thoughts get encoded into our DNA. DNA starts projecting them out. Manifestation may no longer need to take weeks, months or years to happen. Simply think, feel and manifest!

'It is consciousness that creates the material universe, not the other way around' ~ Dr. Lanza

I read about the story of the sunken and destroyed city of Atlantis, a society where everyone had various levels of healing, prophetic and mystical abilities. For those who say it was a true and not fable, warn that we should not become like the Atlantians. We should never allow our inflated egos and Godlike behavior to come in the way of purified intentions and humility.

The words of the Buddhist Monk, ' … We need to start working on our purification.'

Marianne's words of warning, 'We may be given gifts to heal, to prophesy or to create miracles, but it does not mean that we have the Presence of God within us. Even when the presence is gone, the gifts may still remain.'

That sounded dangerous, and in the worst case, disastrous. If the stories about Atlantis were true, when we do develop New Human abilities characteristic of the New World, but then misuse them or separate ourselves from God, history may repeat itself.

From the beautiful experience of receiving a gemstone, I was worrying about a planetary matter that had gone out of proportion. Still, a worst possible scenario had to be prevented. A reinforcement to myself, to all of us, to keep working on our purification, and on our connection with God. And we had to maintain it. To become Towering Golden Souls in the truest sense, without any separation from God. Children of God, Godlings - humble, obedient servants of God, but mighty in His image.

Black (White) Whole, Heaven in the Heart

Singapore
7th July 2014

It was 4:30am and the alarm rang. I woke up with a shock as I would never set my alarm at that time. I examined the alarm setting just to be sure. There were blank entries. Then I realized the date was the 7th of July (7th month) of the year 2014 (year adds up to 7). The time 4:30am (4 + 3 = 7). A quadruple 7-7-7-7! The Mystical 7 in full form.

Why was I woken up at 4:30am? Who had set the alarm? It was certainly not me! Another puzzle to solve. I paced up and down my bedroom. It was too early for a morning walk. It was still dark outside. So what do I do now? What was I supposed to do? I thought back about the recent experiences. So many facts jotted down with some random sketches here and there. Since I could not go back to sleep, I thought I might as well work on compiling those experiences methodically with the supporting illustrations.

Typing furiously on my laptop, I tangled the concoction of scientific and historic facts and figures, with fluid and descriptive words and feelings. As more sunlight brightened up the sky on that auspicious date, I thought I would spend the rest of the morning writing amidst the ambiance of nature. Recollecting the last time I had that online chat with Yasmine, the family of yellow hornbills that lived in the Rain trees of Changi Village were certainly fun to watch. And since I was moving to Sembawang within a few days, I figured that I would pay a visit to the hornbill family once more. After the move northwards, it would be too far away to travel all the way to the East side again.

Arriving at Changi Village, I took a walk up along the Changi Sailing Club vicinity. Close by was the abandoned old Changi Hospital which was an attraction for students vacationing during their school holidays at the government-owned beach-side resorts nearby. There were a couple of chalets and longhouses in the area as well as Black and White houses hailing from British colonial times. The entire vicinity is considered one the most haunted places in Singapore as thousands of soldiers lost their lives there during the Japanese occupation.

Otherwise, the evergreen and peaceful surroundings were perfect. Besides plants and exotic birds, stray cats were also in abundance as compared to any other part of Singapore. An ideal abode for a nature and animal lover like myself. I found a comfortable dark wooden table and bench placed in the outdoors in front of one of the longhouses, lived in by mostly expats who preferred colonial living. I whisked out my laptop, my iphone which contained typed notes as well as some handwritten notes.

As I sat down to make myself comfortable, I had a painful nudge in the center of my stigmatic left palm. Perhaps a message that I was onto something here. A spiraling vortex began to form. I was excited over what God was planning to show and teach me next. This divine lesson plan was getting more and more riveting with time.

I felt a small fireball form in my palm. It stayed there and I waited. Nothing happened. Then I decided to seed it with an intention to create a bigger ball of potent energy. The spiraling vortex intensified as I lifted my left hand up. An invisible fireball created as instructed, growing in size. As it pulsed in greater magnitude, I pictured that anything that it was hurled at in its path would be enveloped by this ball's high frequency circulation of energy. An invisible physicality formed by an energy vortex being released from within me. I was so absorbed in acting out the part of a mystic that I did not realize something warm on my lap. I laughed as I saw a stray cat make its resting place on my lap. It was funny how this dusty gray cat rested on my lap and was staring at my left hand. I was not surprised as cats can see energy and are attracted to higher vibrational frequencies. So I decided to let the invisible ball of energy go. I released the intention and felt the energy dissipate. I gently moved the cat away from my lap, and it scampered off.

Trying to reason it all, my mind became flooded with concepts and vivid imagination. Energy coming out exceeding what is going in – similar to a plastic bag filled with water. When the bag is popped, the gravitational field of energy is so strong that the water will flow out very quickly. There are aspects of our galaxy that is like a vortex. The enigmatic Black Hole with an irrepressible energy vortex sucking up everything on its path and also emanating from them. The White Hole has been highlighted by some researchers. Some physicists say that Black Holes might end their lives by transforming into their exact opposite - "white holes" that explosively pour all the material they ever swallowed back into space. Whether true or not, I sensed it as the Black (White) Hole, and not simply the Black Hole. I imagined "black" represents the sucking in (destruction), pulling from a place we do not want to get near to. Probably an event horizon, of space-time beyond which anything that is sucked into its mega-gravitational pull can never come back out. Next it would be "white" for the release (creation), pushing away by spitting material out and where nothing goes in. I imagined the possibility that the point of creation is sparked when in the Glory realm; or when there is a shooting up of our Spirit Man (Spirit Woman). An exquisite dance of creation and destruction.

In this respect, there may be Black (White) Holes within ourselves where we draw in information and also emanate information. For instance, the formation of gold dust, gemstone or diamond particles emanating from within us. I closed my eyes and tried to visualize the human body mapping it with the Black (White) Hole. The heart is the only organ in our body that sucks and expends substance (blood in this case) with its own powerful vortex. The heart also generates the largest electromagnetic field produced in the body. Scientist Robert Lanza described each soul as a life center for creation through his theory of bio-centrism. Whatever we want to achieve, we can conceive. If the blue gemstone I had was not given by an Angel, then the alternative would be the gemstones and gold dust were being created from within my heart. Our hearts emit electromagnetic fields that change according to our emotions. As Adriana said, we need to have unconditional love and unconditional forgiveness in our hearts in order to have sovereignty to enter Heaven. Emotions of love may create the strongest and highest electromagnetic fields. Powerful emotions of creation.

The dual torus structure within our hearts and brain. Based on this "ring with circular cross-section" structure our brains are perfectly designed to resonate with the fundamental frequencies of the vacuum and it's energetics, allowing us to both receive and send signals to and from the very structure of space-time.

Similarly, even Black Holes had a torus structure due to their infinity. Entropy encapsulating Light. And perhaps the Black Hole is the gravity that pulls it in at its centrifuge. This could be the same tunnel which the Buddhist Monk referred to, advising me to go deeper into the tunnel – the tunnel into the Black Hole.

Then there was this thing about "consciousness".

The past words of the Buddhist Monk, 'Consciousness is the aspect of the mind that is aware. It is the entire ensemble that includes sensation, recognition, processing and awareness.'

Marianne's words, 'The mind is in the heart. Christ Consciousness is in the heart.'

Combined with the synchronization of all areas of thought, reasoning and emotions, something magical may happen where consciousness creates matter. The gold and gem formations are evidence. So in a way, possibly the highest consciousness may bring about the greatest innovation. Considering the ideation of the Black Whole which is based on a grand unification, I would call it, "Black (White) Whole, Heaven in the Heart" – the theory for the source of creative miracles. Since it was all pure speculation on my part, I decided to put in a request to God to reveal more to me so that I could refine this unproven theory with time.

The gold appearing instantaneously, the blood flowing through our hearts, the pulsating center of our aliveness, reflecting reassuringly on the Prophetic Painting.

> '... Surrounding the center
> A blood red crimson shade.
>
> Above the xanthous background
> Of yellow, orange and gold ...'
> ~ from the descriptive prose of the Prophetic Painting of 2008

I imagined a New World where instantaneous creation from pure thought to full physical form to be very possible. What a world it would be if there were more and more people walking and talking like master creators and master alchemists creating something out of nothing, defying the constraints of space and time. Once many of us believe it, creative miracles would become commonplace. Who knows, we may be ruling the galaxies by co-creating with God. We are far greater than what we could ever imagine. It is time for us to accept this as a very natural part of ourselves. We need to start to looking at ourselves as if we have God within our DNA.

To be ego-less, most compassionate, sublime, all forgiving, void of blemishes and much more.

If we emulate or manifest these qualities, we may be able to harness immense power. The "Black (White) Whole, Heaven in the Heart" within us, within everyone. The New Humans with their unique signature - an intent to create, the intent to resolve, and to bring forth new realities.

Speaking Like Sages

I would be lying to myself if I said that my inner work was done. It was far from done. My actions had to be impeccable. My thoughts and spoken words had to be impeccable too. Those "blemishes" had to go if I wanted to have the Christ Consciousness within me.

I was introduced to a form of spiritual fasting which would be stretched over several days without any food (only water). It had its benefits of hydrating the body with more water, referred by some mystics as the river of the Glory. There were testimonials by people who fasted while spending time reading Scriptures and communing with God, and they were able to overcome a lot of their negative qualities by the end of the fast.

Fully convinced, I was raring to go with the water fast. The 1st day was a piece of cake. By the 2nd day, my jaws were aching badly and the top of my head throbbing with pain. I imagined the heavy metals in my blood stream oozing their way out from the top of my head. Finally by the 3rd day, I could see myself effloresce with a whitish glow in my skin. I felt great. Fasting brought out more of my Spirit Woman.

I was proud of myself that I successfully completed my first 3-day water fast. I felt healthier and spiritually more alive. Still, it was no big feat as there were remarkable testimonies of people who completed a laborious 21 days or even 40 days. Some transformed to become totally different people after that, for the better of course. I was not ready for a long drawn fast at that time. However, I had something else arranged for me which I had never planned for.

Virtually by "accident", I found myself in the middle of a spiritual deliverance, and this happened all because of that mysterious blue gemstone.

It was all because I wanted to show the gemstone to someone who had received one before. Perhaps I could learn a thing or two on how they received theirs. Adriana had received many but she was in Malaysia and I was looking for someone in Singapore I could meet with immediately. Fortunately, I found the person through word of mouth, and her name was Stephanie. Small in stature and in her late 40s, but spunky, athletic and youthful. Her auburn-tinted sleek shoulder-length hair would toss side to side as she would speak with bubbling energy and expression. Her pin straight fringe added even more youth to her doll-like looks.

I invited Stephanie to my home so that I could show her the gemstone. When the day came, she was accompanied by a gentleman friend by the name of Tyler. Not wasting a moment, I opened up my jewel box, I showed Stephanie the blue gemstone, the mysterious one that appeared supernaturally as well as the one given by Adriana.

Stephanie said, 'Nice!'

She placed them on her left hand and looked at them adoringly.

'Thanks. But they are so tiny,' I replied.

'Well, let's make them bigger, shall we?' she added.

'Excuse me?' I said in bewilderment.

Stephanie began speaking the words of encouragement to the gemstones, speaking to them like they were little babies, 'Grow, grow. Come on. A little bigger now!'

Now this was getting interesting. Without hesitating any further, I joined in to give the verbal encouragement. Shortly after we saw a slight movement – very faint shove. They expanded intermittently like tiny blow bubbles, hesitating to grow and then building their confidence. They listened obediently! As she osculated both the gemstones, one could almost see the tingling vibrations.

These words came to mind, 'In Heaven, everything is alive, everything has consciousness.'

Through Stephanie's presence, she brought the vibration of Heaven onto Earth.

She turned to me with a playful smile on her face, 'You can do it too.'

Now counting 1,2,3,4,5,6 – 6 out of this world experiences. I was looking forward to more!

This deceptively ordinary looking woman was like a high priestess within. She gave me back my gemstones with the manner of a job well done.

'There you go, let's say they are about one and half times bigger now. Remember to keep asking them to grow,' Stephanie said.

What had happened was commonplace for her. And as she turned her attention to me, she was the first to notice a ring of dark energy circling around my mouth and penetrating deep within my throat.

'Have you done deliverance before?' Stephanie asked.

'No, never,' I replied.

'I see something latching onto you that needs to be removed,' she added.

She told me to stay still and she reached out to her left side and raised what seemed to be an invisible sword. With her was the quiet man who watched from the background. Also in his late 40s, he fashioned a crew cut which gave all the more emphasis to his piercing beady eyes, framed by a pair of deep red rectangular glasses. He tried to read me while she performed.

Stephanie spoke with a seriousness, 'Tilt back your head. Let me get it out.'

Though small in stature, she got up and stood radiating with authority, looking at me the whole time.

'Let me use my sword to remove it,' she said educating me on the process.

She raised what was an invisible and imaginary sword. I was taken aback for a moment but I decided to let her continue. With artful slow movements, she pierced it into my belly and moved the sword upwards through my spine.

With vehemence, she shouted, 'Out in Jesus' name!'

As for her sobriquet, Stephanie was a Spiritual Warrior with an invisible sword that swayed in her hands with style and dexterity.

Amazed by her skill, I wondered why I felt no pain but a very real and uncomfortable force of energy pushing through my organs and up my spine. An intense prayer of deliverance with effect. A sudden feeling of nausea, a sensation of an invisible chain-like object in my throat, in my stomach. Thick and morbid like large intestines, almost ghostly. She placed her hands over my mouth and pulled it out, a gradual pulling of a long chain, almost like a tug-a-war. Whatever was removed, even though it was invisible, it felt real. Its swift elimination left a lightness on my lips and tongue, as if a dark cloud had vaporized into nothingness. I was left with utter disbelief about what had just happened.

Suddenly, Stephanie noticed something and said, 'I see four white stars. Floating a little over your forehead, with a purple glow!'

'What does it mean?' I asked Stephanie.

The gentleman by the name of Tyler, who was with her stepped forward and intervened.

He gave the answer in a rather cybernetic manner, '4 - Father, Son, Holy Spirit of God and You. White stars – represents purity or out of the Earth's orbit. Purple glow - overflowing royalty,' he went on, 'The interpretation is that you are wrapped in pure light of heavenly star power and overflowing with royalty.'

Tyler's words encouraged me despite the torrid flaw removed from within me. I felt light and bright. The recharging of my Spirit Woman by emptying the body of worldly elements, with the entity removed that was a negative emotion of anger and hurt encapsulated to become a living entity. The emotion itself was like a conscious being wanting to live in my body like a parasite. Almost like an invited person not visible to the naked eye. I was overcome by an epiphany of my years of harsh spoken words: words of defense, criticism and complaints, angry outbursts, of being judgmental. They were removed as a living being kicking and screaming not wanting to go.

There was more Truth surfacing. Here we are living in this dog-eat-dog world, we tend to talk loudly to draw attention or to get our points across. Swearing and using curse words in social interaction has become a norm. Though I have never sworn in my life, there were a few occasions when I would lose control of my hurt and anger and lash out with words of anger, disappointment and disdain. This epic incident validated that dark energies reside in our loud, harsh and negative way of speaking nowadays. Just as God's name attracts divine frequencies, these bad words attract low vibrational frequencies. The tongue truly has the power of life and death.

This spontaneous event was certainly an eye opener. I learnt that for us to shift into the New World, we need to be discerning in our speech. We raise our vibrational frequency when choosing good words and talking in a tone that is respectful of others. Participation in any forms of gossip has a whole host of negative repercussions: idle talk, and malicious talk; slander which is an abusive attack on a person's reputation; hearsay which is heard through an indirect source. Cosmically, I could imagine that no word uttered is ever lost as the sound of it reverberates into the Cosmos infinitely.

I asked Stephanie how she had developed the gift of sensing these parasitical entities. I could sense them too but nowhere close to the level as she could.

Tyler intervened again, 'Meditate deep in God's name. Go deep beyond the galaxies. God is there in the realm of eternity. The more you spend time with Him, ask for the gifts you seek and ask for their release.'

When Tyler finally did speak, he would shake the whole room with his naturally loud gruff voice. The teaming up of Tyler, a gifted Singaporean Chinese, with Stephanie, a skillful Malaysian Chinese.

Go deep beyond the galaxies? I reflected on the Black Hole (or Black Whole considering the grand unification). If every Black Hole contains a smaller alternate universe, then going deeper beyond the galaxies may take me to another universe. If I could do that, would I receive greater insights and revelations? Would there be more intense transformations?

I recalled Marianne's words of guidance on meditation, 'Meditate on the Word of God. Meditate on God's testimonies in your life. Meditate on the prophetic word given in your life. And last but not least, meditate on good things as it will fill your mind with memories so that the Holy Spirit of God can move in it.'

Tyler's guidance on meditation was an astrophysical extension to Marianne's. Meditation with different intentions. So far I learnt that there was Meditation in Stillness and Meditation in Movement. And then there was worship which involves music and singing praise. Lastly, prayer where there would be a conversation with the Holy Spirit of God. My ritual had to be upgraded to the threefold activities of meditation, worship and prayer. Perhaps best done with eyes closed as it opened up our mind's eye to see beyond our earthly realm, giving us access to the greatest mysteries.

Tyler continued to speak this time sharing about his personal experiences, 'I survived a heart attack and three strokes. But it left me lost and weak. Then one day I was struck down by a massive force. The Hand of God. Half unconscious, a message received, my planetary task assigned. And I have been prayer walking ever since.'

Elaborating on the point on prayer walking, he said, 'I just walk the streets and prophesy and pray for people. I walk up to those who I am led to by the Holy Spirit of God.'

As he checked his mobile phone, he added, 'Oh yes, I attended a conference a couple of years ago. The speaker shared about how God is raising a troop of Overcomers. They are going to stand in an overlapping place.'

I asked, 'What kind of place?'

Tyler replied, 'Overlapping, is in between the Earthly realm and the Spiritual realm. And these Overcomers are going to go up to the spiritual realm and they are going to grab what they see and manifest that onto Earth.'

I replied thoughtfully, 'I see.'

If Stephanie and Tyler were among the Overcomers, could I be one of them? With so much intelligence in our DNA (with its RNA), I imagined that every cell of our body is designed for overcoming. It just needed to be triggered.

He said, 'We need to understand our true identity. Our true identity is not humanity. Our true identity is our divine nature. And when we begin to see that divine nature restored then we can begin to function without limitation. That means that we are standing at the most critical juncture of all human history!'

A critical juncture indeed, with the tide and turbulence across the globe.

Tyler said, 'My task is for Singapore. A Watchman for the people in Singapore. To help them ascend, so that the nation can ascend accordingly.'

Stephanie cut in as she said in chorus, 'My mission is to use this invisible sword for deliverance! I take it everywhere I go.'

The Watchman was his nom de guerre in the Spiritual battlefield, an Overcomer who watches, inspects and alerts the rest of the troop. Stephanie, the Spiritual Warrior, may be an Overcomer too, but in different way with her stealth and connectedness with Heaven to conquer entities of Darkness.

Tyler said to me, 'We were fated to meet for this spiritual quest.'

'For this spiritual quest?' I asked, 'But why?'

He answered, 'At least for me, I am supposed to be one of your spiritual guides. My job is the watch the spiritual realm and to be the sounding board for the spiritual market-makers like yourself.'

I agreed, 'Really? That's interesting. Somehow I feel that the marketplace is where I play an important role.'

Tyler said, 'Well, I could see that. Let me tell you honestly, when I saw you from a distance, I was wary of you. Because the energy from you was different from the people around you. You are an anomaly. Your intelligence may be limitless.'

I rolled my eyes in shock. Tyler spoke with such conviction and certainty. I thought to myself. It never occurred to me that I had supernatural intelligence. Did that "electrocution" experience in Rural Pakistan have anything to do with it? Was it a gift being released?

'On Earth, we measure by IQ. But you cannot be measured by human standards. Since I can sense that you are a very curious person,' Tyler paused and said, 'Just to let you know I am a "Nathan" type of prophet. I know things. I am also an aspergic. Despite this flaw according to standard education systems, I was calculating at the speed of light without a calculator when I was 7 years old. 186,000 miles per sec. 1 min. 1 hour. 24 hours. 1 year,' he shared.

Taken aback, I stopped him before he would go rambling on, 'Wait a minute. Aspergic as in Asperger's Syndrome? Similar to autism but different.'

'Yes. A kind of lifelong disability that affects how a person like myself makes sense of the world. I see things, process things and relate to other people very differently from ordinary people,' Tyler replied.

I added, 'And highly dexterous with numbers too. Your condition must be linked to this special gift.'

The new super-intelligent prophets among our midst, wrongly classified by society. Gems amongst the seemingly ordinary. Remembering his words, I decided to make an extra effort to upgrade my prayers and meditation.

'It's a mystery to us because of the limitations of our own thinking. We have a tendency to believe that we are human beings with a spiritual experience. When the Truth of the matter is, we are spiritual beings having a human experience. That means that we are eternal beings,' Tyler said.

Those facts I knew. But the fact of the matter is that in our regular lives, we still choose to forget that. We constantly live like humans, neglecting to build on our spiritual side. Many would save and grow money in the bank, but do little to grow and build our spiritual wealth.

'Who you are in the "now" is just a foretaste of who you are in the future now(s) because the future now(s) can be pulled to the present if the conditions are met but these conditions are not generic conditions. It is personal for each individual,' Tyler explained.

Stephanie nodded in agreement throughout.

'So I will bring my future Self now?' I asked.

'Yes, and start living it,' Tyler said.

'I thought about my mission. My task. What I had to do. I am in the midst of writing a book. At first it was purely scientific, but now its shifting with a science and spiritual angle. I am being led to see it as journey somehow …' I replied.

Before I could continue Tyler interrupted me and said, 'There is an Angel standing next to you. The Angel is holding a pen in one hand and a lightning bolt in the other hand. I am sure you understand what the pen signifies.'

I blurted out, 'To keep writing. That I am doing the right thing ... but I don't understand about the lightning bolt.'

'Well, I guess as you continue this path, more will be revealed,' Tyler replied.

My future Self that was brought to the present, writing and crafting on one hand and the very ambiguous "lightning bolt" task on the other hand.

Still thinking about what Tyler had said, he went on to say, 'My God-given gift are my eyes. I can see beyond what others can see. My mission? I am the Watchman for Singapore as assigned by Heaven. My job is through my prophetic abilities to make sure that Singapore moves upwards and in the right direction.'

I replied, 'That is a big responsibility you have on your shoulders. Very few people will understand what you mean by that though. An incomprehensible task for them really.'

Tyler replied, 'It's not for them to understand. As I said, soon more and more will be revealed. And regarding the blue aquamarine gemstone, it could represent you as it was coming out of you.'

His profound words got me thinking.

Realizing how much time had passed, I picked up my bag and said, 'I need to leave as in a few days I will be shifting to Sembawang, so I have quite a lot of packing to do. By the way, that was a great session of deliverance. Thank you both so much. I am not letting those entities on me again!'

Tyler laughed, and said, 'Sembawang! Where the trees look upwards!', he continued reverting back to the topic of spiritual deliverance and protection, 'Just remember to keep shielding yourself from negative energies and entities. Cover yourself with the Blood of Jesus.'

Music, Love & the Mystics

Another day with another euphoric moment. If Tyler was right that the tiny blue gemstone may be a representation of myself, I wanted to be a brighter, polished diamond as the final destination.

Then there was the sparkling gold dust. The evanescent gold.

A thought came through my mind - 'Gold is a transitionary element'.

More revelation coming in! I messaged Marianne instantly since I did promise I would update her on any new discoveries on the gold dust.

While scanning the details on my iPhone like the last time, I wrote to Marianne, 'Gold is in the middle of the Periodic Table. The center of the periodic chart of elements consists of what are known as the "transition elements," meaning that they can transit from metallic to monatomic or diatomic via chemical treatment … or through other means.'

Marianne wrote back, 'And gold is a good conductor.'

I typed, 'Gold is the semiconductor of Light.'

Marianne's reply, 'Hmm … the transition. As we transit, or transfigure into the Glory!'

More motivated than ever about "transiting" in the Glory realm, I continued to meditate and worship in dance with music. In the past I was always shy of showing my dance moves, but it began to come naturally to me while I flowed in worship.

Each time, I allowed the high octave music to play in full blast. So high that I would feel a buzzing across every cell in my body, as it worked from the lower part of my body and upwards. An intense tingling sensation finally reaching the top of my scalp. A ringing and ringing – like a bell. A high pitch and then an even higher pitch. I thought about myself and then the Planet Earth, like an onion with its layers unraveling. The tapping within the layers, with a higher and higher ringing as the layers are removed, into higher and higher dimensions and realms, transfiguring us to become heavenly beings of a greater power.

'The Earth rings like a bell' ~ Nikola Tesla

Above all, love was the feeling and music was the instrument to bring out that feeling.

'Music is love', by American guitarist David Crosby.

The Shakespearean quote, 'Let Music be the Food of Love'.

The highest realms contain only the energies of love. After all, God is Love. With more and more blemishes out of the way, I was still a work in progress. Alongside, Heaven's reflection on Planet Earth also becomes a work in progress. The Glory realm in full form on Planet Earth – where nothing is impossible.

The New World may be a grand assembly of magis and mystics, sages and alchemists, spiritual physicians, priests and great healers. We will be capable of so much more than we are currently aware of.

It was becoming clearer and clearer that this is the time to open ourselves up to God. He is training us for bigger things than we can possibly imagine. Making us leaders and chiefs where nobody falls behind, with no exceptions and no limitations set on the poor or under-privileged. A natural trajectory towards a multidimensional being where powerlessness is relinquished; allowing for a full release of gifts and abilities most of which we have never come across in our lifetimes.

WE
The new Master Creators,
Master Alchemists,
Engaging in the DNA of God,
Embracing the record
Of the dimensions of Heaven.
And releasing it
Into our bodies.

Speaking like Sages,
Au courant of the Truth,
Commanding the DNA to activate,
Transforming every genetic record,

And re-sequencing our DNA
Into a higher alignment.

All towards resonating
With the DNA of God.

Speaking creative words
Into our DNA
Releasing supernatural abilities.
And triggering our innate ability
To transform Matter.

Gold is a chemical element with symbol Au and atomic number 79. When you have two or more gold atoms in a microcluster, it will have metallic properties. But if you have only one atom, it will then have ceramic properties, which means that it becomes chemically inert but at the same time will have superconductive capabilities even at room temperature. The weight of these materials can also change by heating, becoming lighter, even to the point of levitation.

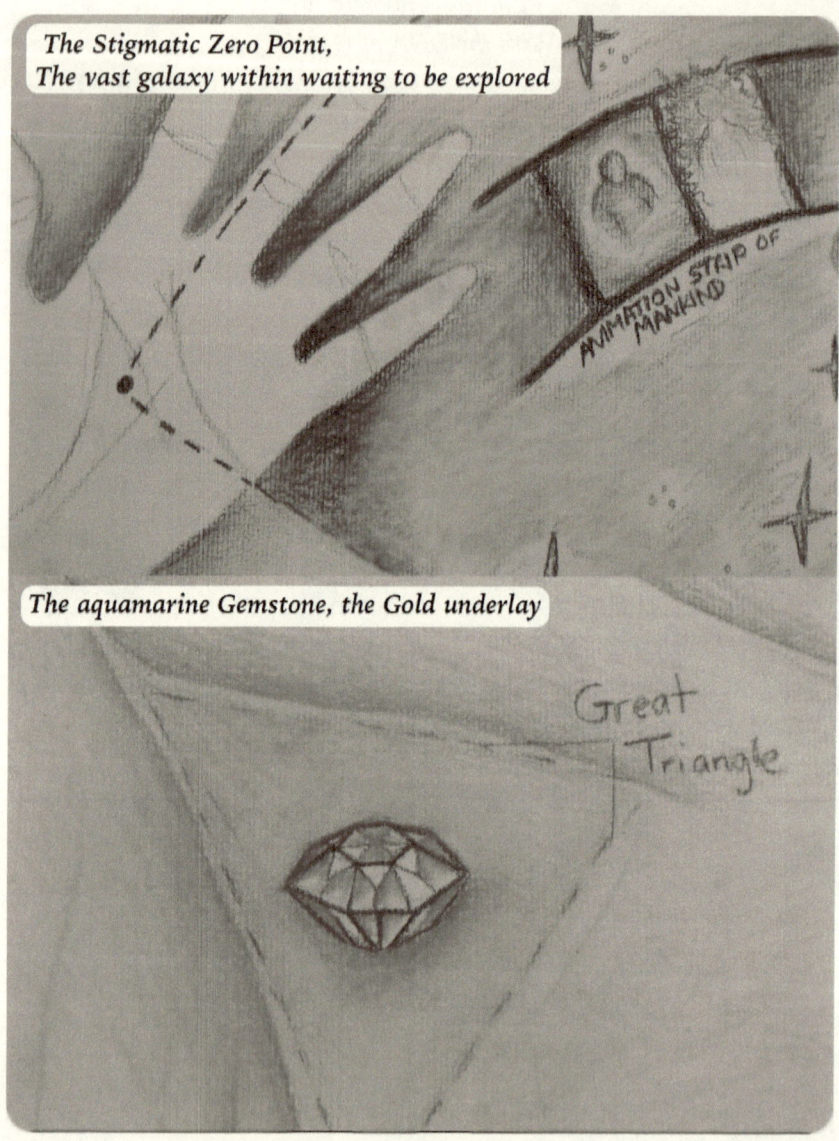

13

Making Technology Responsible

Moving towards Singularity.

Man and Machine,
Man and God.
A Oneness,
An aliveness
More real than ever before.

To be mindful always,
As we advance ourselves spiritually.

To prepare ourselves
For even greater and faster
Technological transformations
Heading our way.

Since the return from Bali, Malaysia and Pakistan, Singapore felt even more of a utopia, especially in terms of its infrastructure and technology. Visually striking with its ultramodern landscape, was the curious Helix Bridge in the world famous Marina Bay area, which linked Marina South to the ArtScience Museum. The latter was an unusual museum shaped like a lotus flower, also known as the "Welcoming Hand of Singapore".

Every corner of the Singapore island was wired up to perfection in every possible way, as it hoped to become one of the first Smart Nations in the world. I was very comfortable with all that - the systematic functioning in terms of processes, and the use of latest technology as widely as possible.

For two decades deep in the technology world, I was personally very much involved in a reputable Singapore-based society that supports the growth and innovation of the mobile technology ecosystem. This fast moving segment, involving smartphones, ipods, headsets and mobile apps, was changing exponentially; more than any other product in the world. With four years dedicated to various roles from an Executive Committee member, to 2nd Vice President, then upwards to 1st Vice President and finally President; as soon as my year long role as President in the was completed, I was ready to step down and hand it over to the new elected person.

Alongside the involvement in this society, there was a sense of satisfaction that a technology startup I co-founded way back in 2002 had a new framework in place. The business shifted from its own zero point to rebirth and upwards, with so much letting go of unnecessary overheads, old ways and outdated systems. With a new positioning and a renewed business plan, I imagined the business rejuvenated as a shining beacon, just as I was hoping to become. Furthermore, I was committed to channeling my new expanding energies into the new season of what God had planned for me. With my new mission in place, I was going to move further with a combined spiritual and technological approach, remembering the 3 keywords of my role always - Writer-Futurist-Innovator. Clutching the book I was still reading "The Agony and the Ecstasy", I was exhilarated as I waited for greater experiences to come to me.

I learned some really valuable things as a technologist. Technology is similar to human beings in a way that it cannot be constrained. It needs to move and should move as quickly as it can. With the release of the Apple Watch, and 3D printers and the like becoming more prevalent, as well as the new era of Quantum devices, technology enhancements are being unveiled in leaps and bounds. The Digital Revolution period (1980s to present) is marked as the most inventive period in human history across centuries. Lagging behind is the Space Age period which started in 1957. Nonetheless, all previous centurial periods did not come close in terms of the scale of inventions.

This made me wonder about a recent vision I had that had close associations with advancement. Vastly different from the world that we are part of, it was a city enveloped completely within a glass shield – an artificial bubble, floating in space. There was a slight glimmer to the city as if it were made of crystal glass.

But the vision was so vague that I could not it see clearly. As my natural eye zoomed in for a closer view, there were several winged horses and human-like beings within the city. A blue facade covered the whole place. The horses stood tall, muscled and majestic, while the men poised beside them were equally strong in stature. Evaluating the vision symbolically, the Pterippus or winged horse signifies aspiring for the greatest heights of accomplishment. Blue, the universally known color of royalty. Blue, the color of the eyes of the Divine Being. The glass covered dome of protection, congruous to a state or a governing body that has the full right and power to govern itself without any interference from outside sources or bodies. A state of sovereignty.

The removal of blemishes, learning to let go and to simply "Be", relinquishing fear and anger and filling that precious space with joy, realizing the true meaning of unconditional love and forgiveness – allowing for the cleansing of our hearts and purification of our souls. The needed soul-centric metamorphosis of myself, and of every other human being. The vision was a reconfirmation that we are being renewed and taken to greater heights. I called it the "Blue Crystal Dome" vision. Regardless of whether it was symbolic, or a real city sometime in the future, or another planet, the encapsulated city was a portraiture of a civilization aspiring to the greatest heights of what they could become.

Tahira Amir Khan

The Vision of the Blue Crystal Dome
Encasing a civilization,
Reflecting the strength,
The sovereignty,
The crowning of aspirations.

Spirituality ahead of the technology

A soul and societal renewal towards a greater responsibility as cumulative technological inventions come into fruition. Technology is not merely Facebook and websites and apps, but instead, the things we can't easily fathom now that are easily achievable ahead. Thus, the impending New World of a technological climax. What should be most feared is an anticlimax due to a technological misdemeanor. We are already seeing that through decades of environmental degradation, war and violence, greed and exploitation of others, substance abuse and addiction, hunger and malnutrition, political oppression and much more.

Some insights on this. Computational technologies extend the reach of human activity through time and space. With the help of social media and communication technologies people can interact with others on the other side of the world. Satellites and advanced communication technologies allow pilots to fly remote-controlled drones over a target in a foreign territory from their ground-control station in their homeland. These technologies enable people to act over greater distances, but this remoteness creates an impersonality that breaks the humanness of who we are. When you are thousands of miles away, and the ties of emotional bondage is invisible, the "feeling" of the consequences is only partial or indirect. The "attacker" would never fully comprehend the significance of their actions. Their original actions in programming the system may have effects on people years later, the problems of "many hands" and "distancing effects" on the use of technology. Even if the technology is responsible, there is another perspective in terms of ethics, as I soon discovered.

Through The Golden Door

I recall one of those nightly business meetings. Not the usual "in office" meeting but at a business lounge of the Hyatt Hotel in Singapore. My team and I were engrossed in a meeting with a potential investor about a new mobile app that we had conceptualized. It could allow the member of the public to quickly capture information from their portable device about a critical incident, and report it as accurately as possible (with minimal tampering) for the police and for insurance claims. We shared about how crucial it was to prevent fraud while protecting members of the public at the same time. The virtue of "No lies, No secrets" was the inspiration for the app.

The potential investor was a technologist and a global player in business and government for over 30 years. Rotund, he was a typical scotch-and-soda gentleman. Whiskey was the elixir of his life as he held a glass in his hand. That was when his babelism which I found wildly amusing would set in – carefully cultivated "highly intellectual" speech which sounded like gibberish at times. Regardless, when he was sober, he was very much on the ball, well versed in more than 12 languages and knew the in-roads of how governmental organizations worked. His name was Dr Rodriguez.

His large greenish-gray eyes rolling with ideas as he tuned into the solution. The insured would be prevented from tampering with photographic evidence they captured on their mobile devices for the insurance company. The insurance companies would be forced to be ethical as they are less likely to find loopholes in insurance claims through the use of the mobile technology. Enforcement would also receive more police reports from the public meaning a greater responsibility at their end to take action and close the cases. Straightening the jackets on all sides, the issue of ethics is controlled through the technology. He felt that in terms of the concept of the mobile app, the timing for implementation was right. He listed countries and organizations which ethically (and spirituality advanced) would be easier to collaborate with to speak to about using this technology.

Dr Rodriguez said, 'Leave out those countries and organizations which lag behind in terms of transparency for now as they may have hidden agendas for corruption. Even if your app collects the reports for them, they might not use it appropriately. Governments need to be transparent and trustworthy, for the people to be the same and vice versa,' he continued, 'So start with Singapore first and work through with the other advanced nations. They will be easier to penetrate.'

He went on to educate us a little about the real world, 'As humans, we are always trying to learn new things. If we do not have the understanding of how something should be applied, there is a danger of abuse.'

Dr Rodriguez had his hands dirtied with a wide range of technologies over many decades, including those for defense and security.

He said, 'There is so much technology out there but it is not being used or disclosed to the public. That is because we are just not ready for them as yet. So it is important to work on our spiritual uplifting now so that we can handle the new technologies.'

With the pluses and minuses of technology advances as clear as day, what do we need to prepare for now?

Dr Rodriquez said, 'Technological advancement is growing exponentially. In the near future, key parts of mobiles and computers are going to be more accurate and faster: light-driven including clocking and sensing! The Quantum Clocks!'

These were some advances which I did not have enough knowledge on, and I had plans to find out more.

He added zealously, 'We are at the beginning of a new renaissance that explores the quantum nature of our shared reality. This new age is fast forwarding us to an era of Quantum engines, devices and systems.'

Dr Rodriquez spoke with increasing excitement, 'And the global race is on. From China to the USA and from Russia to Europe, the race is on to construct the first Quantum Code Breaker, as the winner will hold the key to the entire Internet. From transnational multi-billion dollar financial transactions to top-secret government and military communications, all would be vulnerable to the secret-code-breaking ability of the Quantum Computer that can run a quantum factoring algorithm, which takes an exponentially long period of time to solve. Those Quantum computers that can implement the new mathematics could quickly break our most sophisticated encryption codes protecting the internet based secure info.'

No lies, no secrets justified repeatedly that there could be no more secrets in the near future. Furthermore, the greater emphasis on how things will move at the speed of light literally.

The infinite cap on his knowledge was his greatest charm. I was impressed of course as there was great Truth to his words. Technological change is exponential, contrary to the common-sense "intuitive linear" view. Instead of 100 years of progress in the 21st century, it will be more like 20,000 years of progress (at today's rate). There's even exponential growth in the rate of exponential growth as claimed by futurist and inventor, Ray Kurzweil. As long as the Law of Accelerating Returns holds true, we need to prepare ourselves for anything in the New World. Since a hologram or laser would appear magical to a human 200 years ago, inter-stellar travel, for instance, may become a reality. And who says that we are limited to the Earth's atmosphere. Space farming may prove vital to the survival of our species. Then Star Trek style teleportation opened up a entirely new paradigm. Quantum tunneling, which allows a quantum to simply up and leave and show up somewhere else. There is a very real yet astronomically small chance that all particles that make up us and our devices suddenly decide to zip to the Moon and back, like balls of light. Such fictional technologies appearing all the more real than ever, which circles back to the message of the vision of the blue Pterippus.

'Humankind is on the cusp of a gigantic revolution in quantum technologies. Yet, in parallel, we have ISIS decapitating humans!' Dr Rodriguez said with utter disgust.

The irony of it all. The danger of stunted spiritual growth in the face of the state-of-the-art technologies.

Tyler's own words when we last met, 'ISIS and all – these are just distractions to take us away from our spiritual growth.'

All the more, the crucial message that we need to reach the pinnacle of our spiritual growth before we can use the latest and greatest of technologies. The Blue Crystal Dome, perhaps was the divine reminder. To constantly work on ourselves, our actions as well as to rethink the use of technology so that it helps alleviate human suffering instead of aggravating them.

Everything has Consciousness

So that was my first meeting with Dr Rodriguez. It was intellectually enlightening. From time to time, during my long travel commutes, I would mince upon his words on the highly dynamic topic of quantum technologies. Since the move to Sembawang, the commute to the city would take a lot longer but it was not too much of a hassle as the trains were always fast and efficient.

In terms of the domestic situation, it was a readjustment for me from the luxurious bungalows of my childhood to government apartment living, a forced humbling as part of a learning process. It was a pleasure being part of the neighborhood based on equanimity. I frequented the clean hawker stalls and the coffee shops close to every block, especially the *kopitiams*, which were traditional coffee shops around Singapore patronized for meals and beverages.

Usually plain sailing, my daily mechanical walk was halted momentarily by a cry and a scream. I surveyed the grounds to find out the source of those cries, and the culprits turned out to be a cantankerous Punjabi family who were my neighbors. My neighbors were usually very amicable, except for this particular one. A disturbed and broken family that lived in a manifested Hell of their own. They were up at arms with each other – the parents (actually stepparents) versus the grandparents and the neglected children who were in the midst of it all. I could hear the mother admonishing her adopted son.

Shouting at the top of her voice speaking in *Singlish*, 'You don't listen to me? You don't like me? Hah! You ungrateful wretch! I bring you to Singapore from your grandparent's useless village in India. You are nothing okay!'

Suddenly a loud sound of something falling to the floor.

She snarled, 'Here is the mop!'

Then she threatened fiercely, 'You better make sure you mop the entire kitchen AND the rest of house after that. You do it NOW!'

I could hear the sound of a soft voice, the little boy crying in the background.

She shouted again instilling as much fear as she could, 'You heard me or not? Mop the toilets also! Are you listening? I am going to sleep now and when I wake up I want to see all the mopping done!'

There was some heavy pounding of feet with the hard slamming of door. It just pained me to listened to all that. And that was just one incident. Those poor children! Their home was in a constant state of chaos and despair as the children and their grandparents were tormented by this evil woman. As a hypersensitive, the situation bothered me terribly.

I kept my thoughts on the praying mantis and thought aloud to myself, 'Stay calm ... stay centered!'

Then I did a silent prayer to God for protection to create a shield of spiritual protection around the children, the grandparents and myself.

Trying to remain calm in the midst of the chaos, I kept walking. I focused my mind on the recent happenings with regards to the blue gemstone, its appearance and growth; and with the Dr Rodriguez's sharing on the Quantum era we were entering into. Whizzing through the door as I turned the key to unlock it, the first thing I did was to seal the windows and block out the perpetual noise from that family. With more atmospheric peace returning to the home, I made myself cozy in my bed as I reached out to the jewel box on my dressing table.

Admiring the tiny blue gemstone as I rolled it around with my fingers, it was amazing how Stephanie coaxed the gemstone to grow as though she was speaking lovingly to a small child. And how it grew bigger and bigger! An inanimate object coming alive - alive with a consciousness, with a personality of its own. Bewildered that I was witness to this, and how she had done it so casually as though it was no big deal. I tried to understand the deeper meaning behind it.

If this Truth applied to all things, all inanimate objects other than gemstones - rocks, a glass bottle, a wooden chair, for instance - then the concept of singularity (man and machine/things unified and alive) becomes more real than ever before. Is there a possibility that the real and the unreal start to merge? The distinction between "virtual" reality and "real" reality becomes confounded as fog-lets come into common use, allowing immediate assembly or disassembly of all sorts of physical objects. The future may involve machines and computers starting to disappear as distinct physical objects, as they become closer and closer to being embedded within ourselves, and they will be more alive than ever.

Reflecting on the month of Dec 2012, a milestone in history when everyone was talking about the end of an era based on the Mayan calendar. The overall theory was that it was the end of era and the start of a new one.

It was a time when Marianne referred to as, '… the opening of the veil'.

Nonetheless, the Dec 21st 2012 auspicious date was all over Facebook, Twitter and all other social networks. Yet, there were many who chose to ignore it considering it just a doomsday paranoia. There was a flood of status updates and group emails from friends to 'Wake up!' before the date-specific transition to a New World or the anticlimax of the end of the world. The next day, it was once again all over the social networks, about those who had expected something visible to happen, and their dismay at the anticlimax.

To be more exact about the timeline, it was two days before this auspicious date when I had a vision that appeared rather extraterrestrial in nature. I named it the "Octopus Spaceship" vision. A craft with multiple legs of an octopus. A machine or mechanical "silvery" contraption of some sort that was very much alive. A human being, or some hybrid, was entering the contraption in some way. While the being prepared to seat himself, the interior design came alive. An irregular shaped malleable substance similar to Play-Doh emerged from the interior of the craft. Rising from the floor of the craft, it shaped itself as an enlarged seat before molding itself around the hips of the being locking him or her securely in place. Consequently, the same substance appeared from the low roof of the craft and created a hand shaped mold over the being's head. Like plaster, it hardened to become a helmet. Biologically connected somehow, it functioned as a mind-reader as it extracted the command to launch from the pilot. Almost instantaneously, the craft was spurred up into action, flying up projecting itself into the sky and vanishing within a fraction of a second. Driven by thought, the man and machine had become one and alive, both alive with a consciousness as they worked in harmony together.

Resembling the Avatar movie, where the indigenous Na'vis from the planet Pandora where able to channel their thoughts with the wild and uncontrollable flying dragons, as they were tamed into full submission to fly with a machine-like precision. The "Octopus Spaceship" vision. A futuristic vision. Or perhaps an invention already available now.

So that vision was recorded in my diary back in Dec 2012. I was still in touch with Dr. Rodriguez. Catching him online, I told him about the blue gemstone that appeared out of nowhere and how I saw it grow when spoken to. He was almost glad that I shared this novel experience. A junkie technologist who delved into everything and anything, he went straight to answer with what he knew.

He said, 'Hmm ... gemstones. Diamonds. Interesting. Did you know colored diamonds are a novel way forward to developing Quantum Technology 2.0 devices that work at room temperature?'

Diamonds, an interesting reference point. If diamonds can power Quantum Technology, then if we are figuratively transforming ourselves from coal to diamond, then there is an unlimited quantum power within us.

I relayed the spaceship vision to him.

Dr Rodriguez's reply, 'Read the book "Chariots of the Gods". It explains everything especially about the higher technological knowledge that we are supposed to have access to.'

The existence of structures and artifacts that have been found which represent higher technological knowledge than is presumed to have existed at the times they were manufactured. The author Von Däniken maintained that these artifacts were produced either by extraterrestrial visitors or by humans who learned the necessary knowledge from them. Interpretations of ancient artwork throughout the world as depictions of astronauts, air and space vehicles, extraterrestrials, and complex technology.

The Singularity of God, Man & Machine

It was a time when Christmas was just around the corner - a universal holiday celebrated by many in Singapore. Just like festivity with family and friends during Chinese New Year and Hari Raya (*Eid*), many people would celebrate regardless of their religious background. Singapore, a truly cross-religious city state as everyone I knew was looking forward to Christmas.

I promised the two young children of the Punjabi family Christmas gifts as I sensed their stepparents would not be around, as usual. The stepparents who warred with each other constantly, left the children home alone with their helpless grandparents. A 9 year old boy and a 5 year old girl, both adopted from a village of India, they were brought to Singapore with the aspirations of a better life. So those stepparents were negligent of a true parental role for children at such tender ages.

While I had to deal with my tests, these children were battling their own. I asked God to spare them any more pain and trauma from such irresponsible stepparents. I prayed that they be shown miracles, just as I was. As I was uplifted giving me hope, I wanted them to experience the same. The children were both intelligent and great talents in the making.

I saw the young boy and struck up a conversation with him. I was friendly with the two children and their elderly grandparents, but I stayed away from their stepparents like the plague.

'How are you?' I asked.

He disinterested reply with a *Singlish* accent, 'Okay-lah.'

I asked again, 'What would you like for Christmas?'

The Punjabi boy replied in a resigned tone without making any eye contact, 'Anything.'

'You sure?' I asked as I did not believe him.

He nodded almost defiantly. I knew that he was keeping up his strength.

Then he opened up, 'We are moving again.'

'What happened?' I asked.

'My stepmother had a big fight with my stepfather and they both refused to pay the rent. We have not paid the house rent for 3 months. So we are being evicted from our place,' he replied.

'Where will you be moving to?' I asked.

He shrugged and said, 'Don't know. But my stepmother and stepfather do not really live with us so they don't care.'

The poor boy with his sister and grandparents were in a state of flux.

'Just after New Years Day we will have to move,' he said.

'How do you feel?' I asked.

'I don't know-*lah*,' was his nonchalant reply.

I could see the loneliness in his eyes, the feeling of not knowing where they were headed to next. He did shed a few tears earlier, suffering from another round of scoldings from his stepmother. That was a tough question for a 9 year old to answer.

Our conversation ended there and he went over to his sister to join her at play. They were playing with coins and marbles, a divergence from the usual toy cars and action figures. The familiar buzzing of my left palm. The Holy Spirit of God was speaking to me as I looked into my palm. I turned my head and saw the young boy playing with a coin as he sat on the floor of the doorway of the apartment.

I called the young boy over feeling led by the Spirit somehow, 'Try this. Take one of the coins and try to make it stay on the wall magically. Just say - "I command this coin to stick on the wall!" When you say it, think of God's name in your heart.'

The young boy looked at me with just the faintest risibility, a gleam in his muddy eyes.

I coaxed him, 'Go ahead! Just try it. Believe that the power of God is within you and the Angels are around you to help you. Come on try!'

His eyes slowly widened with excitement and he placed the coin on the wall.

With a coercing tone, I said, 'Have no room for doubt!'

Turning to look at me again for reassurance, he recited the verbal commandment before releasing his finger. The coin held and it stayed there. Bewildered, we both looked at it, and it still continued to hold itself up.

I said, 'Now that's something!'

He grinned from ear to ear. And that grin stayed transfixed on his little face just as the coin stayed up on the wall without a budge.

Quickly noting down on my iPhone and adding to the list. Now counting 1,2,3,4,5,6,7 – 7 supernatural experiences! And this time the little boy was the miracle maker. It was ironic that I was guiding them when for decades I was the biggest doubter. That hindering voice of Ego saying 'Won't happen!', or 'Can't be done!' and so forth. Time to get rid of feelings of doubt once and for all!

I watched his next move. With confidence he did it again, with no faltering. The coin obediently stuck on the wall, as if pressed hard by an invisible magnetic force. Jubilant his face shone with an exuberance. I was stunned myself. How did that happen? I tried it myself, but the coin kept falling again and again.

'You can't do it because you are unhappy,' he said.

That same knowing look written all over that tiny childlike face. He was now mocking me. The insight of this 9 year old certainly caught me off guard. After all, he did notice my tear-stained eyes the other day as I was off to work.

What a precocious little boy. His intuitiveness was impressive. And yes, I was still unhappy. He was absolutely correct. I was still complaining and grumbling from time to time that my life could be better. And this was despite the black spot appearing and disappearing from my palm as a divine sign, despite the blue gemstone appearing the night when I was worried that I would lose my things, despite the divine visitations and despite the new objective to do what I loved. The esoteric coin that stuck on the wall with a God-powered instruction – that was another wake-up call for me in an indirect way.

Christmas came and went, and soon it was just past New Years Day in Singapore. The breathtaking spectacle of lights, music and fireworks that spanned across the famous shopping district from Orchard Road all the way to the Marina Bay, came to a close. I was curious what happened to their move. I nosed into their affairs again looking for the boy. He was outside about 50 meters away from his apartment, walking with authority ahead as his grandfather trailed behind. Dressed in the spanking new T-shirt I gave him for Christmas with matching shorts, he had a new spunk in his stride.

He explained without me asking, 'We just returned from Singapore Power. Our electricity was cut off. We had no lights and could not turn on the fan the whole day.'

I asked, 'Okay. But weren't you supposed to move?'

He replied, 'Not yet. My stepmother did not bother looking for a new place for us. We received a summons to move out tomorrow. The owners of the building will seal the place by 3pm tomorrow afternoon.'

After laying his bag down from the outdoor adventure of paying bills, he sat next to the wall opening up his bag of coins to play the "Coin on the Wall" game. I wanted to scold him for saying that I was not happy in my heart, but I restrained myself. He was right. He was so right. This little boy was a survivor and he was going to grow up with great promise.

Concerned, I asked, 'Where do you go now?'

He laughed, 'We don't know. Most probably we will have to shift to one small room and rent it from another family - if anyone wants to take us.'

Shocked, I asked, 'All four of you in one room?'

The young boy answered speaking almost like an adult, 'Yes. Haha. I have been going through this all my life since I was brought to Singapore from India. Hmm, about 5 years now,' he paused and continued, 'But I am not worried anymore. God is there watching over me and my Angels are there with me helping me everywhere I go.'

That was his cheerful reply.

Relieved that he was handling the domestic crisis quite well, I said, 'Good. Since you are now a powerful yet humble (I must emphasize that) boy, make sure you do some reading too. I know your parents are hardly ever around to guide you, but do listen to my guidance at least, and read.'

He quickly replied, 'Yes, I just borrowed from my school library a book on Astronomy. It has lots of pictures and explanation on the Solar System and the Star Systems. I find it really easy to understand.'

I replied, Great!'

He picked up the book and showed it to me. Flipping through the pages, a section on quasars appeared.

I said, 'You know what? You little boy are going to grow up to become larger than life like a quasar. I am certain of it … that is if you keep up with your reading. Now find out more about quasars. I will quiz you the next time we meet.'

He replied, 'Yes, Aunty.'

The young boy put his book away and went back to the game.

He released a silent command as he placed a coin on the wall. It stuck yielding to his telepathic instruction. It reminded me of the being in the "Octopus Spaceship" vision as he telepathically communicated with the control panel of the vehicle. A firm silent instruction with clarity of thought.

The young Punjabi boy's little sister appeared from within their apartment proudly wearing the Hello Kitty bedroom slippers I got her for Christmas. Dressed in a matching frock with tiny red heart prints all over, she was secretly watching what was going on with the coins earlier on.

She jumped up and down full of delight, and shouted 'Sticky-icky! It sticky-icky on the wall!'

Thrilled to see the joy all around, I said to the young boy, 'I think the Angels were probably helping you the first time round. Perhaps now, they are letting you do it on your own?'

He listened and looked up at me.

I said, 'Perhaps it is because there is so much of the Presence of God with you. What do you think?'

My words of encouragement were his elevation.

'Yes!' he said with greater hope and faith in God.

He grasped the concepts easily. The emergence of the new genre of children such as this young boy. The breed of the super-intelligent coming in.

I recall Olga's words that her young son, ' ... would take care of me.'

That was when Olga's son took me on a tour around the paddy fields of Ubud entirely on his own. A prolonged tour covering a large expanse and distance of the village, knowing every nook and corner, every touristy detail, he was probably the youngest tour guide I ever had! When I asked Olga later on, she would insist that her son was a crystal kid. I checked that out and discovered that crystal children are supposed to be one step ahead of ordinary children in everything – intelligence, intuition - all abilities. They have a greater knowing. And this young Punjabi boy had the same inherent knowing in his eyes.

Researching more on crystal children, I discovered that they were being born since 1990s and beyond, and there was some evidence that they had sometimes 10 times the power of the original DNA. One of the theories of the crystal children is that there is no box that could limit their learning and how fast they learn. With that sense of knowing, they had a sense of mission - all linked to an elevated consciousness. Perhaps this young boy was a crystal kid with an enhanced DNA structure. Or perhaps it was simply divine intervention to show a miracle to this boy who needed that miracle so badly at that time. Several possibilities, all with good reason and a great outcome. As plainly as the boy observed, the sadness in my heart was holding back my ability to carry out instant miracles as quickly and easily as he could. If I could just sort my heart out once and for all, I would be able to do so much of what God had planned for me with flawless effort.

Thinking aloud to myself, 'A flawless effort due to a flawless heart.'

That was revelation. Considering the inherent power within, if the coin was a weapon how dangerous it would have been in the hands of the wrong person. This incident alone with this young boy showed the awakening reality of singularity: God-Man-Machine. With the technology available to us, it means that we need to be responsible. The spaceship vision felt like a clear message of singularity, where the human and the mechanical living furniture and devices were becoming One. In the worst case, an elaborate science fiction portrayal such as "War of the Worlds" or the dismal earthly state shown in the "Terminator" movie. From that perspective, singularity is coined as nebulous and ominous yet embodying an ever-steeper rate of technological change. It hints at impending sociological, economic, and political disruption and foreshadows a transformation in the impending future when advances in artificial intelligence, robotics, cybernetics, and nanotechnology may progress so drastically that some of us cannot even begin to fathom what life will be like beyond the veil.

Without getting carried away with wild imagery of destruction, I went back to the message behind the revelation – '… flawless effort due to a flawless heart'.

Was this the secret weapon that could command any machine to work? Or could the heart be tainted or be without the Presence of God and still be able to command a machine and things to happen?

I remembered the words of warning by Marianne as it replayed in my mind, 'We may be given gifts to heal, to prophesy or to create miracles, but it does not mean that we have the Presence of God within us. If that presence is gone, the gifts may still remain. Hence we need to be careful. We must always have the Presence of God with us. Always!'

That added another complexity which I could not figure out. As I always did, I asked God for the answers to be revealed to me as He willed. All I knew is that with true singularity, where it is God-Man-Machine, the worst case example of the Terminator would be prevented as we would be spiritually ahead of the technology. We would be All Knowing, All Merciful and more, in the image of God, with the assistance of machinery. In fact, the supernatural proof and visions had their useful place in confirming that Man and Machine are not really separate, but both pulsating with an aliveness. Machine as an extension of ourselves as we create them – from computers, the mobile phone, our car, stereo system, the kitchen cooking stove. The ideal combination would be the empowerment with a divine alignment as in God-Man-Machine. As long as the union with God is there, we would head toward a bright future.

And from the perspective of creation, the more we create, the more we grow our consciousness. I could almost imagine that. I was beginning to see that singularity is consciousness coming together and becoming more and more One. Perhaps a good comparison with the fractal which shows the multiplication through self-similarity. The universe spiraling towards singularity in all scales from galaxies to atoms, from hurricanes to flowers, to human beings. The Golden Mean. The new paradigm – a transformation in the way humans exist like the 6 million dollar man - developing an interface between the human eye and the brain which would allow people with faulty eyes to see, but also to see beyond human limits, to see with quantum eyes.

The infusion of humanity (Man), technology (Machine) and God, with God leading the way. We may reach a point where our civilization changes so much that its rules and technology are incomprehensible to previous generations. The minacious point of no return if the divine element played a lesser role.

A Time of Arising

The young boy was not done yet. He was still going strong with a whole row of coins esoterically and relentlessly sticking on the walls.

With the 7th coin holding itself up, he pointed encouragingly at his little sister, 'You can do it too! Remember, you are powerful in God and you are never alone!'

He learned well. I was so proud of him. His sister smiled with a big grin on her face, matching perfectly with her "abound with love and joy" red-heart-designed frock.

I bent down forward toward her so that I could reach to her level, and said adoringly to her, 'You are all heart aren't you?'

She nodded vigorously keeping her grin wide. I noticed something on her forehead. Gold sparkles!

I exclaimed, 'Wait a minute! What's this? Is that gold on your forehead?'

The little girl's face beamed with the attention focused on her. The same "gold speck on the forehead" phenomenon of the 12 year old village girl in Pakistan to a 5 year old adopted Punjabi girl in Singapore. A wonderful coincidence. A happy day for all three of us!

As we had our moment of joy, I reflected upon the young boy's unintended cutting statement - 'You can't do it because you are not happy.'

A highly perceptive statement from a young child. Unforgettable words of wisdom. An interesting notion that our human and planetary civilization advancement could be linked to happiness. The art of happiness as an atonement for our lives as preached by the Dalai Lama. Our Arising right now.

With the inevitable growth and development of singularity, it is essential that the heart should always rule first. The spirituality of our human race has to be ahead of the technological breakthroughs in singularity. The dangers lie when we allow technology to overtake our spiritual uplifting. Science, a very sharp two-edged blade where it can be used for good or bad, especially when the decision to use technology for aggression lies in the hands of the policy makers. Everything that is created for technological purposes should be used only for the advancement of the human race, and more importantly for a more secure and peaceful coexistence for not just some but all Mankind.

With singularity inevitable, and tripartite singularity an absolute must – God-Man-Machine, and that was veridical. God, the ultimate highest frequency. This or nothing! Leave out the God element, there will be a high possibility where the technology available in a race will exceed the level of spirituality. The human race may eventually destroy itself. Without the union with God, we may enter an era where we are at the mercy of technology. The union (and intimacy) with God teaches us intimacy in our human relationships too. The Zombie culture most feared by Einstein where relationships start breaking down. The impairment on our emotions, a skill that goes down with lack of practice when we allow technology to take control. Emotions, linked to our hearts, to be treasured as it is the greatest gift of Mankind.

I wanted to be like the young Punjabi boy. How he commanded the coins to do as he wanted. How he remained centered despite all adversity. A pure heart undefiled by sadness or grief. If it did, it would only be momentary and not a permanent corruption in his heart. My learning from the young boy to finally let go of the losses of the past. But most of all, the encounter with the Divine Being that I felt was arranged to take me higher - the eyes of living water, quantum powered and eternally flowing. The basic Principle of Resonance that is when two frequencies are brought together the lower will always rise to meet the higher.

Olga's words, 'Love unconditionally.'

Adriana's words, 'Forgive unconditionally.'

All leading to the words by Jesus Christ, '... be like Me....'

To become Towering Golden Souls deeply interwoven with our mechanical and very soon-to-be quantum powered inventions so that we can do so much more good in a far more efficient, precise and powerful way. The quality of our lives will improve significantly as technology becomes more and more at One with us, with the God-Man leading for the good of Mankind.

Principle of Resonance when two frequencies are brought together, the lower will always rise to meet the higher. Matter is organized by waveforms and frequencies. Two violins that are tuned exactly the same, and if one string is plucked, it will produce a field of sound energy that will trigger the vibration of other violin's matching string, and produce the same sound. This is called "resonance" and it happens naturally. Another way to look at it is that everything is made up of atoms, which are made of particles called quanta. At a micro level, quanta are described as energy vibrating at a certain frequency, which tend to come together or gather with other quanta vibrating at the same frequency.

Vision of the Blue Crystal Dome

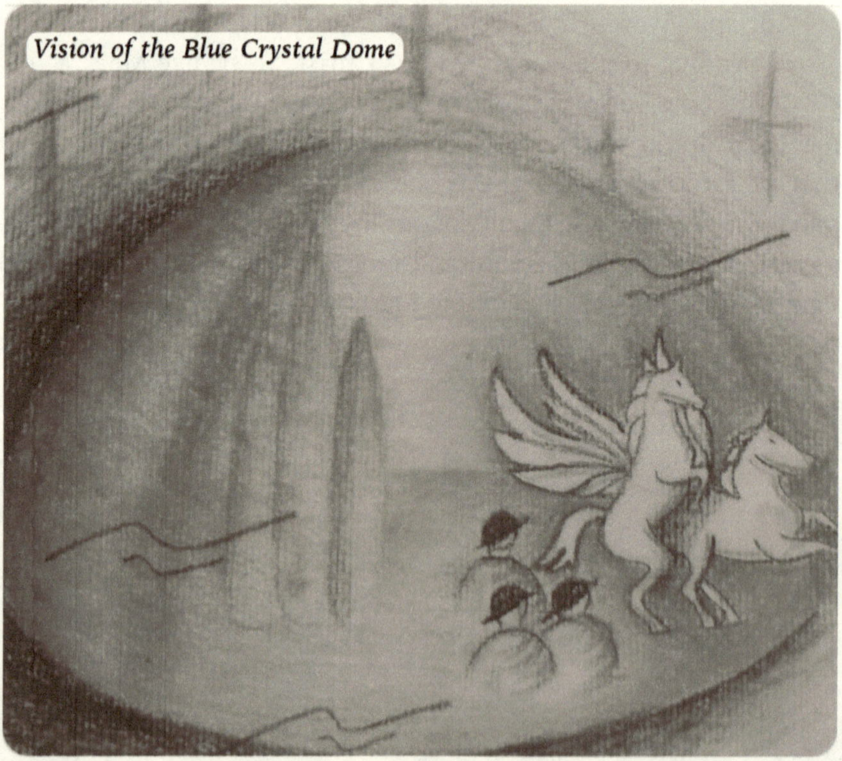

14

Making War Unthinkable

Once we are awakened,
War is no longer needed.

The War and strife
That we battled inside
And outside
Is over.

The vision of a view of an immense amphitheater – a well-organized conference of hundreds or maybe even thousands of beings. The stage of the amphitheater emulating the front of a court room with several throne-like chairs. The stage had an opulent setting for a monarch to preside in majesty over official ceremonies. I could see individual cases involving conflict presented with respective justifications, conducted with decorum and proper protocol.

Was this a supernatural vision of the Heavenly Courts? Or some kind of Galactic Court? The court rooms, hierarchies and its legislation. Perhaps members of such a Council sitting in their seats while the amphitheater was filled with other beings. They appeared to have human-like features, and were dressed in what seemed like intricate costume, and there were others in white linen. The council members who were seated emanated a persona of benevolence. They appeared fair in their dealings. Everyone appeared to have a duty assigned, performing them with diligence and focus without breaking boundaries. Naturally empowered, they did not need to be pushed to perform their tasks correctly. There was an overall feeling of peace, order, honor and empowerment. An ethereal example of how issues are resolved judicially. On Planet Earth, we have had our judicial systems yet we are still at war. If that vision was a depiction of the judicial system in Heaven, we were not completely mirroring it on Earth where there are gaps, from scandals and corruption to hidden agendas for control.

An email message came from Faryal who sent a blind-copy broadcast to her friends.

Her email read, 'I heard from my family in Pakistan. Marshall law may be back soon! This means that soldiers have orders to shoot if they see anything suspicious. Sometimes they make mistakes too.'

It was the year 2014. Such severe political upheaval was still the norm for years on end. It was nothing compared to the aura of the Heavenly Courts. A Hell and Heaven difference.

Faryal wrote in her email sounding infuriated, 'Oh God. This does not create peace for us – certainly not! All these wars, centuries of it. It's just so despicable! According to some study I read, all the major wars in the 20th century, with a recorded total of at least 194 million earthlings killed! What's wrong with us?'

She continued on in her email sounding enraged, 'I feel driven out of a country I love. The constraints, the lack of freedom, the political instability. Of course, I come from a background of wealth so I suffer from it at a very minimal level. The lower middle class and the desperately poor who make up the majority of Pakistan are the ones who are chained.'

So much evidence that Ego was primarily the driving force behind the centuries of wars. Two worlds existing in parallel - one was the doom and gloom world obsessed with among other things terrorist groups around the world, and the other was for peace and harmony, which the spirituality inclined were striving and struggling towards.

Faryal's email read on, 'Otherwise I am getting through. I heard that you had a good trip to Pakistan. I just arrived for a month long reunion with my family. To be honest, it's a been an uninspiring one, with one person pitted against the other. Some inheritance matter that has dragged on for two decades. Old grievances that are breaking us apart! We are at our own war. I can't wait to leave, even to be with my dogs in Kuala Lumpur. Anything for some peace!'

So it was more than just societies and nations. Our own souls were at war between positive and the negative energies. Our families at war. Not uncommon at all to hear about the story of siblings spending their whole lives at odds with each other . Family fortunes wither due to greed and simple refusal to compromise, accept and move on.. The question is – When Does It End?

I shared the Amphitheater vision with Faryal.

Her response, 'Well, Pakistan really needs a good judicial system. But to be fair, not just Pakistan but worldwide. There is an appearance of fairness in some first world countries, while there is corruption hidden at the core.'

A great deal of work has to be done in this arena for our pathway of peace and justice into the New World. I decided to do a little research on the state of peace in the world. This was what I discovered. According to the Global Peace Index for 2014 by the Institute of Economics and Peace, the Scandinavian countries, Singapore, Australia, New Zealand, Canada, Japan and some parts of Europe lead the way. On the downside, the organization also declared that since 2008, 111 countries have deteriorated in terms of levels of peace. With the exception of these countries, peace was far from the ubiquitous paradigm across the Planet Earth.

It was time for this lower denser realm of Planet Earth, a perpetual stage for centuries of war and conflict to become a reflection of the Heavenly Realm. Faryal's message on Marshall Law in Pakistan worried me. I hoped that my two little birds in rural Pakistan were safe and well.

Fortunately, Marianne's message gave a sense of hope – at least for Pakistan and other countries around Asia, 'Singapore is one of the launch-pads for Heaven on Earth. There are other cities chosen too, though Singapore is one of them.'

The peaceful little red dot of Singapore with an important mission. If Marianne was right, I was at the right place at the right time as important work had to be done. Singapore, the launch-pad, the nucleus for a positively charged quantum entanglement to its neighboring countries and the rest of Asia including Pakistan.

The New Judicial System

Through connections with family and friends, I tried to seek out someone who can shed light in the areas of judicial systems and conflict resolution. I was given the name and email address of an ethnic Malay, by the name of Rizwan. With only five years as a practicing lawyer, I was hesitant at first to write to him. However, after I heard that his ability to analyze and collate information was exceptional, I went ahead. Moreover, I wanted a fresh mind in the legal field to consider a new way of looking at things, especially from the New World perspective. A battle of ideas between highly experienced but rigid thinkers set in old ways would not get me very far. Other than a critical thinker from what I heard of him, he had the credentials to back him up as a law graduate from one of the top universities in the UK.

Rizwan's home was in Malaysia. Newly married for about two years, he and his wife always stayed close to each other as they traveled everywhere together. While he worked as a corporate lawyer for a large pharmaceutical firm, his wife worked as marketeer in the same firm. Fortunately, Rizwan replied to my email that he and his wife would be in Singapore for a couple of days and they would be doing some shopping along the famous Arab Street, not far from the city center.

In a few short weeks, Rizwan arrived in Singapore with his wife. Physically, he was well-built and of average height. He spoke in clear and crisp sentences, and had a rather universal accent. Most of all, he was very polite and extremely gracious in his manners. From a warm handshake, running to open the door for a lady, to standing up to respect her departure. I could see why his wife cooed with contentment.

I tagged along with Rizwan and his wife as they browsed the eclectic array of shops along the street. I took the opportunity to interview him while we did a little window-shopping on the side. As we walked leisurely from store to store, he shared with an exuberance about how after his break from work to visit Singapore he would be heading over to finish off the balance half of a postgraduate specialized program at an IVY league university in the United States. It was his long-awaited dream to be immersed in that illustrious and much sought-after academic atmosphere.

I asked Rizwan, 'What's your course about?'

He replied briefly but proudly with his chest out, 'Conflict and mediation.'

Answering matter-of-factly I said, 'Well, that should be really useful in this day and age.'

Rizwan shared, 'I am just barely halfway in the post-graduate program. So far, I realize that conflict is so complicated and how people deal with conflict is equally complex.'

He continued to share what he had learned so far, clearly showing his passion in the field, 'I learned that there are 5 essential tendencies for people facing conflict and we all have bits of each tendency. My style leans towards Fairness, Unity, Fidelity and Peace and Compromise whereas there are some genuine personalities who look at conflict completely differently. We are just heart-wired differently from birth, depending on birth order, depending on life experience and depending on things that are important to us.'

'A very human aspect, indeed. So how we are spiritually and how we have been brought up have significant effects at the world level,' I commented.

Rizwan replied, 'Precisely,' he paused and said, 'Taking another angle, conflict resolution works well when there is consensus. And consensus works as long as the root cause, selfishness is dealt with. If not even an ideal conflict resolution mechanism will be impinged as each party vies to ensure their self-interest.'

Moving along with his statements hoping that it would shift towards a spiritual focus, I said, 'So we need to move towards selflessness?'

'I suppose it does. In some way linked to "selflessness", I would say that we need to have a more duty-based mindset. Of course, everyone has a different idea of what is fair. Thus, there will always be a need for an authoritative entity, a leader vested with the final say on any matter,' Rizwan replied.

I noticed that he spoke in a very structured legal way, mindful and selective with the use of his words. I also realized that the topic was getting a little heavy while on a shopping spree. So I suggested we take a break for lunch.

There was a little restaurant with delicacies from Yemen and Morocco. We thought it would be great to have some Middle Eastern food. As we entered the restaurant and browsed through the menu, we ordered a healthy platter of mainly vegetarian dishes before I opened up the topic again. This time I shifted gear into my Amphitheater vision except that I described it as a dream. Perhaps later on, as I got to know him and his wife more, I would be more open that it was a real vision. At this stage, I was not sure how he would fathom the concept of the Heavenly Courts or the Men in White Linen or perhaps a Divine Council. Thinking it through, I decided to leave those labels and perceptions of mine out from the description.

'Recently I had a dream where I saw some kind of judicial system. Perhaps it is an ideal system,' I said.

I described the dream to him in full detail, from the colors, the ambiance to the beings that were present.

'They seem very fair ... and empowered,' he said.

Clearly a thinker, Rizwan paused for a moment and then elaborated with a response, both powerful and profound, 'I see that "empowerment" will overshadow "rule". As long as empowerment is done in a positive manner, for instance, only beneficial industries that nourish the progress of humanity are empowered, and not harmful industries that stunt progress instead. Ruling needs to be done with morality, fairness and justice, and governments would still need to carry out their duty. Technically speaking, the government may be ruling according to the laws of the land (carrying out its duty to rule) yet, this is done without thought for proportionality of the punishment to the crime.'

Rizwan expounded, 'Even if "empowerment" overshadows "rule" where everyone is duty-based, we still need both. You still need leaders – good leaders. A world without that will devolve into chaos as like-minded individuals begin to form into different interest groups and division will return. And with it, conflict too will return. Unless there is some authority which can break a dead-lock, we will get nowhere.'

I added, 'Ruling with the heart as a key requirement.'

Rizwan replied, 'Well, it is idealistic. So yes.'

Thinking about the Golden Door, I said, 'We do generally aspire towards utopia.'

Rizwan said, 'Yes, we do,' he paused, 'Now, if everyone is duty-based and as you say "ruled by the heart" then having mini-councils and decentralizing decisions to smaller and smaller units would be successful. But are all countries ready for that?'

I replied, 'We could work towards it through education, spiritual awareness and more. Start from the young. Also, to make it a requirement that how spiritually evolved a person is as an important attribute for leadership.'

Rizwan smiled, 'Yes, all leaders whether heading mini-councils and then upwards – all visionaries, with a deep connection and understanding of consciousness.'

I agreed, 'That's right. And that is cohesive.'

Rizwan added, 'There will still be hierarchies, however most conflict resolution will be resolved at the grassroots level.'

I said, 'I can imagine that. A highly duty-based society with its leaders at all levels "ruling by the heart", a pure undefiled and selfless heart of course. That would take any nation many steps higher. Peace, harmony and prosperity in abundance.'

After he said those words, I pictured "Let's be Self-less" campaigns abounding. A global awareness to revamp every human mind from selfishness to selflessness. After all, a solipsistic world where selfishness and individualistic thinking is the norm, war will always exist.

Rizwan continued to speak sounding a little frustrated this time, 'I mentioned earlier how I discovered through my coursework how conflict is so complicated and how people deal with conflict is equally complex. Some may lean towards Fairness, Unity, Fidelity, Peace and Compromise, whereas there are some authentic personalities who look at conflict completely differently. We are just heart-wired differently from birth, depending on birth order, depending on life experience, depending on things that are important to us,' he emphasized, 'It is all about perspectives, neuroscience, life experience, cognitive bias, interests, need and wants all competing for expression.'

His thoroughness and natural depth made it easy to penetrate all angles of the topic.

To delve a little deeper into the topic, I asked something which perhaps would have sounded off-tangent initially, 'Have you heard of the Global Consciousness Experiment?'

Rizwan replied, 'No.'

I explained, 'Well, it is an international, multidisciplinary collaboration of scientists and engineers. They collect data continuously from a global network of physical random number generators located in up to 70 host sites around the world at any given time. The data are transmitted to a central archive which contains more than 15 years of random data in parallel sequences.'

I felt I lost Rizwan for awhile as he was not adept with scientific research as I was.

So I said simplifying the explanation, 'Okay in layman terms it works on collective conscious thought. It brings together conscious thought during a moment in time, and things start to happen. In this respect, we can push and use it in a much bigger scale for selflessness, empowerment and eliminate war as a consequence.'

Rizwan looked lost in thought while he continued to eat his food. Then suddenly he started speaking again.

'Pardon my silence earlier. I was just thinking about how it would be like if the judicial systems all around the world were truly duty-based and ruled by the heart. Perhaps we in the legal and political professions need to deeply understand scientific methods like the Global Consciousness Experiment to really see how we can shift hearts and minds – at the individual level and organizational level. And that includes organizations such as the United Nations,' he said.

I said supporting his statements, 'Then perhaps all conflict could be nipped in the bud. Of course, we have to be very careful as it requires very ethical political leaders. Very very ethical. If it works, this world would certainly be cohesive. We would be more at One with each other.'

Nodding his head, Rizwan said, 'Yes, I would like to be part of that world,' he added, 'In Spiritual Islam, we talk about *ikhlas* being the purification. We need to achieve the Oneness.'

A New World where a duty-based society that is selfless and geared toward Oneness. As more and more of us allow for our spiritual development to speed up, the lighting up of our hearts and minds, more and more of us will drift towards taking the right course of action, towards conflict resolution rather than conflict instigation and escalation.

A realization occurred to Rizwan compelling him to say these words, 'Being duty-based is in itself not the entirety of the solution. Duty, while a noble concept, is just as susceptible to corruption as any other concept. It is just as open to interpretation as any other concept. What is needed is a standard, a line in the sand which clearly should not be crossed, either out of love for doing goodness or out of fear of the consequences that may befall a transgressor.'

This followed on with a few more moments of silence as he continued to gaze around the store. Rizwan was a quiet man. But when he was fired up with a topic of his interest, he would take it with great heart and speak volumes.

As soon as he was ready, he spoke and stated a key point, 'A shift in intention is needed. Intention that is based on the goodness of the heart, followed by proper action is how real progress and justice can be achieved.'

Encouraging his contributing thoughts, I replied, 'Quite true.'

I continued to let him speak as this was his passion and area of interest.

Rizwan said, 'A duty-based society is where every entity is focused on making sure that they are truly giving others what they are owed. A government understands that it has a primary duty to ensure fairness and justice for all under its authority. The people understand that they have a collective and individual duty to the government and to each other. Moreover, this applies to companies too. Companies understand that they have an overarching duty to ensure they carry on business in a responsible and fair manner. The concept of instilling selflessness through a duty-based society would play a part in preventing future conflicts.'

I added, 'With Oneness as one of the symptoms of a duty-based society that is "ruled by the heart", we shift from competition to cooperation. I can imagine the end of wars instigated by land ownership.'

Rizwan said, 'The spillover effects are huge! To think we are talking about something so simple, so basic. That is operating from a pure heart!' he sighed and continued, 'Just look what has been happening in Kashmir. One of the longest standing territorial disputes in current world history.'

The dispute between the government of India, Kashimiri insurgent groups and the Government of Pakistan over the control of the Kashmir region, out of which three wars have been fought since 1947.

I empathized and said, 'Sad I know. I imagined "ruling by the heart" would mean to love, to share. If that is the case, then in such a world, let's call it the New World, such disputes would be unheard of. Sharing means it is freely given. No real title deed to it, or price tag to it.'

With those words, Rizwan's face shone a little brighter.

He said, 'Well, I just might bring up this topic about the "ruling with the heart" and "sharing" at my program. Fairness, Unity and Peace is one thing. But really following it through is another – truly at the "heart" level. To be truly pure in our actions.'

I was happy to hear that. I could see him becoming a man of consequence. This shared universe that he and I and everyone of us is a part of, this links back to our spiritual uplifting - to shift away from material accumulation even at a political level, to the matters of the heart in terms of sharing and caring. A New World where decisions are made in smaller and smaller units. A New World where it is all about the good heart and good works for peace and harmony at the grassroots level. Perhaps there may be no more need for intermediaries such as City Councils, State or Provincial Legislatures, National Parliaments or Congresses.

Global Consciousness Experiment is an international, multidisciplinary project between multiple scientists and engineers. It collects data constantly from a worldwide network of physical RNGs located all over the planet. RNGs had the largest effects ever recorded by the Global Consciousness Project during major world events, like 9/11. Its purpose is to examine subtle correlations that may reflect the presence and activity of consciousness in the world. We hypothesize that there will be structure in what should be random data, associated with major global events that engage our minds and hearts.

RNGs are random number generators created to respond to intentions of individuals. Peaks of order are commonly recorded during moments of shared attention and emotions.

The New Politician

I was fortunate enough to be invited to the home of a reputable gentleman in Singapore. A large plush home furnished with beautiful East Asian artifacts and designed to be highly functional. A Patriarch, as no other title suits him more. A mix of Arab and Indian origin, his first name was Aminuddin. I respectfully call him Mr Aminuddin. A highly successful business owner, active leader in Singapore society, as well as the son of the reputable founder of a multimillion-dollar publicly listed conglomerate.

Amongst the pioneers of Singapore, the octogenarian was impeccably dressed. His pet topics ranged from politics to religion where he had immense knowledge and perception. An assiduous attendee of Friday prayers at the famous Sultan Mosque near Arab Street, he was a true equalizer at the same time. He showed great respect and knowledge for all other beliefs and religions. As a result, when the lines between politics and religion crossed in the wrong way, he would get himself riled up, full of positive will and energy to explore ways to resolve matters. He could extemporize on any topic. A philosopher in his own right, he wanted to see a progressive move forward in the world. What was going on right now was just not acceptable in his eyes.

Mr Aminuddin shared, 'In 2005, the Amman Message - Resolution 154 was signed. The resolution highlights Islam's position of extremism, radicalism and terrorism in the world. It has been signed by over a 100 countries includes the whole of the Middle East. But look at where we are now! It is now 2014, the age of the birth ISIS. This completely contradicts the Amman Message Resolution signed! What happened to the maintenance of the agreement? What happened to keeping your honor and your word!'

Too many countries not honoring their word? Or was it essentially, a corrupted judicial system that gave a false portrayal of functioning well. The dishonoring and disunity in the world from the resultant wars got him even more furious. He stood by Truth and honor like an iron pillar. It was not just talk, but he "walked the talk" and he did that fearlessly. I could see how he was bombarded with calls and emails from all corners of world inviting him to speak at conferences and events. Admitting to himself that he was not possessed of genuine, innate sangfroid, he nevertheless firmly resolved to behave always as a fearless man would be.

Standing his ground, he said, 'I say what needs to be said, and do what needs to be done!'

Mr Aminuddin was determined to spread the idea that Honor, Truth, Peace and Unity needed to prevail in this world. A self-ordained communicator, he would speak with brutal honesty to people at the top of the hierarchies.

He said with disappointment, 'These religious divides have gone too far!'

His words justified. Religious groups across the board, with not just one to blame, were in various degrees in conflict, and they were causing more division and harm than ever.

To lighten the topic, I switched it to something a little different, yet related at the same time. This was my topic of investigation on how we had a choice to shift towards Heaven on Earth as well as the other overlapping perspective on Type I Civilizations and beyond. I tried to explain simply the concept of how it was all happening at the same time depending on our own personal choices. Despite his advanced age, he was open and fresh in his thinking, although it did worry me initially if he would think it was all a bunch of outlandish hocus pocus.

I went on to share about our needed inner transformations so that we move towards becoming New Humans in upgraded biological containers, that is: our bodies. I explained about the reality of the crystallization of the human skin as we shift from Carbon-based to crystalline-based human containers. I shared with Mr Aminuddin about Dr. Max G. Lagally's theory about how all of our cells had to be transformed from carbon to silicon crystal so that we can withstand the tremendous amount of Light that will be streaming into the Planet. And through the process unleashing a power within us to create and manifest instantly, with powerful gifts of God coming from within.

A look of bewilderment on his face as I excitedly sped through the facts and information. When there were moments when my stories sounded a little too sensational, he would throw in a few jokes.

He jested, 'I hope that I become like those mystics. Sounds far-fetched though. But it would be great to become like a crystalline being and never age and decay! I could do with some of that!'

Mr Aminuddin looked good for his age, except for a small problem with his legs.

He complained, 'I have always been as fit as a fiddle. But this leg of mine. Urgh! It's the only thing that is giving me some trouble. A pesky problem just getting in the way of my daily activities.'

Looking at his aching leg, I went on to share about spontaneous self-healing from dengue.

He received that notion quite well and said, 'I agree that there are some forces that are intangible but their existence cannot be denied. And yes, that includes healing'.

Since he was receiving the information so well, I felt that I could go a little further. My thoughts were on the floating neon green Ball of Light that came before the red flaming Fire and the blue aquamarine-eyed Divine Being.

I said, 'I feel that in the near future, we might be transporting ourselves as levitating balls of Light.'

Another look of bewilderment. But he listened intently as I continued to speak.

I said, 'I know. I know. Call me crazy, but I am so sure that this will happen in my generation. In fact, it could have happened a long time ago. Maybe the technology was held back from us because we were not spiritually ready.'

He persuaded, 'Hmm. I am listening.'

I looked into his eyes and said solemnly, 'I feel it will happen once Planet Earth becomes peaceful and war unthinkable. Because if we had such abilities or access to such technologies based on what we are now, societies and nations still at war with each other, it would be very catastrophic. Just the same way as we were not ready for nuclear energy and it was used the wrong way.'

Besides the Divine Being encounter, I shared everything else. All the 7 supernatural experiences. I gave him an earful! Thankfully, Mr Aminuddin was a humble and patient listener to my grand theories and bizarre tales of encounter. Similar to Faryal, who did not allow her restricted environment to keep her mind from being open, with a philosophy of "I Know that I don't Know". He did not allow his advanced age and more traditional background to prevent him from being open to hearing and receiving new information. I was deeply appreciative of that.

As a man of prestige and position in the Singapore society, he was a coveted guest at events and ceremonies in Singapore and across Asia and beyond. With stacks of voluminous books embedded in ornate bookshelves across the walls, he not only had wisdom from books and education, but divine wisdom. Larger than life many times over, that if he achieved greater transcendence, he would be so expanded and so magnified in his Spirit Man that it would fill an entire hall and beyond!

I envisioned the new politician of the New World, and that's how they would be. Despite all the testing circumstances and situations, the new politician remains pure and undefiled, strong and compassionate, with a mind wise beyond measure. Feelings and thoughts surpassing all inclinations toward war, greed or dominance. The Heavenly Courts encounter blessing with the insight that the New World political leaders will be like the judges in a courtroom - benevolent heads of true to heart fairness, disassociated from greed and corruption in all forms. In the language of quarks of the universe he would be the very old, rare but refined quark. Most other old quarks would have died out, while he remained. The New World for only the refined quarks, old or new.

With all that heavy-duty sharing out of the way, we then spoke about personal matters.

Mr Aminuddin said with a beaming smile, 'I am so blessed. I love what I do. I know that I have given so much over the years and people respect me for that.'

A lover of humankind. A true believer that building a strong family foundation is the core of all growth, success, happiness and Unity. He spoke with warmth, love and praise for his family, his sons and daughter with their spouses and grandchildren. Mr Aminuddin shining his paternalistic nature in all aspects of his life.

He said, 'Oh, I have the most amazing grandchildren. They are so great. I am learning so much from them. Sigh. I am glad that my late beloved wife and I got it all set up for everyone.'

He quietened for a brief moment, reminiscing. He could not help bring up the sensitive topic that almost totally wrecked the family's business and its legacy. The billion dollar business was almost torn to pieces. The long-standing family war, the meaningless feud based on disagreement and misunderstanding resulting only in pain and massive financial losses. His eyes, clouded with strain as he furrowed his brow. The strong man inside him holding up the family torch so that it could burn in full force again.

Mr Aminuddin was not ashamed to elaborate, 'We stumbled, yes, and lost millions! What a ride! But we came back and re-united and re-built. We may have lost the great family empire we built before, but what we have re-built is a new empire of our own. It is not as big but it is sufficient and more importantly the family is happy and we are building it together; united and in harmony.'

From the expression on his face I could hear the unsaid words, 'No more warring. The family has been there, and done that'.

The imminent 1000 years of peace. His choice, the choice of the family. As I thought so, our individual choice for Planet Earth as well.

Mr Aminuddin asked, 'Based on all what you experienced, I am sure you need to do something with it. Don't you think so?'

Not a surprising question from a man who lived larger than life.

I replied, 'Well I was writing a book on new planetary civilizations. It was going to be called "Transit to Type I". We are not just shifting towards a new civilization, but we are moving towards Heaven on Earth. Alongside, we need to transform individually – body, soul and spirit,' I continued, 'Then came the vision of a Golden Door. I believe the Golden Door is twofold. The pathway towards our spiritual uplifting, and the pathway to a New World.'

He said, 'And this New World is Heaven on Earth?'

I replied, 'Yes, that is what I am referring to. We may not arrive and we may reach a different destination which may not be so ideal. We may even go backwards. And even if we do go through this symbolic Golden Door, either (individually or collectively), I imagine various degrees of Heaven on Earth manifested.'

I reached out to the sketch I did on Mankind's evolution. That was the sketch of my stigmatic left palm with the an animation strip and the inner-galaxies in the background.

I explained, 'As Mankind evolves we may also go through a "repeat procedure" to start all over again. It is quite true as we see repeats in our own lives. Things go wrong, we have to try all over again to make sure that we do it right. We can't afford to do it wrong and miss the boat. Would we want to go back to the early 1900s or even way beyond that so that we could go through the whole process of learning again and making sure that we do it right this time? I certainly would not want to in my personal life. I have learned a lot that I had to fix in my life – No Fear, No Anger, Unconditional Love, Unconditional Forgiveness, and more. Those are like keywords pasted on my heart all the time for a constant reminder. And I am sure you wouldn't want you and your family to go through those same losses due to mistakes made in the past.'

'Of course we wouldn't. It took a lot out of me and my family,' he said.

'Correct!' I acknowledged and added, 'The world has gone through so much pain the past few decades. Now it is about reaching the best possible outcome.'

I elaborated based on the research I did on the Many Worlds Interpretation, 'With the repeats, there are also permutations to everything – even our worlds. We could move along together to the same New World, or maybe different ones. In this Multiverse, we have infinite web of alternate timelines which are constantly branching off and creating distinct and coherent worlds. We could manifest a world with no wars. It's possible. We live in a Multiverse of gargantuan proportions!'

Before going any further, I emphasized on what was really important, 'Very simply, it would be great if we reach our best possible outcome. Be it Heaven on Earth and/or a Type I Civilization and beyond. For us to finally have access to unlimited energy around us – that free energy. Think about it, we would not be warring anymore. It would no longer be about the "oil" agenda,' I continued, 'But not just that, it is time to unleash the divinity within ourselves, giving us access to a limitless potential.'

I paused for a while. I had been talking too much. But I could see that he was still listening attentively. That encouraged me to continue.

'I was shown the vision of the Golden Door, I was told these words " ... there are many doors waiting for you ... there is one very special door, the Golden Door, and it is waiting to be opened." Many opportunities or many worlds open to me for my choice. So I feel that the Golden Door has manifold meanings. The Golden Door as the golden opportunity for our highest Selves. The Golden Door as the doorway for entry to the New World of Heaven on Earth. Both versions somehow in-sync - not asynchronous, but in synchronicity – as if tied to each other,' I explained.

Affirming further, I said, 'Planetary-wise, we simply need to make sure that Heaven on Earth becomes a reality. It is "our" New World. To discover the Keys to opening the Golden Door to this New World of "ours".'

Mr Aminuddin nodded slowly and said, 'And now we need to go through this transition carefully and make sure we make the right decisions.'

Although he appeared pleased to learn something new, there was a distinct strain on his face. I knew that he had a lot to critique about what I shared. There was so much that went against traditional thinking.

He finally said, 'I will think through what you shared with me. I can't say that I agree or disagree with everything. But it is very thought-provoking. It sets your mind thinking.'

I informed Mr Aminuddin, 'These are simply experiences and observations. I believe that with time, God will reveal more. We need to just keep our hearts and minds open so that we can receive more.'

He said, 'Valid point. Now, may your New World and my New World be the best world possible ... so I will wait for the book "Transit to Type I"?'

I had not yet informed Mr Aminuddin about the change from the trusty mnemonic of a book title "Transit to Type I" to the new ethereal and mysterious name.

I replied, 'Actually, I have decided to change the title to "Through the Golden Door". I felt it was apt due to all the visions and divine interventions. I discovered that it was not just science. It is the spirituality with the science, and what happens in the spiritual realm determines what we see and experience in reality,' I continued, 'Anyway, I was misled before by my earth-bound mind. Thankfully in 2012, God intervened to steer me in the right direction. It's the heavenly realm driving the changes. Science simply explains the building block. Earth is the physical.'

He acknowledged my words, 'Makes sense. What will be the overall theme of the book?'

I shared, 'The slogan of the book will be "The Doorway to Our Advancement." My advancement or uplifting as I see it alongside with people around me, society and nations. I see it all inter-linked, and happening at the same time, not one without the other. I want to feature the Keys for this advancement, this elusive Golden Door. I am still trying to discover what they are.'

I put in my last say before we closed our enlightening discussion, 'So through this book, I will share what I have experienced, discovered and learnt from the people who I feel have been arranged to meet with me to pass on this valuable information. I will consolidate everything and add my observations. All we need to do is work on reaching our highest Selves, discover our God-given gifts and talents and pursue the tasks which were assigned to us diligently so that we can altogether, as One, manifest Heaven on Earth.'

>
>
> **Many Worlds Interpretation** is that each universe branches into innumerable new universes every time a quantum measurement is made. All possibilities are therefore realized. Scientifically, it postulates simply that the wave function never collapses; it simply branches into its own unique world-line, resulting in every possible outcome of every situation existing in physical reality.
>
>

Peace in the Heart

Very much like Mr Aminuddin, my father was very passionate in giving his opinions on the state of the political affairs. Atypical of seniors of the Singapore Pioneer Generation, my father was in his early 70s and he had seen the full spectrum of what Singapore a tiny young nation has gone through. From its own painful zero point experience and then rebirth towards growth and prosperity. He was amongst the small pool of pioneering witnesses of the rapid transition from war and strife in the 1940s to peaceful, simple community living in the 1960s and finally to the fast-paced (and still peaceful) urban living from the 1980s onwards.

In his lifetime, he saw Singapore reach 1st world from the 3rd world country he was brought up in. He could share how Singapore had transformed significantly. Yet, politics was not his main focus. He was at peace with his love for oriental rugs and Persian artistry. Yet, even greater peace was derived when he spent time in prayer and reading the Holy Qur'an. I dropped by his store at midday after several morning meetings. Located in the rustic and eclectic Kandahar Street (close by Arab Street), as I walked in, he was sitting on his favorite Chinese antique chair. Where he was sitting was partially blocked by a towering pile of historical, art and religious books which he collected and referenced over the years.

On his desk sat his old fashioned FM radio. The BBC radio station was tuned in and a feature came up on the escalating threat by the ISIS, among many other pending torments the world was going through. I could see a sense of sadness in him as he listened in. Reminiscing, he shared a valuable point that we have created our own hell on Earth through conflict and wars. He continued to talk about how he was barely a two year old toddler when the most prominent event in the history of Malaysia and Singapore occurred; the invasion by the Japanese Imperial Army, where many Singaporeans and Malaysians regardless of race, language or religion took to the jungle to resist and defy the invaders. Many died heroic deaths, tortured and executed by the *Kempeitai* (military police arm of the Imperial Japanese Army) rather than live as traitors and slaves. They were fighting for their right to be free.

We discussed about the peace and tranquility that Singapore has been experiencing for many years now. There is no longer a need for an average Singaporean to fight to be free; to the point that it has reached an enviable level compared to other countries around the world. Even though the fact is that society, in general, tends to gravitate towards conflict. Conflict between ideologies, conflict between religions, conflicts of self-interest. That shifted my mind towards the mass media. Just turn on the TV. In our sitcoms we watch people who live their lives constantly at odds with each other. In our reality television programs, most are fueled with drama and conflict with each other. Movies of bloody warfare become box office hits, and let's not forget the animated video games that bring to life fantastical dreams especially to the teenage demographic who are the most susceptible. Information out in the open that some governments spend most of their time and money on exacerbating conflict.

From the mountainous book pile, my father dug out a book titled "The Forgotten Warriors" compiled by Captain S. S. Yadava of the INA (Indian National Army). The sub-heading "Indian war of independence 1941 – 1946". The book featured my grandfather. He had sailed the Komagata Maru alongside 150 passengers in his 20s from Hong Kong to Vancouver. Enduring two months of hardship and sometimes at the brink of starvation, facing hostile press and the failure of their legal battle, the passengers were finally forced to return to India on 23rd July 1914. After which, they undertook another arduous journey and finally landed in Singapore. The land of promise and opportunity, trumpeted as the gateway to Asia. With the nightmarish yet battle hardening experience of the Komagata Maru, my grandfather was so determined to liberate India from the British yoke that apart from giving financial aid to the liberation movement, he also sacrificed his three elder sons to join the INA.

In light of all this, I was grateful that I was born and spent most of my life in a country where conflict to the level of a war was virtually unthinkable. The Oct 2013 riots in the streets of Little India was probably the worst that we could fathom, the riots started due to the loss of an Indian labourer's life when he was run over by the bus driver who refused to let him board the bus. It was enough to shake Singaporeans up.

There were times when my father would feel disturbed by what he and his family had gone through. The early years in Singapore. As such, I changed the topic to speak about Heaven on Earth, explaining it with the same recounting of events as I did with Mr Aminuddin. I emphasized that when Heaven would be created on Earth would be entirely up to us. We had to do the works to make it happen.

I spoke with idealistic values, 'Imagine no wars, no world hunger, only world peace and Unity'.

I shared with him about my very recent vision of the Heavenly Courts and about how it gave me insights about a heart ruled duty-based society which deals with conflicts in an ambiance that may be considered the archetype of judicial courtrooms, both in decorum and procedure. I went on to share about the explanation of the scientific scales explaining how we were in the transition from a Type Zero civilization to a Type I civilization and beyond. I made sure I explained slowly as there was a lot of new information for anyone to absorb.

As I looked up, I glanced at the Persian miniature painting that hung just below an old wall clock my family had since the 70s. The painting depicted men on horses in battle. The image of the Horses played on my mind. First the winged horses within the Blue Crystal Dome vision, then the Akhal-Teke golden horse statue at the Art Festival, and now this painting of Persian battle horses. Perhaps a sign? Could the Golden Horse be a Key, perhaps a symbolic one to opening the Golden Door? A symbolic representation of the profusion of energy within this planet, the quantum power of God within ourselves.

I took out the blue gemstone from my bag and placed it on my palm for him to see. A daring move as I knew that it would be hard for a person of the older generation to accept, let alone most people on average. Many would strike it off as a farce. I did not want him to think I was into gemstones or diamonds or gold, based on some kind of perverse obsession or for the sake of material gain. I had no attachment to physical things. I wanted him to know that it was just a proof of what we and the Planet Earth were meant to become. Most of all, I wanted to continue sharing as I did with Mr Aminuddin and some other people who I felt were ready to hear my story.

Next to the Persian miniature painting was a distinct carpet that hung on the wall. A rare and antique Persian rug with pure gold interwoven. My father had shared with me in my younger days about how the foundation of that carpet was of fine 24k gold thread, intermittently woven along the warp thread (the thread in-laid).

His words way back then, '... the warp thread is very slowly combed down with a wooden comb so as to not damage the gold thread.'

That made me realize that we were likewise - gold was the foundation of ourselves with the gold particles weaved within our skin; and how we were gradually transforming as we allowed ourselves to be combed down to our zero point.

My father asked inquisitively, 'Where did these gemstones and gold coming from?'.

I pulled out my "Black (White) Whole, Heaven in the Heart" theory explained in simple terms.

I replied, 'Gemstones and gold may be created from within, the power of our heart. Or they could have been given by Angels ... as a sign.'

I stumbled through the sentence hoping my replies would be well received. Then some news from the radio interrupted. It was broadcasting a stream of events – depicting Hell on Earth; suffocating the lives of millions. I went onto share about the vision of Heaven – the Golden Road, Trees with Golden Canopies, the Towering Golden Spirit Man (Spirit Woman) floating in and out of the realm.

'It is a time for us to become like Towering Golden Souls,' I stated openly.

I explained the visions on the Golden Souls, the Portal, Open Heaven and more.

I concluded, 'The question we need to ask ourselves is, how do we ever expect to resolve issues between nations when we are unable to resolve issues within ourselves and our families? If our hearts are at war, we would not be able to experience Heaven in our hearts. What we have in our hearts is reflected out and manifested in the physical. I believe that if more and more of us realize this, we can literally create Heaven on Earth.'

That was my simplified explanation.

The topic of the gemstone would have been hard to swallow by any one person, but I was glad that I could open up and share. I prayed that the fragments of evidence of a brighter world gave him a sense of hope. I also decided to give him the blue gemstone as a gift. Perhaps a blessing. What I received in distress to comfort me, I decided to give to him. A quantum entanglement of positivity from one particle to another.

Seeding the Idea

There was another vision that was shown a number of times but with a different setting from the Amphitheater vision. I was shown a room, and at the center of the room stood a long table with chairs. The room was large enough to seat perhaps 10 or more people. I could not see the number of chairs clearly. I wished I was more attentive and had counted them carefully. They were all beautifully carved arm chairs, but what was significant was that the seats were empty.

I did not think much of the vision at that time. Moreover, I could not understand what that room was or even where it was. As it was shown again and again, it made me wonder about its significance. Clearly the room had a special purpose. If the Amphitheater vision was a view of the heavenly judicial system, was this vision a view of a room for discussion, decision-making or arbitration? Perhaps a room for communion between beings to discuss an important task for resolution.

I consulted Tyler, the self-declared Watchman, to get his view on this. He had the immediate "no need to think and analyze" answers as he claimed to capture answers direct from the Holy Spirit of God.

Tyler's laconic reply, 'These are our seats.'

'Our seats? I have seen this vision many times over the past one year or more,' I asked.

'It's an invitation,' Tyler explained.

'Really? That's a pity. I have been ignoring that invitation all this while,' I whimpered.

'Each person is numbered. Once the person sits on it, the density changes,' he said.

I toyed with the idea of this Special Room and said, 'Perhaps the room with its seats are for discussion, arbitration, or for Watchmen like you. Maybe it is an invitation for the Overcomers as you mentioned before?'

'When one sits, one will know,' Tyler replied in his usual robotic and emotionless manner.

I thought for a moment and replied, 'Well, the next time this room is shown to me, I am going to pay serious attention to it.'

I thought again and said, 'However, based on the limited knowledge I have now, I feel that it could be for governance.'

'Maybe,' Tyler said.

During one of my online discussions with Marianne, she had made this statement, 'A spiritual battle that has being going on in higher dimensions. It is now going on in the 3rd dimension, here on Planet Earth!'

Higher dimensions as in 4th or 5th dimension, or higher? Whatever the purpose of those spiritual seats, it was time to fill them. If there is a spiritual battle going on that is invisible to the naked eye, then we had to re-think how we fight war.

Marianne's thought-provoking words, 'Not by Might. Not by Power. But by Spirit! God is shifting the way we do War.'

That stayed with me. I made it a plan that the next time I meditated and if that room appeared, I would ask what governmental protocol should I learn if I decide to take a seat. If it was a room for governance, by taking a seat I could play a part in directing the battle of Light over Darkness. Through my Spirit Woman, specifically around matters related to war between nations, war between societies and religions and more. On the contrary, if a seat is not offered to me, I would simply continue with my standard prayers praying for the speeding up of my awakening and of my families' as well as everyone else's on Planet Earth, so that a manifested war on Earth would indeed be unthinkable.

Our battles could be limited to the spiritual level, in the heavens between Light and Darkness, with no bloodshed in the physical realm. While fighting the war by Spirit, in the earthly realm we had to carry out some real actions for peace. Perhaps the criminalization of and global ban on war and armed conflict. Or the permanent ban on the design, production, or sale of weapons systems including nuclear weapons, space-based weapons, and conventional weapons including the maintenance of offensive armed forces. How about the imposition of heavy criminal penalties for violation and astronomical fines, for individuals, organizations, and nations who break these laws and fundamentals? Other than actions, ideas to play a significant role too.

Actor and comedian Robin Williams once said, 'No matter what people tell you, words and ideas can change the world'.

Everything we see in our physical world started as an idea, an idea that grew as it was shared and expressed. I saw the idea of war being unthinkable growing and manifesting into the physical, through a number of steps as part of the order of the New World. The idealistic destination being where nations unite to become global families of love. The combining of the three water worlds: the Indian, Pacific and Atlantic oceans. The harbinger of the new epic of humanity through the realization that "Love" is the solution for everything. First and foremost, Love, Respect, Caring and Peace all start in the family. It is where parents teach their children the right values to have respect for everyone and each other. That is the nucleus which forms society and spreads into a wider spectrum.

Marianne's words, 'The greatest form of government is Love!'

Thinking about "Love" which brings peace, and its nemesis "Hate" which triggers war, I remembered the harrowing tragedy of the 3 year old Syrian boy who was the victim of chemical weapons in December 2013.

'I'm going to tell God everything!' were his screams of pain and turmoil.

The Syrian boy's last words that scattered across the news media worldwide.

Marianne's words highlighted this, 'We, as in YOU and I, are an expression of a realm of government that God is choosing to host on the face of the Earth. The omniscient, omnipresent and omnipotent God actually chooses to live within us.'

Those who lead or initiate war, they are so far from their true expression. As hosts for this realm of government, we as individual human beings need to have perpetual feelings of "Love" in our hearts. This goes back again to the very basic nature of who we are – Unconditional Love. And this leads naturally to the notion that "war is unthinkable" burning in our hearts.

As we continue on this Golden Road for ourselves and Planet Earth, we may reach a time in the New World where it will be more glorious to fight against ignorance than to die on the field of battle. Perhaps the countries we once wrote off as being in a perpetual political upheaval and war would have a chance to finally redeem themselves. Every country will experience peace as it will be the flavor of the new era of the Golden Planet. The discovery of a new scientific Truth will be more important than the squabbles of diplomats. Even the newspapers of our own day are beginning to treat scientific discoveries and the creation of fresh philosophical concepts as news. The newspapers may give a mere "stick" of a column in the back pages to accounts of crime or political controversies, but will headline on the front pages the proclamation of a new scientific hypothesis.

The Golden Door towards a realm where spirituality and worldly life overlap. It is duty-based, where every individual and entity owes duties to each other, based ultimately on the overriding duty to promote justice and fairness so as not to transgress the limits of God. Hence, "Love" through justice and fairness.

15

The New Commodity

*A renewed marketplace,
An elevated consciousness,
No hidden secrets,
No extremities or misuse,
No mine or yours,
No longer everyone for themselves.*

*Opening up to a new paradigm
Of transparency and Truth
Of cooperation and sharing.*

*Reflecting back on a catastrophic world event
March 2014*

A mysterious plane disappearance that shook the world on the 8th of March 2014. It was the MH370 flight from Kuala Lumpur, Malaysia to Beijing, China. On that day itself, after its alleged disappearance or crash, there were no signs of passengers and no sign of the plane.

I recall, during that time, how my heart sank as I realized how so close to home was this unfortunate event. Three days passed since the tragedy and it was sad to hear that there was still no sign of the passengers as well as any hopeful discovery of the plane. The MH370 was a Boeing 777. Consequently, the MH17 which happened only a few months later on the 17th of July, and which crashed killing all on board. The number '7's dispersing all over sparking my inner thoughts about the Mystical 7.

In terms of the MH370, I remember tracking down the news broadcasts of all the latest developments. There were a whole host of theories of what could have happened including some mind-boggling conspiracy theories - from pilot error or suicide, engine failure, cabin fire, electronic warfare experiment, terrorism, military strike and more. There was also the speculation about corporate espionage as there were claims that 10 passengers were all from the same company holding patents.

When the third day came, with the news that the plane was still missing, I had spent hours and hours of cogitation thinking back and forth about what could have happened. So distraught by the event at the time, that I had pressed on God asking Him for the Truth. I recall how within minutes I was caught in the Spirit. Snapshots of the scenes appearing in a random order. There were some very lurid and disturbing scenes. And there were some which were almost scandalous. What if more people did what I did, that is, to go into meditation and ask for the Truth to be shown? What if that ability became the norm amongst human beings? The media that is scattered with so much speculation of what could have happened. The New Human could freely tap into the information themselves if and when they wanted verification.

The last time I met Mr Aminuddin at his home, I had showed him abstracts of the book "The Forgotten Warriors" where my paternal grandfather and his two sons (my uncles) were featured. Mr Aminuddin knew that the upcoming seminar would be within my interest. It was about the uncovering of the secrets of the disappearance of Netaji Subhas Chandra Bose. Netaji was the Prime Minister of the Provisional Government of Free India based initially in Singapore, and then in Rangoon (Burma). Netaji and my grandfather were colleagues at the INA branch in Singapore. The precise circumstances of Netaji's death remain shrouded in mystery.

There was the scholarly view that Bose died in an air crash and that theories that state otherwise are incorrect, speculative, mythical, and possibly fabricated. Very similar to the MH370 case with many possibilities on the table. Taking it as another invaluable learning experience, I made it a point to attend the seminar.

An Order for the Truth

The day of the seminar arrived. It was attended by a small group of people and started off with a welcoming speech by Mr Aminuddin to a mix of patriotic and historically curious audience. He then passed on the microphone to the main speaker. The main speaker began to speak at length and with boldness about all the evidence uncovered coupled with contradicting eyewitness accounts.

The main speaker said, 'There has to be a movement towards Government declassification as government files are meant to be public property!' he added, 'There were voluminous files in the government office out of which several were Top Secret and some so sensitive that even the names could not be disclosed.'

He showed snapshots of the confidential documents on the projector screen of the seminar room. He highlighted how the wordings of the documents were long-winded and evasive. The reports appeared doctored to the point that some of the sentences were white-inked or taped on to make them illegible.

Flabbergasted, cringing his forehead and waving his hand as if it was utter nonsense, the speaker said, 'Oh and they said disclosure may lead to havoc in the law and order of the country!'

As the main speaker closed his speech, an avalanche of questions from the audience poured in. The common question was why the Truth was only coming out decades after the reported death of Netaji.

Reflecting on the main speakers words, ' ... lead to havoc in the law and order ... ' and simultaneously reflecting on the series of 111 and 1111 that were consistently flashing toward me.

A psychoanalysis of repeated numbers from a floor number 11 to the time on the clock of 11:11. The appearance of this series of numbers would spread across computers, microwave ovens, cars, documents, and more. Each time as I noted down their occurrence, I would try to decipher their meaning. The number 11 may represent chaos while the number 12 may represent order. Chaos before the order. A little shakeup in the nations creating chaos, before order comes into place.

Based on previous experience, when I was revealed the Truth about Siva the corrupt businessman, I was given more and more evidence that we are entering into a New World of no lies, no secrets. I imagined that to be the new order. With the constructs of the Global Mind, the releasing of gifts for people to see and prophesy as they develop deeper and deeper connections with God, eventually nothing can be truly hidden and swept under the carpet.

Marianne's words, 'God does not want anything in secret!'

The hundreds or thousands of Cloud of Witnesses who are watching everything from Heaven. They know the Truth as they see what is really happening. But most of all, with the Truth unveiled, it is about doing the right thing. And that is where the new commodity or the Heart-driven Commodity lies.

From ownership to sharing

The patent conspiracy related to MH370. The Apple versus Samsung smartphone patent wars. The patent monopoly of pharmaceutical giants. The established concepts of proprietary rights, intellectual property, copyrights, and patents manifested in corporate entities and in the sovereignty of nations. At the other end, there is the need for a free exchange of information that is necessary to meet global challenges – matching the free, abundant, limitless energy synonymous of a Type I civilization and beyond.

The delicate balance on a tendril between the two where free access and no ownership is mandatory for anything that is a basic human right. A tiny imbalance would break the symmetry of how the universe functions. Like the frost crystals that occur naturally on cold glass forming elaborate fractal patterns, copying and repeating each other. In the world of business, nothing can stop another from learning, copying, replicating from each others' ideas and innovations, and adding a small mark of individuality.

Faryal's words, 'What we create is for sharing.'

Olga's words, 'We do not own anything.'

Right now no one wants to admit that they own nothing. From one angle, it necessarily entails that we face the reality of our mortality. As we lightened our hearts, sharing and growing would come naturally like the frost crystals. Ownership becoming less and less, leading to its eventual demise as a wild possibility. The purpose of patents themselves may be redefined from legal protection and ownership to primarily a stamp of recognition and honor for the unique creation by the individual.

As we develop an increasing detachment from materialism, we may attain a global universal realization that it is no longer about control and ownership. In the process, we are hit hard so that we are forced to advance accordingly. Just as I had shifted over the decades from a lavish lifestyle to a small humble home for simpler and more nimble living.

Playing on those noble-minded concepts, I thought back on the stimulating discussions with the young lawyer, Rizwan. Meeting him again to get some insights on this would probably be a good idea.

And so we did. Instead of lunch like the last time, we would just have a coffee for a slight caffeine boost as we had so much more to discuss and mentally dissect into. We returned to the same Moroccan restaurant at Arab Street as it offered a quiet and conducive environment to talk. This time his wife would not be joining us as she had to return to Kuala Lumpur to attend to work matters. He had a few more days before he would return to the USA to complete the final leg of his short course at his university.

Enjoying the quiet and cool restaurant, intermittently disrupted by a cacophony of music and the distant sound of fighter jets. The serious practice sessions for an outstanding performance for the

49th Singapore National Day just around the corner in August 2014. The short but noisy interruption and the flood of tourists filling the streets created a foisonous ambiance of festivity and achievement. More so, a feeling of achievement and abundance.

Holding onto that thought, I said, 'In Singapore, we have been on the road-map for abundance for awhile now. Though I believe that as we allow for our true Selves to emerge, our spiritual Selves, we will change how we perceive "abundance",' I continued, 'Abundance perceived in different forms. Not just assets which a traditional bank would place a value on. Remember the last time, I mentioned about a hypothetical New World. Well, I would view it as achieving Heaven on Earth or a Type I Civilization and beyond. Or both.'

I explained the definition of Type I to him as he admitted that he was clueless about astrophysical scales.

I elaborated, 'Based on Type I, we have found the means to tap onto infinite energy sources within our planet. Not just discovering it but actually implementing it in most parts of the world. No depletion and no destruction to our planet. From another perspective which is also based on the foundation of no limits and abundance ... I see as a symptom of Heaven on Earth where the necessities of life would be available freely. Freely shared. No ownership.'

He nodded and said, 'True. In fact, the concept of ownership would be of no advantage whatsoever in a society of abundance.'

Rizwan showed that he had his criticisms about the concept of abundance, particularly how it is used in society.

He added, 'Abundance needs to be taken from the right context,' he continued, 'Without the overarching importance of duty to counter-balance the desire for self-aggrandizement and self-interest, "abundance" merely becomes a word used by new age spiritualists and multilevel marketing representatives.'

The loud piercing sound of fighter jets suddenly hit the skies again. The music played in the restaurant stopped and we saw people just looking up into the skies enjoying the show of the fancy moves of the fighter jet pilots training hard for their D-day. Rizwan walked out to the open door of the restaurant to enjoy the sights and sounds, while I stayed inside thinking through the notion of abundance and ownership.

The New World based on abundance for all, with the right intention and a duty-based approach. There may be sharing and applying all of the new technologies for the benefit of all nations. Who knows? The whole concept of funding may change to a greater focus on the project's impact on society rather than impact on profits. With such a culture in place, it may lead to the demise of the buying of a politician. The phasing out of such a common practice in many countries in order to win mega projects or to get a business agenda forward for further wealth accumulation.

Furthermore, I imagined that through the death of ownership, we make ourselves closer to becoming a society of givers. The Golden Planet based on the actual skills and talents of the individuals in the society. A collaborative sharing not based on who owns what, but who knows what. Perhaps a greater price tag placed on the latter rather than the former.

A heart-driven economy

We touched on judicial systems. Then ownership and sharing. This time, Rizwan and I planned to dig deeper into the topic of advancing societies.

Despite his busy schedule as a lawyer, he did an ample amount of volunteer work in his free time. His main voluntary activity involved fighting for the rights of a class of people which the government of his country did not officially recognize: the refugee and asylum seekers. These people had gone through tremendous trials. First, they faced persecution in their own home countries, necessitating them to flee. Second, most of them would end up living in desperate conditions. I could see the sympathy he had for these people. He felt their pain that they would arrive thinking they might be safe in a relatively stable country. Only to find that when they complete their long journey, they are extorted, harassed, detained (many of them indefinitely) and subject to administrative whipping which is in itself a terrible torture that destroys the mind and body. All because they did not have a slip of paper.

'We need a virtuous society,' Rizwan added shaking his head in dismay.

I empathized with his disillusionment. Rizwan was the archetypal "innocent" character. Although he was highly educated and very well read, he grew up as a child with a privileged and uneventful life. His recent exposure to real life after graduation and working shook him up. His "I want to save the world" gusto deflated a little, as he was naive to the distortions of the Old World. Young and barely street smart, he was suffering inside.

My own family from two generations before were immigrants. And his probably too. Though anyone would say that he would be too young to care, he did care. Contrary to the generally held belief that lawyers were cold and calculating, he felt the hearts of the people.

Rizwan said, 'Every one of us is a valuable member of society with worthy contributions in our own right.'

He was clearly referring to the refugees and asylum seekers. And I concurred with him. There is a flawed sense of entitlement in society. It's the same message all over again. For a society to heal and repair, the individual needs to be sorted out. Right down to the soul level of knowing what to do and what not to do in the right way. Going back to infusing the lessons of unconditional love at all levels, expanding into a caring society and a paternalistic governance.

To lift his spirits, I changed the topic on reading. I sensed that he was an avid reader.

I asked, 'Speaking about societies and governance, do you have a favorite book?'

Something we could dive into as I finally completed the deliciously enjoyable novel "The Agony and the Ecstasy".

He jumped to give the answer, 'Plato's best known book 'The Republic' of course! You must have read it?'

I shook my head. Although I was familiar with some of Plato's literary works, I was no cognoscenti of the vast topics he covered.

Rizwan was clearly a step above as he was an enthusiast and admirer of the great Thinker.

He spoke with elation, 'I thoroughly enjoyed his book. I would call him the father of governance. He was a great mind who was a philosopher, scientist and mathematician all rolled into one.'

Rizwan lectured, 'Plato defined the 5 regimes of government. Oligarchy was the system which distinguished between the rich and the poor. The rich became the administrators. From what I know, it was allowed in their constitution to own property and thus to both accumulate and waste money. Money is valued over virtue, mainly because of its immense pleasures. As a result, many times the leaders of the state seek to alter the law to give way and accommodate to the materialistic lust of its citizens.'

Rizwan noticed my questioning brow and quickly came to Plato's defense, 'Of course, Plato was not supportive of oligarchies at all. He abandoned its political power to seek out virtue,' he continued, 'From the Empire of Production to the Empire Consumption. We started borrowing to maintain a level of consumption as well as an empire we could no longer afford. The tantalizing illusions of the consumer culture vanishing as we head towards collapse!'

His theoretical explanation making sense for a menacing collapse (if has not happened several times already). I had seen it myself, investment bankers blink in confusion when questioned about the morality of the billions in profits they made by selling worthless toxic assets to investors. We need to start substituting the illusion of growth and prosperity for real growth and prosperity, pushing us from the new found appreciation for money to the new found appreciation for the abundance associated with our hearts.

He continued with magniloquence, 'The center of all modern society in current times is the economy, not the government. People do not care who is in government if they are starving. The economy is the structural system through which self-preservation is restored. Every economy functions by an economy of exchange. All nations are built based on the structure of the economy.'

Rizwan's harping on the word "economy" to prove a point. From stricter banking regulations as a form of reaction to the financial upheavals towards a transition to a softer and minimalist approach. The borrower will no longer be a slave to the lender as it is seen to destroy relationships. There may come a day commemorated as the World Debt Forgiveness Day where there is global forgiveness of all public and private debts. Perhaps a faster launchpad towards the New World where there is an alleviation of all rules, systems or activities that create fear and anxiety keeping us in survival mode. If only this would have happened years ago, those invisible shackles around my heart, the heavy burden of debts would be gone. Now that I had taken years to clear that off, it made perfect sense that the heaviness of debt would simply hold us back from becoming lighter beings.

Rizwan gave an example to explain another point, 'If people were stranded on an island that was abundant with natural resources producing more than the necessities for survival, then a monetary system would be irrelevant. It is only when resources are scarce that money can be used to control their distribution. In a resource-based economy all of the world's resources would be held as the common heritage of all of the earth's people, thus eventually outgrowing the need for the artificial boundaries that separate people – this is the unifying imperative.'

The fall of the Upside-down Kingdom (Old World) where "who owns more" rules, winnowing falsehood from the Truth. The idealistic New World based on a truly resource-based economy empowering each and every person on the planet to transact with whom they want to transact with, without being constrained by location. It allows them to be the very best they can be, not to live in abject subjugation to a corporate governing body.

I noted down what we had talked about and learned so far, perhaps it would be useful for my book. Rizwan was a mentor of another form. He was a perceptive intellectual I could bounce my ideas off. What he spoke about were practical concepts for implementation. However, the other element which I felt was just as crucial, if not more, is changing how we observe things. Abstract as it may sound, by simply "Be"-ing and alternating our spiritual eyes to see things in the best possible light, it can create a dramatic shift in our physical world.

The Double Slit Experiment, which involves a series of single photons (light particles) fired at a solid plate, demonstrates this perfectly. Explained in a highly summarized and simplistic way, the results of the experiment shows that our physical reality is based on what we observe. The observation creates the reality (the particle). Like a conscious being it is aware that it is being watched. So if we observe that the society we are part of is "virtuous" then we manifest a "virtuous" world as part of our reality. So based on what we observe, one world becomes the reality, even if there are many world possibilities.

Thinking aloud to myself, 'If I shift the way I observe "things" in this world – money, abundance - the world I will be part of will switch.'

Almost too theoretical and too impalpable to imagine in reality even though the experiment proves it. Changing the way we "observe" things is crucial, though I could never forget how the "death" of myself changed and switched my entire world literally.

Feeling that it could be the right time, after all we had met twice so far, I said to Rizwan, 'I would like to share something with you, Rizwan. It's a little off the topic, but it's relating to this world in a way.'

'Sure, go ahead,' he said.

'The last time I told you about my dream of a judicial amphitheater. But much more than that, I had the experience of the "death" of myself. I felt a major awakening, a resurrection of a "new" me after that as a result,' I shared.

'I see,' he said.

'So liberating, so freeing, I can't explain.' I said trying to describe the sensation.

As I opened up a little more about my zero point experience, I could see Rizwan's IVY league mind processing the information sedulously.

I explained, 'The New World, as the truly "virtuous" society you are talking about. I feel that it reflects perfectly well that this Old World is going through a death too, a resurrection to something new.'

Rizwan answered quickly, 'When we die, we awaken. Death is the doorway to Truth, to Reality, to Transcendence. The doorway to the True Reality. The challenge is to transcend the falsehood, the life of this world (*Dunia*) and awaken to that True Reality.'

I added, 'The falsehood of the materialism of this world. The True Reality that resides within our hearts.'

A flashing "heart" symbol instead of the "dollar" symbol in my mind's eye. I imagined Adriana the Mystic had accumulated many "heart" symbols representing unconditional love and unconditional forgiveness. Both shaping our True Reality.

A reminder to move away from the entitlement modal to a shift in ideology that entitlement is from within. With that in mind, I imagined a New World's economic system that will be about nurturing relationships through compassion. A system that is almost alive with a heart, where love, joy and peace are a by-product to churn out greater creativity. A stronger economy built on the multiplying effect of creativity, not the multiplying effect of numbers. If the heart is the commodity, then it is the time to transform our hearts to seek righteousness and humility. Our walk and our talk - patient, mild and compassionate like the saints of the past, like the Men in the White Linen.

An awakening realization from the fallacy of the external to the real treasure which is within ourselves waiting and ready to be manifested. The gold manifestations embedded within the skin as a sign to us that the gold was the wealth emanating from within our hearts, our DNA.

'All gold which is under or upon the earth is not enough to give in exchange for virtue' ~ Plato.

An eager volunteer from the Singapore Heart Foundation approached our table asking for a donation.

The Foundation's simple slogan, 'Your Heart, We Care'.

Synchronicity in action to fortify the message that the heart "rules". A sustainable commodity that could one day even be measured as our hearts already have an intelligence code embedded within. And this heart code generates a quantum field with each cell imprinted with memories. To keep working on cleansing our hearts. To allow that torus energy flow to become more expanded and harmonious as we expand our Spirit Man (Spirit Woman). Regaining respect through the pureness of a person's actions, no matter how big or small.

Taking it further, to cooperate in loving partnership rather than to compete. I could see a greater meaning blossom out from the vision of the Blue Crystal Dome. The sacred geometry designs engraved on the dome's surface depicting the coming together of human soul parts by the billions. A cooperative tapestry of souls where everyone is doing something different but is not aware of it consciously. The remoulding of the Darwinian principle of "survival of the fittest" to shift to cooperating to become the fittest. Cooperation is abundant in nature. A New World where cooperation reaches full form, not just in tattered pieces here and there as it is now. Becoming the New Human as elevated beings with a passion to deliver to the best of their individual ability without the need to compete with other. Each person enjoying the fruits of doing what they love during most hours of the day.

With full blown cooperation, there may be no pull towards deception, secrets and lies. If our consciousness was nurtured as a valuable commodity, heartwrenching situations such as the MH370 or the disappearance of leader such as Netaji, may one day be unheard of. Corporate espionage obliterated as the need to gain or hold onto power would be out of the question. Alternatively, if the cause of the flight disappearance was engine failure, it would have been prevented as the correct measures would have been taken. For more and more of us to work towards more heart-conscious acts, with the need to give, rather than extort. A re-positioning that the nation that has the highest proportion of human beings with a high level of consciousness become recognized as the most advanced.

Double Slit Experiment: In this experiment, a series of single photons (light particles) are fired at a solid plate that has two slits. On the other side of the solid plate, a photographic plate is set up to record what comes through those slits. If one neglects to observe which slit a photon passes through, it appears to interfere with itself, suggesting that it behaves as a wave by traveling through both slits at once. But, if one chooses to observe the slits, the interference pattern disappears, and each photon travels through only one of the slits. It goes back to acting like a particle. In other words, the observer collapsed the wave function into a particle simply by observing, and that creates the existence of particles. Light fluctuates between a particle and a wave. The observation creates the reality (the particle). Like a conscious being it is aware that it is being watched. As a result, quantum physics debunks materialism, debunks realism.

This is where the **Many Worlds Interpretation** comes in for some justification. When we observe, one world becomes the reality, even if there are many world possibilities.

16

Unity

God as the Vine
While we are the Branches.
A unified Tree of Life.

A spiritual integration
A God-Man Singularity,
Commanding things to happen.

During the tough times of entrepreneurship, I used to stay at times at backpacker hostels. Times when one did not have a choice. This was during a business trip with the motive of trying to save every cent. It was funny how I would pack my business attire along while the residents at the backpacker lodge were all casual. Brought up as a child with a silver spoon, this was a test of my Ego pushing me down to greater humility.

There was an Olde Worlde backpacker's hostel in Little India which was just a short walk from the Arab Street vicinity. It was nestled among the Singapore shop houses still standing with grace for at least 50 years on. Because it doubled up as a cafe, whenever I was around the area I would make it a point to have a taste of their gourmet coffee. I enjoyed the coffee and I enjoyed revisiting hostels as it reminded me to stay humble and always be grounded.

Singapore
Early August 2014

There was an Indian lady who appeared to be living there as I did see her a few times. I sensed her watching me more out of curiosity. Thinking that I was from India, she struck up conversation with me hoping that she could find another person she could speak to in her mother tongue.

She introduced herself shyly as Deepa. A soft spoken lady, petite with long tightly braided black hair, Deepa looked like she was in her late 20s or early 30s. Dressed conservatively, she was in that way a younger replica of the wife of Siva. A trained linguist, she decided to forgo her profession for her domestic duties in her marriage. Despite her career sacrifices, and leaving her family in India to be with her new husband in Singapore, he mistreated her with a life of neglect and humiliation for nine years. Love and joy were absent from her life throughout her marriage. So now, she was in the midst of a divorce battle. The mounting unpleasantness of accusations and lies hurled at each other made it even more challenging.

Awake everyday at the crack of dawn, Deepa would tuck herself away to the farthest corner of the hostel balcony and diligently recite chants from the Hindu Scriptures. This she did both in the mornings and evenings. She reminded me of the Balinese women I met in Ubud who were known to dedicate one-third of their lives to ceremonial offerings and prayers, taking a fair amount of discipline and devotion.

This dainty linguist was from a wealthy Hindu family in Kerala, India who had unfortunately disinherited her after her decision to get a divorce. They considered her a failure and refused to see her or offer her any help during this ordeal. As the legal battle took months, Deepa had to self-finance her stay. She was willing to stay in a hostel packed with bunk beds with 20 women in a large room, and lived like that for months. Unlike my stay which was just for up to two weeks. I found it dreadful at times as there were just two bathrooms to share, and the lights in the bedroom would sometimes be on all night making it really hard to get a good night sleep. By far, she was ahead of me. I would not have been able to handle it for 6 months as she had.

While Deepa struggled with her divorce battle, she devoted her free time mentoring other women who suffered at the hands of abusive men. She would make an effort to speak to a troubled stranger on the street to find that she could help transform their life. Any extra time was spent at homes of girls and women who were either abandoned, impoverished or homeless. An epitome of humility, with a philanthropic nature in the sense she gave as much of her time as she could. Sharing the same religious heritage as the well known chef-turned-social worker Naranayan Krishnan, being born a Brahmin which is considered the Hindu upper class. While Naranayan gave up his prestigious job as a top hotel chef to feed the homeless and mentally disabled in Tamil Nadu (India), Deepa was an unknown doing charity at a much smaller scale. Also a close resemblance to Adriana, who did not allow her personal traumatic life and the fact that she was "only" an Indonesian maid, stop her from taking the chance of doing great things.

Deepa said, 'Simply staying at a cheap hostel has been a shock for my family. They simply cannot understand. They would say to me "How can you share a room with so many strangers!" I don't know. But this experience has made me realize that we all come together. Here we are casteless, ageless, genderless and so on. Men and women sleeping in the same hall together. All with the same bunk beds, no bigger or smaller. No barriers created by money or status,' she continued, 'Most times it is peaceful, with very few complaints of disturbances. And if there are any, they are rather minor. This is how the world should be.'

I could not agree with her more. Not too long ago during my business travels, I had the privilege of staying at luxurious 5-Star hotels where the residents at my floor level were dressed in glamour and glitter, overshadowed by the blank look on their faces with a rare hello. Deepa was wise beyond her years. I felt that I could mentally connect with her a lot better than some of the wealth-ridden entourage at these big hotels.

Deepa said, '$18 per night at this hostel. Yet, I feel the warmth and love which you rarely feel in a society like Singapore. Face it, people have little time for each other here. People in big cities can be cold, with some exceptions of course.'

I agreed.

She reminisced, 'But I found warmth in a hostel, like you would feel in a village in India, which I know sounds so strange.'

As soon as she said that, a casually dressed slim silver-haired gentleman, possibly in his mid 50s, walked in the cafe lounge area of the hostel.

Deepa recognized him instantly, 'Oh hi Peter! Meet my friend from Singapore.'

She gestured with her right hand calling me forward to meet with her fellow hostel mate. We shook hands.

Deepa said without hesitation, 'Incidentally I was talking about the warmth of 1-Star living in a hostel. Peter here is a visiting Chemistry professor at a local university. He is from Germany. Although Peter stays at a 5-star hotel, for about one or two weeks during his quarter-yearly visits to Singapore, he spends almost all his free time mingling with us at this backpacker's hostel. Now, who would think that?'

The Professor said, 'In these big hotels, there is so much separateness. Tourists come in their bus loads and there is very little interaction other than within their own tour group. Being extra friendly with a chat at a big hotel is much less likely. The facilities are great, yes, but I come here to feel the heart, the Unity of the residents. I just come to this hostel after work for the coffee and company, then when it is time for bed I go back to my big hotel.'

As he gave out a joyful laugh, Deepa smiled and added, 'And I thought I was the only one who felt that way.'

She turned her head around to look around the hostel lounge. A couple of the laid back residents acknowledged her glances smiling back.

Deepa said, making a friendly hand-wave at the other hostel mates she wanted me to meet, 'Now that's Mehran from Iran, Syed from Egypt and Feroz who is originally from Afghanistan! His family shifted to Paris when he was 5. And you see there – it is a group of Indonesian students from an all-girls school backpacking together to explore Singapore.'

The Indonesian students waved back with great delight expressed on their faces. Dressed in jeans and T-shirt, with a stylish *hijab* pinned with crystal brooches, they were enjoying themselves interacting and meeting with the inter-racial concoction at the hostel.

Satisfied, Deepa turned to look at me, 'A heart to heart connection – a communal feeling of genuine caring. We are all at the same level. In that sense, I feel free here.'

An uncomfortable experience of sharing a large room with 20 other people for a period of six long months was her private revelation. She discovered freedom and Oneness. Free from the shackles of her community embellished in what is expected for a particular caste, status and materialism. She was at One with people of diverse backgrounds.

Segregation removed, transcending all of the artificial boundaries that separate people. Breaking the mold of a plastic society so that we can join in our hearts and minds. Towards a New World where human energy bubbles stick together because they have a common purpose and match in frequencies rather than being based on esteem, prestige or the value of their bank balances.

United in prayer

Singapore
10th August 2014

'I see a Banyan Tree. I see the number 7-1-1, 7-1-0', a prophesy spoken by a first time acquaintance. What did it mean? I did not quite understand. Yet, I was very soon to have my questions answered.

Singapore
14th August 2014

An email message from a family member, 'Dad had heart failure!'

My father was enrolled in ward 710-711 of the Intensive Care Unit (ICU). The Mystical 7 making its presence known. Was this another sign from God?

I arrived at the intensive care unit past midnight. Fortunately, the medical staff let me in. They advised me to wait until he woke up on his own and then I could go and see him. He woke up at 2am asking for some milk. They called me in and I rushed to hug him. Gently, of course, as he was wired up with tubes and needles all over. A moment of divine love. The MerKaBa of unconditional loving energy that filled the gray and gadgetry room. The medical staff tried to revive him. 14 recorded cardiac arrests.

Other than his heart, the incident had damaged his liver and kidneys. There were fears that, due to the high number of collapses, his brain may have been damaged too.

My father went through a double bypass surgery. Meanwhile, my family and I posted on Facebook inviting everyone to pray for his rapid recovery. We had response from over two hundred individuals and organizations from various religious organizations and ministries. There were even strangers (friends of friends) praying. There were emails coming in from elders of churches saying that they were arranging a special congregation just to send prayers of healing. Several *mosques* added a prayer in their service for my father. Prayers were recited at a *Gurdwara* as well as several meditation groups.

Words spoken by a family friend, 'I saw your father collapse 14 times in a span of 2 and 1/2 hours. Yet, he survived. All I can say is God was on his side that day.'

Another family friend emailed saying, 'When I heard the news, I stopped all my work and went straight to my church to pray.'

My father was soon shifted from ICU to a regular ward, which was a great relief for us all.

By the 7th day, exhausted by the drama of it all, I decided to take a break from all those days sitting at the waiting lounge of the ICU.

To capitalize on the healing power of sound, I left my iPhone next to his hospital bed to play in the background music resonating at 528 Hertz. "528" the healing frequency of love, also known as as the "miracle" tone which brings remarkable and extraordinary changes with the ability to repair damaged DNA. Putting to test my readings on Dr. Horowitz's research work with mathematician Marko Rodin on genetic structuring. Even then, we were showering him with so much love. As energy beings, we are all personifications of sound with our own unique tone, with the prayer intention of miraculous healing and love in the hearts. We were just adding greater power to the music with the frequency of love. The God-Man-Machine combination playing a part in shifting his DNA to its original and perfect state.

Taking a short break from the tumultuous turn of events, I sat with my family at the Starbucks cafe of the hospital. I was so thankful that a stream of people had come together virtually in prayer. Some of whom were complete strangers dropping a note that they had organized dedicated prayers in their place of worship. What an honor. The feeling of gratitude sank in. I opened my palms and let myself be absorbed into its beauty and repose. As far as I remember, a soft light warm and radiant swept over me. This time it was different. There was no longer an effort to sit in the right posture and keep my mind in focused meditation. It happened at an instant as a reflex action. The Spirit making its presence felt. In the midst of my reflection, it seemed to grow gold dust - in the center of my left palm, within the Great Triangle again!

The appearance of 111 and 1111 accelerated. From that day, it popped up 2-3 times a day! What did this mean? The miracle was that my father's brain was completely intact. The 2nd miracle was that his damaged liver and kidneys had healed within days. The 3rd miracle was that after being discharged from hospital, after a week's recovery at home, he was walking and back at the store. Recording in my iPhone diary Counting 1,2,3,4,5,6,7,8 – the 8th most amazing out of this world experience so far.

This really made me question the overpowering message on Unity. Was this what God really wanted us to achieve right now so that we could have a faster, smoother transit to the New World? If I had prayed alone, would my father have been alive today? If my family had prayed alone without the united strength of others, would he have recovered so quickly? The Global Consciousness Experiment confirming that shared attention and emotions have powerful effects. The tapestry of God in our DNA coming together. The consciousness, through the conversion of possibility into actuality.

I messaged Tyler and Marianne keeping them posted about the developments.

Tyler's words of response, 'This whole incident was arranged. A better word would be "pre-arranged".'

Pre-arranged? Thoughts swarmed in – the quantum entanglement, the earthly guides and mentors, the spiritual helpers and guides from the Men in White Linen to Angels.

Tyler wrote, 'Pre-arranged to perfect you. To perfect your father. To perfect your family.'

Marianne's response completed the picture on the matter of Angels, 'Definitely the presence of Angels assisting. Many people don't realize how useful they are. Do you realize that even if you are committing a sin, Angels are actually standing there waiting? They have no opinion or participation in sin whatsoever.'

As I contemplated on her words, Marianne elaborated, 'They are just waiting for the Glory and the Light to come out within you and then they can be given the mandate to do their job. Angels have been around for years and years and years, but they have not been able to do their job because we have not been able to respond correctly. And they are waiting. There are hundreds and thousands of Angels connected to your destiny that are waiting to do their job.'

Just what I needed to know about Angels. Marianne turned out to be more than a mentor. She was a true mother-figure as she gave her guidance consistently and with great care and love as I went through my journey. With the greater involvement of the Angels I could see appearing in my life and my family, I (and my family) were on the right path of bringing out the Light. An elevated Light Being I was hoping to become. Strangers, friends, family and other loved ones coming in prayer. The involvement of Angels coming in to heal. A miraculous healing hoped for and received, all beyond our wildest imagination.

Returning to the Tree of Life

The Banyan Tree was a Tree of Life. The carpets depicting "The Tree of Life" were amongst my father's finest collections. A prophetic message that he would soon be in a hospital room and ward, 711-710. After all, it was he who taught me the historical significance of the "Tree of Life". About two years before this event, he had shared an interesting perception on the "Tree of Life", intellectualizing the concept.

My father's words about two years before, ' ... interosculating between the three world levels of the ancient orient: "Paradise in the sky", the world of men (on earth) and the world below. It was believed that the three are held together by a great Vertical Axis through the center. The depiction of the Earth's axis as a Tree is very ancient in European and Oriental mythology.'

The destiny of humanity, the Planet Earth, like a carpet being woven on a loom. Underneath one cannot see what the pattern is coming out, but perhaps if we could see on high, the pattern that was beginning to show. So if we keep our hearts pure and golden, the destiny of Man will be golden. The Chinese symbolism of gold being tolerance, patience and wisdom.

There is an old Chinese saying that goes, 'With great tolerance you will be able to attain the highest esteem (position).'

If we could see with our mind's eye in the higher realms, we may see a tapestry woven of living threads of the eternal souls of Man. The Tree of Life could represent that everything starts with consciousness. The trunk of the Tree of Life may be the consciousness itself, the ground of all being. A transcendent consciousness where the material world branches out from there. When many people came together with freewill, either physically or virtually to pray a heartfelt prayer, they were united in their consciousness. The prayers strengthened with causal power to manifest.

Now reflecting that on Earth, where we should be tightly integrated and at One.

Singapore
20th August 2014

The overwhelming emotion that went into the prayers, those closest to my father crying our hearts out. After having spent several days and nights at the ICU, I felt that I had pushed myself to exhaustion.

I decided to go back to my home in Sembawang to catch up on some sleep. I had also left things in shambles and they needed sorting out. As soon as I reached home and just as I was about to close the door, I felt the raging fire of a very angry person. On my right, there she was, sitting on her sofa glaring at me through the gaps of the bars of the door of her apartment. It was the young Punjabi boy's stepmother.

His stepmother was a very large woman. Her eyes appeared cold. Her fists were clenched tightly as if ready for a fierce duel. She stood up and screamed, furious that I had intervened with her adopted children. She spewed out cutting words with the attempt to break me. One after another. If those words had form, they would look like silhouettes of demons charging from her side to raid me. All of a sudden, I felt a sharp jab through my lower abdomen. I froze as I felt handicapped for a moment. The pain lingered on for a few minutes, and then persisted on.

As soon as her screams ended, I apologized and I went into my home. I entered my bedroom and I had to lie down. I felt totally drained of all my energy, whatever was left of it. And as I lay down, I could still hear her screaming from outside. She went on and on and on.

What a verbal attack! Yet, I was still very grateful for the few miraculous days at the hospital. I told myself to keep my mind focused on those positives.

Singapore
22nd August 2014

As our families spent long hours at the hospital waiting room, we saw other families who were equally anguished.

Some were waiting with urgent questions, ' … will our mother make it?' or, ' … will our child survive?'

The intensive care waiting room was like the Black (White) Whole, where nothingness existed and everything existed at the same time. Nothingness in terms of the distinctions of race and class melt away. Everything existed as it was all about love and nothing else. It was about patiently or anxiously waiting for a loved one to recover, to return and to heal. It was about loving someone. Selfishness was the one thing that did not exist in the room. A transitory room that magnified a moment that we had to remind ourselves constantly.

It was then that I was reminded of my new friend at the Backpacker's Hostel. I thought I would go see her and share the news. The travel from my home this time was painful. The jabbing pains would come and go. At times they would intensify to become like stabbing pains, so much so that I would find it hard to walk and had to drag myself step by step. But I stayed quiet, and just hoped that it was a temporal health setback in light of an emotionally turbulent week.

As soon as I arrived at the hostel, I asked for Deepa at the reception. She had been staying at the hostel for many months so the hostel staff knew her well. They called her from her bunker. Shortly, Deepa appeared dressed rather sophisticatedly in a green chiffon *sari*, enhancing her pear-shaped figure. She was unconcerned that she was a misfit dress-wise amongst the very casual hostel residents.

Looking pale and drained, she said, 'I was just going to change and go to bed early as I had a full afternoon of interviews looking for jobs at Indian jewelry stores and boutiques. But I am very happy to see you.'

Deepa gave me a tired smile.

In no time at all, I related the entire episode to her – the full gamut of events from the vision of the Banyan Tree, heartfelt prayers by many to the stream of miracles. Injected with a dose of happiness, her tiredness just melted away. She nodded repeatedly as I described what had happened in detail, her small delicate face shone from paleness to glowing as she listened to the sheer miraculousness of it all.

Deepa added, 'In terms of coming together in Unity, as a linguist, I can relate this best with languages. Across world cultures, the first thing that creates the divide is the spoken language. However, even based on the history of languages, it proves how connected we are. There is a historical relationship between languages. The tree metaphor describes it best. An ancient source (say, Indo-European) has various branches (e.g. Romance, Germanic), which themselves have branches (West Germanic, North Germanic), which feed into specific languages (Swedish, Danish, Norwegian),' she continued, 'We have so many words, so many languages, so many dialects. For instance, ask yourself why do Eskimos have so many different words to describe "snow"?'

A polyglot description of a tree metaphor with its components which she tried to use in the real world.

She said, 'Take a look at the people of this hostel – the variations in races and languages – but all coming from a source. The Banyan Tree aka Giant Tree with its branches - a perfect fit.'

The unifying factor of the English language is one of the reasons why Planet Earth is on the transit towards a Type I Civilization and beyond. But if we look at achieving the holistic destination of Heaven on Earth, it is the unification of our hearts.

Deepa said, 'Diversity is a fact, and is necessary. If we could just remove that linguistic divide which is just an illusion, just imagine how close we all are. Our hearts so close.'

Hearts talking to each other electromagnetically. Every beat of our heart sends out a 360 degree spherical bubble at the speed of light. We are immersed into each others' heart beat. Every individual heart is closely connected with and affecting all others as well as being affected in its turn. The language of prayer with feelings being a truly universal technology. Most of those people who had prayed for my father did not know him personally at all. But they prayed with feeling. As we made our call for prayer and shared our pain sending it like a vibration through the words, they could feel the pain too and wanted to do their small part. The results proved everything.

As I was about to leave and return to check on my father at the hospital, there was a verbal buzz at the hostel about a horrific massacre of a large number of Syrians during the first two weeks of August. At least 700 members of a tribe in eastern Syria, with a majority of them civilians. Deepa and I watched the news with a numbness in our souls. As I saw my family and hundreds of friends and strangers unite in prayer for my father's recovery, at the same time I could see that there was an ongoing hidden political or religious agenda to break any Unity within societies. Disunity stifles the growth of the branches of the Tree of Life. It is only nourished when we are united in our hearts and love one another unconditionally.

A procession of quotes from the various mentors:

Marianne's words, 'We are at time where God is calling us for Unity as we bring Heaven on Earth. Heaven and Earth will become One.'

Stephanie's words, 'We are moving from Self Consciousness to World Consciousness to God Consciousness!'

Olga's words, 'We are not beings separated molecularly. We are all One.'

I looked into the palm of my hands as the sensation of a tingling electric current from the lower left side of the palm disseminating through the fingers. A possible validation from the Holy Spirit of God. Unity through singularity between Man and Machine with God. "I in You and You in Me", God is Oneness, and Oneness is God.

As if the depressing news on the killings was not enough to swallow in one day. My Whatsapp was buzzing unceasingly.

'We need a miracle now!' a message from a friend of mine.

She was the one who sent my family an invitation to the beautiful Sikh wedding at the *Gurdwara* in Singapore.

She spoke with a desperation in her voice, 'A close friend of my daughter-in-law has a large tumor in her heart! She was rushed to the ICU experiencing breathlessness, persistent cough, blue blacks, nose bleeds and drastic weight loss.'

Listening to my friend's sorrowful cries, she continued to speak, 'Oh such a wonderful happy kid, so gracious and so full of life! And to think she just got married. I feel so bad for her and her family! Please I need your prayers. I am so devastated. We are just praying.'

Coincidental heart collapses hitting both the young and old. Through my father's incident, I discovered that it was certainly not my prayers alone. No lone thaumaturge, it was certainly not the glorification of myself. I could see that it was his strong mind, his will and belief that miracles do exist, coupled with the united heartfelt prayer of many that created cohesive conduits speeding up the creation of miracle.

Hence, the formula of the Unity of prayer being tested all over again. The rounding up of individuals and groups into prayer. The Human Consciousness RNG Experiment all over again. I asked for her permission to call on the mighty hearts of prayer of the people and groups I knew, my own family included.

My friend gave out a vociferous, 'Yes!'

I said to her, 'Do tell this girl who is sick that she needs to believe deep in her heart that she will be healed completely. By believing in the miracle she will receive the miracle.'

My friend replied insistently,'Yes, yes, she does!'

And so it began. The receiver of healing and the senders of healing marrying with the agreement to be healed. The same prayer with fervor amongst family and strangers. The same calls on Facebook and emails shooting out to everyone and every group I knew who was willing to pray for a stranger or friend of a friend. The formula that was proving to work yet again.

A Whatsapp message from my friend the next day, 'She is breathing a lot easier now!'

The unbreakable formula of a united and communal society, giving hope for a New World where barriers don't exist. Unity, the true essence of who we are. We are the branches of the vines of God, designed to be genetically united.

Scientist, David Bohm (1917-1992) believed that the reason why subatomic particles are able to remain in contact with one another regardless of the distance separating them is not because they are sending some sort of mysterious signal back and forth. But because their separateness is, in fact, an illusion. Bohm suggested that at some deeper level of reality, such particles are not individual entities, but are actually system components of the same fundamental something, which we call God!

Moreover, Dr Masaru Emoto declared how crystalline structures (clusters) reflect the tight bonding with the purpose of maintaining the integrity of the information and to function with greater power. The tightness was the Unity. A possible movement towards the formation of a more tightly woven crystallized Tree of Life.

So we think we are separate, when we truly are One. Now is the time to get rid of all divisive man-made boundaries and concepts. The Tree of Life, a unified field of the energy of consciousness creating a tapestry that commands things to happen. The power of Unity had shown its face in full form. I in You, and You in Me. God is Oneness. Oneness is God. The bridging of the egoist-utilitarian where the utilitarian reach for a greater good.

With "I in You and You in Me" in the New World, the fusion may go so deep that there may no longer be a separation between "You" and "Me". How can even the most selfish person or community logically remain separate when the Truth is every being of consciousness has the God code in their DNA?

The prayers were in Unity that was sparked by unconditional love. As I was discovered through my own elevation since the Stigmatic Zero Point, the attributes of unconditional love were taken to a heightened elevation through the Divine Being. I had a sense that the Divine Being had a part to play in arranging those startling play of events; with an agenda to send out a message: a call for Unity. His message about unleashing the quantum God effect through Unity. I recall how the encounter pushed out those thoughts and feelings of "I am alone" out of me. There is no such thing as "aloneness". We are being called to return to becoming more communal. Unity within families and societies, the essence of making war unthinkable at a national level. Unity within our soul and spirit with a higher divinity.

The New World of living, working and praying in Unity; and more intimately thinking, feeling and being in Unity. Shifting our perceptions to view things in a bigger picture. The bigger picture of "Us", that is all encompassing fitting into the full harmony of the All that is.

Clusters According to Dr Masaru Emoto it refers to the crystalline structure of water. The smaller the clusters, the longer the water will retain its memory. If there is too much space between the clusters, other information could infiltrate within the space between the clusters, making it hard for the clusters to hold the integrity of the information. Other microorganisms could also enter the space.

17

Free, But Responsible

The Hallmark
Of our advancement
Comes with Unity.

But our Flowering
Comes with Freedom.

Freedom instills confidence.
Freedom inspires responsibility.

With time it brings forth an order
Sublimely free and flowing,
Self-organizing and autarkic.

Down and out three times in row with severe upper and lower abdominal pains. This time the pains so excruciating that I could barely walk. I was lying down most of the time. Desperately trying to massage the pain out of my abs, I would find myself doubling over in agony throughout the day.

Maybe this was due to the strain of almost losing my father. Or it could be due to the verbal attack by the young boy's stepmother. I was certainly not as strong as I thought I was. And based on what happened, my anxiety level shot up bringing my body's vibrational frequency to a very low level. My nights were spent in anticipation. I made requests to God to activate the spontaneous self-healing within me. If I could heal myself from dengue in a day, it was possible now as well. But I was wrong. Nothing happened! I was confused. Perhaps I had not channeled enough emotion into the prayer. Or perhaps God was planning to teach me something new.

Singapore
Early September 2014

I finally made it a point to visit a hospital for a full and complete set of medical tests. Nothing cancerous and life threatening was discovered. If I was not ill, there was something else going on with me. The instantaneous healing from dengue was God's sign to me on the new era of self-healing. Then the situation with my father was a message on being united in prayer, a greater healing power in numbers. What was the message behind this?

The appearance of 111's and 1111's continued to show multiple times daily. As the numbers accelerated, the pains escalated to match in congruence. Words that ran through my mind - 'Release! Now it is time to release!'

I called on Mei Ling to step in and help facilitate so that we could combine healing power. I believed that I could heal myself, however I was struck down so badly that my willpower was not strong enough to do it on my own. I felt I needed reinforcement. I went over to her home and saw that she had prepared a bamboo mat for me to lie down on. Her Balinese-inspired home with its eclectic scents of essential oils and Tibetan chanting sounds helped me sink into relaxation.

Mei Ling pulled out a translucent disc with concentric circles on it and placed it on my abdomen.

She explained, 'These discs will harmonize the frequencies.'

I asked, 'Hmm. I have seen this before. From what I know, they contain infused silicon crystals.'

Mei Ling continued to explain, 'Four of these discs create the quantum field and that pushes frequencies to a much higher level.'

Four to create the base shape of a pyramid.

'Place the disc standing upwards, and you get a counterclockwise flowing energy that is expansive,' she added.

Reminiscent of the swirling Persian dervishes and the spinning leaf formations on ferns.

Mei Ling said, 'Place it in reverse and the energy is shrinking and absorbing.'

With the disc in place, she closed her eyes and called on the Holy Spirit of God. As the energies raised and the momentum built up, she swayed gracefully. I felt my left hand come alive with my index finger tapping on the surface of my abdomen. Perhaps a phenomenon of self-induced surgery that was invisible to the eye. The disc was lifting up normalizing the frequency of my body to a healthy state. The 7 concentric circles on the discs. God-Man-Machine (disc).

Mei Ling brought me back to the reality of why I was there with her in the first place.

She said, 'You are releasing in acceleration. I believe it could be a decision made at the soul level. When did this all start?'

I looked back and the severe pains started as soon as I had made the decision to focus on work and activities that allow people to experience Heaven on Earth. One of them is through the book I was writing and the other through innovative technology startups I planned to be involved in.

She added, 'Well, if you are going to play a role of preparing people to experience Heaven on Earth, then you need to be prepared for it yourself.'

Mei Ling shifted the disc higher up my abdomen. I felt the tingling created by the structure of the object and the infused crystals, as the electromagnetic waves spiraled on. Based on my earlier research on the Junk DNA, crystals tap onto this dormant segment our DNA to unleash hidden memories and untapped human abilities. The activating qualities of crystals, the majestic trees in Ubud with their empowering natural energies. God-Man-Machine-Nature (Crystals/

Trees). The great intertwining. God, the CORE of everything! More evidence that God and Man had to infuse to become One, while the rest (Machine-Nature) were simply the enhancing peripherals. They were like the devices, tools or constructs as part of the mechanics of the universe. The peripherals could only do so much and take us so far. They can never be a replacement. Even if we have physically fit bodies, and supernaturally intelligent minds, the support of machinery, technology as well as nature, the real mileage depends on our intimacy with God.

Mei Ling spoke in a calm soothing voice, 'Those pains are your chains. Release them.'

I had to free myself of those invisible chains - the remaining fragments of negative emotions still left in my system.

She said, 'This is an important time to release all those emotional pains and to prepare your physical container, your body, since we are shifting to a higher dimensional Earth.'

I perceived the higher dimensional Earth asynchronous with us as a higher dimensional being. There are also discussions about the triple helix DNA. Some geneticists claim that humans may one day have 12 strands. If so, our internal biology is being altered towards a multidimensional liquid light-based crystal structured system – bringing about an expanded awareness within a perfect physical structure to contain and store the Light of God. My thoughts were spiraling like they were in a space-time continuum of their own, trying to blend all the facts together. Then I recalled Dr Rodriguez's words on our DNA during one of our intellectually inspiring meetings.

His words, 'Most of us are operating at only 2-4% of our DNA.'

Now what if 10% or 25% of our DNA is turned on? From our internal system becoming more multidimensional light-based liquid crystal, to more of our DNA utilized, it would be remarkable! Our capabilities would skyrocket. But then if that happens, we need to be responsible.

Mei Ling unintentionally broke my cognitive flow of thought as she said, 'Welcome the new energies, quieten the mind, surrender the heart and allow the inevitable changes to take place.'

I replied, 'Yes.'

Mei Ling reminded me, 'Do not swim against the current. Go with the flow. Free yourself!'

Breaking those chains that imprison, stopping the movement in circles. Finally releasing the pain that holds back the freedom. I had to allow for my physicality to experience its full metamorphosis. With all those affirmations in my mind, little did I realize that two and a half hours just whizzed past. I was feeling so much better. Lighter. And the throbbing pains were mostly gone.

As we hugged and said goodbye, Mei Ling said, 'Keep working at it and become like the Akhal-Teke. Strong, golden and beautiful inside out!'

I had to be responsible for my own health. I knew the facts and figures. I understood the scientific theory. I just had to encapsulate it as part of my very being.

Moving up the levels

Tyler heard about my collapses and he gave me his two cents worth, 'In the past three years, so much has been shown to you. You have progressed so far. Don't let these negative entities bring you down. They don't like it when you move forward.'

I stayed silent.

He advised, 'If you keep dwelling in the past, it is not going to help you. Anchor yourself in that hope so that it can propel you in the future.'

His words worried me. Was I moving backward or forward?

Tyler said, 'You are reverting to the original you.'

I almost yelled, 'No! I don't want to go back to the old me!'

Tyler said, 'It's a process of purging. An arrow is pulled back and then shot. The pull back and holding takes a lot of effort. You are this arrow and the archer at same time,' he continued, 'People of your nature, once fired up, you become very held together. Only when you start to thinking nonsense, you get the jitters.'

I understood Tyler's words.

He explained, 'There are different levels. When you are Level 1, and you think you are Level 4, you are going to attract the Level 4 demons to come and test you.'

Tyler frightened me for a moment. Move up the levels, and I was going to be tested even more? It sounded like the logic behind a digital video game. That was the last thing I wanted!

He pressed on with his words hoping to drive home a message, and said, 'You made a mental choice to go up the levels. Spiritually you need to match the level you think you are.'

The higher, the greater the tests. Seemed perfectly logical but it sounded daunting to me.

Tyler explained, 'Demons are more aware of the Presence of God than humans. It's us, humans who are doing much of nothing - thinking that we are doing things the right way, blowing our own horn, in this committee or that committee. Demons don't care much for human works but when a Spirit-filled person is around, they move away or run because it's like standing in front of a bonfire.'

I replied jokingly, 'Demons, just one of the dominion "villains" for my testing in this Upside-down Kingdom. I am done with them!'

Silently making an affirmation to myself, 'May my Spirit Woman be a towering one and burning unrelentingly!'

Tyler said after turning his head left and right scanning the spiritual realm, 'You are aware that you are being watched?'

Feeling more curious rather than nervous about it, I asked 'Who is watching me? The Men in White Linen? Or these maddening demons you are referring to?'

Tyler didn't answer, leaving me to figure it out on my own. I was hoping that it was the Men in White Linen.

I was getting a little overwhelmed by the conversation about demons when Tyler said the timely words, 'Focus on the Light, not the demons."

Thinking of the "Light", I remembered the time when Stephanie saw a beautiful display of four white stars with a purple glow floating across my forehead. Correlating the Human Uplifting Scale with what Tyler interpreted the stars to be royalty, I imagined that to refer to the higher levels on that scale. Perhaps there was hope for me to move up.

I asked, 'How many levels?'

He replied scanning with his cybernetic eyes as he always did, 'Probably thousands of levels. Many humans on Planet Earth are not even on that scale.'

He spoke with gravity, 'Vibrate so high that you cannot be touched. My interpretation from Matthew 6:33".

I checked out the exact words in the Biblical Scriptures and this was what was written:

'Seek first His kingdom and His righteousness, and all these things will be given to you as well' ~ Mathew 6:33

Divine reminder to focus on the heavens, to vibrate within the high octaves of the Glory realm.

He added, 'Once you reach a certain level, you may be untouchable. Perhaps that is Level 5 or 6. After that level, nothing can really stop you as it may be upwards all the way.'

As he explained, I imagined it to be like driving a car or riding a bike. Once we pass the basic test, it's just about fine-tuning after that. In that sense, freedom. Freedom as I could become untouchable. Responsible freedom as I had to be responsible for my new strengths and new capabilities.

It was all so fascinating. I tried to see if Marianne was still online to see if I could get further validation on the concept of levels and scales, but she wasn't. So I sent her email on this matter, and fortunately within a couple of hours she replied.

Marianne's words, 'Royalty, kingship is not about position. It's about serving. It's about responsibility to the solar system. Kingship is about who you are in the full measure of God.'

Moving up the levels to attain the full measure of God, yet staying humble and grounded always. As the divine message declared, as long as I stayed IN God, tasks and tests may come against me from left to right but they could not touch me.

Thinking about the "full measure of God" statement, and intellectualizing on the Kardashev Scale again. From what I researched this scale had at least 6 recorded levels (Type Zero to Type V). Of course, there is some mention though that it could go to hundreds of levels. Now, Type IV (Four) beings who can control or use the entire universe or Type V (Five) who control collections of universes. So Type V is when we become literally like Gods, authorized with a kingship by having the knowledge to manipulate the universe as we please. The Type V civilization would outgrow its own universe. A multiverse culture, capable of harnessing the energy of multiple universes, it would span countless parallel universes, being able to manipulate the very structure of reality.

If we ever reach that level, we'll most likely not resemble ourselves as we are now. We would be so different, so "alien" to our current thinking, that it's mostly beyond our current ability to imagine how we might evolve into that. The infinity of everything. Perhaps thousands of levels on the Human Uplifting Scale. As we moved up this scale, I imagined us becoming freer and freer - a kind of holistic freedom.

What level was I? Was I even on the scale? If over the past few years I had advanced the levels, I was certainly not going to allow myself to move backwards!

While my mind whirled with thoughts on the current topic, Tyler shifted his serious tone to a more jovial one. For an eccentric man with great depth, who would usually speak of bizarre facts relating to the spiritual realm with a lack of emotion on his robotic beady-eyed face, he suddenly put on a comedic persona of himself. I could see his split personality emerge as he started cracking one joke after another.

I stared at him feeling a little perturbed by his inconsistent behavior, and asked, 'Weren't we in the midst of talking about spiritual and planetary scales?'

Tyler tossed his head back laughing heartily, 'That's the objective!'

Embarrassed about his reaction, he said apologetically, 'Sorry for being sneaky. You see the more you laugh the easier it will be for you to shift from one level to another. It may not be the prime factor for our spiritual uplifting but it eases the chains a little so that you can loosen them off and move up.'

Of course, how could I forget? The emotion of "joy", the highest vibrational frequency of 540+ Hertz. My two little birds in rural Pakistan who were my teachers on "joy".

He asked with a kiddish look on his face, 'What's your favorite cartoon?'

A few seconds of silence. Do I answer that silly question?

I replied, 'Well ... I do love cartoons. And I have a very quirky choice of favorites too, and funny animal videos. The only thing is that I don't give enough time to watch them.'

He spoke with seriousness about a somewhat whimsical topic, 'We should be watching cartoons regularly, if not daily. Hey, I am going to be 50 but I thrive on being this child-adult.'

Being as joyful as possible – noted and not forgotten this time! I was mentally consolidating everything that was discussed so far.

I said, 'So I must add joy and laughter as part of that daily regime.'

Tyler said, 'Relax, go with the flow and just mentally be aware how important it is be joyful every moment. We tend to forget.'

I replied, 'You are right. I went through a time almost losing my father last month. I should have remained centered. No matter how difficult times are, to be joyful always.'

He emphasized, 'Yes, and keep a clear mind and your body strong.'

Justifying my past endeavors, I said, 'I have started consuming more fruits and vegetables to lighten my body and raise its vibrational frequency. And drinking more water too. I have been working on keeping my thoughts and words positive.'

Tyler said, 'Good. You realize that as a Watchman, I am only here temporarily to be your Spiritual Guide, as I am for a handful of others. Once you reach what you are meant to become, and do, I will move on. My deed will be done.'

'Yes, I understand. Thank you,' I replied with gratitude.

Previously erratic in the past, I had to be a little more structured and disciplined so that I could manage on my own. Yet not too rigid that I lose the fluidity and freedom needed during the process of my uplifting.

And so, I pulled out my iPhone to list down the activities I would follow as a guideline. A disciplined self-empowering program to strengthen myself spiritually, mentally and physically. A daily endeavor with joy and laughter as part of that regime:

- Worship, meditation and prayers (that was a standard I was practicing daily anyway)
- Each morning two glasses of water. Bearing in mind of Dr Masaru Emoto's water crystal theory, I would speak words of prayer onto the water. This act of creating holy water by enhancing the crystalline structure of the water.
- Body strength and stretching exercises.
- Barefoot walking on earth for several minutes each day. This activity makes us "grounded" human beings so that we are able to connect to and receive direct benefit from the infinite free electron source generated directly from our planet.
- Water fasts are known to improve immunity and give longevity. I decided to practice intermittent 1 to 3 day fasts every 3 months or so.
- Deep breathing exercises to strengthen the breath, raise the energy level and more. I would also breathe in high vibrational frequency essential oils such as rose and frankincense.
- A diet with lots of raw fruits, vegetables, nuts and seeds.
- The Joy – Laughter exercise. Getting a daily dose of cartoons, animal videos, comedy shows or a fun hangout with friends for a good laugh.

Several weeks passed since that enlightening discussion. I was stumbling and tenderfoot with the activities initially, but soon I got the hang of it. Within a few weeks the abdominal pains were within control. My skin gleamed with more radiance and my hair was salubrious. And spiritually, I was shielding myself against attacks of any nature that would come in my way. By manifesting Heaven in my heart, only then could I really heal, only then could I pursue my mission effectively. A revitalized Writer-Futurist-Innovator with plans to help others to move up these challenging scales.

Awareness Of Codes Of Conduct

'I guess it only happens when we see things as they really are and decide to change our lives. No one else can do it for us.'

My mother's words were a message for both of us. She had previously made a daring move and took up the position as an expat educationist in the cities and rural parts of Pakistan. The project was done and she was willing to do it again. Since the positive shift she had made in her own life, I could not help feel immensely proud of her. It was one thing to see myself break new grounds in my spiritual uplifting, it was even more fulfilling to see my own mother shift accordingly. In several weeks she was going to pack her bags to leave for Pakistan. A noble but risky educational quest, she had no qualms about tackling her own emotional tests. She was fearless.

I woke up with a realistic dream the same night my mother was set to fly off. It was a long dream and it felt as if it stretched for hours. The dream portrayed a serene vista of a sprawling emerald green park. In the horizon, there were several buildings but the scene was too unclear to figure out who or what they were. Standing in the midst of the park was a tree with a circle of children sitting under the tree. Their teacher was standing and, at times, sitting down with them. Most of them were pale and light-haired dressed in soft light garments. The teacher was tall and pale too and wore similar soft light garments. It appeared as though those garments were not really a fashion statement, just very light and flowing to match the very light beings.

Between the students and the teacher, there was a telepathic conversation going on. Among the children, there was one boy with distinct aquamarine eyes. He detected my presence and looked straight at me. I watched him as though he might evanesce at any moment. His bright eyes searching and expectant.

A pledge was being recited by the gathering of students in unison.

The words of the pledge, 'To become self-regulating and responsible. Simply knowing what to do and what not to do. Becoming truly self-confident and free. Being responsible for oneself.'

Those liberating words – perhaps a pledge that every human being of the New World would abide by. Whatever world that was, in the future or another dimension, another world, it was recited dutifully in their schools. I imagined that the same pledge would be followed with earnestness right up to adulthood. No one was forced to abide by it, yet it was adhered to, with joy. Perchance a planetary pledge flashed visually and telepathically to every human as a reminder on daily living. Or perhaps there was more.

A simply knowing what to do and what not to do.

And besides, there may be a decorum that all would follow, 'Respect your home, respect yourself and respect each other.' Three basic codes of conduct as acts of love, crafted to bring freedom.

Creating the Self-Regulators

Kuala Lumpur, Malaysia
Late September 2014

A call buzzed on the land line and I went over to pick it up. We had a visitor at my mother's home who was on her way to bid her farewell. This lady was a teacher at one of the schools in the suburbs of Kuala Lumpur. In fact, the vicinity where my mother lived, it was filled with teachers, many of whom were expats. Her name was Kathy and being a kind soul, this was the first thing she asked as she removed her shoes at the doorstep to enter the apartment.

Kathy asked tenderly, 'Oh how are your abdominal pains? Are you feeling better now?'

I nodded and said, 'Yes, much better. I had a good healer who helped work with me to heal. I told myself to stay positive and optimistic, and I drank lots of good structured water. Of course, lots of other stuff helped too.'

I shared with her the daily routine which I tried to follow as much as possible.

Kathy said, 'Very good! Good hydration is important and all that other stuff you mentioned too.'

Casually dressed in pale blue denim, and her blonde hair dressed as a bob, Kathy had a nurturing presence about her, making her easy to talk to and open up to. She was a big believer that dreams and visions provide subliminal messages. She had been following my visions and dreams for awhile. To add to the previous ones, I shared with her about the latest one regarding the school children out in the field, with all the obscure details.

Kathy exclaimed, 'What an interesting dream! The part about the pledge ... hmm. It will take awhile before we as humans can become truly self-regulating,' she paused to think, 'I do agree we are moving towards that direction, and we need to!'

Kathy was very much enticed by the dream. Extremely vocal and pronounced in her British accent, her prime objective was about getting her voice heard. Yet she was a charming middle-aged lady, who was simply disillusioned by standardized education in many countries after being immersed in it for over 20 years. She wanted to focus on the nurturing of a child's consciousness and leadership at an early age, with a healthy level of freedom. With some success, she had set up a non-profit Non-Governmental Organization with the intention to create a compassionate community between international Educators with a group of Nepalese children.

As Kathy settled onto the living room sofa, we prepared some tea.

She kept her thoughts on the dream, and said, 'There is some sense in the dream that the children are taught the pledge to drive in self-regulation at a very early age. That kind of mindset may create some fear amongst certain political leaders as they think that the children would grow up to become difficult to control. That is completely untrue of course. In fact, it raises up a new generation with self-regulation deeply ingrained within them.'

'True,' I said in agreement.

'In order to enable people, we need to do it first by enabling children, and that instills the self-regulation from young,' Kathy explained.

Kathy's spirits were suddenly lifted as the topic on "self-regulation" made her remember from a childhood a teacher who inspired her.

'Her name was Mrs Plant and she treated me like I was special, a genius in my own right. Mind you I thought I was just an average student. But that was her way of expressing an unconditional love. She had no reason to enable me. She just enabled!' Kathy shared.

It was funny that she would say that. I thought I was just an average person until God shook me out of my comfort zone and enabled me. Ten years ago it would have been unthinkable of what I knew and was capable of now. Now, He was teaching me about responsibility and self-regulation - the act of knowing what to do and what not do. As a system, the educational sector had to be put in place. More than ever before with the big changes we were already witnessing in Mankind and Planet Earth. Deep inside me I felt that perhaps the message behind the blue-eyed boy staring at me meant that it was time to enable the youth. The young Punjabi boy and his sister were the first on my mind. They were going to be my pioneering students. I had learned so much that I was going to pass on my knowledge to them. With their hearts and minds like sponges, they were going to be on a fast train!

Kathy spoke aloud thoughtfully in a deeper more serious tone of voice, 'Considering your dream ... since it must be a view into the future ... by then, can anything be withheld from children anymore? As an educationist for so long, I find that nothing can truly be hidden from them anymore.'

The New World where there will be a transparency of information like never before. Even now, it is hard to withhold anything from children as so much is out in the open. From telepathy and the Global Mind to the mass media taking its next level of birth in 2016 and beyond. What's more important is for children to be given a thorough education on the correlation between science and spirituality, validating and experiencing the true nature of

God. Quantum Mechanics made easy into bite sized chunks and application in their lives.

My spiritual discovery started when I was 19. In this current era, it may be much earlier. Children will be learning and reading everything and anything on top of solving problems for themselves. Besides, everything in the universe is in relative motion with everything else. Similarly, education should be in relative motion with everything else in this world where nothing is held back. Always be in tune and never be out of sync. Everything that we think, do, see, feel and touch should revolve around education. Education at the highest level, available to everyone following the few effulgent examples in the world.

With a combined total of 30 years of teaching, my mother had experiential view points from two very different worlds, Singapore and Pakistan. Her mind wide open to possibilities as she had already seen so many sides of the issue. She was listening to the conversation as it steered towards education. That was when she added an elementary point which was worth its weight in gold.

My mother said, 'Each experience has a seed of learning in it,' she continued, 'Confidence is needed if you want to build a society of self-regulators. Nothing damages a child more than when he or she is treated as lesser than another, simply because he is a child. Adults should talk to a child like an adult to build his confidence and strength. Schools no longer become just proxy baby-sitters. An education system that fosters dependency steals the child's ability to stand up on their own. As children are the next level of consistency for the human race, this is so important.'

Kathy concurred with her point.

Hoping to get deeper answers for the dream, I shared, 'Speaking about self-regulation, in the dream I felt that in that small group there was a friendship, a trusting bond between the teacher and students. It felt so close.'

Kathy caught onto that quickly with a reply, 'The adult-adult relationship between the teacher and the students,' she added, 'Part of creating that adult-adult relationship to inspire a performing student to go higher.'

That reminded me of how the late Minister Mentor of Singapore, Lee Kuan Yew, propagated decades ago that the Singapore education program follow the mandate that classes with superior performing students should be allocated the best teachers who were intellectually on par or higher. Though it received some initial resistance, he knew what he was doing as he was way ahead of his time.

The "adult to adult" communicative relationship is backed by the Principle of Resonance. When two frequencies are brought together, the lower will always rise to meet the higher. The communicative relationship should be applied everywhere - not just in schools, at home as well as in the work environment. That adult to adult relationship proven as the average Singaporean is brought higher with the presence of an advanced paternalistic leader. An average Singaporean is honest and transparent and would feel uncomfortable littering. Petty thefts and crime in general is low.

But not just Singapore alone or about realigning education systems, I saw this "arising" in my own personal life. The sense of loneliness disappeared as soon as I discovered the "adult to adult" relationship with God as I began to speak to Him daily. Perhaps, the visitation of the Divine Being intervening in my life to raise me up the levels so that I could work towards reaching the full measure of God.

Nothing for control, nothing for distraction

I shared with them my decision to focus on innovation, to reinvent the old with the new. I shared also that I would be focusing on writing and communicating through books the heralding of a better future (the new) to the present. A futurist in that way, prospecting the Heaven on Earth optimal and ensuring that it becomes a reality in the marketplace.

Kathy supported me, and proclaimed, 'And that's what you love. That's what drives YOU!'

I answered, 'Yes, and that's God's greater purpose in my life. It is me in a much bigger way than I realized. I was thinking within my earthly capsule mindset all this time.'

Kathy shared, 'All schools should teach this very early on,' she continued, 'Schools should teach students the purpose of life is to live in line with their purpose and highest excitement. It brings freedom.'

As we took the last sips of tea, I turned on the old DVD player to play some *Qawwali* music from Ustad Nusrat Fateh Ali Khan's most prized musical creations. An acclivitous musical ending to an enlightening discussion on the crucial role of education in creating a society that is self-regulating, responsible and free. The advent of the New Human, nurturing such children now to be the best that they can be for the sake of our planetary advancement. Children on the path of this Golden Road so that they are free and encouraged to pursue the ambition or dream they cherish without interference. Children given an inner spiritual grounding that is uniting and tolerant. Children free to make their choices spiritually as they mature. School behavioral guidelines based on universal human values or virtues such as honesty, compassion, Unity, forgiveness, gratitude, tolerance and so on.

The sororal bond between two inspirational women, my mother and Kathy, was uplifting on its own. In just a few hours my mother would be heading off to the Kuala Lumpur International Airport to board her plane for Pakistan. I recall in my childhood how she would open up to me about how she felt that she was "going around in circles" as she found herself constantly making the wrong decisions. That itself was a valuable reminder to me that I had to keep moving forward by learning from my mistakes and to be careful not to drift into a loop. I was going to move up, not down.

And that goes for all Mankind as well. The only thing that we need to repeat in circles would be to build and enhance our relationship with God and the important people in our lives. Learning from our mistakes should be linear experience, part of an essential growth experience, but as long as we are responsible enough to try not to repeat the same mistakes again and again. A heedlessness that itself tightens the chains holding us back from better possibilities. Huge societal mistakes which we cannot afford to repeat. Why did we allow for gun licenses or authorize nuclear power for widespread use for that matter? Why did we repeatedly allow organizations to get away with corruption? Why do we keep funding war?

Speaking about war, I was still heartbroken about the brutal mass killings in Syria. Why did so many civilians have to die? I was determined to find who, what and why. Driven by a pursuit to uncover the Truth, that same night after my mother boarded the plane, I did a prayer asking for the unveiling of the Truth. Taking account of what happened so far, the details of the Bal Thackeray funeral was shown as a Black & White movie strip. Consequently, the MH370 vision was shown as multiple static images. This time it was different. It was a startling series of blinding flashbulbs revealing secret places, hidden information. I was astounded by the exploits. Fraudulent secrets making us forget who we are and what we are supposed to do.

A remote viewing experience complete, and as soon as I visually floated out of that ambiance, I shook my fists with vexation. I was disturbed by what I was shown. Nothing should be for control. Nothing should be for distraction. No more muting any entity, person or persons. No more placing humans on a tight leash. According to the Uncertainty Principle of Heisenberg, even a quantum particle cannot be coerced! It might even boldly go where no particle has gone before. Nothing is certain. Everything is possible! Even Quantum Mechanics disagrees with control, which brings us to another fact. Freedom is the most fundamental principle of the universe.

Humanity has been lost in the viscous circle of being self centered and lacking responsibility. To halt the process and to set ourselves free!

Tyler the Watchman's words, 'It's time to relinquish control. If you don't let go of control, it will be hard to ascend. Even if you find "I AM", the "I AM" will be yourself!'

Adriana the Mystic's words, 'When the Spirit of the Lord is in our hearts, we have freedom! Let our hearts be the freest place on Planet Earth!'

Our surroundings becoming free because our hearts are free. The checklist was growing and it was an important one. It was then when some sense arose from the words of advice by Faryal.

Faryal's words, 'Sometimes we find ourselves being hit hard or opposed by someone or some people equal to or stronger than us. Just remember this. Diamonds cannot be refined without friction with another diamond. Gold cannot be purified without fire.'

The past hurdles and suppression was for our personal perfection of a 10-10-10, away from the 6-6-6, the Sign of the Beast.

A tempestuous journey to the finish line. A refinement after a quark slaughter in the universe. The divine purpose to make us stronger, wiser and more compassionate.

'Our flowering comes with freedom. To release ourselves towards freedom – allowing for the flowering of our Spirit,' Faryal's words in the past as she unleashed herself from the prison of never being able to do things on her own.

Uncertainty Principle of Heisenberg states that you can never simultaneously know the exact position and the exact speed of an object, because everything in the universe behaves like both a particle and a wave at the same time. According to the Uncertainty Principle of Heisenberg, even a quantum particle cannot be coerced. If it chooses to do so it will end up where only 1% of the particles end up.

Mutual Trust Is Prevalent

God showing me answers in a unique way every time. By allowing the Holy Spirit of God to lead me, I was accepting God's sovereignty upon me. I was walking MY path as a free sovereign being. The new Heaven and the new Earth, a planetary society where everyone's free choice and freewill is respected. Education systems nurturing confidence, giving access to information, and structured based on self-regulation and responsibility. Governments serving the freewill of the people – a self-regulated and responsible people.

Responsible and free. A New World of perfected mutual trust.

How many people we meet today still say 'I don't trust anyone', or 'No, I will not start anything without a written contract'?

Probably many. The vision of the Heavenly Courts inspired a duty-based society where all the agreements were abide by both parties. Mutual trust prevalent in all aspects. In some societies, it could be easy to implement, in others much more difficult or even impossible. No need for contracts with just a verbal or telepathic agreement. All payments received with projects completed to satisfaction. The disappearance of corrupt organizations and people who would be considered as, at one time, the vultures of society who thrived on the absence of mutual trust. And now with the advent of robotic technology, doing things in a more regulated, responsible manner becomes easier. Systematic processes so that corruption is prevented. With the correct Man-Machine empowerment, it disintegrates any control structures that have detrimental effects. The removal of middlemen motivated to swindle and extort.

Mutual trust, an attribute of a heavenly nation. If Singapore is one of the heavenly blueprints, I imagined that it could shift higher into that direction if the right moves are taken. I recollected how our company did business mostly based on a verbal project contract with a Scandinavian firm. The only contract was a non-disclosure agreement as enforced by their end customer. A smooth sailing partnership that has continued for more than a decade without any broken agreements. Joyful and gifted with a freedom as it left certain things open to discuss, with no hidden agenda to circumvent or extortion for more money.

However, with "go" or "no go" enforced written agreements and highly extensive legalistic jargon, the business collaboration would become nothing more than a lengthy marriage vow chained with a strict prenuptial agreement allowing for little fluidity and growth in the relationship. Perhaps the people behind this company were 1 or

2 levels up in the Human Uplifting scale. But I could clearly see the benefits of responsible freedom in the business context.

This steers us back towards the purification of our Golden Souls. No amount of material or man-made effort can create foolproof protection. It is like being involuntarily caged behind bars in a prison, where we would end up spending a large amount of our time looking for means to escape. Lack of mutual trust could be a callous roadblock towards Heaven on Earth. Such a simple notion that mutual trust brings freedom. But above all, the intimacy with God taking precedence. We become so filled in Him and covered by His Grace that we are guided towards the people we can trust. More and more of such people start to enter into our lives and become part of our physical reality. As I was led by the Holy Spirit of God, I was brought to the Buddhist Monk and Marianne who guided me. I was led to Mei Ling who I trusted to work on healing me. Same for Tyler and most recently now Deepa and Kathy with their words of wisdom. These were people I barely knew and all through chance meetings. No long testing periods to trust or not to trust. There were no suffocating chains of high expectations.

> 'Good people do not need laws to tell them to act responsibly, while bad people will find a way around the laws,' quote Plato.

To trust is to be free. With mutual trust, we transmit a purified and liberating quantum field that is passed on.

No longer deceived and disillusioned wondering souls lamentably declaring, 'Why did they do this to me?'.

God-Man-Machine like threads of three-ply wool, inextricably mingled with our life on Planet Earth reacting upon each other. A global community where goodness "within" is released to the point where everyone (or almost everyone) becomes self-enforcing and self-policing. These are the seeds for a Golden Planet, transcending all that we currently know and entering a realm of supreme efficiency and self-realization.

To discover the Keys for entry into a world of the Moral and Upstanding, where the inner planes are much more attuned and responsible freewill for societal and planetary survival are manifested. A world that is joyful where none of us are afraid to have a good laugh or even to laugh at ourselves. A world where we can ease the chains that bind and limit us and allow us the freedom to move up the levels.

The humming of the ballad, 'Light of the world, shine on me. Love is the answer. Set us free ...'.

18

Thriving, Not Simply Surviving

We grow
With the nourishment of Love.
We strengthen
With the power of Unity.
But we flower
With Freedom.
Then finally we Thrive.

Singapore
October 2014

My Spirit Woman was floating way up in the sky looking down. Yellowish city lights shimmering in the dusky night sky. Technicolor rainbows birthed on the city surface. Innumerable shapes in Lilliputian proportions, crisscrossing in all directions.

Rainbows epitomize good things to come, an abundance in store, a beautiful life ahead. A vision of freedom, a vision of thriving. An imminent possibility of a world with rainbow abundance, as I progressed month after month, gradually flushing out the harmful and low vibrational emotional and physical toxins within my body, heart and mind.

I heard from Dr Rodriguez again that he was coming to Singapore on another trip. He had some issues with a large technology infrastructure project which he described as a perpetual headache.

'Meet me at the Marina Bay. Glutton's Bay sounds good!' he said.

An unusual location this time. It was not the usual Hyatt Hotel but a traditional hawker center, an outdoor assortment of food shacks catering authentic Singaporean and Malaysian cuisine. Dressed down in casuals, he was not the least bit bothered about appearances this time.

Dr Rodriguez groaned, 'I have had my fill of formal business meetings at hotels. This will be my last trip to Singapore on business. After this I am retiring.'

He emphasized, 'No, I mean it. I have given my life to these mega projects and they have just sucked the life out of me!'

His words punctuated by an uncontrollable series of coughs. A toll had been taken on his health.

He chose a place that was certainly not conducive for a meeting. By the early evening it had turned into a fish market, full of tourists crowding the place for local Singaporean delicacies. I suggested we walk down to the Marina Bay Sands to one of those quieter bistros overlooking the Marina Bay. As we settled down with our orders, he latched onto his pet topic of money and politics – in particular, the trillions that made the cities on Earth function and how he wanted a piece of the pie.

Dr Rodriquez complained, 'We are supposed to thrive!'

He stopped short at the end of his sentence with a heavy sigh of frustration. The millions he made in his early days now seemed elusive. The mega projects he co-owned around the world were faltering in deep debt and bleeding him dry. His attire reflected just that as he was dressed shabbily, a stark contrast to Mr Aminuddin who kept himself impeccable to the tee. The wear and tear in his clothes and even his wallet, ripping on the sides, matched the wear and tear in him. He was struggling and it showed.

Dr Rodriguez sat down on the sofa at the cafe releasing another big sigh. His inner turmoil was much too obvious.

His face looked gaunt and tired, his eyes lifeless, and said, 'I may talk about millions or billions of dollars, but look my state!'

He confessed, 'My mistake was that I wanted to keep the wealth to myself. I wanted security. Okay, call it self-serving! Something is not allowing me to keep it for myself!'

He turned his face to me, looking lacerated, 'One after another, these projects would mount huge debt. Either we were cheated by not being paid, or something unexpected had to go wrong. Now, we are just bleeding uncontrollably! It was never like this years ago. How do I stop it?'

Dr Rodriguez would question, but he already knew all the answers. He just wanted a sounding board to vent out his frustrations. He was a verbal advocate for communal sharing, doing what we loved as well as divine healing and more. None of the preternatural and supernatural experiences I shared with him surprised him. In fact, he claimed to be quite the divine healer himself with prophetic gifts. It was he who was trying to educate me on the Heavens through the novel "The Chariots of the Gods". Supposed to be a forerunner spiritually, he backtracked as his heart hardened and mind stayed locked in pride, keeping him chained to destructive ways. His healing and prophetic abilities withered to weaker levels. His ability to create and thrive shrinking down alongside. His dark hoarding intentions went against the grain of what God is calling us to do – which is Unity and communal sharing.

Apparently, his past glories were for trumpeting to the world, ammunition he kept handy even though he had now lost all his wealth, plunging deep into debt. And he did just that as he was irritated by the slow service at the busy bistro. Angry despite his numerous calls, the waiters were not responding as they rushed around to assist the earlier guests.

Dr Rodriguez cursed disdainfully, 'These impudent dimwits should be fired! This place could do with better service!'

He stood up defiantly and began to throw his weight around, bloated with an ugly pompousness, and shouted, 'I will buy your bistro, and then we will see some real changes around here!'

He topped off his statements with a few expletives. Those brief moments made him feel almighty and superior as the waiters and the bistro manager ran to his attention with a flurry. I looked at him utterly perplexed. Earlier on, he was confessing his mistakes, and now he went back in full force into his "all too familiar" arrogance and rage - breaking away from humility all over again.

It was sad to see Dr Rodriguez like this. In a hopeful New World of magis, mystics, healers and sages, he was a magi gone wrong. He knew more than the fundamental laws of science to understand how to transform situations. Instead of galvanizing his energy for good, he fell to alcohol addiction. He used manipulation and fear as a sociopath would do to get what he wanted. His nemesis was Mr Aminuddin, the blossomed magi who aligned himself with the cosmos, transforming, creating and rebuilding what was lost all over again. Dr Rodriguez was clearly being pushed down to his own zero point. As his pride was so huge, he would reach the brink of it, but never really leveling down to the full "zero". He would never want to show his vulnerability, or resume to humility as that would not be acceptable to his egotistical Self. Yet the sad part of it all, was that he was being pushed down repeatedly, collecting those tombstones representing his "near" demise. But never bearing fruit as demonstrated by the Buckminister Fuller's tetrahedron whose construct is the state of absolute equilibrium representing nothingness, the Zero Point, yet it is the brink of a pure potential (abundance) to be released.

Satisfied that he shook the little bistro up, he looked at me knowing what I was trying to imply to him, 'The path of a coward,' he retorted with a scowl on his face, 'Me? I will never take that path. I will never break!'

Dr Rodriguez was stuck in a rut. It was a highly undesirable place as people began to drift away from him. The support mechanism he relied on before became frightfully absent. Even his brilliance could not save him. It was ironic though. As he spoke about the owners of the wealth of the world who kept most of the wealth to themselves, he was no different. His deep relationship with God had fizzled out as soon as financial abundance materialized into his life. With his addiction to Darkness, he steered clear of the Light.

"We can easily forgive a child who is afraid of the Dark; the real tragedy of life is when men are afraid of the Light,' quote Plato

I wanted to say 'I told you so!' but I did not as it was not for me to judge.

I had to keep my Ego in check so that I could keep moving up the levels. Though my issues were mostly fear, anger and anxiety more than anything else, there were times in my past when I did suffer from an inflated pride.

Learning from my own mistakes, I had an urge again to voice out and say, 'Allow yourself to break … so that the Light of God can enter into your heart,' but again I held back.

Those words were certainly not rocket science. They were just plain and simple words of wisdom. However, as he continued to ramble on with angry curses and swears, lashing out opprobrious remarks, I held back again. Perhaps another time when he was more receptive. But if I lost that chance to convince him, I would just pray for him.

Adriana the Mystic's words, ' … pray for those who hurt you'.

Although Dr Rodriguez had not hurt me in any way, he was so wrong to lash out verbal abuse at people who served him. These were blue-collar workers who could not answer back, or else they would lose their jobs. So I did pray for him. I prayed that not only would God's grace cover him, but also that he would see the Light and embrace it mightily, never to return into Darkness again.

Shifting from Scarcity Thinking

For decades we have been conditioned to the notion of scarcity thinking. I've heard it all and I used to believe it myself. At one time, I thought that if I made a lot of money, peace and happiness would evade me.

The fear of having too much stemming from the commonly heard statement, 'Money is the root of all evil ...'.

Random statements spoken by people, feeding my mind, and sometimes even uttered by my own tongue, 'I don't have enough' or 'That is too difficult' or 'There is no solution to this problem.'

Those statements were excuses reflecting scarcity in all shapes and forms.

It was when I started doing prophetic prayers for people ranging from loved ones to strangers, did I discover that scarcity thinking was a unanimous problem faced by many. My prophetic ability was still in its infancy, as compared to Tyler the Watchman and Marianne who were light years ahead of me. While they could prophesy in a split second, most times I required a few seconds or minute or so of being in stillness before I would receive the message. There were a few occasions when I would be so filled with the Holy Spirit of God that the message would come instantly. I was longing for that to happen more often.

Through visions I was shown the causes and issues related to scarcity. They were remarkably heterogeneous, which made me wonder. Each time I looked up into the night sky, I could see the glaring disjunction between how the universe is designed and how many of us think consciously. Scarcity is totally delusory because the universe is limitless and designed to stretch with abundance. There are at least 100 trillion galaxies in the multiverses. We are each made up of 100 trillion cells, which are each made up of 100 trillion atoms, that were created in the center of the stars. Like a cosmic Russian doll, our universe nested inside a Black (White) Whole that is itself part of a larger universe. Based on my research on the Black Holes found so far in our universe, whether microscopic to super-massive in size, they may be doorways into alternate realities. Abundance within the abundance.

One of the prophetic prayer visions showed a mountainous pile of cash. A dwarf-like man appeared emerging from the pile of cash holding a pair of binoculars. Although he was drowning in a cascade of crisp currency, he looked left and right but he could not see the cash eagerly waiting for him. It was bizarre! Perhaps it was a message that we are blind to the abundance available to us. It is already there. And since everything is energy, we need to simply match the vibrational frequency of the abundance in order to see it and receive it.

There was another vision which showed a tall pile of gold bars. I was shown tiny snakes slithering under those bars hidden from full view. Symbolically snakes are seen as hidden threats or betrayal. They may also represent fear as they can strike anytime without warning. I interpreted it as the need for us to stay on the straight path, to work or associate with the positively charged people. In other words, Golden Souls who have gone past the need to betray or deceive as they walk in righteousness.

Then there was a queer vision that I recall vividly. It was a display of multiple crystal balls lined up as in Newton's Cradle. However, instead bouncing off each other in unison from left to right, they were just hanging there quivering in all directions. A possible message that we need to have a clear direction in order to lead us to abundance. We had to be very clear in our objectives in both our hearts and minds, as vagueness leads to poverty. Perhaps another divine sign showing the end of being a jack of all trades (and master of none). A reinforcement that we need to specialize and do what we love.

Deceptive associations, unclear intentions, attachment to security, old ways, old systems, e pluribus unum. It was just the tip of the iceberg. The scarcity thinking mindset of the Upside-down Kingdom, if mapped to the universe it would probably be like the early universe which is a lot smaller than the universe today. Many particles zipping about at such high speeds that no particle was able to travel very far without being intercepted by some other particle and blasted into oblivion. If not, bursts of other particles that zipped off, collided, decayed, were replaced by others (in reality - mindsets, people and situations trying to block the abundance). Particles zooming about to get this done, and then that and so on and on and on. If translated into the context of the real world, it would be about getting that car or that house or that much sought after status in society. Life becomes a tiring endless struggle till we get blasted into nothingness, leaving behind a less desirable version of ourselves overshadowed by Darkness.

A robotic lifestyle with an iron cage around us when we needed to start opening the doors of our cages into becoming a thriving community which is a close match to what the universe is today. It is a lot bigger with so much more room for us to move, grow, thrive and to be in the Light.

What is the true meaning of security? A question that was clearly part of my quest to discover the Keys to opening the Golden Door. The Buddhist Monk's teaching to simply "Be" - to learn to let go. The united prayers of boundless healing love for my father's recovery as well as the young new bride. The immeasurable love embodied within the bonds between families and friends. To do what we love, to set up loving environments, to create loving and trusting working relationships – the answer bringing me from the tip to deeper and deeper levels to reach the base of the iceberg holding the kernel, the solutions to thriving. That is the true meaning of security.

I had one more person who asked for a prophetic prayer that day. As I placed my hand on this gentleman's forehead and closed my eyes in silence, a vision slowly appeared. There were thousands of beings dressed in white. They were cheering! What was this? I could not understand. Their mirthful faces, the cheers that were going on and on till I could no longer hold onto that vision. As soon as I finished the prayer for this gentleman, I typed furiously on my iPhone a Facebook message for Marianne describing my latest vision of the cheering beings to the very last detail.

Catching her online as most of my contacts were always connected virtually, she answered, 'That could be the Cloud of Witnesses. If they were cheering for you, it means that you had made the right decision about something.'

Perhaps they were cheering for all the learning and my growth so far. Close to 3 years had passed and I persisted throughout despite the challenges along the way.

Marianne explained, 'The role of the Cloud of Witnesses around us is to testify over your actions, to rejoice over your victories and to testify to the manifestation of God within you,' she continued,

'Just because we don't see the Cloud of Witnesses around us, doesn't mean that they aren't there.'

Marianne elaborated, 'They are cheering us on the righteous decisions we make, simply because they can see it all,' she continued, 'The Men in White Linen are part of that and they are involved in every major event of history – you call this transit to this New World or Heaven on Earth.'

I added, 'Yes, the transit to Type I and beyond ... and in Scriptures, Heaven on Earth.'

Marianne asked, 'I see. Are they the same thing?'

I replied, 'No, there are not the same. The former is a hypothetical astrophysical scale. I do see some overlaps in terms of access to unlimited energy, Unity and more. Though I have to admit that I am still learning,' I continued urging her to proceed her explanation, 'But please go on. Do tell me more about the Men in White Linen.'

Marianne explained, 'Alright. Now, only when you encounter God, can you speak to those Men in White Linen and commune with their brethren. And remember they are real. They are going to bring Truth to you. You need to acknowledge them. They have secrets of Heaven to empower us of what needs to be done on Earth. Once they see that you are standing up to righteousness, they will be helping you with what is around your life. There will be supernatural intervention!'

Apparently, there is no scarcity in getting help from Heaven. What could I say? I counted 8 out of this world incidents while the most recent one involving my father was a classic case. The Men in White, the Angels, our divine ability to create instantaneously, the quantum entanglement, and more. The complexities were adding up.

I asked, 'How do I engage them for more guidance and education?'

Marianne replied, 'Talk with God during your prayers. He will send them accordingly. But it is up to Him.'

The Flow of Abundance

So that was Marianne with her enriching teachings, all based on decades of learning and real experiences. Then there was the sprightly and unforgettable Stephanie. As I got to know her, I nicknamed her the Spiritual Warrior. A tiny person with a giant spirit, she held an invisible sword in her hands as she swayed it masterfully for a spiritual task to be completed with a magnanimous triumph. I called Stephanie this time to keep her posted on my progress. I wanted to thank her again for the session of deliverance.

Stephanie reminded me what she had taught me before, 'Remember what I said about being discerning in your speech?'

I replied, 'Oh yes, I am now very watchful about my thoughts, spoken words and even the written word.'

It was about a year after I had returned to Singapore from Bali in late 2013 when I had my very first and only spiritual deliverance with Stephanie and Tyler. I recall how after the session, she mentioned briefly that she was getting out of debt and was doing reasonable well. We did not talk about it at length at that time, but this time we did.

Stephanie opened up and shared, 'I had a $20,000 debt. And I was jobless,' she added, 'I had a deep desire in my heart for all my debts to be cleared. All I know is that my negative bank balance was canceled out by a deposit made by some anonymous person. Also, the job I needed so badly fell into my lap. It was not the perfect job but it was good enough to help me move up from a zero balance to some savings so that I could breathe.'

Stephanie let out a sigh of relief as she relived that stressful time in her life.

She explained, 'It all started coming together as soon as I took the path God was leading me to.'

The path of her highest Self. Her own Golden Road.

Stephanie said, 'Greater and greater things started happening in my life. I realized that God wants us to be greater than what we are,' she paused and said, 'You speak about planetary advancement? You can say that I was advancing.'

I assumed that she was moving up the levels and had to tread carefully.

I was right as Stephanie elaborated, 'I had to be more discerning than ever before. I am careful with whom I interact now. I made some mistakes in the past by going "off the path" when I surrounded myself with worldly and devious people. I saw the blessings stop pouring in. But when I was back on the path again, it was as if I was back in the Light. Whatever I would ask in prayer would manifest quickly.'

Her experiences were a reflection of my own experiences. I tried to make sure as much as possible that I surrounded myself and collaborated only with those who were pure of heart.

Stephanie continued, 'Well all's well that ends well. As the blessings began to pour in again, this time I made it a point to give.'

I could not understand why, but when she said that a thought hit me about the two aquamarine gemstones I received. The one Adriana gave me was kept in my bank safe deposit. The other I had given to my father. At that moment, I was drawn somehow to check if they were still there. I had a very funny feeling about the entire situation. When I checked with my father, he said that he had kept it carefully in a box in his safe. However, he searched high and low, but there was no sign of the gemstone. When that happened, I just knew what to expect when I immediately headed off to check if the other gemstone kept at my bank safe deposit was still there. Just as I had suspected, that one disappeared too! Well of course, if they could appear out of thin air, they could vanish too! And that phenomenon is well supported by Quantum Mechanics. And even if it was due to Angelic intervention, what was the reasoning behind their disappearance?

I asked Stephanie about what happened to her gemstones.

She replied, 'I gave all of mine away. I did not keep them. Money, gold, gemstones and all forms of abundance are energetically charged and need to be moved.'

I knew what she was trying to imply. It was not about giving everything away. The underlying message was about "circulation".

With that in mind, all of sudden I received a revelation. I wrote it down while putting on my scientific thinking cap:

'Vacuum in a circulation state becomes matter. Matter is a product of CREATION. Hoarding breaks the circulation state. It goes against the law of nature. So when we circulate what we have, a greater abundance is created. To keep giving as our wealth grows.'

Was this even correct? Where did that thought come from? Perhaps Heaven was teaching me something. Circulation is the fulcrum for an abundant New World.

Stephanie explained a little more about the energetic concept of giving.

She said, 'To give is not enough. Our money, when we release it we give it the voice of Heaven. Heaven embodies instantaneous creation. If we don't get rid of the fear in our hearts, the bitterness and feelings of unforgiveness, our money will release that same testimony of fear and bitterness.'

Stephanie emphasized, 'It is important to give with a joyful heart. Intention is key!'

An entrepreneur like myself, she had her fair share of dealing with cash flow problems. Inherent in any business that has flaws within its structure, flaws in the hearts of the founders, she believed in the structure of giving to the right people and the right organizations.

I asked her, 'For us to thrive together, the question may arise - how much is too much money to give?'

Stephanie's candid reply, 'Nothing is ever too much. It is simply whatever amount that puts us in a place that we start to feel a slight twitch of pain. That's when we stop.'

Everything is energy. Everything vibrates and releases a sound. I imagined that our money would have to release the right sound. Attach it with resentful giving, and it will pass on a low vibrational energy which is a destructive force rather than a creative force.

Stephanie added, 'Give into a person or organization that you believe in with your hearts, and not based on hearsay or popular preference. And give a little more till you feel that pinch, pushing you to take that leap of faith.'

It was all about releasing fear. The revelatory message to "circulate" the blessings, the lifeblood of the Giant Tree of Life, from the vine to the branches, from branches to other branches. A continuous flow of "give and receive" revved up by the emotion of joy and fueled by faith.

If the Giant Tree of Life were personified singing a hymn, I would imagine the words, '.. sow onto me, and I will self-sustain. And so will you.'

Vacuum is space that is entirely void of matter. However, in practice achieving complete emptiness is impossible. Even the outer space is not empty of matter. The source of dark matter vacuum field is the circulation of the energy of spinning matter.

Dark matter is a hypothetical kind of matter that cannot be seen with telescopes but would account for most of the matter in the universe.

Breaking the Wisdom Barrier

Singapore
November 2014

I met with Dr Rodriguez again. A long stay this time. He was in Singapore winding up some pending business projects. As part of our preprandial discussion, I wanted to share with him some of my newly gained wisdom acquired over the months and see if it could help him in any way. He was frustrated that he was getting more and more ill by the day.

With fierce resentment he shared, 'I was hiring and firing people every week to the point that I was numb to people's feelings and emotions. When you are responsible for billion dollar mega-projects you have to watch your back every single day. You just need one or two corrupt officers who would screw you out of millions!'

Dr Rodriguez concluded, 'I was beginning to develop "eyes" on my back. Who do I trust? Who do I not trust? It was getting crazy!'

I explained to him what I learned from Tyler and Marianne, 'I was told that the higher up you go, the harder the tests … with the Cloud of Witnesses watching this race. I think when we make a righteous decision, they cheer.'

Displeased with my words, Dr Rodriguez replied in biting anger, 'Oh these tests!'

I said, 'But as you said yourself this era we are living in is an important time.'

He replied, 'Yes I Know! I know! Nonetheless I am bored with their "Oooh he is failing his test again". When am I going to get those cheers!'

His verbal crudeness was coming out in full form.

He retorted impatiently, 'I am done with this entertainment routine!'

The gradual hardening that made him literally a tough nut to crack. His heart was becoming stone hard on the outside, and dark and murky on the inside. I could understand the place where he was. I was at the exact same place before the vision of the Golden Souls through the Portal at the Gardens by the Bay. The arduous two months of only seeing morbid scenes associated with Darkness. My heart used to be dark and murky as his was now. Thankfully I was out of it. He was still a victim of the survival-driven Old World. His heart was hard. I could imagine the seeds of abundance literally bouncing off. The hardening was counter-productive, breaking the spin of circles of the MerKaBa, creating stagnation in the heart giving it no room for creation. When there is no room for creation, there is no place for true abundance.

When Dr Rodriguez took the path of wisdom in the past, he thrived. As soon as he switched, his finances switched to barrenness. I had to be watchful myself. His lessons were for my learning too. It was all too clear. The Wisdom Barrier was the fine line between surviving and thriving.

The words of Marianne, 'We need to break the Wisdom Barrier. And that applies to everyone of us.'

As she said that, I imagined a kind of wisdom that enhances the brains of all humanity to a point where most minds can agree on things that they never even knew before. All this without actually being taught. Activations and downloads happening naturally and invisibly.

Marianne's guiding words, 'In prayer, other than praying for a new car, a house, a new job, money, spouse, children, we move towards requests for faith, influence, peace, love of others, patience, forgiveness of others, knowledge, understanding and wisdom. By verbalizing these requests and transmitting an image of that into our minds, the abundance can manifest itself, but as long as there is zero doubt and if we walk in righteousness.'

Allowing for our consciousness to evolve as we make a consistent effort to request for blessings of a spiritual nature from God. Of course, doing the work to make it happen is important. Learning the lessons on thriving, I began to get in touch with people and organizations I believed in and trusted. To these, I gave a small token amount every month as a circulatory offering. I had barely much myself, so I gave very small amounts that I could spare. With time, I would increase the amounts little by little.

Concurrently, I continued to take up projects that gave me the greatest satisfaction. And naturally I worked on them with great joy. I worked on my relationships with people, offering more and more of my heart. Pouring out more love and more sincere praise than ever before. The mechanics of the heart, the mechanics of the 7 ringed disc were my testament for learning. All releasing a torus energy pattern that can sustain itself. The tornado, a smoke ring in the air, or a whirlpool in water. A torus structure of giving and receiving to create a sustainable flow of prosperity and abundance.

Ascending to Thrive

I took my worship sessions in music and dance very seriously. Sometimes in the evenings, and at times in the wee hours of the morning. The visions would escalate and become more and more stunning each time. Each time I would enter the Glory realm, my body would feel softer and lighter as I danced with feathers on my feet. I was finding myself more relaxed in the process as I taught myself to get my senses going rather than just seeing in the Spirit.

Singapore
Early January 2015

There were two visions that left me speechless. First in sequence was a breathtaking spectacle of beautiful white horses bridled with jeweled armor and regalia. The horses were galloping across the fields. And in the background were the tall Cloud of Witnesses, standing and watching.

I imagined the Cloud of Witnesses saying, 'Be free and wild like the gallant white horses! Hold yourself up with honor. Allow no fence, bush or any form of obstacle to break your graceful gallop down.'

> *The Cloud of Witnesses,*
> *The bejeweled White Horses,*
> *Galloping with speed,*
> *Unblocked by an encumbrance,*
> *Unstoppable and free.*

I took a step back relishing that moment. Followed on by the second vision which was just as stunning but different. Initially, all I could see was flowing silhouettes of air waves creating a misty atmosphere. As I looked closer, I realized that I was in an enclosed chamber and there was something ahead of me in the background. It was barely visible as it slowly emerged to be seen. A large crystal block, very much like the block of crystal hanging around Olga's son's neck, only this one was at least a thousand times bigger. This galactic chunk of icy crystal had shapes like bottle tops or anemones protruding from all sides. Remembering the fine details, that night before I went to bed, I sketched out the peculiar vision.

A clear Crystal Block
Of galactic proportions,
Sparkling incessantly,
Perhaps a secret to be revealed.

I awoke the next morning with an unusual dream. It had nothing to do with the galloping horses or the large crystal block. In fact, the dream was so elaborate that I was very surprised that I could remember the words spoken verbatim. This was how it went:

A voice spoke, 'Get in touch with the old man!'

Suddenly, I found myself in a fancy office. Sitting at a regal polished teak desk was a man who looked like the eccentric genius Dr Rodriguez. In front of him, a classic leather sofa redolent of the Presidential office of the White House.

This man sitting at the desk said, 'I was expecting you here.'

The man behind the voice spoke like Morpheus in the Matrix movie.

He instructed, 'You need to look for the old man.'

Which old man? I was confused.

He spoke again, 'The old man owns a large expanse of property. In fact, he owns the property which rented an office space to you.'

That reminded me of that same expensive office space my company had canceled the lease on.

The man said, 'The old man is deep in debt. Summons after summons have been sent to him. He is supposed to be filthy rich but his company cannot pay up.'

In the dream itself I felt sorry for the old man he was referring to. Somehow, I wanted to see him. I was advised to get in touch with him.

Then almost instantaneously, the scene in the dream switched to a grand white mansion up on a hill. As I walked up the entrance of the mansion, I could see the old man from the window on the second floor. His body had expanded in size. It was severely bloated.

As the scenes switched, I could no longer see the man at the desk, but I could still hear his voice as if he was monitoring me in the background.

The voice spoke again, 'The old man is locked in his own massive home as his body is "leaking".'

Leaking? What did that mean? I looked at the old man again. He looked very ill with the smell of death around him. As the voice of this man described, the old man's body was leaking a toxic white substance.

I saw myself standing at the door of the mansion. I knocked and a young man opened it.

The young man said, 'The old man is dying. He is not bothered at all about all those summons.'

Apparently, the young man was among the caretakers. He started talking about a secret related to crystals which I could not quite catch. Something I needed to know about. I awoke from the dream at 4:23 am.

The next day, I told both Dr Rodriguez and Tyler about the dream as well as the "Crystal Block" vision.

Dr Rodriguez words, 'Crystals? Hmm. Crystals release memories. Memories locked within your DNA.'

Tyler's words, 'You ascended. The "old man" was you, the old you struggling in transit. Fusion/fission. Crystal memory and/or formula.'

What both of them said made sense. I was tapping within my own layers shedding a layer symbolic of the old man and old memories. I was tapping within the layers rewriting the code within my DNA. I was tapping onto the voice of the Holy Spirit of God. I was shifting away from the voice of Ego that the Buddhist Monk warned me about. I was discovering the "I AM" just as God washed away the blemishes. The "I AM" ready to move up the scale.

Through The Golden Door

I let the day pass thinking about that dream. Although this was more than a year from the Stigmatic Zero Point experience, I was still re-birthing.

Tyler continued to advise, 'Now you can rest instead of helping as you are still re-birthing. Part of your problem is that you have this "helper" image. This is why you broke down in the past. If a caterpillar is trying to hatch but has not gone through the proper metamorphosis, its transformation into a butterfly may be stunted. REST and let your new Self blossom so that you are strong enough to start helping the world.'

Tyler's words shook me up. Apparently what I was doing in the past was not enough. I had to spend more time in prayer, meditation and worship. As he described, I was like a caterpillar in a cocoon in hibernation mode. So more rest was needed. And so I did.

I spent more time in prayer, meditation and worship. I remembered to dance as I was earlier guided to by an Angel. When I was a little more adventurous, I would spin counterclockwise soaking in the higher vibrational energies. From time to time, before the start of the worship, I would sing even though I would never ever sing due to sheer embarrassment. Trying to sing a little higher each time, hoping to tap onto the higher octaves to collectively raise the vibrational frequency of my cells of my body, the atmosphere in the room. And each time, the Holy Spirit of God would make His presence felt as the atmosphere would suddenly shoot up to an even higher vibrational frequency. A soothing chill in the air. Perhaps the perceived as a Quantum Glory realm where the power would extrapolate to an entirely different level. How I got there was another puzzle on its own.

As the months passed, it was getting easier and I was getting the knack of it. At times the elusive twisting tunnel would appear, like a wormhole. The feeling of being gravitationally sucked into a Black Hole. Graphically, like the inner funnel of a torus field, where I would enter at one end of the funnel and out the other. As soon as I would emerge, I would see a panoramic view of an inner-galaxy within an inner-universe.

Tyler's past words of guidance, '... go deep beyond the galaxies. God is there in the realm of eternity ...'

Like a lone galaxy swimmer, free-floating and sightseeing. Throughout my thoughts and words of worship were on God, thanking Him and praising Him. I discovered that when I place myself in full focus without distractions in between, the results would be greater. There would be a visual clarity of the higher realms. Downloads of revelatory thoughts, ideas and visions would come through more easily and with greater precision.

Several weeks later, I noticed a change. I was feeling an abundance that I did not have for a long time. A kind of abundance that was in perfect harmony with what I wanted, what I felt, what I needed. It was like everything was beginning to happen at the right time and falling beautifully in place. New technology startups for mentoring coming my way. And they were all in areas to disrupt the old way of functioning into the new way of operating. All in line with the aspirations of the New World - the breaking of barriers and structures, the greater flow of capital, the greater freedom for a happier people. On top of that, instead of wasting hours on administrative matters as I did in the past, I had more time to meditate on and research on futuristic ideologies. To feel, to analyze and to put them in writing.

The Thriving Contagion

I thanked Tyler for offering so much guidance. He had such minimal earthly desires. In fact, they could be so low to the point of discomfort – at least from my point of view.

I asked in a concerned tone, 'Don't you have financial constraints when you do all this volunteer work?'

Tyler answered, 'What is "financial constraints"?'

With a genuinely puzzled look on his face, he could not understand the meaning or the relevance of those words "financial constraints", as if they were totally alien to his vocabulary.

'You know what I mean,' I replied candidly.

Tyler said objectively, 'I have very simple needs and desires. Firstly, I have a roof over my head. Secondly, there is always a place I can get a free meal in Singapore. Not a day has gone by when I had to starve,' clasping the cloth of his shirt with his two fingers he continued, 'This branded shirt you see me wearing right now – it was gifted to me. So what else do I need? I am taken care of one way or the other.'

Tyler may call himself a Watchman for Singapore and the nations, but I could see the other side of him. He was a bold modern day prophet with his introverted hermit-like lifestyle. He would release prophesies and words of depth that could leave anyone in awe and wonder. He said that his mission was to guide and watch over spiritual market-makers like myself and many others. I was beginning to see the fruits of his guidance. His purposeful life quest was being served well. And it was not just him, Marianne too. She was one busy lady speaking in conferences and groups week after week. She was truly amazing.

Then there was Adriana with her similarly simple needs and ways. From what I last heard, her employer (the lady of the house she worked in) sponsored her for a diploma in nursing. They also bought her bi-annual air tickets to Indonesia so that she could see her children more often. She was ecstatic as her dreams were coming true. As a citizen of Heaven, her earthly life was becoming more and more like the heavenly version she would visit in her dreams every night.

Singapore
Late January 2015

I was returning to the transient home in Sembawang feeling thankful for all the guidance I was receiving. I was truly blessed. I felt like this prima donna heroine who kept falling into bouts of negativity as I scoured through my quest, while I had these faithful and wise wizards who gave out timely advice so that I would complete it. In that sense, I was thriving in receiving such abundant assistance from multiple people, a selfless group of mentors and guides. This was a huge amount of help daily, on-the-fly and totally voluntary. To me, it was absolutely unbelievable as I had never received this amount of help in the past. But then again, perhaps it was because now (unlike before) I was walking on the path of my Golden Road.

On top of that, I was also feeling pleased that I was shifting to a new home. It was just a small apartment as quaint as Faryal's, but it was comfortably intertwined with nature and it was in a nice neighborhood. I could not deal with my chaotic neighbors at my old place, as much as I wanted to help them. Finally, the life I wanted.

As I walked toward my home, from a far distance, the 9 year old Punjabi boy caught a glimpse of me. He called me, flailing his arms and cavorting with intensity. His bright eyes and face amidst the dark shade of his skin glowing like a beacon.

Shouting ecstatically, 'Aunty! Aunty! More amazing things happened today!'

Sharing his elation, I asked, 'Sure tell me? What happened!'

The young boy said, 'You know that day when I did a prayer and placed the coin on the wall and it stuck magically?'

I nodded. Of course, I remembered that magical day.

He exclaimed, 'Guess what! Since that day more miracles have happened. My stepmother who has never bought me anything for 3 years bought me a new schoolbag, new shoes and brand new clothes!'

The hope, the faith and confidence he gained on the landmark "Coin on the Wall" day. My prayers for the boy may have triggered off a magical quantum entanglement. With the soft heart of a child, he received the seeds of abundance easily. The young boy was so encouraged that he was even more motivated to learn.

The excitement continued to reverberate in his voice, 'I am reading more on astronomy as you told me to. I did not forget.'

I replied with elation, 'Good. I am so proud of you.'

He said, 'You know what? I found out that Earth is a liquid water world.'

I said, 'Yes, that is correct.'

The young boy pulled out from his brand new schoolbag the astronomy book he was reading, turned to a chapter he had bookmarked and read aloud word by word, and said, '77% of the earth's surface to be covered with water.'

Then he pointed to a page, and said, 'They said here that Planet Earth is the ONLY place in the Solar System where Liquid Water appears on the surface at this time in the history of the Solar System. Not gas, not solid.'

He closed his hardcover book and asked looking up at me, 'Is it true?'

I replied, 'That is incredible what you shared with me. Yes, it is true that the Planet Earth is abundant. Now your question – is Earth the only place in the Solar System were Liquid Water appears on the surface? Well, we may never know what we discover next. We are only limited by our thinking.'

I could literally feel his tiny little heart pound with excitement.

I elaborated, 'For instance, it is said that if humans are planted on a barren planet with no water, that planet may soon start developing water. That's how powerful we are. I believe now scientists recently discovered Liquid Water in Mars.'

The Human DNA (and its RNA) displaying its powerful effects - wherever it is carried, it will gradually alter the environment.

He looked at me starry-eyed and said, 'Wow! We are special.'

I replied, 'Yes, indeed we are. From what I know, as long as we have the Presence of God within us, I believe that we will remain abundant and thriving ... regardless of which planet we are in!'

The young boy's heart was pulsating for more to learn. The softening of our hearts to receive the seeds of germination. The entanglement, the circulation - give, receive, give, receive. To give and to keep giving consistently. Creating an abundance and creating more room to carve out lives of meaning, rejoicing and thankful about the blessings. Like the circulating vacuum energy that hits everything else with everyone else, and everyone else with everything else. And everything in the universe spins. Spinning energy has the property to change energy very quickly. Spin, a non-classical degree of freedom. Clockwise spin draws energy, while counterclockwise spin expands energy. Energy that nature uses to express itself – to shrink or to grow. Energy simply IS. God is All that IS. "I AM" the "I AM" expanding and expanding to become thriving Towering Golden Souls.

As the months passed, finally the long awaited prayer vision of barren land erupting and transforming into a wide expanse of plantations. In the sky, there were fireworks on display. If that was a vision of the New World, the old adage of scarcity had finally phased out of commonly accepted thinking. If it represented myself, I had finally let go of my poverty mindset.

'May the Glory realm hit the nations!' were the words of a song that played on my mind.

The end of old structures and the beginning of real change. As humanity we need to work together to ensure that the majority of money is put to good use, as much at least for society and ecology. We need to realize that life is about Oneness, and that we thrive when we are in Unity. We need to push for the eventual elimination of institutional control mechanisms that segregate and stifle circulation. Bringing Heaven on Earth means that responsible freedom should be part of the new structure. And where there is freedom, there is little need for control.

Marianne's words, 'Planet Earth has gone through seasons of germination, growing, bearing fruit …'

A time to bear fruit. The Golden Door was so close. Perhaps a New World where there is no segregation between rich and poor, just different levels of abundance suiting each person's needs. Not a single person is impoverished. The Golden Door of Harvest for the planet, it felt so ready to be opened. The good thing was that I figured out the Keys.

19

The Golden Door Opens

For centuries,
We walked in Darkness,
Stuck in a time chasm
Captive in a mimesis
Of events destructive.

The countless times
We stumbled and fell.

It is time for us to now
Pick ourselves up
To reflect and to learn
To break away and to flower
As we discover the Keys.

Singapore
February 2015

A seeker searching for a better life, a believer of God and a perfectionist who hoped to co-create with Him a better world. I was a purist in that way, striving to understand the planetary Truth along with its corresponding Keys. Finally, I was a heroine battling my own tests, keeping myself shielded and crossing swords when I had to, not in the physical, but with my Spirit Woman.

I resonated with David. He was the helpful mentor who I met very early on in the journey, the visionary philanthropist who found his answers in Bali amidst the trees and the dolphins. His vision attained in flying colors as he allowed himself to be led by the Spirit. Moreover, I was inspired by him to think out-of-the-box, to be creative by tapping into my thoughts, ideas, revelations and visions. I also resonated with Yasmine, the Cancer Survivor-Hero who fought through her own journey against the challenges of disease as they tried their best to annihilate her. I was not going to let my sicknesses rule me. I aimed to be like her - a fearless ruler of her destiny, creating an order and structure in her life so that she could achieve the ultimate, coming out looking more resplendent than ever before.

Alongside the other heroes and heroines, I saw my whole family becoming heroic in their own way. My quest for the answers was parallel to their journey which was unique and special in its own way. It was during one of those Skype chats with my mother when she shared her sentiments about "us". "Us" as in myself and my siblings. She said that all of us had changed so much that we live simple lives dedicated to our passions at work as well as prayer and worship.

'Yours seems the same too ... amazing!' she said.

'Mine too?' I asked.

'Well yes, so much prayer, meditation and simplicity,' my mother answered.

'I find it enjoyable. Peace in the heart gives a certain kind of joy,' I replied frankly.

'But you children lived in the lap of luxury growing up. Unbelievable!' she added.

Those huge bungalows with chauffeur driven cars. And every Saturday night it would be a lavish dinner out at the Shangri-La Hotel. And to add to that, as young children we attended grand luncheons and extravagant charity balls.

Now such extravagant affairs are very much toned down. Socializing is not always a grand pompous affair, though enjoyable from time to time. It is great for meeting up with the upper echelons of society, the influencers, the movers and shakers. Our lives have become more balanced. A little more time spent with the less fortunate, from praying for and healing the sick, helping the disabled and homeless, or simply spending time with them like family. And the rest of the time, interacting within groups of high-minded people who want to learn, share, collaborate and create for a common purpose. A tapestry of teamwork living, working and enjoying this important time of transit towards a New World. All in line with the Heaven and Earth balance of being heavenly minded while living an earthly life.

My mother was absolutely right. The changes in my family were no passing observation. There was less of an obsession for material accumulation, but more of a contentment to do well, to live comfortably and be happy.

I saw the play of quantum entanglement as we influenced each other. As I learned to let go, they learned to let go. As they shared their divine experiences, I was impacted and vice versa. We were transmogrified toward a renewal.

My reply to her, 'Yes, our lives are totally opposite now.'

My mother said proudly, 'Your lives are so different from what it used to be as kids. It is quite amazing. It seems as if all of you grew up in one world and now live in another world.'

I reflected upon my discussions with Mr Aminuddin, businessman extraordinaire, and how he touched on the matter of family, as he said, ' ... more importantly the family is happy and we are re-building the business together; united and in harmony.'

The communal approach towards Heaven on Earth. It was truly a family endeavor. I could see it in his family's life, and I could see it in mine. In fact, many of us are already witnessing transitional shifts. However, I was waiting for the big one. The full blown New World. This time I knew the Keys. They were reiterated during the turn of events, from an initial state of vagueness and disarray to the point where the Keys were shown in full clarity. What's more, as my visions were rife with symbolism, the Keys had to be symbolic too.

The Towering Golden Souls

The first key is to become like Towering Golden Souls. Eliminating fear and anger within ourselves as well as all other low vibrational negative emotions, keeping our tongues and words immaculate through no lies and no secrets, eliminating harsh and angry words. Relinquishing attachment, while keeping a healthy balance with the material world. Attachment keeps us anxious, and we cannot become like Golden Souls if we are constantly anxious. To learn to love unconditionally and to understand the power and the depth of divine love as displayed through the Divine Being's visitation. The heart code wired in our hearts is powered by a divine love that grows our Spirit Man (Spirit Woman) to become as large as it can be.

With so much work that we need to do within ourselves, it needs to be in our thoughts daily to consistently bring us closer and closer to this "Towering Golden Souls" reality. My transformation agenda was on my mind every single moment of the day. There was always more inner work to do, so much more to be healed. And I wanted to hear more of what others had to say and what they were experiencing.

Deepa the Linguist sent a message, 'There is one person at the hostel who wants to meet with you. I told him about your experiences. He has been having experiences too. I barely know him. I believe he is new to Singapore. We were just chatting casually while having breakfast and he kept saying that he had an important message to share, some urgent things to do and that he needed to get support or just to talk to someone. Someone or some people who would not think he is crazy.'

I replied, 'I know where he is coming from.'

Meeting with and opening up my heart and soul to acquaintances who were practically strangers was something I was getting quite used to. Based on my feeling, he was sincere which was why I agreed to meet.

Soon after Deepa connected us virtually, we agreed to meet at City Hall. It was close to the financial center of Raffles Place, and just a few blocks from Arab Street. The last time I was in Raffles Place, I had silently explored the cosmic meaning of Stigmatic Zero Point as I doodled on my sketchpad - with the inner-galaxies and the Animation Strip of Mankind. This time it would be City Hall – the crossroad, the temporal urban meeting point for quest holders like myself and others on a similar spiritual agenda.

Five minutes before our meeting time, I spotted a heavyset tanned man looking like a fish out of water. He looked terribly lost. So I knew it had to be him. I would have not been surprised if he was so new to Singapore that it was just barely days after his arrival. Facially European, he stumbled to introduce himself carefully, pronouncing every word very slowly, making sure that he would construct the sentence correctly. Accentuating his words with a hybrid Italian-French delivery, which made it hard for me to place where he was originally from. Despite the mixed slang, I understood him well. Finding a place to sit, we went straight to the meat of the discussions.

This new acquaintance said, 'I did not know why I was being led by the Spirit to come to Asia first. It was not clear yet which part of Asia. I heard about you from this lady at the Hostel. I traveled from my homeland in Europe, then to Macchu Picchu, then Bali, and now I am here in Singapore. I am searching for answers.'

He introduced himself as Han. His blue eyes danced around with excitement as he spoke. Although Han was confident and presentable with slick gelled back hair and dressed in a well-ironed Polo shirt, within him I could see a very pure soul. By the way he spoke and his mannerisms, he was a fragile being with an intent so pure that he was aching to follow an intuitive calling.

Han said, 'Deepa told me that you were talking about Heaven on Earth. The return of the Garden of Eden. Hmm ... there is something I am supposed to do here and I do not know what it is. But I do know that it is something for the Planet Earth.'

I replied, 'Yes, I was talking about that. And yes, a lot of things are being revealed now on how we need to prepare ourselves for the changes – the needed changes in ourselves, our societies and Planet Earth.'

A little lost in thought before he continued, 'Speaking about ourselves, they said that we need to reduce eating heavy red meats. This is why I have become a vegetarian. If you really want to eat meat, have the lighter white meats like chicken or fish.'

The material universe comprising of the Golden Planet with our heightened consciousness creating it. Lightening ourselves up, cleansing our hearts and minds is not enough.

I listened as he went on, 'But most of all, we need to find what task God has assigned each of us. It is different and unique. They told me to stay away from vocations of Darkness. We should certainly not support or be part of any business that can indirectly create family disharmony like the gambling industry, prostitution, environmental destruction and so on.'

Each time he referred to as "they", and I wondered who "they" were. Were "they" the Men in White Linen, a Divine Council, some other Inter-Galactic Council, familiar spirits or extraterrestrial?

Han said, 'Almost all areas of my life were going through severe ups and downs. I was so traumatized that I was tested to the limits,' he continued speaking with a deep strain in his voice, 'I realized that I had to change myself. I had to fix myself. So I stopped my business for a while and went to Macchu Picchu for a couple of months. I stayed there, visited the sacred sites to learn about the lives of the natives. My hope was to heal myself and to discover who I am. Along the way, I went through some very strange experiences where I was shown in dreams of other sides of myself in other physical realities,'

I said with appreciation, 'I know you hardly know me, but thanks for sharing this with me. Many I have met and know are going through their own trials. We are being pushed to wake up. To move into the Light. To transform, to change and become what we truly are.'

Han said, 'That is so true. I have been in Darkness for too long. I have now chosen to follow the path of the Light. In those dreams, I was shown what I was supposed to be doing.'

I explained to Han about the Overcomers. Perhaps he was one of them. He was a man with a mission, as I imagined many of us would be in our unique way. Any vocation, that we are part of right now that has a hint of Darkness, must be cast aside. Our right to choose so that we can keep our vibrational frequencies at its peak. As our Spirit Man (Spirit Woman) grows, we can shine our Light and help bring out the Light in others, inducing a positive infection. I imagined that Jesus did that with all he spoke to, his disciples as well as the people in the street. They were like charcoal transformed with pressure into brilliant diamonds. Each of us becoming like diamonds, dispersing Light so greatly so as to project out as Towering Golden Souls.

We no longer become bogged down by lower vibrational energies of Darkness. We have entered a time that is ripe to put on the armor of Light. The Punjabi boy was shining with happiness in his heart, despite the torments at home. The magical night when the aquamarine gemstone materialized. And so much more before and after.

Han said, 'I am willing to travel the world to find people to work with me, or to speak to, or just as a sounding board to achieve my mission.'

Glancing hastily at his watch, he said, 'I need to rush for an appointment. It's a pity we only have a short time to talk. I have so much more to share with you. Also, I would like to meet people who are the Overcomers as you mentioned. I feel so alone. I want to meet others with whom I can share my experiences as well as to learn from.'

I replied, 'There are several people I know and I am sure there are many others. I will keep a look out for them. Do keep in touch and I will keep you posted.'

Throughout our discussion, he remained solemn and serious about the whole thing. It was not a game for him, but his new life mission and he took great risks globetrotting for that noble purpose. My mystical journey started off with a message from a stranger and ended with another message from yet another stranger. Both messages were invaluable. While the MRT Stranger pushed me to get started quickly, the meeting with Han was a push to start mentoring others more proactively.

As Han picked up his wallet and phone from the table where we sat and talked, he said, 'By the way, just to let you know, before

I came to see you today, I had a strange dream last night. Your face was shining like there were diamonds emerging and popping out from your face.'

A surprising statement that left me speechless.

'That was what was shown to me,' Han spoke with a softness in his voice.

Those words stayed in my mind for days, in fact, for weeks and months later. A satisfying feeling that this new stranger could become a supportive friend in the future, and vice versa. We exchanged business cards.

Han was among the pioneers in an assembly of awakened and gifted individuals who were going to be part of a future sharing cum support group. Soon after I met an Australian lady whose life was just as melodramatic.

Trying to maintain a savior-faire, this lady said, 'Bizarre is the word, what will people think of me?'

Followed on by a chance meeting with a South African male this time saying the words, 'Please don't think I that am crazy, but I have been going through some pretty bizarre experiences. When can we really talk? I want to tell you everything. I have been keeping it inside me for too long.'

All of them were pushed to zero point. All of them were faced with supernatural experiences in the past few years. All of them were getting early signs of gifts. Some could not be absolutely sure who "they" were that were speaking to them.

From a mentee to becoming an mentor equipped with preeminent wisdom and vigilance, my apprise to all of them, 'No matter what, always ensure that you are led by the Holy Spirit of God. And that you are IN God. Never ever allow the Presence of God to diminish within yourself.'

That was the basic starting point of a Golden Soul. We could have all the gifts in the world, but without the Presence of God, we become an empty vessel. The mechanics of the universe, the improved dietary habits fill the vessel, however a "Towering Golden Soul" reality may, figuratively speaking, be the Total Internal Reflection – the complete reflection of the Presence of God within us.

> **Diamond** is a polymorph of the element carbon (C). Diamonds are crystalline in nature and have a three dimensional arrangement of carbon atoms linked to each other by strong covalent bonds which results in a high refractive index and dispersion of light. The magnificent brightness of a diamond is due to the refraction, total internal reflection and dispersion.
>
> **Refraction** is the bending of a wave when it enters a medium where its speed is different. The refractive index of a diamond is a measure of the speed of light in that diamond. It is expressed as a ratio of the speed of light in a vacuum relative to that in the considered medium.
>
> **Total Internal Reflection** is the complete reflection of a light ray at the boundary of two media, when the ray is in the medium with greater refractive index.

The Quantum-powered Golden Horse

'Diamonds popping out of your face ...'

That sounded utterly divine, yet unreal and just too good to be true. Was Han just giving me a dose of man to woman flattery? I was more than flattered, of course. But by the seriousness of the way he spoke about the dream, it left some food for thought. Maybe it was a prophetic sign for a phenomenon that could unravel more Truths.

Thinking about diamonds, I recalled the words by Dr Rodriguez, 'Did you know that colored diamonds are a novel way forward to develop Quantum Technology 2.0 devices that work at room temperature?'

The mysterious link between quantum power and diamonds. Standing with my back to a digital clock, something made me turn around. The time was 11:11. The appearance of 111 and 1111 accelerated to every day now even higher to up to 5 or more times each day. My thoughts were being manifested at record time. Perhaps, I was shifting into a faster world of thought indeed! Quantum speed? Was this a foretaste of the New World?

Moving towards a faster world of "thought" with a greater pulsating of the Global Mind. With our accelerated powers to manifest, and our thoughts opening up with no mask, I shudder at the realization that our thoughts return like boomerangs, potent and immediate in their effects. As a thought comes into mind, it is solidified into immediate action. A scary thought as in the human mind, a negative thought can creep in and insinuate itself between all of one's good intentions, lying apparently dormant. Imagine that it becomes a nucleus attracting to itself thoughts of similar content until it takes a semblance of force through emotion; later results, physical and material are manifested. If negative, the consequences can be devastating.

The potency of thought is stepped up into a frequency which permits no side-stepping. The thought pattern becomes determinate of our welfare, our progress, our happiness and joy. Creative "thought" or destructive "thought"! That made me think. I had to stay on those on planes of higher frequency so that I could be in a creative "thought" state.

Now, Dr Rodriguez had finished his work in Singapore and returned to his home in France. From his updates, his financial situation was slowly but surely getting resolved. I managed to catch him on Skype as he was settling back in his office. Without doubt, his lectures were enticing, and I would patiently listen to him as he gave me an earful on space, time and the quantum field.

He emphasized again, 'We need to move quickly! There is much for all of us to do. Time is moving faster and faster. The lens of the Black Hole of our galaxy has distorted time. Just look at the massive changes in the last 18 years. Now it is about the next 18 years. The battle of the swords as we get rid of the old energy as its flips and flies and dies hard. See what is coming! I believe that it is not moving backwards. What we are seeing are things being tried that don't work.'

Control, corruption and secrecy was tried, tested and did not work. There was so much coming out into the open, so much evidence that control, corruption and secrecy are flawed.

Dr Rodriguez shared, 'Just like a treadmill, that starts on slower speed. We step on and move with the rhythm. As the velocity of the treadmill increases, we need to move along with it. As the years go past, from 2015 to 2016, then 2017 and beyond, the treadmill will go faster and faster,' he continued, 'The downloads started happening decades ago and it is trickling down faster and faster! We have to match the speed of this hypothetical treadmill, or we will stumble and fall off.'

Based on his word, I imagined that if we do not shift to match the frequencies of the New World, we may simply miss it and be left behind. If he was right, it is important right now to ride the wave and not just hang back. We had to move along with stealth and speed, much like the Golden Horse, to catch up with the higher frequencies so that later on it does not become overwhelming for our logical minds and our physical bodies to catch up.

Dr Rodriguez added, 'The measurement of time has gone up to perhaps 11 to 12 pulses per second, or faster. I am quite certain that the frequency vibration of the Earth is no longer at 7-8 pulses per second.'

Marianne expressed this urgency too, but differently. She took it from the perspective of a race for completion during an important time. As I sent her those questions by Facebook Messenger, she responded with an interesting analogy to a relay race, something I could relate to very easily as I was an avid track athlete in school.

Marianne wrote in her message, 'We are on a race – a relay race literally. The fastest runner is usually the first runner, while the last runner is among the fastest but also the one with the greatest strength and perseverance to finish the last leg of the relay. God has reserved the best in line to finish the race. You and I are one of them!'

A justification for speed and timeliness reinforced by two influential people. Marianne did share in the past that we were the best DNA reserved for this time. I presumed to finish this race we all played a part in our own unique way to break through this Upside-down Kingdom and manifest the New World,.

Marianne's message continued to read, 'You were in a relay race as a young athlete weren't you? The race is ON. And time is of the essence! This is the last leg for the baton. We can't drop the baton. We need to complete the race.'

We do not have the luxury of time. There is a need to accomplish so much more in less time. So many lessons to learn. Free and responsible, we need to be in charge of our own future. Awareness that the time is now. The past like an old frame, an old photograph that we can refer to for lessons learned, but to which we have no attachment. We have to keep moving higher, always higher, always progressing in an upward trend. To reach a point where our meditations have gone to such a deep level, our minds become more and more luminous. Like a newborn child, the Truth reveals itself.

With an elevated excitement in his voice, 'Just imagine a high voltage current passing through you. See how that feels. A greater power will be within the spirit, our soul energy field, to accelerate and decelerate at will!'.

Feeling the energy of his words, and visualizing the urgency, I imagined us responding to change and to move forward like Quantum-powered Golden Horses. Moreover, I imagined that the shared energy frequency in the New World would be much higher than before.

Dr. Rodriguez asked a rhetorical question, 'Did you know that there is an unofficial fact that knowledge doubles every 2.5 years on average, where before that the knowledge of Mankind would double every 2000 years?'

A superlative in terms of acceleration. Perhaps, the theory and practice of horology may become outdated.

He added, 'What's the new invention for the next 18 years? WE are the new invention! You and I ... well if I am still alive that is. Our ability to see Quantum Energy. As it is revealed, it is going to blow everything we know out of order! Every single theory will have to be rewritten. All of it. Physics, Biology, Chemistry. When we begin to see with Quantum Eyes, it will be like the beginning of radio. An ability to tune into something that we never really could tune into before.'

With those words said, Dr. Rodriguez clasped his hands together and gave out a big sigh of contentment. An important message passed on. An impressive deed of supernatural intellect presented and delivered.

I thought back to my own electrocution experience with the flood of visual binary '0's and '1's while in the rural colony in Pakistan. There was an astuteness and sharpness of my mind since then. Even my father's near death experience made him realize that miraculous physical transformation can happen at any advanced age. The last I saw him, he looked fitter than ever before. Shortly after he was vacuuming the carpets and lifting them up single-handedly, refusing to ask for help. A profound confidence and stealth breaking all barriers set by age. Mentally and physically stronger, an ageless human that has moved many steps above the faculties of knowing and uplifting.

I listened intently as Dr Rodriguez rambled on with his polymathic gift.

He said, 'It will happen slowly like radio tune into the sound, and TV into pictures. We will be in communication with the rest of the Galaxy, teaming with life. Anyone with a quantum receiver will hear you. In a quantum state communicating across the star systems in real time.'

As Towering Golden Souls, with speed and strength of quantum-powered Golden Horses, we could stretch out far into the galaxies; communicating with our inner and outer universes, all at the same time.

Dr Rodriguez continued by making a mysterious statement, 'See the Grid. See the Crystalline.'

I listened attentively.

He added, 'See the life that we never thought existed. And all along you thought you were alone. Really? Look out your window.

See the trees. See the sky. Do you feel them standing there and looking at you?'

A cold shiver ran through my spine as he said this. The exact feeling I had of "being looked at" as I lived in the villa with the deep surrounding forest of the village in Ubud. And there was Tyler's description of the trees that look upwards in Sembawang, Singapore. But what was this Grid? The world energy grid, the communication grid of the trees? And what was the Crystalline? Was he referring to the Crystalline Grid, the energetic lattice that covers the planet?

Dr Rodriguez intercepted, reading my thoughts, 'Visualize the grid as a geodesic sphere, of pentagons and triangles, sparkling as a faceted, brilliant diamond.'

I scrambled through the pages of the Web erratically. An article came up describing the Crystalline Grid as a seed crystal of new form, the double penta-dodecathedron. A highly complex shape with 144 facets (a number within the Fibonacci Sequence). The number 144 was the number of Christ ascension, and is considered a sacred number integral to all of creation. Perhaps, like a perfected crystal, a diamond, it is a number that works in harmony with our vibrational field bringing in a balancing effect to dimensional receptivity, encoding full brain thinking or a whole conscious experience. A 144 "galactic" frequency weaving itself through all of Creation.

For a moment I felt numb. The seeding – the tiny blue aquamarine gemstone. Seeding for an acceleration – an ascension. The triple '1's and quadruple '1's.

Dr Rodriguez went on further, 'As you evolve you will allow yourself to see with Quantum Eyes. Like a bird's ability to navigate using the Earth's magnetic field lines.'

Some researchers think birds might be able to see the magnetic field via photosensitive proteins in their retinas. The theory is that when a photon strikes one of these proteins, it creates a pair of oppositely charged ions, which separate for a fleeting moment before recombining. Each of these ions contains electrons with a quantum property called "spin". Initially, these spins point in opposite directions – but in a magnetic field, they tend to become aligned. When the ions recombine, this alignment triggers a specific biochemical reaction, which gives the bird information about the magnetic field.

That reminded me of the Olga's words on seeing people like energy beings with their auras and all. Quantum Eyes, eyes that that could see beyond the structure and deeper into the quantum energy. More than the eyes of the eagle, it was the eyes of the Divine Being that had that Quantum Eyes effect of a totally different level. A seamless, nontheatrical but overflowing burst of love. Some would call it the "The Sight of the Lord". The sacred presence, touching me in a very loving way.

It was Dr Rodriguez's prophesy that we would become like that, quantum-eyed New Humans. I had a taste of it through the blue eyed boy in the dream of the students at a school making a pledge.

Dr Rodriguez lectured, 'Children who are born without structure. We call them autistic. Some say that in their brain the structure of 3 dimensions has been removed. These are quantum individuals to the max. They respond very badly and poorly in a 3-dimensional structure. Some of them do not even want to put words together. The Spirit is testing the waters!'

At once I was reminded of Tyler and Marianne. I felt that they were all very early versions of the Golden People with an emerging development of quantum eyes, heart and much more.

I asked with an open-ended objective, 'The Golden People?'

Dr Rodriguez replied, 'Yes, possibly. A Golden People with a super-intelligence beyond what you can imagine. Though the super-intelligence would be conscious in principle, since the neural code is akin to a computational code, thoughts could well be embedded in a silicon-based substrate.'

Silicon-based? Of course, the carbon to crystalline theory.

Dr Rodriguez added, 'A silicon-based intelligence would also have tremendous implications for long distance space travel.'

Riveting information indeed.

He said, 'By the way, such highly intelligent beings here on Earth include the dolphins. We could learn from them.'

The example was shown through my visionary Bali friend David, whose love for the dolphins, as they led him to his salvation. The intertwining with nature where all the answers lie.

As soon as my Skype video call with Dr Rodriguez ended, I did not hear from him for several weeks. From what I heard, he had fallen gravely ill. Despite his awe-inspiring gifts of profound knowledge and linguistic ability, Darkness enveloped his mind and body. He failed to stop drowning in alcohol. I could almost imagine his body crying for its life as sickness took over. If I could just inject that quantum horsepower into him, and get him back up on his feet, all fired up with his usual intensity. Unfortunately, all I could do was pray that he would be okay.

The Giant Tree of Life

In my mind, the third Key is the Giant Tree of Life. It is a majestic symbol emanating purity and stability, projecting a world that is a reflection of the true nature of our collective Self. The tree of life is a concept, a metaphor for common descent, and a motif in various world theologies and philosophies. Biologists use the DNA sequences of modern organisms to reconstruct the tree of life and to figure out the likely characteristics of the most recent common ancestor of all living things — the "trunk" of the tree of life. Speaking about the DNA, the 3 letter genetic code, CGA and GCG, are the same in every creature, every life form. Everything has consciousness, where only humans have the creative potential (or full potential) of the Spirit of God.

As such, I imagined it as not just a tree of life, but a Giant Tree of Life with its golden canopy and eternal branches, powered by the Holy Spirit of God as we function as parts of each other yet like independent branches clear with our purpose and playing it out perfectly. It was perhaps a haven for not only my own healing and solace, but the same for everyone else as a place of love, a place of succorance with a bond between caring parties, to commune and connect. Moreover, its lifeblood may "circulate" the blessings - from the vine to the branches, and from branches to other branches. A continuous flow of give and receive.

A recollection of the words of knowing that came through while in Bali, '... to grow your roots deep into the soil of your origin. To draw the sap - the core of your soul, undergoing change the same way that the sap of a tree is chemically transformed in the trunk of the tree.'

We would tap into the sap of God, as we are all chemically and spiritually transformed for eternity. This would bring us back to our inherent nature, which is communal and compassionate: as we would not send each other out to war, we would not let each other starve and we would not deceive or lie to each other.

Marianne's words, 'There will be clarion call of God from the pulpit. We will say a thing and people will be changed in a twinkling of the eye! People who were in opposition are going to come together as different facets of a diamond.'

There was immense power in those prophetic words. Depicted by the Giant Tree of Life, there is a potential for whole world standing united! Speaking like sages, creating with magnificence like the magis, scanning the spiritual realm like the Watchmen and the list goes on. A holographic New World finally comes into form as it is super-charged with the long-awaited Unity, a power distributed to many.

To take the Golden Road

The Golden Road is perhaps the fourth and final Key. An imagined version of myself standing on that long glimmering golden pathway, stretching out, meandering between the golden canopies of trees. As I stood on that road, it meant that I had already made the right choices. I had moved away from dark pathways representing old ways, destructive habits and archaic levels of thinking. I had shed my old Self for good.

Along the way, an imagined voice of Stephanie echoing with authority, 'Stop wavering! Let your "Yes" be "Yes" and your "No" be "No"!'

Three bipolar years of contrasts and extremes. I found myself moving forward and then backward again. My soul screaming, 'Festinate! Move forward!'

I realized that once I made the decision to say 'Yes', I had relinquished my Ego and let God guide me.

Bringing to mind, Marianne's words, 'Faith brings about possibilities'.

Faith is linked to saying 'Yes'. The old pathway is like quicksand under our feet, dragging us down instead of uplifting us. The Many Worlds Interpretation where we switch from one physical reality (world) to another physical reality (world) a billion times a second. In a chaotic system, very small changes in initial conditions lead to radically different trajectories. Protracted by the Double Slit Experiment, the motion of the electron after it has passed the slits is chaotic in just this sense. As a matter of fact, even a diminutive thermal fluctuation in an electron's interaction with the slits can cause the electron's future motion to be unknowable to us.

"The minute that you begin to do what you want to do, it really is a different kind of life,' quote R Buckminister Fuller

The appealing different kind of life made through positive intentions. With each decision made, more possibilities branch out. The impending choice of the Golden Door which was that elusive. I had to stay with the guidance of the Holy Spirit of God to lead the way, and I had to stick with it, believe in it with all my heart with no turning back.

Stephanie advised, 'Everything comes with a price, whether it is great wealth, fame or even advancement. We have to be prepared to let go of the old to bring in the new, no matter how uncomfortable we are with it,' and then raising her voice with insistence, she exclaimed, 'So stay focused! Stop over-thinking and go with the flow!'

To become a Towering Golden Soul, staying united and communal as represented by the Giant Tree of Life, and with a Golden Horse powered physicality and speed, choosing to take the elusive Golden Road. A potent assemblage.

The Symbolic Keys

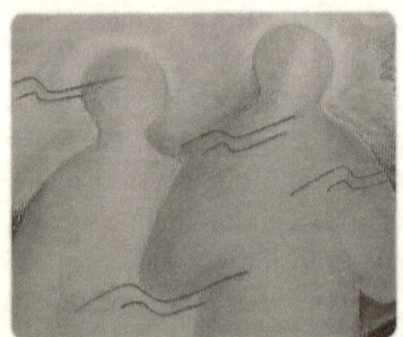

Towering Golden Souls

Quantum-powered Golden Horses

Giant Tree of Life

Golden Road

Moving at Unstoppable Speed

Mentally weaving through the curves and downturns, unrelenting and unstoppable. Maneuvering with precision as in my dreams. And as I walk I pick up the specks of gold dust on the surface of the road, picking up the fragments of golden lessons along the way.

I imagined the feeling of Jesus holding my right hand guiding me through the road whispering to me to stay focused, to be unwavering so that I would reach the Golden Door at the end of the road.

Stephanie reminded me, 'Watch for the signs. If you are on the right path, more signs will show themselves. To stay in the zone, we need to continually spend time with God and converse with Him. Focus your thoughts on what you wish to create, rather than what you do not wish to experience.'

An imaginary repeat button playing an image of myself walking down the Golden Road.

Silent affirmations to myself, 'I have chosen my path and I am not stopping for anything!' - marking my unwavering decision when suddenly a message from divinity came in consanguinity.

A message received,"God is smoothing the path for you now!'

The imaginary road smoothing and straightening out its meandering curves, padded and cushioned, supportive, every step of the way. The smoothing of my path may look like an infinitesimal part of Planet Earth's smoothing path towards advancement. The Double Slit Experiment proving big trajectory changes in an electron. My change could shift me invisibly into a totally different world. Many different permutations of the New World. Or many different permutations of the current world degraded further. Not by chance like the roll of a dice. A freewill of real concerted effort. The Golden Door led to my most desired world.

The Golden Door Opens

Sealing my eyes, in moments, I was deep in my inner space. Suddenly, the interception of multiple strands of curved lines buzzing and vibrating as they stretched across the dark space horizontally. I knew immediately that it was the strands of the DNA. It appeared beyond the double helix formation, perhaps triple helix or beyond. I was stunned.

What was going on here? Was it my own transfigured DNA shown to me? Or was it a sign that the DNA of my body was being scanned for qualified access to the New World? If it was not referring to me, was it the DNA of the New Human required for entry? From some speculative research I had uncovered, when a third strand is activated, a human may experience the 4th Dimensional reality, and after activation of a 4th strand of DNA, the 5th Dimensional reality may be experienced. These 3rd and 4th strands of DNA have remained dormant within the DNA structure, and are being activated throughout our planet by energies currently bathing our world.

With those energies, perhaps "doors" would open or "veils" would lift. I envisioned many who have gone through this before me, and many who were going through at the same time, and a number waiting to get access. Like an invisible Judgment Day with long queues of souls waiting. "They" decide if you are ready for the New World. "They" telepathically scan your body, soul and spirit to check if you have qualified. If you are "In", you are led through. I imagined those who could not go through were given another chance another time. Was this the same queue of souls as in the "Portal and the Golden Souls" vision?

Marianne's words, 'Judgment is not punishment. Judgment is just verdict. Judgment always gives an opportunity for life to change to come into the fullness of God.'

Then a duskiness enveloped my view. In the far distance, a pitch black curtain (perhaps the veil) that was drawn came to view. The curtain started lifting ever so slowly. It was the unveiling of something secret, something untouchable, something new.

Marianne words in the past, 'There is an ever thinning veil between Heaven and Earth!'

Marianne did share previously that several veils were going to be lifted. I remembered that on the Prophetic Painting I did in 2008, I sketched the four arcane doors opening to the center painted in bright red. Were those four doors the four veils? And was this vision of a lifting black curtain another one of them?

> 'Four arcane wooden doors
> Opening on all sides ...'
> ~ from the descriptive prose of the Prophetic Painting of 2008

The planetary Golden Door was symbolic of the opening veil, as though all the four Keys were unlocking in-sync for a great revelation. I felt light, expanded, overflowing with joy and gratitude. I kept my eyes locked on the lifting curtain. Inch by inch the curtain rose, displaying a shimmering Crystal City in view. Undoubtedly, it felt like the New World. A Crystal City formed at some moment in time. There were several tall towers and buildings. All crystalline with one which was the tallest sitting in the center amidst the grand display. Perhaps the giant Crystal Block I was shown earlier was used as a building block for this shimmering city. A stunning view surrounded by pitch blackness.

Scrutinizing the futuristic scene with an intense curiosity, I could see sparkling crystal lotus formations closed tightly to seal something. Impressive large constructs, their sextuplet off-white petals were shaped like the curved walls of the Sydney Opera House. More accurately, a union with the palm-like Singapore ArtScience Museum to form a hybridized composite form. The walls appeared to be built of clear crystal, or perhaps even diamond. In entirety, they were ostentatious but positively miraculous.

The walls which were closed in like a lotus bud began to open up. As I waited to see what was within those walls, all of a sudden I found myself in a hall with dome-shaped pathways. To my dismay, I was unable to make a full 360 degree scan of the area as the visual scenes of the city switched in flying speed way beyond my control. From the hall, I found myself abruptly on one of the pathways. It was clear that each pathway was leading to different locations, that is, other hallways or rooms. And considering the curvature of its supreme architecture, I was so sure that I was inside one of those large lotus formations.

As I looked around the enclosed pathway, the looming walls were even more astounding. The same clear crystal formations with fine lace engravings, with each block of crystal molding and reflecting light from different angles. Mentally tuning in to see with more clarity, I could see sacred geometry engraved onto the borders of the crystal walls. Sacred geometry, the secret language of life. All in all, it felt out of this world. Mesmerized, I continued to admire the intrinsic beauty, harmony and perfection of the shapes with awe.

Slowly I drifted myself out from the vision and back into reality. I was physically tired as if I had gone on some astral journey. The soles of my feet were trickling with sensation even though I had not moved an inch. Not to lose an ounce of the visual and audio discoveries, I sat down with my sketchpad to draw out the vision of my observations, excavating new meanings and revelations hidden within. I kept reflecting back on the huge Crystal Block that I saw the last time when I ascended. If it was not just a piece for building construction, where was it? It could have been in one of the rooms which pathways led to that branched out from that 6 sided hall I was shown.

The 6-sided hall leading to 6 different locations. Each location may have a unique meaning. Switching into rational thinking to find some answers, the Metatron's Cube came to mind instantly. The number 13 (of its equal circles) may signify purification, alternatively, the death of oneself and the birth of the spirit. The reborn and the renewed New Humans. The lotus formations similar to the carved formations of the Flower of Life which is associated with the Metatron's Cube.

The 6-sided Hall
Leading to 6 pathways
The circumference of the Metatron's Cube
The Perfect Blueprint.

Within those circles, there were 5 platonic solids. The Number 5 signifies radical change as well as Grace. Now delving further to explore the circles. If each circle's center is considered a "node", and each node is connected to each other node with a single line, then there will be a total of 78 lines. The Numbers 7 and 8 separately may mean the Presence of God - completion and abundance. Was that the underlying meaning?

All of a sudden, I felt a piercing sensation in the middle of my left palm. Perhaps the invisible stigmata signaling a message. Was it related to the crucifixion? A possible theory that the cross was actually a cube unfolded. The cube possibly the representation of the universe, or a perfectly balanced Euclidean space.

Bringing it all together, it just may be that the symbol for sacrifice is derived from the concept of unraveling perfection towards this Crystal City and its people. A symbol to allow for our rebirth and our renewal. Not to resist or to hold on to old ways or old ideas as it may be the only pathway for a changed New World where everything is expanded and magnified; with constraints broken down and harmonic creation in abundance. The New World, defined by the Holy of Holies, a destination so sacred, so special.

The sparkling Crystal City
Marked by a foison,
Governed by the New Commodity
Of the Heart

Fruit of Life is a 3 Dimensional structure containing 13 circles. 13 represents Unity and transition between worlds and dimensions. In the chromatic scale of the 12 notes, the 13th note is actually repeating the 1st note but on a higher frequency. When we attain a higher octave, we enter a higher dimension. If we connect all the centers of the 13 circles, the result is 78 lines which creates a structure called the Metatron's Cube. This structure contains all 5 platonic solids. This geometry of Metatron's Cube is set to underlay the quantum vacuum or "void" and it is fundamental to the creation process at the quantum level. The zero point. The Tree of Life also exists within the Fruit of Life pattern.

Metatron's Cube is a name for a sacred geometric figure composed of 13 equal circles with lines from the center of each circle extending out to the centers of the other 12 circles. It is considered the fundamental geometry of the universe. It is the Holy of Holies which is the place considered most sacred, most special.

Triple helix DNA The famous "molecule of life", which carries our genetic code, is more familiar to us as a double helix. However, now the triple helix DNA is a hot topic. Some researchers say that the Human DNA is now evolving from a mere two strands (which are responsible for lower dimensional traits such as survival and procreation), to three, four, or even twelve strands of DNA fully activated. Some research says that a human with two strands of DNA activated is plugged into a 3rd Dimensional reality which we have experienced here on earth. When a third strand is activated, a human may experience the 4th Dimensional reality, and after activation of a 4th strand of DNA, the 5th Dimensional reality may be experienced. These 3rd and 4th strands of DNA have remained dormant within the DNA structure, and are being activated throughout our planet by energies currently bathing our world. Please note that there may still be speculation in these claims.

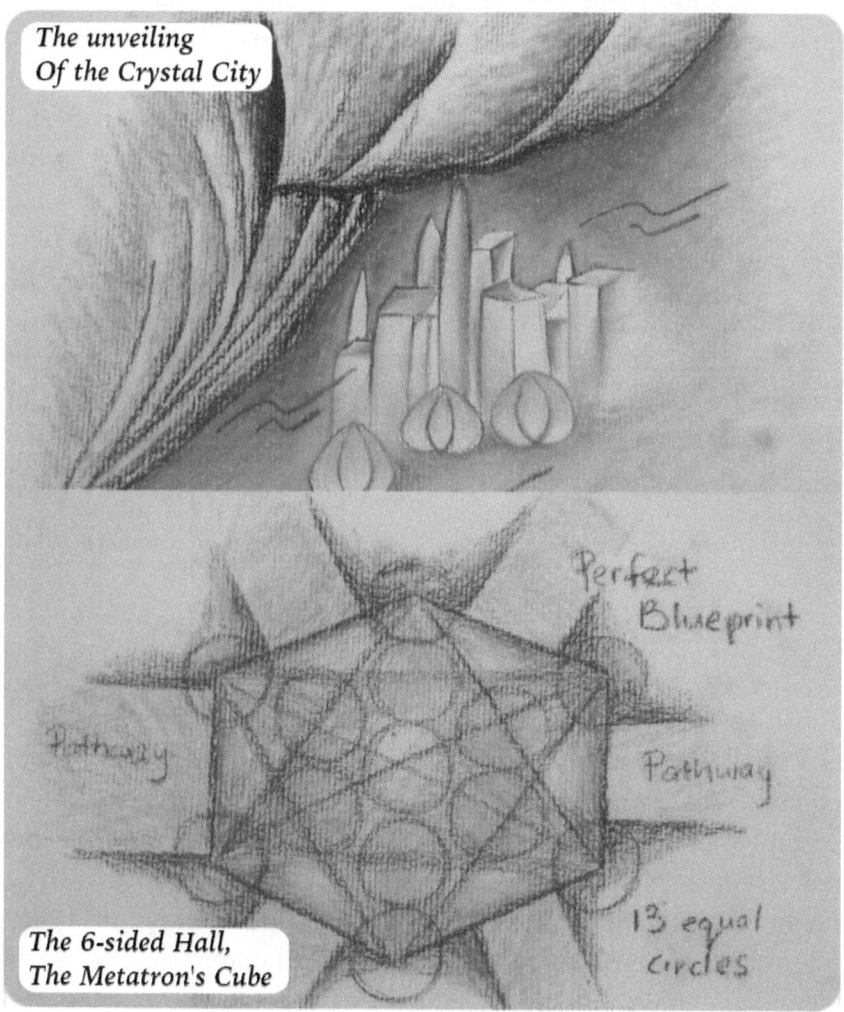

The Golden People

Still I was not satisfied. I wanted to see more. I wanted to know more about the people. That same week I went into meditation, prayer and worship asking to be shown more. I breathed in some frankincense essential oil to ease the process by raising my body's vibrational frequency. Soon after the vision showed itself. First a large expanse of land. Subsequently, vast areas of sea could be seen.

Soon the vision was clear enough and I realized that they were land continents separated by oceans. And on the land appeared uniformly-sized pyramids scattered all around.

Then I noticed something. I wanted to zoom in to see closer. I saw many bubbles of energy floating. Zooming in further. In the center of the bubble were human souls! They were just freely floating from city to city, continent to continent. There was an energy field penetrating from the bottom to the top of each soul bubble. The torus field of energy more fully utilized as souls floated freely and trans-located anywhere and everywhere, flying as if there were no undercurrents in the air. There was a spark within the center of those floating people which made me think of the MerKaBa - the wheels within the wheels.

Citizens trans-locating freely
Driven by the divine Light vehicle,
The crystalline field
Of the efficacious MerKaBa.

The MerKaBa, an inter-dimensional vehicle consisting of two equally sized, interlocked tetrahedra of Light with a common center, where one tetrahedron points up and the other down. This point symmetric form is called a stella octangula which can also be obtained by extending the faces of a regular octahedron until they intersect again. Also coined as the Star Tetrahedron, since it can be viewed as a three dimensional Star of David. Some research describe this "Star Tetrahedron" as counter-rotating, through meditative state activating a non-visible saucer shaped energy field around the body.

Within the MerKaBa, is a crystalline energy field that is comprised of specific sacred geometries that align the mind, body, and heart together. This energy field created from sacred geometry extends around our bodies over a great distance. These geometric energy fields normally spin around our bodies at close to the speed of Light, but for most of us it has slowed down or stopped spinning entirely due to a lack of attention and use.

Floating souls showing their unlimited energy source within. Heaven on Planet Earth and Heaven in the Human Heart as a direct reflection of each other, dependent on each other where one cannot do without the other. The break in the separation between "I" and "You". The quantum God effect. And with that in mind, we need to make sure that the technology of God is always present. As we are part of an open world and we have the ability to create multiple worlds, the essence of this is so integral.

One of them being Heaven on Earth, the planet and the cities with a crystalline grid structure, magnifying all existing energies. Tied into Heaven is the Human Heart where the citizens are so consumed in the purity of God within their hearts that they are emanating in His Glory. They are washed off of all the black dots of blemishes, and they are more in the zone than ever before. There is a sense of urgency intertwined within the personalities of the people. People of all walks of life wanting to taste the infinities of existence. They begin early but never slowly. They are constantly reading new books, studying new trades, trying new things and discovering new places. At the same time, wanting to indulge in the infinite span of time. Time with a different meaning. The Old World chronological time invaded by the New World time where there may be minimal or no decay.

I wanted to see more, but that was all that was shown to me. A greater preview of a preview. I closed my eyes again fantasizing what I could be shown next time. Emerald tablets laden across the Crystal City displaying commandments and pledges titling from the "Law of Non-Interference" and more. I imagined Human "Light" Beings assembling in the halls conversing, with a gold and white Light covering the Hall. I imagined a misty spray that filled the air, as people would be hydrating and nourishing themselves unconsciously as they consumed through their translucent skin.

'This City is what it is because our citizens are what they are,' quote Plato

Plato's words perfecting the explanation of the citizens of the Crystal City.

Marianne's words, 'God says ... You reflect my Glory!'

The Crystal City was a reflection of God's Glory. I imagined that in the Crystal City we had gone beyond religion, beyond politics. A harmonious and cooperative civilization of at least a Type I Civilization or beyond. The Crystal City came about because it was a reflection of its citizens. Every citizen had to know and have the Symbolic Keys. Every citizen had to unlock the Golden Doors in their hearts.

Citizens trans-locating freely

20

The Secret Key

The God-Man Oneness.
An upraised beingness.

The underlying Key
For all transformation
Of all precepts
Of all order.

With its absence
The whole sidereal system
Would fall into a void.

Singapore
March 2015

Returning to 2013, the time of the death of my old Self, which was the real beginning of my transcendence. I was also earwitness to an unforgettable beckoning voice of an Angel:

Commanding Voice, 'God is sending a lot of messages to a lot of people right now!'

Divine messages going directly to many, as audible voices, as visions, as downloads and as a knowing. To myself, to my family and to my mentors and guides who I met along the way. And thanks to God I had grown in my knowing.

The new found learning of the Symbolic Keys was a pleasant uplifting on its own. The dreams and visions of the Crystal City perhaps symbolic with a deeper meaning or a very real premonition, I was not quite sure. Setting aside my wild imagination, time would tell. Nonetheless, there were so many tests tackled in my envisioned Upside-down Kingdom reflective of the Old World. I had battled numerous "villains" of that dominion – the screaming stepmother of the young boy, the deceiving businessman, the near fatal sickness of my father, my collapses, my negative emotions and the craving to hold onto things. Not finished, but an eternal battle that fortunately gets easier over time.

Still floating mentally, I drifted over to the front of my bedroom mirror. My face and body chiseled further. It had been a roller coaster ride. If I had to travel back in time, would I have recognized myself? A transfiguring three years. A hard push against the will of my Ego in many respects. I lost material things when it was things that I clung onto for self preservation. Things were never the true source of security. As a result, it was about discovering "beingness" and to let go of the old, to live in the moment and bring my future Self to the Now.

The divine leading to Bali to discover God through nature. The wake up call to look at things and to do things in a new way that would be light, easy and joyful for me. The learning from Faryal that we can find joy in even the simplest things. It was about learning to surrender to God instead of always wanting to take control. Olga and Adriana opened up my eyes and heart on unconditional love and forgiveness. Rizwan along with the MRT Stranger and the new visitor to Singapore, Han taught me to be zealous in taking action. Dr Rodriguez's message was about keeping up with change and moving fast, along with Stephanie's about thriving and creating a circle of giving and receiving. Mr Aminuddin taught me about openness, transparency and pursuing Truth. The young Punjabi boy, his baby sister as well as my two little birds from Pakistan taught me about filling our hearts with only joy. Yasmine and Mei Ling were teachers on self-healing and self-empowerment. Deepa's inspiration on Unity. Tyler and Marianne's spiritual guidance every step of the way. My father's dramatic yet poignant experience was on the power of miracles. And finally my mother's ennobling was that even the most fearful can overcome fear.

All towards the aspiration of discovering the true nature of my soul, and to unleash my Spirit Woman. The unopened spiritual eyes, the untapped wisdom, the undernourished supernatural intelligence and other gifts waiting to be released, no longer held back by daily drudgery.

Marianne's words when I first met her, 'We have been soul driven for too long. We have reached a point of time that it is now about developing the Spirit Man or Spirit Woman.'

The discretionary listening to the guidance and words of spiritual teachers, including random strangers. The life-altering encounter with the Divine Being. The unified message of hope, faith and unconditional love. The discovery of divine love which pushed me up to become a Towering Golden Soul for a sweeping moment. Growing my wisdom higher and higher, and allowing the Holy Spirit of God to lead me placing me on the fast track of the Golden Road.

Joining of Hearts

A clear skied Saturday morning on the 7th March 2015. It was another momentous gazing into divine eyes. A second time recurrence, a renaissance of a coming together which I relished deeply.

The moment was tender and blissful. So soft a moment that I gave it little importance. But as the days passed, I felt a filling up and expansion in my heart. I always thought I had a healthy heart, but the undulated expansion and the slight pains worried me. This was different. My heart felt double in size, with an indescribable magnetic energy covering my entire chest area. I did not think much of it in the first week. However, as the second week came by, it felt like a physical Oneness with the Holy Spirit of God. A flaming Fire as the energy filled more and more of my heart, the corresponding magnetic energy shifted to my hands leading to much greater pains than I had before. Biologically wired with a bilateral almost quantum powered energy flowing through – heart to hands, hands to heart, heart to hands so on and so forth.

I sensed a furtherance to my faculties with a greater need to lay my hands on people, to transfer that excess energy which I could not understand and could not handle within my physicality. Even when I was reluctant, but forced somehow; forced by a greater presence. I shared this new phenomenon with both Tyler and Deepa.

I shared, 'I don't understand what is going on with my heart. Since it started happening, the first thing I did was go to my doctor and she did an electrocardiogram (ECG) to test the performance of my heart. It turned out all normal.'

Tyler's observation, 'Remember many months back I saw an Angel standing next to you holding pen in one hand and a lightning bolt in the other hand?' he paused and said, 'Well, I think you are supposed to transfer the energy.'

When I asked Deepa, she said nothing. I told her what Tyler interpreted it to be. She listened with great thought and interest at the same time and was curious to understand more. My initial gut feel was that it was a union with the Holy Spirit of God. Then again, I could be wrong. It was also possible that Tyler was right about carrying out a transfer of that energy. Then again, he could be wrong. So I was going to try it out and see what would happen.

I asked Deepa if we could meet so that I could have her permission to transfer some of the "divine energy" to her. She agreed without hesitation. We arranged it immediately that afternoon.

I went over to her hostel and as we sat at a quiet corner, I said, 'Let's just hold hands, close our eyes and see what happens.'

As I closed my eyes, all I saw was a shining light. No visions, nothing else but just overflowing gold and white light flowing, bouncing and playing off each other.

About twenty minutes later, I released my hands from hers and asked impatiently, 'What did you see?'

'I saw so much Light. White Light,' Deepa answered.

'Anything else?' I asked.

'No ... nothing else. Though I feel very much at peace,' Deepa said.

While Deepa was the first, I discovered that during each transference session of "divine energy", the discomfort in my heart lessened and I felt at peace with myself. Perhaps, a deed done. I felt almost like a human electrical conductor passing on something divine. Of course, that is if what Tyler said was right, although it made a lot of sense as I practiced it. When I would resist, I would find myself agitated and the discomforts in my heart would start again. I was forced to be in obedience. So without resistance, I continued to do that to a few other people who were willing.

A few days later, that potent energy in my heart had subsided to a more comfortable level. Within two days, it went back to normal. But that was not it. The heart extending to the palms. The heart and hands connection. The gold sparkles in the Great Triangle of my left palm. The black spots that would appear and disappear in my right palm, which any Palmist would be fascinated by. God speaking to me through my hands - so close, so coalesced with me. The divine intimacy that was beyond measure.

Hence, the revelation of the Symbolic Keys, but the even greater discovery of the Secret Key – our intimacy with God. The Symbolic Keys represent the effort involved to go through the Golden Door, but the Secret Key makes the transition possible and easier. And to bring me up, it was the Divine Being, who I felt was Jesus. He was assisting in holding my hand along the Golden Road and through the Golden Door. Secret would be the right word, as it is hidden and sometimes unknown - it is underlying everything. The magnified energy in my heart was possibly another sign of a new human attribute. The remote viewing, the self-activated healing and more. Quantum eyes as illustrated by Dr Rodriguez. Then it was about the vision of humans trans-locating. Trans-location, perhaps just one of the many abilities that are being returned to us, once we become purified spiritual beings. Becoming translucent in our skin as we become more crystalline. All bizarre but perhaps real now and in the future. WE are the "new" technology with the God-Man Oneness.

It was never about limitation. It was never about division or ownership or even entitlement. All false precepts to create separation and fear. The all important God-Consciousness we have to carry in our hearts always. A confirmation that everything circumvolves around our hearts. The union of our hearts with the divine. The rest Machine-Nature were simply enhancing peripherals. They were like the devices, tools or constructs as part of the mechanics of the universe. The overwhelming benefits of machine through technological advancements; nature through the trees and crystals. The peripherals could only do so much and take us so far. Even if we had physically fit bodies, supernaturally intelligent minds, the support of machinery, technology as well as nature, the real mileage depends on our intimacy with God. The technology of God pushing Man up to become god-lings of a New World where Truth and righteousness rules.

I had to become more humble, more obedient, more joyful and so on. I had to develop a robustness of health more than ever before. I had to move with greater alignment with God at rocket speed! I had to create more and make more positive things to happen miraculously. My eye on becoming eternal like Jesus. As I felt the Oneness grow in my heart, at times I would have a paramnesia between illusion (of Heaven) and reality (the real world), as I fluctuated between both realms. With heavenly eyes, I was looking into the earthly activities of the world. I could see a lot better how it could be improved and remedied.

The God-Man Oneness that is so crucial as the underlying Secret Key. It was the layer underneath that layer of the Symbolic Keys to open the Golden Door of Planet Earth. The destination waiting for myself, and each and every one of us. All synchronizing together mysteriously appearing at the right time as soon as we are ready. That state of readiness achieved through all the preparations we have made for ourselves.

The Battle Won

That precarious night of the 7th of July 2014 when I was woken up at 4:30am stayed with me. I never understood why I was woken up at that time. Finally many months had to pass before I realized that it was also a circumstantial instruction from God (through his Angels) that 4:30am was my assigned sacred time with Him. I was frustrated by the perpetual time lag in coming into certain realizations, my wisdom still rough around the edges.

Henceforth, the daily alarm set on my clock at precisely 4:30am. The same deafening shrill in every dark morning to wake me up inexcusably. The only difference was this time is that I knew the objective. A renewed assurance and endeavor to move forward.

I stood on my prayer rug. I asked repeatedly and fervently in prayer, 'Dear God where am I now? What more do I need to learn? Please teach me. Show me.'

He would always be there. He would always come.

And at times, when I would go into pure stillness, I would always be shown what needed to shown, and what had to be learned. I was never let down. My relationship with Him so close, that I would never allow anything to break that sacred bond. Thus, those sacred 4:30am mornings proceeded. Sometimes I would fail to wake up, sometimes I wouldn't. To make regular time for Him was the unceasing discipline. I was thankful one morning when there was one thing I was shown that was totally unexpected.

At the blink of the eye, another vision appeared. It was the vision of a battalion of a tenfold or more demons heavily decked in bronze armor surrounding me in a full circle. Their large round heads, the ill-shapen and furious stare on their faces. Their bloodshot eyes locked onto my eyes. Their large throats releasing silent screams of rage. A ghastly battalion enveloped within a dull gray mist that surrounded them as they surrounded me uninvited.

They were not pleased at all. Not one bit. But no, I was not afraid. With God's grace I was protected by a divine shield. They tried their ways, but I would soon become untouchable. Not there yet. Still a long way to go. I had to remain committed. I had to keep persevering. I had to keep that shield strong always.

My silent yet firm words to the defiant battalion, an abstract from Psalm 7:10, 'My shield is God Most High, who saves the upright in heart ...'

Inviolable and untouchable by Darkness, so that I could keep transcending. To become more purified, more shining, more golden.

Marianne words, 'Many of us will be purified and made white.'

The white or clear crystal visions shown repeatedly in different forms. The Blue Crystal Dome. The huge clear Crystal Block. The sparkling Crystal City. Recording the milestones of my uplifting, I reached out to the amethyst bracelet I was wearing and replaced it with a precious malleable gold bangle around my left wrist. It was a passed on inheritance from my paternal grandmother.

Incidentally, I was reminded of the most recent acquaintance, Han's dream where he saw diamonds popping out from the skin of my face.

Reminiscing John Lennon's song, ' ... Lucy in the sky with diamonds ...'

Seeing diamonds and finally "being" a diamond. A hopeful vision of my future – the diamond-cut and polished Self. After all, diamond hearts are simply divine.

The Grid, the Crystalline

I checked my iPhone and found that a frantic email had come through from the wife of Dr. Rodriguez. He was critically ill in hospital with liver failure. It was uncertain whether it would be his last days, his last breath. His early departure would be a waste of a great soul. Without a doubt, he was brilliant and way ahead of his time.

In moments, a call came in and it was Dr. Rodriguez's wife.

'He left you message. It was an email, but it was on the Outbox folder. It was not sent yet,' she said.

'What was the message?' I asked.

'Wait, let me forward it to you,' she replied.

In two seconds, my iPhone buzzed and I opened up the email to read it - ' ... I told you about the Grid. Just imagine Planet Earth as a Giant Crystal ...'

I could interpret it almost immediately. He was clearly referring to the Earth Grid. It was about the planet, about crystals and indirectly about us. Crystals magnify energy. Crystals are the building block of who we are.

The phenomenon of the overwhelming energy in my heart with the astounding feeling of expansion. I did the right thing and passed the energy. I had to keep building that energy through greater and greater unification with God. Not just to build, but to pass it on. The Metatron's Cube in our hearts to reflect the Heavenly realm. New Humans with a quantum-powered spinning MerKaBa in their hearts residing in a Crystal City that expands the energies further. We, Planet Earth and the universe are all a mirror of each other, and that the Earth is inherently crystalline, while we are all inherently crystalline. With all the signs and visions of crystals and the crystalline, I saw it as a message that we are being called to return to our base elements.

Like crystals, we are built based on structure and order. Like crystals, we contain unlimited information and memory within our DNA. Like crystals, there is a fluidity of Light that permeates through. The God consciousness. I imagined that Light penetrated and expanded many times greater within a crystalline membrane rather than a carbon-based membrane. I imagined the carbon structure would diffuse and absorb the energy.

Stephanie's words, 'We are shifting from Self-Consciousness to World-Consciousness to God-Consciousness.'

At that instant, my hands and my chest pounding with energy. A painful intensity. An arising with goosebumps on my skin. I had to catch my breath. A feeling that Jesus was holding my hand, teaching and guiding. A timely message that God-Consciousness (or the Oneness with God) would aid us to return to our crystalline true nature.

I continued to read Dr Rodriguez's email - 'We spoke about this before, that Planet Earth rings like a bell – that was the great insight of Nikola Tesla. Just imagine how the world would be if the right tone of music was ringing through this crystalline Earth ...'

His email ended there. His message was about the right tone of music with its subliminal effects. Because the human body is like a sound chamber, there is so much that needs to be done to tune our sound to the optimal frequency, that "divine sound" to create a divine Earth.

> The Earth was claimed to be envisioned as a "Giant Crystal" by a group of three Russian scientists in the 1960's. There are claims that decades after, researchers have defined the **New Earth Grid** as a formation of hexagonal geometric shapes that exist within a crystalline sphere. This new Crystalline grid is based on an infinite number – one that is built according to sacred geometry, the divine blueprint. Anthropologists may have found that the planetary grid of Earth is the shape of Metatron's Cube (also known as the Sphere of creation), which is a sacred geometric energy form that includes all other forms including the Flower of Life, Tree of Life, and the list goes on. Earth functions like energy lines that follow sacred geometry patterns and when put together represents a Sphere that has energy grids that move in a "wheels within the wheels" design as depicted in many ancient texts around *the world*.

The Divine Signs of Intimacy

A message 'Spend more time with God, and you will see what will happen!'.

While I prayed for others, I had a prayer done on me. And that was the message. It was one commanding instruction to another. I was being pushed to interface further with God.

All of sudden, a buzz on my iPhone. A Facebook private message from Mei Ling, the Qi Gong Master.

'Guess what! There was an announcement that the Schumann frequency just hit 16.5 Hertz (up from 7.83 Hertz). Wow! This demonstrates that the Earth itself is changing and is literally speeding up!' Mei Ling exclaimed.

If the Earth experienced a spike, I experienced my own spike with the doubling or tripling in my heart's magnetic resonance through what I felt was the union with the Holy Spirit of God.

Then came the landmark date. March 23rd 2015 marked the passing of the political giant Lee Kuan Yew who led Singapore to become a free and responsible nation. March 23rd 2015 (23 + 3 + 2015 which reduces to a single digit 7). The Mystical 7 staccato that presented itself numerous times in my personal and family life during the course of the events, and now appearing for nationalistic reasons. The Number 7 representing the Presence of God. A divine presentiment for the people of Singapore. The late leader did a commendable job in laying the bricks, and now it was the start of a new era. A time for the citizens to elevate themselves with a great God intimacy and to take their transformation into the marketplace.

To bring forth the Crystal City, the possible full manifestation of blueprint of Heaven on Earth. Singapore is drawing these highly sensitive and deeply spiritual souls for a unified purpose. The Buddhist Monk, Han and the other travelers who were led by the Spirit to come to Singapore. Was Singapore like the Antioch? Perhaps that was why the Buddhist Monk shared in the early part of my journey that Singapore was, as he said, "more ready". A spiritual gathering place to prepare for a greater elevation, perhaps its own inner and outer crystallization, while the neighboring countries such as Malaysia and Indonesia follow suit. Concurrently, the shakeup and the start of the purification of Pakistan, one of the many hearts of the world. Just like the tiny growing gemstone that was throbbing and coming alive.

Centuries had to pass before there is a universal realization that only love has any validity or any real alignment. Any disputes were peacefully resolved through non-violent judicial format like the Heavenly Courts. Under the tutelage of political leadership with a world view that was unified, coherent and in sync with the hearts and minds of the people.

A calling for a deeper divine intimacy across Planet Earth. The Secret Key was becoming more and more real, and more and more evident. As I was coming out of the woodwork, the Secret Key was itself revealing after centuries of being set aside as secondary to the worldliness and materialism. The four white stars with a purple glow across my forehead. Perhaps the Father, Son, Holy Spirit of God and Me, coming together for an outpouring of purity and out of the Earth's orbit. An overflowing. My personal transfiguration together with the societal and national transfiguration, symbiotic of Planet Earth's transfiguration in concurrence. The eventual rise of the spiritual citizens – the new citizens that are master creators and master alchemists coming into the marketplace.

Dr Rodriguez's words spoken earlier, 'WE are the new invention! You and I ..."

The New Humans with the new energies, reflections of the Golden Horse for stealth and speed to respond, awaken, change and strengthen mentally, emotionally and physically. More so, the double or triple expansion of hearts working as "Black (White) Whole, Heaven in the Heart" of a higher altitude. From quarks to quasars, from zero point to stretching out to becoming Towering Golden Souls. Breaking all the false divisions so that we can commune and become united for the further blossoming of the Giant Tree of Life. New Humans with fingertips of golden energy, loving and influencing others. Free and happy beings in a healthy communal state of sophrosyne.

And at the end of the road of transformation, though we do not know when that would be, I imagined that one simply rests in natural ground of our esse, which can be called "pure consciousness". Planet Earth may have transcended to reflect higher and higher through the realms of Heaven; while our bodies self generate through time and dimensional shifts. From 5th, 6th, 7th dimension and beyond as the Human DNA re-coded itself automatically with the transit. Crystals doing their part to activate. Perhaps we would be transcending up the realms of Heaven to enter the realms of Eternity. Eternity where there is no end and no beginning. We would have raised our vibrational frequencies to the level that we are able to fully harness an unimaginable amount of divine energy within ourselves. Perhaps, by that time, we may not be eating at all. We may not have names. Our identity felt and sensed through our energetic heart code as nameless, vast, boundless Light.

Sensing, feeling, seeing, thinking and becoming like Light, Light and more Light, magnified by the crystalline, the no longer obscure elemental constructs of the divine, I pulled out the manuscript of my book, and typed in the words "Part 1" in front of the title "Through the Golden Door". Thence the blood, sweat and tears of an embryonic phase sealed and done, and may the next phase of an odyssey for knowledge acquisition and spiritual uplifting begin.

21

Your Personal Golden Door # Action Plan

I am a mere quark in the entire planetary uplifting, just 1 out of about 7 Billion or more. A rainbow colored tapestry of human souls. You and I are the threads, our colors are different and our textures vary. Let the New World be that masterpiece. I hope that this book becomes such an expansion of my Spirit Woman that it inspires you to seek your Personal Golden Door. It may be time to experience the shooting star resemblance of your Spirit Man (Spirit Woman). It may be time for you to be as expansive as a mighty quasar so that you can reach your spiritual limelight. It may be time to join in with other God-led hearts for a planetary advancement upward.

Homework on Chapter 1 'The Old World'

Personal Exercise #1: List down the personal challenges you are facing in your current world (Old World)?

Group Exercise #1: List up to 10 things that would best describe what you would like to see in the New World. Form a small group of up to

5 members and share this within the group. You might be surprised what you can learn from each other.

Homework on Chapter 2 'To Simply Be'

I described the Old World as an Upside-down Kingdom as shown in my vision, '... an upside down world with boundaries and limitations.'

Personal Exercise #2: What boundaries and limitations are there in your life? From now on, refer to that list from time to time and meditate on how you can resolve them.

Personal Exercise #3: Next, just as I had done, consider letting go of the unnecessary things in your life. Prepare a list and see how you can work on them. Take baby steps as letting go is never easy.

Homework on Chapter 3 'Growing The Spirit Man'

The essence of Chapter 3 is to give you some awareness on the your Spirit Man (Spirit Woman). It is all about frequency – linking everything together, mind, body and soul. The purpose of the mind is to empower the Spirit Man (Spirit Woman) to function.

Personal Exercise #4: Keeping stress under control is crucial to allow our minds to work on this function. An abstract from this chapter, 'To reduce stress by letting go of work situations that no longer serve. To make healthy choices in the associations with people as a conducive fellowship raises my vibrational energies.' Access how you can resolve this in your own life.

Personal Exercise #5: Another abstract from this chapter, 'Physically, I had to lighten and strengthen my body through oxygenation, hydration, occasional fasting and any activities that induced the removal of toxins. Eating raw or live foods, moving away from heavier foods.' Work out a daily diet and exercise plan for you to strengthen yourself.

Homework on Chapter 4 'Intertwining With Nature'

An abstract from this chapter, 'Wildlife needs to be protected as they are God's way of using nature to direct us to the right path.'

Group Exercise #2: **Protecting nature is** everyone's responsibility in one way or the other. Within the same group, discuss how you (and the group) could play a part in conserving wildlife in the neighborhood, city or country you live in. Appoint a group member who is most passionate to take the lead in this topic, and ensure that actions are followed through as a team effort.

Homework on Chapter 5 'Everyone A Healer'

Regardless of what your situation is, I believe that everyone can heal themselves. But of course, we need to be ready for it. Allow the Holy Spirit of God to guide you.

Personal Exercise #6: If you experienced a similar "spontaneous self-healing" phenomenon as I have, that's wonderful! If you have not, when you go into prayer and make that your intention. Ask God to allow you to experience spontaneous self-healing. As the saying goes, 'Ask and Thou Shall Receive!'

Homework on Chapter 6 'Reaching Zero Point'

At this point, keep going with the daily prayers, meditation and/or worship.

Personal Exercise #7: If you have seen any visions, had any dreams, heard an audible voice, received any revelations or messages in unusual ways, write that down in your journal.

Personal Exercise #8: List down the mentors and guides assisting you with your progress so far. It is important to recognize who they are. Describe what they have taught you and what advice they have given you. Anyone can be a mentor or guide. An Angelic presence can come in various forms. But it is important to be discerning on who guides you. Get your spiritual leader to assist you with this. At the same time, keep your senses open and alert always.

Personal Exercise #9: Now let's turn the tables and list down the tests you have faced so far. Describe how they have come into your life to cause a hindrance in your spiritual uplifting. Meditate and pray requesting for guidance on dealing with them. Consider what you learned in Chapter 2 – To Simply Be, the segment on letting go of things, situations, relationships that are toxic and slow you down.

Homework on Chapter 7 'Loving Unconditionally'

Personal Exercise #10: Record any supernatural or preternatural experiences you have had so far. If some have made you uncomfortable, just remember that it is always mind over matter. It is always about intention. If you do not put in energy into the thought of demons, then they may not affect you or be part of your life.

Personal Exercise #11: Here is an exercise on meditating on God's Word. Quieten your mind and visualize your Meditative Secret Place. Then meditate on these words on "Love". *'Love is patient and kind; love does not envy or boast; it is not arrogant or rude. It does not insist on its own way; it is not irritable or resentful; it does not rejoice at wrongdoing, but rejoices with the truth. Love bears all things, believes all things, hopes all things, endures all things.'* 1 Corinthians 12:4-8

An abstract from this chapter, '.... when individuals become secure in love, societies as a whole become secure and happy, and this pushes forth progress of Planet Earth to the next level.'

Personal Exercise #12: Assess whether you feel secure in love right now.

If your relationship with your parents is weak, it may pose as a hindrance in your spiritual uplifting. Since your parents brought you into this world, while God is your spiritual Father/Mother, building a loving intimate relationship with both God and your parents is integral. If it is impossible to build that relationship with your parents, or they have passed on, simply ask for forgiveness and that you have forgiven them unconditionally. Keep working on parental issue resolution until you feel your heart is cleansed of all the pain and hurt from the past. Nothing is more fulfilling than a resolved and healed relationship with our earthly parents and our spiritual parent (God). It will lift you up many times higher as it had for me.

Homework on Chapter 8 'The Golden Door' and Chapter 9 'No Fear, No Anger'

To deal with our destructive emotions is the next stage of the purification process. The Old World is what it is because of fear and because of anger. It is the manifestation of these core emotions and all the other emotional reactions tied to it.

Personal Exercise #13: If you are ruled by fear, explore ways how you can deal with it in your life. The same applies to anger.

God speaks to us in different ways. In fact, He may speak to us in ways that we are most familiar with. I have always had an affinity with numbers, visual images and I knew the art and science of reading palms. I received the message from God through my palms when I was anxious, to guide me. I was also shown spectacular visions. I received signs through repeated numbers.

Personal Exercise #14: As you ask for the Holy Spirit of God to fill you and to come into your life, to teach you and to guide you, watch for the signs. Be patient and stay committed with your heart and eye on the Holy Spirit. You may be surprised by how God decides to "speak" to you - perhaps in a unique way.

Homework on Chapter 10 'No Lies, No Secrets'

I spoke about how we are entering an era where nothing can truly be hidden anymore. There is no escaping it as it is going to be more and more prevalent. We need to make speaking and acting in Truth a part of our daily lives.

Personal Exercise #15: Do you feel in any way that you have to lie in order to protect yourself or to get ahead in this world? If so, meditate on how you can do without lies and live with honesty.

Group Exercise #3: Explore how you can drive a policy of "No Lies, No Secrets" in your workplace. Consider setting up an Action Committee.

Homework on Chapter 11 'Doing What You Love'

Personal Exercise #16: Record any supernatural experiences, dreams or visions you have had so far.

Personal Exercise #17: List the things you enjoy doing (up to 10). Choose the top 3 things you love or are deeply passionate about. Work out a plan on how you can consider making them part of your daily activities.

Homework on Chapter 12 'Master Creators, Master Alchemists'

Now is the opportune time to step up on your prayers and meditation. Feel free to follow these exercises for your own guidance.

Personal Exercise #18: Exercise of meditating on God's testimonies on your life. These can be recent ones or ones from the past. Note down the feelings, realizations or revelations that you receive.

'God is raising up a troop of Overcomers who are going to stand in an overlapping place, and they are going to stand between the earthly realm and the spiritual realm and they are going to go up into the spiritual realm and they are going to grab what they see and manifest it on Planet Earth.'

Group Exercise #4: If you feel that you are an Overcomer, discuss and share with your group what you feel your role could be. Welcome feedback from others about your role, and be open on what kind of help you need from others.

Homework on Chapter 13 'Making Technology Responsible'

The Zombie Apocalypse we are faced with right now, where more and more people are staring at their mobile devices and tablets, family members sending each other Whatsapp messages even though they may be living in the same house. When personal intimacy and bonding weakens, it also weakens societies. Do note that this is just one example.

Personal Exercise #19: Evaluate the various current and upcoming solutions for God-Man-Machine unification. And note down how it can be applied the right way so that we can prevent this Zombie Apocalypse.

Some of you may be aware that there are technologies out there which many of us are spiritually not ready to handle wisely. Hence, we need to prepare ourselves to be evolved enough to deal with the big leaps and bounds in technology that will suddenly be accessible in the very near future.

Group Exercise #5: With this in mind, share with your group how you are progressing with your spiritual journey, and what steps you will take to advance further.

Homework on Chapter 14 'Making War Unthinkable'

An abstract from this chapter, 'We, as in YOU and I, are an expression of a realm of government that God is choosing to host on the face of the Earth. The omniscient, omnipresent and omnipotent God actually chooses to live within us.'

Personal Exercise #20: At this juncture, it is important to meditate and discover Who You Are, and what you have inside of you, and how you can truly be an expression of God.

Group Exercise #6: Discuss within your group how would you seed the idea that war is unthinkable. What campaigns and activities would you propose in your neighborhood, city or country?

Homework on Chapter 15 'The New Commodity'

As Rizwan the Malay lawyer said, 'We need a virtuous society ...'

Group Exercise #7: What are the top 5 things in your city, town or country that need resolution in order to achieve this? How do you feel you could play a part?

An abstract from this chapter, 'The nation that has the highest proportion of human beings with a high level of consciousness become recorded as the most advanced.'

Group Exercise #8: If you agree with it, consider seeding the thought with others you know. We need a particle to create a wave. Let's make waves! Discuss with your group on how to churn out noble ideas to make the New Commodity of the Heart of real value in the marketplace. And if you are a student, in your school.

Group Exercise #9: This is another follow on exercise for your group discussion. The New Commodity of the Heart - right now it is subjective. How would you make it measurable?

Homework on Chapter 16 'Unity'

An abstract from this chapter, ' ... how crystalline structures (clusters) reflect the tight bonding with the purpose of maintaining the integrity of the information and to function with greater power. The tightness was the Unity. A possible movement towards the formation of a more tightly woven crystallized Tree of Life.'

Unity provides manifold desirable results. This chapter shares a touching story of how Unity played a role in saving a life, in allowing miracles to happen and in creating happiness. The New World is a world where miracles would happen everyday and that would be a normality.

Personal Exercise #21: Coordinate groups together in your social networks, neighborhood or amongst your friends to pray for the sick. You may just do wonders.

Personal Exercise #22: Is there disunity in your personal or work relationships? If not, work out an the action plan to resolve it.

Homework on Chapter 17 'Free, But Responsible'

An abstract from this chapter, 'Lack of mutual trust could be a callous roadblock towards Heaven on Earth. Such a simple notion that mutual trust brings freedom.'

Personal Exercise #23: Lack of trust between people slows down our advancement as information cannot flow as freely as we would like it to be. If you cannot trust others, how can you expect them to trust you? Reflect on how you can achieve mutual trust with the people in your life. It will not be easy as we need to understand that it starts from ourselves.

'Humanity has been lost in the viscous circle of being self centered and lacking responsibility. To halt the process and to set ourselves free!'

Group Exercise #10: List the things humanity has been irresponsible on, and what should be done to rectify them.

'... there may be a decorum that all would follow, "Respect your home, respect yourself and respect each other." Three basic codes of conduct as acts of love, crafted to bring freedom'.

Group Exercise #11: How should the "Three basic codes of conduct" be applied to your organization or school?

Homework on Chapter 18 'Thriving, Not Simply Surviving'

All of us will need to break through our Wisdom Barrier. Once we reach one level, it's on to the next, higher and higher. I would associate it with the hypothetical Human Uplifting Scale, as wisdom has a significant impact on all areas of our lives, and one of them is enabling us to thrive.

Personal Exercise #24: Read the story of King Solomon. Solomon, also called Jedidiah, was a king of Israel and the son of David. King Solomon was the wisest man who ever lived and also one of the most foolish. God gifted him with unsurpassed wisdom, which Solomon squandered by disobeying God's commandments. Discover how the attainment of wisdom helped him thrive.

Personal Exercise #25: Consider areas of your life where you have felt that you lacked wisdom. Reflect on it and assess how you could have approached them differently. In prayer, ask God for greater wisdom in your life. Besides, with wisdom comes all things.

An abstract from this chapter, 'The revelatory message to "circulate" the blessings, the lifeblood of the Giant Tree of Life, from the vine to the branches, from branches to other branches. A continuous flow of "give and receive" revved up by the emotion of joy and fueled by faith.'

Personal Exercise #26: Work out a circulation plan of giving and receiving – only if it is within your means. List out who or which organization would you like to support. Go for those who are pure in their intentions. Always use your discretion. Remember Stephanie's words when she spoke about this? She emphasized that your intention when you give is important too.

Group Exercise #12: Discuss the structures and systems that should be disrupted (or revamped) for the benefit of Mankind. Each member of your group can choose a different segment, perhaps on their highest excitement. If it is in the field of manufacturing, choose that. One approach would be to dwell upon and meditate on each of your selected segments, and to meet another day to share and discuss your thoughts and ideas.

Homework on Chapter 19 'The Golden Door Opens' and Chapter 20 'The Secret Key'

An abstract from Chapter 19, 'I imagined that in the Crystal City we had gone beyond religion, beyond politics. A harmonious and cooperative civilization of at least a Type I Civilization and beyond ...'

Group Exercise #13: Now just imagine what the world would be like if we had finally gone beyond religion and beyond politics, and focused primarily on building our intimate relationship with God within. This would result in the biggest change in human history. And it would literally change everything. Reflect on this and share your thoughts with your group.

Personal Exercise #27: Have a clear understanding of the Symbolic Keys and the underlying Secret Key. Apply them into your life. Most importantly, to allow this time for REST. Spend more time in meditation and reflection. Give a little more of yourself to the hobbies and activities that you love. This will allow for your metamorphosis so that you may unleash the beautiful butterfly that is YOU - your True Self blossomed. Keep flowing with your work passions and your spiritual pursuits through meditation, prayer and worship.

As soon as you feel that you are ready (and you will know), compare the before and after of your spiritual journey – the experiences, changes and new learning.

Note down your Personal Golden Door: _____

_____

Epilogue

When we are seated up in Heaven,
God starts doing things
Through us,
And with us.

The vibrational frequency of God
Carried within us.

We become an Oracle of God on Earth.

We begin to frame things at Will,
And they will start to happen.

Planet Earth
Simply the Training Ground.

While soon
We will be tackling
The Galaxies.

~ Tahira Amir Khan

Bibliography

Books

Wormhole – Stargates: Tunneling Through The Cosmic Neighborhood, Eric W. Davis, Ph.D., FBIS. Kurzweil, Ray (1990). The Age of Intelligent Machines. Cambridge, MA: MIT Press.Mathematics of Bioinformatics, Theory, Practice, and Applications by Mathew He, Sergey Pethoukhov

Universal Truth: Thinking Outside the Box, Book2, Peter C Rogers, Dr, PhD

Between Death and Life, Dolores Cannon.

The Isaiah Effect, Gregg Braden

The Mystery of Life, and how Theosophy Unveils it, Clara M Codd

The Convoluted Universe 3, Dolores Cannon

Power VS Force, Dr David R. Hawkins

The Magic of Awareness, Anam Thubten

The Mental Universe, R.C. Henry

Testimony of Light, Helen Greaves

The Quantum Phaith, Jeffrey StricklandDark Matter: New Research, J. Val Blain

Striving to be Nobody, Venerable Acara Suvanno Mahathera (1920 – 2007)

The Holy Bible, the Holy Q'uran and other holy text

Videos / Articles

Wikipedia.org

'The Renewed Mind' Youtube video, Bill Johnson

'You are not alone' Youtube video, Ian Clayton

Acknowledgments

My heartfelt thanks go to:

The distinguished Ameerali R. Jumabhoy
for writing the 1st Foreword.
Dr Eric Wilding for writing the 2nd Foreword.

Mickey Chiang as the Advisory Editor.
Adil Naeem and Flaviana Chelliah as the Co-Editors.

Thanks to loved ones or family who have seen me evolve through my journey. Thank you for your unconditional love and support (in alphabetical order): Anisa Mirza Khan, Joseph Khan, Naseer Ahmed, Saud Fariz Sultan, Taher Amir Khan, Thang Siew We and Zahira Amir Khan.

And thanks to all other loved ones, family members, close friends or new friends or contacts with generous hearts. Thanks for assisting, inspiring or reviewing the manuscript. Thank you most of all for your love and support (in alphabetical order): Ama Lia Lee Wai Ching, Harjit Kaur, Inna Reevatar, Jeff Yuen, Julia Fraser, Kristen Daria Zuriel, Kristen Naeem, Kirthi Madhok, Michelle Bliss, Nicola Ransome-Goh, Madeline Tan-Yeo, Patrick Neo, Sanmuga Thavamoorthy, Saraswathy Devi and Sumitra Thinagara Sundram, Subra V. S., Tammy Teh, Terence Nicholas Tham, and Yassmen Kicchlu.

And last but not least, my heartfelt thanks to all those I interacted with from friends to new acquaintances and random strangers such as the real person/s behind the characters: "MRT Stranger", "Han", the "Buddhist Monk" as well as all the other characters. For some of you it may have just been a one-off meeting, but you played a part in shaping this once in a lifetime journey.

Contributors

Amir & Sons Pte Ltd (facebook.com/amir1921)
HRD Gateway Management Development (hrdgateway.com)
Kristen Zuriel Ministries
Soakability Supernatural School (soakability.com)

Glossary

angkor wat is a temple complex in Cambodia and the largest religious monument in the world. It was first a Hindu and later a Buddhist temple.

azan the Muslim call to ritual prayer, typically made by a muezzin from the minaret of a mosque.

baji elder sister

chowk bazaar

chai a type of Indian or Pakistani tea, made especially by boiling the tea leaves with milk, sugar, and cardamom.

charpoy a bed used in India and Pakistan consisting of a frame strung with tapes or light rope.

darbar sahib the main hall within a Sikh gurdwara.

dupatta over-the-shoulder scarf worn with a shalwar kameez.

Dunia language of origin is Hebrew-Arabic. The meaning of Dunia is "life".

Eid a Muslim festival.

ghazal North Indian Urdu or Persian love lyric

ganga is a great river of India. It flows from Gangotri to Brahmaputra river. The river is also referred to as goddess Ganga.

gulangan is a Balinese holiday celebrating the victory of dharma over adharma. It marks the time when the ancestral spirits visit the Earth.

gurdwara is the place where Sikhs come together for congregational worship. The literal meaning of the Punjabi word gurdwara is "the residence of the Guru", or "the door that leads to the Guru".

hijab a head covering worn in public by some Muslim women.

ikhlas the purification of a Muslim person's motives and intentions so that their actions are not tainted by anything other than seeking the pleasure of Allah.

kahwah is a traditional green tea preparation consumed in Afghanistan, northern Pakistan.

kebaya is a traditional blouse-dress combination that originates from Indonesia and is worn by women in Indonesia, Malaysia, Brunei, Burma, Singapore, Southern Thailand, Cambodia and the southern part of the Philippines.

kopitiams traditional coffee shops found in Southeast Asia, patronized for meals and beverages.

lah In Singlish, the ubiquitous word **lah** is used at the end of a sentence.

makara is a sea-creature in Hindu mythology. It is generally depicted as half terrestrial animal in the frontal part, in animal forms of an elephant, crocodile, stag, or deer, and in the hind part as an aquatic animal, in the form of a fish or seal tail.

mosque a Muslim place of worship.

peer is a title for a Sufi master equally used in the nath tradition. They are also referred to as a Hazrat or Shaikh, which is Arabic for Old Man. The title is often translated into English as "saint" and could be interpreted as "Elder".

sari a garment consisting of a length of cotton or silk elaborately draped around the body, traditionally worn by women from South Asia.

shalwar kameez a pair of light, loose, pleated trousers tapering to a tight fit around the ankles, worn by women from South Asia, typically with a kameez.

sindh is one of the provinces of Pakistan. Sindh was home to one of the world's oldest civilizations, the Indus Valley civilization.

singlish The English slang of Singapore. The vocabulary of Singlish consists of words originating from English, Malay, Hokkien, Teochew, Cantonese, Tamil and to a lesser extent various other European, Indic and Sinitic languages. Also, elements of American and Australian slang have come through from imported television series and films.

satyagarha is the idea of nonviolent resistance (fighting with peace) started by Mohandas Karamchand Gandhi (also known as "Mahatma" Gandhi). Gandhi used satyagarha in the Indian independence movement and also during his earlier struggle in South Africa.

qawwali a style of Muslim devotional music now associated particularly with Sufis in Pakistan.

Theories and Definitions

Consciousness 4
Quantum 4
Quantum mechanics 4
Black hole 15
Black Whole 15
Space-time 15
Kardashev Scale 19
Vector equilibrium 22
Crystal 35
DNA 35
Junk DNA 35
DNA phantom effect 39
Electromagnetic 50
Fractals 50
Flower of Life 54
Holographic Universe Theory 54
Sacred geometry 54
Fibonacci sequence 60
Golden Mean 60
RNA 77
Dr Emoto's water crystal experiments 80
Antimatter 87

Quark	87
Quasars	87
Merkabah	94
Quantum entanglement	103
Law of Vibration	112
Energy levels of emotions	123
Love healing frequency	128
Schumann Resonances	138
Torus	168
Octave	175
Gold	195
Principle of Resonance	218
Global Consciousness Experiment	229
RNG	229
Many Worlds Interpretation	238
Double Slit Experiment	260
Many Worlds Interpretation	260
Clusters	276
Uncertainty Principle of Heisenberg	295
Vacuum	311
Dark matter	311
Diamond	332
Refraction	332
Total Internal Reflection	332
Fruit of Life	348
Metatron's Cube	348
Triple helix DNA	348
New Earth Grid	362

Alphabetical Index

A

Amman Message 230
Angels 12, 69, 73, 155, 156, 177, 210, 212, 242, 268, 269, 307, 359
Astrology 2
Astronomy 2, 212, 320, 321

B

Bali 40, 41, 42, 44, 45, 48, 49, 50, 51, 55, 58, 59, 62, 67, 71, 116, 120, 127, 139, 169, 170, 171, 172, 174, 197, 308, 325, 328, 339, 340, 354, 401
Bal Thackeray 140, 143, 294
Bible
  Biblical Scriptures 27, 108, 155, 283
  Holy Bible 3
Black hole 12, 15, 134, 181, 182, 188, 317, 333
Black whole 12, 13, 15, 183, 188
  Black Wholes 13
Blue Crystal Dome 204
Buckminister 20, 22, 85, 167, 302, 341
Buddhist 3, 13, 14, 16, 17, 18, 19, 20, 24, 25, 26, 27, 37, 56, 65, 79, 90, 108, 119, 144, 179, 182, 183, 297, 306, 316, 363, 387
Buddhist Sutras 3

C

Carbon 29, 31, 32, 33, 125, 231, 332, 338, 361
Christ ascension 337
Christian 29, 52, 82, 172
Cloud of Witnesses 250, 306, 307, 312, 314
Clusters 275, 276, 374
Consciousness 1, 2, 4, 21, 45, 46, 47, 50, 54, 66, 73, 76, 78, 85, 90, 123, 129, 150, 177, 178, 182, 183, 184, 185, 204, 205, 207, 213, 215, 225, 226, 227, 229, 247, 259, 268, 269, 270, 273, 274, 275, 289, 313, 329, 339, 358, 361, 365, 374

Christ Consciousness 88
Global Consciousness Project 229
God-Consciousness 361
Self-Consciousness 361
World-Consciousness 361
Cosmos 22, 58, 60, 91, 166, 168, 188, 302
Crucifixion 82, 347
Crystal 32, 35, 39, 48, 80, 132, 155, 165, 177, 199, 200, 204, 213, 231, 241, 259, 265, 280, 286, 305, 314, 315, 316, 337, 345, 346, 354, 360, 361, 362, 363
   Crystal City 345, 347, 351, 352, 377
   Crystals 80, 251, 278, 279, 316, 358, 361, 365
   Diamond 32, 182, 193, 207, 295, 332, 337, 340, 345, 360
Crystalline 29, 31, 32, 33, 34, 35, 79, 165, 172, 231, 232, 275, 276, 286, 332, 336, 337, 338, 345, 350, 351, 358, 360, 361, 362, 365, 374

D

Dark matter 15, 311
Darwin 35
   Darwinian principle 259
David Bohm 275
David R. Hawkins 123
Divine Council 224, 329
DNA 31, 32, 33, 34, 35, 36, 38, 39, 66, 67, 74, 75, 76, 77, 93, 128, 133, 134, 135, 141, 157, 167, 168, 169, 174, 175, 183, 189, 194, 195, 213, 258, 267, 268, 275, 279, 280, 316, 321, 335, 339, 343, 344, 348, 361, 365
   Double helix 344, 348
   Junk 34, 35, 67, 76, 279
   Triple helix 280, 344, 348
DNA Phantom Effect 38, 39, 157
Double Slit Experiment 257, 260, 341, 343

E

Earth grid
   Grid 19, 46, 54, 336, 337, 351, 360, 361, 362
Edgar Cayce 55, 111
Edward Snowden 141
Einstein 21, 28, 58, 76, 149, 159, 177, 217
Electromagnetic 27, 46, 50, 78, 134, 138, 164, 166, 167, 182, 279
   electromagnetic force 27, 50
Emoto 78, 80, 275, 276, 286
Euclidean space 168, 347
Extraterrestrial 19, 134, 155, 206, 208, 329

F

Fengshui 2
Fibonacci sequence 58, 60, 135, 337
Flower of life 53, 54, 346, 362
Four Foundations of Mindfulness 13
Fractals 47
Francis Harry Compton Crick 36
Fruit of Life 348

G

Galactic Council 155, 173, 329
Galaxy 15, 19, 88, 89, 181, 317, 318, 333, 336
Gandhi 28, 389
Giant Tree of Life 311, 340, 342
  Giant Tree 48, 50, 58, 59, 74, 76, 122, 127, 272, 311, 339, 340, 364, 376
  Tree of Life 160, 161, 261, 269, 273, 275, 339, 348, 362, 374, 376
Giordano Bruno 166
Global Mind 129, 138, 139, 140, 141, 142, 250, 290, 333
Glory realm 171, 172, 174, 177, 182, 193, 194, 283, 314, 317, 322
  Glory 29
Gold 147, 253, 258, 339
Gold dust 30, 31, 33, 127, 176, 182, 267, 343
Golden Door 129, 146, 147, 148, 149, 151, 225, 234, 235, 236, 237, 241, 246, 306, 322, 324, 341, 343, 345, 357, 358, 365, 370, 377
  Golden Doors 352
  Personal Golden Door 366, 377
Golden horse 163, 241, 334, 342, 364
  Quantum-powered Golden Horses 335, 336
Golden mean 37, 58, 60, 128, 215
Golden people 338, 349
Golden planet viii, 27, 245, 253, 297, 329
Golden road 13, 242, 245, 293, 308, 320, 340, 342, 343, 355, 357
Golden souls 23, 24, 25, 26, 27, 28, 36, 37, 40, 48, 59, 62, 64, 68, 74, 79, 83, 86, 93, 102, 141, 146, 147, 148, 151, 160, 179, 217, 242, 297, 305, 312, 322, 327, 344
  Golden Soul 34, 96, 126, 331

H

Hawkins scale 123

Heaven 28, 76, 77, 81, 84, 91, 97, 98, 99, 100, 101, 102, 105, 121, 125, 141, 146, 147, 149, 150, 151, 159, 165, 166, 167, 170, 171, 172, 173, 174, 176, 179, 182, 183, 184, 185, 192, 194, 220, 222, 231, 234, 235, 236, 237, 240, 241, 242, 250, 252, 272, 273, 279, 286, 292, 295, 297, 307, 310, 319, 322, 326, 328, 344, 351, 358, 363, 364, 365, 375, 379, 402

Heavenly Courts 219, 220, 224, 233, 240, 296, 364

Heaven on Earth 28, 76, 91, 101, 102, 141, 149, 165, 170, 222, 231, 234, 235, 236, 237, 240, 242, 252, 272, 273, 279, 292, 297, 307, 322, 328, 351, 363, 375

Hindu 52, 140, 262, 263, 387, 388
  Hindu Scriptures 262

Hippocrates 38

Hologram
  Holographic Universe 54, 147
  Holographic Universe Theory 54

Holy of Holies 347, 348

Holy Q'uran 3

Holy Spirit of God 92, 142, 143, 164, 166, 187, 188, 189, 209, 243, 273, 279, 295, 297, 304, 316, 317, 331, 339, 341, 355, 356, 363, 364, 368, 371

Horowitz 78, 128, 267

Human Uplifting scale 150, 282, 284, 297, 375

I

INA 239, 240, 248

Islam 227, 230
  Islamic 27, 82, 131
  Islamic spirituality 82
  Muslim 111, 130, 387, 388, 389

J

Jedidiah 376

Jesus 30, 52, 69, 74, 82, 83, 92, 96, 154, 171, 186, 192, 217, 330, 343, 357, 358, 361, 402

John Hagelin 174

John Stuart Reid 128

K

Kardashev Scale 17, 19, 150, 284
  Type I 17, 18, 19, 28, 150, 157, 231, 234, 235, 236, 237, 240, 250, 252, 272, 307, 352, 377

Type I Civilization(s) 17, 19, 28, 150, 231, 235, 240, 250, 252, 272, 352, 377
Type II 19
Type III 19
Type V 284
Type Zero civilization 17, 18, 19, 240, 284
Kundalini 14
Kurzweil 203, 381

L

Law of Accelerating Returns 203
Law of Non-Interference 351
Law of Vibration 111, 112
Leonardo Da Vinci 88
Light 13, 23, 24, 27, 30, 32, 33, 34, 37, 38, 39, 50, 52, 73, 74, 79, 82, 83, 87, 91, 92, 93, 94, 95, 96, 98, 103, 105, 112, 122, 124, 134, 135, 151, 153, 158, 164, 172, 175, 182, 187, 190, 202, 203, 222, 231, 232, 244, 257, 260, 267, 268, 271, 273, 280, 282, 287, 298, 303, 306, 309, 329, 330, 332, 346, 350, 351, 354, 356, 357, 361, 365, 387
Love healing frequency 125, 128

M

Malaysia 91, 92, 96, 97, 98, 100, 106, 107, 116, 120, 158, 160, 162, 169, 185, 197, 239, 247, 288, 364, 388, 401
Many Worlds interpretation 235, 238, 260, 341
Marko Rodin 128, 267
Mathematics 22, 133, 203, 401
Max G. Lagally 32, 231
Men in White Linen 155, 224, 268, 282, 307, 329
Merkaba 94
MerKaBa 102, 104, 177, 266, 312, 350, 361
Merkabah 93, 94
Metatron's Cube 346, 348, 361, 362
Michael Hutchison 138
Michelangelo 158, 159, 162, 166
Mother Theresa 28
Multiverse 235, 284

N

Naranayan Krishnan 263
Nassim Haramein 15
Netaji 248, 249, 259
New Humans 102, 137, 174, 184, 231, 338, 346, 361, 364
Nikolai Kardashev 19
Nikola Tesla 38, 78, 194, 362

O

Octahedron 350
Octaves 174, 283, 317
  Octave 81, 175, 193, 348
Open Heaven 242

P

Pakistan 1, 56, 107, 108, 111, 112, 113, 117, 118, 119, 120, 122, 127, 129, 130, 131, 132, 140, 142, 146, 156, 161, 162, 164, 169, 171, 190, 197, 216, 220, 221, 222, 228, 285, 287, 291, 293, 336, 355, 364, 388, 389
Palmistry 2, 122
Particle 76, 87, 144, 159, 242, 257, 260, 294, 295, 305, 374
  Particles 4, 24, 27, 50, 84, 85, 87, 103, 137, 159, 182, 203, 218, 241, 257, 260, 275, 295, 305
Penta-dodecathedron 337
Plato 28, 173, 254, 255, 258, 297, 303, 351
Poponin 38, 39
Portal 24, 25, 26, 27, 29, 62, 83, 93, 147, 154, 172, 242, 312, 344
Principle of Resonance 217, 218, 292

resonance 77, 78, 112, 138, 164, 170, 218, 363

Q

Qi Gong 162, 163, 363
Quantum 2, 4, 38, 75, 93, 100, 102, 103, 159, 177, 198, 202, 203, 204, 205, 207, 215, 217, 222, 238, 241, 242, 259, 260, 276, 279, 291, 294, 295, 297, 307, 309, 317, 320, 326, 332, 333, 335, 336, 337, 338, 339, 348, 351, 356, 357, 361, 381
Quantum Energy 335, 338
Quantum entanglement 103, 159, 222, 242, 307, 320, 326
Quantum-eyed 338
Quantum eyes 215, 336, 337, 338, 357
Quantum mechanics 2, 4, 103, 177, 291, 294, 309
Quantum physics 4, 75, 260

R

Refraction 332
Reiki 41, 49, 67
RNA 76, 77, 81, 133, 189, 321
RNG 274
Rumi 135
Ruth Ward Heflin 172

S

Sacred geometry 5, 54, 93, 104, 128, 167, 259, 346, 350, 362
Schumann Resonances 138
Secret Key 353, 357, 358, 364, 377
Self-healing
  spontaneous self-healing 66, 70, 76, 77, 111, 172, 177, 232, 278, 368
  Spontaneous self-healing 70
Sikh 94, 95, 274, 387
Silicon crystal 32, 231
Singapore 1, 4, 5, 10, 13, 16, 17, 23, 24, 29, 34, 41, 42, 48, 62, 63, 67, 71, 74, 81, 83, 87, 92, 94, 107, 116, 117, 118, 120, 122, 130, 139, 141, 142, 146, 153, 158, 162, 163, 169, 171, 172, 176, 177, 179, 180, 185, 190, 192, 197, 198, 201, 202, 204, 208, 211, 216, 221, 222, 223, 229, 230, 233, 238, 239, 240, 248, 252, 258, 261, 262, 264, 265, 266, 270, 271, 274, 278, 291, 292, 296, 299, 300, 308, 311, 314, 319, 324, 327, 328, 333, 337, 345, 353, 354, 363, 388, 401
Skh
  Sikhs 94, 387

Socrates 28
Solomon 376
Space-time 15, 102, 174, 181, 182, 280
Spirit Man 23, 26, 36, 37, 38, 57, 89, 125, 147, 148, 150, 166, 182, 233, 242, 259, 327, 330, 355, 366, 367
Spirit Woman 26, 36, 37, 38, 57, 69, 89, 95, 126, 147, 148, 150, 166, 182, 184, 187, 242, 244, 259, 282, 299, 325, 327, 330, 355, 366, 367
S. S. Yadava 239
Star of David 350
Star tetrahedron 167, 350
Stella octangula 350
Stigmata 82, 83, 123, 146, 156, 172, 347, 401
Stigmatic Zero Point 86, 88, 92, 102, 151, 275, 317, 328, 401
Sufi 27, 97, 108, 171, 388
Symbolic Keys 352, 354, 357, 358, 377

T

Theory of Everything 138
Three Basic Codes of Conduct 375
Torus 167, 168, 182, 259, 313, 317, 350

Total internal reflection 331, 332
Towering Golden Soul 331, 342, 355
Towering Golden Souls 102, 146, 147, 148, 151, 179, 217, 242, 322, 327, 330, 336, 364

U

Uncertainty Principle of Heisenberg 294, 295
Unified field 137, 138, 144, 275
Unified Field Theory 137, 138, 139, 140
Ustad Nusrat Fateh Ali Khan 171, 293

V

Vacuum 112, 167, 182, 310, 311, 321, 332, 348
Vector equilibrium 20, 22, 85
Venerable Acara 13, 160, 381

Victor Showell 128
Von Däniken 208

W

Wheels within the wheels 93, 350, 362
Wisdom Barrier 311, 313, 375

Z

Zero point 401

About the Author

Tahira Amir Khan was born in Singapore where she spent most of her life, other than residing in Australia, Bali and Malaysia. She studied in Australia graduating from the University of Western Australia, with a double major in Computer Science and Mathematics. This followed on with an MBA in International Business from the University of Melbourne.

With several years in corporate for global multinationals, she made her shift into business. A co-founder of a technology consulting company, MicroUsability, which is in the field of user experience consulting and design, in operation now for more than 10 years. Concurrently, from 2012-2014 she took on a voluntary position as Vice President and subsequently as President of Mobile Alliance Singapore, a pioneering society for innovators and service providers in the mobile communications industry.

So heavily immersed in the fast-paced world of business, she began to lose touch with her true Self, her true identity. It was in 2013 when she finally faced a profound spiritual transformation that virtually pushed her towards the "death" of her old Self. A divine intervention to bring her down to zero point, which she redefines it as her Stigmatic Zero Point. A phenomenon which included a shocking experience of receiving stigmata, the nail-piercing wounds of Jesus Christ, and bringing her to a gradual rebirth which radically changed the course of her life.

Followed by a series of tumultuous events, she was finally placed on the path she was meant to be. It is the path of storytelling to share divine and prophetic revelations, and bringing this knowledge to the marketplace by conceptualizing technology innovations and mentoring startups that are in line with Heaven's reflections on Earth. Her ability to correlate science and spirituality with the real world, makes her writings a valuable read.

This book encompasses her own personal journey in the advancement of the human soul and the Planet Earth, as well as what is needed to facilitate it at greater speed. Tahira is now working on the sequel of this book.

Email: tahira@throughthegoldendoor.com
Web: www.throughthegoldendoor.com

www.ingramcontent.com/pod-product-compliance
Lightning Source LLC
Chambersburg PA
CBHW021758220426
43662CB00006B/105